1992

THE GLOBAL CONFLICT

In memory of my parents, Reginald and Kathleen Bartlett

THE GLOBAL CONFLICT

The international rivalry of
the great powers, 1880–1970

C. J. Bartlett

LONGMAN
London and New York

Longman Group UK Limited
Longman House, Burnt Mill, Harlow,
Essex CM20 2JE, England
and Associated Companies throughout the world

*Published in the United States of America
by Longman Inc., New York*

© C. J. Bartlett 1984

First published 1984
Sixth impression 1990

British Library Cataloguing in Publication Data
Bartlett, C. J.
　The global conflict
　1. International relations – History
　2. World politics – 19th century
　3. World politics – 20th century
　I. Title
　303.4'82　　　JX1395
　ISBN 0-582-49069-3

ISBN 0-582-49070-7

Library of Congress Cataloging in Publication Data
Bartlett, C. J. (Christopher John), 1931–
　The global conflict.

　Bibliography: p.
　Includes index.
　1. World politics – 19th century. 2. World politics –
20th century. 3. Europe – Politics and government –
1871–1918. 4. Europe – Politics and government –
20th century. 5. Great powers. I. Title.
D397.B327　　1984　　909.82　　83-14920
ISBN 0-582-49069-3
ISBN 0-582-49070-7 (pbk.)

Produced by Longman Singapore Publishers Pte Ltd.
Printed in Singapore.

CONTENTS

LIST OF MAPS

ACKNOWLEDGEMENTS

It would be a hopeless task in a book of this nature to acknowledge the help of all those who have contributed to its making. For reasons of space the bibliography is not exhaustive, and refers mainly to the sources cited in the text. I am much indebted for ideas to colleagues and students in the Universities of London, Edinburgh, the West Indies, St Andrews and especially Dundee, and to a number of American friends. My family has shown its usual patience, has offered constructive criticism, but above all has provided the ideal environment. What more can one ask?

C.J.B
Broughty Ferry
November 1982

'The more deeply we search out the causes the more of them we discover; and every cause, and even a whole class of causes taken separately, strikes us as being true in itself, and equally deceptive through its insignificance in comparison with the immensity of the result.'

TOLSTOY, *War and Peace*

'The repercussion of every important blow in any part is felt in every part. In the future every great question must be a world question.'

HALFORD MACKINDER (1916)

INTRODUCTION

Historians must always be conscious of F. W. Maitland's warning, 'Such is the unity of history that anyone who endeavours to tell a piece of it must feel that his first sentence tears a seamless web.' But periodization, however crude, is still a necessary historical tool, and it is submitted here that a useful purpose may be served by treating as a unity great-power rivalries in the period from the later nineteenth century to the 1960s – a period which spans the so-called 'new imperialism', the two world wars and the Cold War.

In these years the imbalance between the developed peoples and the rest of the world reached its most extreme point in modern times. This imbalance had been developing since the fifteenth and sixteenth centuries, and is reflected in the first great expansionist drives of the Portuguese, Spaniards, French, English and Dutch. Hegel was able to observe that the Europeans had circumnavigated the globe, and were equipped to seize most of the territories which took their fancy. As it was, throughout the early- and mid-nineteenth century the British, Russian and French empires, and the United States, continued to expand, but it was only in the last two decades of the nineteenth century that the scramble for colonies reached its climax. It was then that many began to talk of a virtual partition of the world between a few great powers, and the consolidation of perhaps five or six invulnerable empires. Some, indeed, already believed that even the European empires were doomed, as they lacked the huge territorial home bases of Russia and the United States. In these circumstances, and given these expectations, it became necessary to think in terms of a global as well as a European balance of power.

This competition for empire was encouraged by other considerations. As industrialization spread, so too did the concern for markets and raw materials. Protectionism began to make inroads at the expense of free trade which had been in the ascendant as long as Britain was the world's workshop. But while the industrialized powers were greedy and ambitious, their appetite was also fed by the

1

relative ease with which large areas of the world could be brought under their control. Much expansion took place because it was relatively cheap and painless, and because rivalry in Europe in the late nineteenth century was not sufficient to absorb all the energy and attention of the powers. Thus, in addition to the complex motivation which lay behind the drive for empire, one must take account of the opportunities which presented themselves.

Yet, important as the global struggle had become by the early twentieth century, it was not the prime or immediate cause of the First World War. This, both in its origins and character, was influenced mainly by European events and circumstances, by the extraordinary political and social changes and by the economic and technological revolution which had been sweeping through Europe – especially in the last fifty years. Indeed, Raymond Aron has argued that it is more important to ask why the war became 'hyperbolic' – or total in character – than to investigate its origins in obsessive detail. Winston Churchill complained that war had been spoiled by industry and democracy, implying that the one made total war materially possible, while the second reduced the scope for compromise and restraint. Certainly the war did much to complete the destruction of the old monarchical–aristocratic order, opening the door to communism and fascism as well as widening the opportunities for parliamentary democracy. At the same time the war was resolved in the end only by the intervention of the United States, while the global balance of power was further affected by the temporary eclipse of Germany and Russia, and by Japanese advances in the Far East. In fact, no stable status quo resulted from the war, whether in Europe or the Far East, and by the 1930s both German and Japanese governments were convinced that new windows of opportunity were opening before them – all the more tempting because they seemed likely to remain open for only short periods of time before the Russians and Americans began to realize their full potential. A new partition of the world was thus attempted – perhaps even a bid for world hegemony on the part of Hitler – with the result that the advance to superpower status by the Russians and Americans was accelerated (rather than slowed) by decisions made in Berlin and Tokyo.

In the years immediately following the defeat of Germany and Japan it seemed that those who had prophesied the division of the world between Russia and America would be vindicated. Certainly world affairs were at first dominated to a remarkable degree by two blocs, led respectively by Moscow and Washington. Each feared further encroachemnts by the other, and Washington, for instance, was not the only western capital where one heard worried references to Halford Mackinder's warnings that the power which controlled the 'heartland' could control the Eurasian 'world island', and that the ruler of the 'world island' could control the world. Fears of a third world war increased in 1950–51 with the Korean conflict, the alliance between Russia and China, and the intensifying struggle between East and West for the resources of south-east Asia.

Nevertheless in the early 1970s many could speak confidently not only of the ending of the Cold War but of the replacement of a bipolar world by a multipolar structure. The rift between Russia and China had provided the greatest single shock to the bipolar model, but there had also been lesser rifts within each bloc, not to mention the decolonization of most of the Third World. The failure of the United States to defeat communism in Vietnam was the most dramatic demonstration of the new limitations to the power of even the greatest nations in the face of determined nationalist opposition. At the very least the costs of superpower intervention in many parts of the world were rising, so that while Russia and the United States remained in a power league by themselves, their ability to destroy civilization with nuclear weapons did not automatically give them the same degree of influence over weaker peoples as in the past. The imbalance throughout the world was still acute, but with the spread of nationalism in particular the imbalance between the greatest nations and the smaller had been lessened to a significant degree. Although the global struggle for influence between the superpowers would continue, and would indeed be intensified from the later 1970s, autonomous or semi-autonomous regional rivalries retained their importance. The story of international relations from the 1960s was no longer monopolized by the greatest powers and their global rivalries to quite the same extent as it had been since the 1880s. A unique period of great-power rivalries had ended – at least for the time being.

Chapter 1

FROM A EUROPEAN TO A GLOBAL BALANCE

THE LAST YEARS OF THE EUROPEAN BALANCE

Modern Europe, between 1815 and 1854 and again between 1871 and 1914, experienced the longest periods of peace between the great powers it had yet known. Even the wars which followed in quick succession in 1854–71 were limited in aim and character. Naturally the years of peace were frequently punctuated by war scares and panics. Contemporaries certainly believed themselves close to conflict, yet war was avoided again and again.

There was a number of reasons for this relative freedom from major conflict. For the period down to 1854 some credit must obviously be given to the peacemakers in Vienna in 1814–15, though the balance which they formalized owed much to chance. Nor was France entirely appeased by the settlement. Even Bourbon ministers looked for opportunities to extend the frontiers of France – only to find that their country was too weak and their opponents too united. Britain's wealth, and her interest in European peace and stability were often assets, but she in her turn was dependent upon European allies and propitious circumstances. While France was frequently isolated, Prussia was still relatively weak and lacking in self-confidence: Russia and Austria were often restrained by fears of financial collapse if they risked war. Of great importance, too, was monarchical Europe's fear that war, especially one involving France, might entail a renewal of revolutionary disturbances on the scale of the 1790s. In short there existed a number of powerful deterrents to war, especially when, before 1854, no power had a pressing desire to upset what was undoubtedly a tolerable balance in Europe.

The situation after 1871 was rather different, and certainly more complex. Germany had gained too much by that date for the balance to be as satisfactory as that before 1854. But for the next forty years no power had the will or, apart from Germany, the strength to mount a serious challenge to the European status quo. Some historians, indeed, have argued that growing interest and rivalry in the wider world acted as a safety valve, and decreased the risk of war in Europe for a generation. There is some truth in this, but it will be argued in detail later (pp. 9–15, 31–2, 76–80) that there was a variety of reasons why the powers talked, planned and prepared on a grand scale for war without taking the fatal step – until 1914.

Even such wars as were fought by the great powers in the nineteenth century were restrained affairs in contrast to those waged between 1792 and 1815, or after 1914. The controversy surrounding the origins of the Crimean War is itself testimony to the uncertainties and confusion in the minds of the monarchs and ministers who blundered hesitantly into war in 1854. Admittedly some were more belligerent and ambitious than others, but it is significant that Palmerston could never win substantial support for his desire to push Russia bodily and permanently eastward. His aim was to confine Russia within her frontiers of the mid-eighteenth century. Many Germans entertained similar thoughts in 1914. As it was, the Russians were able to make up much of the ground lost in 1856 by 1871. More important after 1856 was the failure of the Habsburgs and Romanovs to revive their pre-war alliance, with the result that Cavour, Napoleon III and Bismarck found it much easier to pursue their ambitions at the expense of Austria. Thus the unification of both Italy and Germany was facilitated and perhaps even accelerated. Maybe, too, the Crimea suggested that war need not necessarily prove so dangerous to the existing political and social order as many had feared after 1815.

Indeed, Cavour, Napoleon III and Bismarck appeared to act on the assumption that a vigorous foreign policy, with limited war among its possible instruments, would protect and improve their positions at home. Bismarck's foreign policy between 1863 and 1871 was profoundly influenced by his desire to preserve the ascendancy of a Protestant, aristocratic, monarchical Prussia. Cavour's devious and complex foreign policy owed much to his determination to prevent the emergence of a republican Italy. Both victors and vanquished in the wars of 1859–71 kept a careful eye on the possible domestic consequences. Thus although Bismarck talked of stirring up popular unrest in Austria during the war of 1866, he was well aware that this could prove a double-edged weapon. Once victorious, he hastened to make peace, fearful that an army of occupation might provoke a mass rising. The Paris Commune following the Franco-Prussian War of 1870–71 was a reminder that revolutionary forces might flourish in the confusion caused by international conflict. Bismarck himself, after 1871, was not insincere when he invoked the revolutionary threat as he looked for arguments to impress Vienna

and St Petersburg with the advantages of peace. Even General
Helmuth von Moltke shared his concern, and warned the Reichstag
in 1890 of the dangers that would arise once any war became
dominated by mass emotions. Others shared his fears that wars would
become more violent and uncontrollable as the political consciousness and sense of involvement of the masses grew. An Austrian
Foreign Minister declared in 1887 that 'the republican and socialist
menace would sweep through Europe . . .' in the event of a French
victory over Germany.[1]

On the other hand, Bismarck's wars encouraged the belief that it
was both possible and desirable to plan and prepare for short, decisive campaigns. The warnings provided by the long-drawn-out American Civil War of 1861–65 were not heeded. The Germans, and
especially the Prussian General Staff, supplied the models for the
future. The secret of success, it seemed, lay in careful prior preparations, in excellent staff work, in rapid and efficient mobilization,
in speedy and skilful deployment helped by intelligent use of railways, all directed to the task of winning decisive battles in the first
weeks or months of a war. The consequences of the Franco-Prussian
War therefore went far beyond those reflected in the terms of the
Treaty of Frankfurt of 10 May 1871. As Michael Howard has pointed
out: 'Germany's magnificent and well-deserved victory was, in a
profound and unforseeable sense, a disaster for herself, and for the
entire world.'.[2] For Germans it confirmed an already excessive faith
in the military and all their works. Other powers strove to emulate
Prussian methods – their general staff, system of conscription, rapid
mobilization and deployment. They aspired to create great armies,
designed to deliver mortal blows in the shortest possible time. Yet
only the French could hope to approach the German level of efficiency. The French, however, could no longer match Germany in
population or in industrial strength. The Russians and Austrians
could do little to match the quantum leap forward of the Germans,
but did what they could with their more limited skills and resources.
The British army remained small and designed primarily for imperial
purposes. Nevertheless some of its leaders became impressed by the
importance of speed in contemporary warfare. In October 1898,
during the Fashoda crisis with France, a British general warned of
the danger of a French attack without prior notice. Howard
concludes: 'It was this inherent military insecurity, rather than the
single factor of Alsace-Lorraine, which was to make the peace [after
1871] . . . so uncertain . . .'[3] A new generation studied the methods
of Bismarck and Moltke uncritically. Bismarck's debts to fortune and
special circumstances were undervalued.

The growth of the armed forces in Europe in the next generation
was disturbing. By 1897 the German war establishment had almost
trebled to 3.4 million. The French had more than doubled to 3.5

million: the same was true of Austria-Hungary (to 2.6 million) and Russia (4 million). National increases in arms spending were rather less, though still significant. In Russia and Germany it had risen by some 80 per cent; in Britain and France by about 45 per cent, but only about 20 per cent in Austria-Hungary. Russia and Austria were most conscious of the economic strain. Russia's war with Turkey in 1877 was financially crippling. But France's problems were also multiplying. By 1914 she had a population of only 39 million against a Germany of 65 million. Germany was producing three times as much iron and steel, and was now ahead of Britain in these and some other sectors of industry. Yet even as Germany raced ahead in Europe, so she was outstripped in the world by the United States. While Americans were not yet translating this wealth into military and diplomatic power – at least not outside their own continent – some observers already felt it was only a matter of time before this colossus joined the great game. Bismarck thought it significant that Britain and the United States shared a common language. In time they were likely to join forces.

One must be careful not to exaggerate great-power competitiveness after 1871 compared with, say, the period between 1815 and 1854. The British, for instance, found themselves engaged in serious naval competition with the Russians in the 1830s and the French in the 1840s. There were recurrent invasion scares in the middle of the century. The other powers experienced several war panics. On the other hand, peace movements began to gather strength in some countries; serious efforts were made to enlarge the scope of international law; international co-operativeness of all kinds expanded from the most humdrum matters to high politics themselves. Although few shared Gladstone's faith in an idealized view of the Concert of Europe, the powers, whether through international conferences or at other diplomatic levels, were alive to the appeal and uses of the Concert for more pedestrian purposes. One must not forget that there was continuity as well as change in the relations of the European powers in the nineteenth century.

This ambiguity is exemplified by John Westlake in his *Chapters on International Law* (1894). Only in the medieval age of chivalry, he wrote, had there been comparable progress in the control and mitigation of war. He was impressed by the advance of international law itself. At the same time he feared that the replacement of dynastic by national war was leading to 'a public impatience of all laws' – it seemed that the nation must be allowed to triumph at any cost. Even international lawyers were now joining generals and admirals in attacks on the agreed restraints on war.[4] There existed, for instance, the contrast between the Declaration of Paris of 1856, with its efforts to provide more shelter under international law for commerce at sea in time of war, and the theories of the *Jeune École* of French naval officers. They were arguing from the 1880s that commerce-raiding was the best answer to British naval supremacy. There was talk of night attacks without warning by torpedo boats on unarmed merchant ships, as well as the bombardment of undefended coastal towns. Even at the Hague Peace Conference of 1899 a British admiral was full of 'the might is right' argument, insisting that it was nonsense to try to humanize war. Colmar von der Goltz, in his well-known *Das Volk im Waffen* (1883), declared that the supremacy of the political arm over the military in war, as argued by Clausewitz, was anachronistic in a Europe of increasingly armed and aggressive nationalities. As early as 1853, in German editions of Clausewitz's *On War*, passages on political supremacy were being altered or their meaning obscured. When the French took up Clausewitz after 1871 they did the same. Within the German Foreign Ministry in 1900 Holstein did not concede everything to the generals, but contented himself with the guarded comment: 'If the chief of staff . . . considers such a position to be necessary, it is the duty of German diplomacy to adjust to it and prepare for it to the degree that is possible.'[5] In practice, of course, the influence of the Schlieffen Plan upon German foreign policy was to be of the utmost importance in 1914.

But it was not only the military who set the pace. If many governments feared the impact of city life, the growth of trade unions, literacy and cheap newsprint upon large sections of their populations, placing the loyalty and patriotism of such people in doubt, they were heartened by the militant nationalism of the middle classes. This arose spontaneously and as a result of prompting from the top. Armies, navies, imperialism and an assertive foreign policy seemed to have a special appeal for those who felt menaced by socialism and trade unions from below and big business from above. For those whose income and status were threatened by the new industrial society, patriotism seemed a natural refuge. Similarly the armed forces and colonies promised new openings for the young from such backgrounds. Over and above this, certain sectors of the economy stood to gain from heavy arms expenditures – especially on navies – and from an aggressive search for new markets or supplies of raw materials. In Britain, despite the efforts of Cobden and Gladstone over the years, support for naval expansion was relatively easy to mobilize, and patriotic belligerent feeling was not in short supply at the beginning of the Crimean War, or in the war scare with Russia in 1878, or during the Boer War. Herbert Spencer lamented the growth of interest in militarism and war in the last twenty years of the nineteenth century among his countrymen.

Charles Darwin's theories on natural selection through struggle and 'the survival of the fittest' were eagerly and crudely exploited as supposedly scientific proof of the inevitability and indeed the desirability of great-power rivalry. In fact few read Darwin. Most had only nebulous impressions of his work, and these were freely mixed with other ideas. But Social Darwinism was a tempting pseudo-scientific argument to add to current pragmatic and ethical justifications. In Germany it combined with many pre-existing intellectual trends to encourage respect for the state, power and efficiency.[6] Hegel remained perhaps the most potent single force. He had interpreted history as a process which revealed the divine purpose. Right would prevail through the superior might which legitimately belonged to it. Just as Greece and Rome had enjoyed dominance in the past, so would Germany in the future. Prussian and German experience from the eighteenth century seemed to confirm his argument that struggle was the final arbiter. In the 1860s Bismarck and Moltke had succeeded where the less single-minded and ruthless liberals of 1848 had failed. But one must not forget that arguments of all kinds for expansion were being put forward elsewhere in Europe, with many commenting on the 'natural tendency' for 'civilized peoples' to expand at the expense of the more backward or those who were in decline. Gorchakov, the Russian Chancellor, claimed that his country's Asiatic expansion was 'irresistibly forced, less by ambition than by imperious necessity'. This was in 1864. Sir John Malcolm used a similar argument for the British in India in 1815. Social Darwinism easily made headway against this background and in the emotive imperialist atmosphere of the later nineteenth century. Thus Max Weber, the German sociologist, came to describe world politics at that time as a ceaseless struggle between autonomous cultures. International relations were not about morals but power. Naked force would soon be the only deciding element in the struggle for markets. Views of this kind were especially common among German intellectuals. Not surprisingly the German peace movement was very weak. But militant nationalist sentiments were commonplace among the educated classes of many nations – not even the United States was immune by the end of the century. Britain in the pursuit of her interests from Egypt to South Africa, and the Gold Coast to China was as ruthless as the occasion appeared to demand. Not even Gladstone could insulate himself from imperialism and power politics in the early 1880s, and he was driven to resignation in 1894 when his Cabinet colleagues insisted on the maintenance of a large naval programme.

Threats to the peace of Europe in the first generation after 1871 came from two quarters – the possibility of a second Franco-German war, and great-power rivalries in the Near East. An Anglo-Russian war scare in central Asia also had repercussions in Europe. The most likely belligerents appeared to be Britain and/or Austria-Hungary ranged against Russia. Bismarck hoped that he would not be forced to choose between Russia and Austria-Hungary, but many of the

German leadership, especially among the military, feared and made preparations for a two-front war with France and Russia. Despite moments of serious Franco-German tension, war seemed most likely to arise from a breakdown in the efforts of the powers to accommodate themselves to the decline of the Ottoman Empire and to the problems posed by the successor states in the Balkans. Apart from Russia, however, it was never clear from one year to the next which other powers might be involved in a war originating in the Near East, or how far such a war would spread. Bismarck, in particular, was intent on the localization of war, not least because he believed that once Germany was involved in a war in the east, war with France was likely to follow. Thus fortunately for the peace of Europe the power that was best prepared for a war on the continent was the one most interested in the preservation of the European status quo. Even when Bismarck spoke of possible Austrian or Russian gains in the Balkans, he was thinking in terms of preserving the existing balance between those powers.

Bismarck down to 1871 had been in the happy position of being able to exploit Russia's determination to reverse the Crimean War settlement. The test which Russia applied to her relations with other powers was their stance on this issue, and by this test no power was able to offer more than Prussia. But with the revocation of the Black Sea clauses in 1871, Russia was free – and indeed compelled by the emergence of the new Germany – to pay more attention to the overall balance in Europe. As early as 1874 a number of diplomats were noting and commenting upon hints that the Russians were troubled by German strength and anxious to counterbalance it. There were several forewarnings of the stand that Gorchakov was to take against Bismarck during the War in Sight crisis of 1875 when some feared that Bismarck was looking for an excuse to go to war with France for a second time.[7] Bismarck tried hard to play the 'honest broker' between Russia and Austria-Hungary during the Near Eastern crisis of 1875–78, but by 1879 the deterioration in Russo-German relations had persuaded him to make sure of the Habsburgs by means of the Dual Alliance. Even so he hoped that this step would persuade the Russian government to seek better relations with Berlin. The League of the Three Emperors was always his preferred solution, in that it isolated France and assured him of more influence over the chancelleries in Vienna and St Petersburg. When Austro-Russian differences in the Balkans made the League's renewal impossible in 1887, Bismarck negotiated the aptly named Reinsurance Treaty with St Petersburg, so determined was he to try to preserve a link of some kind.

Nevertheless, Bismarck's efforts to preserve the peace in Europe often confused – and alarmed – contemporaries, and have caused no little controversy among historians ever since. Norton Medlicott for one argues that Germany's position in Europe between 1871 and 1890 was so secure that it did not require his 'complicated subterfuges' in its defence.[8] So complicated had his dealings with the Austrians and Russians become by 1890 that some scholars doubt if even Bismarck could have run in harness with both St Petersburg and Vienna for much longer. But it is to Bismarck's credit that he should have refused to succumb to the fatalism which began to dominate the thinking of much of the German leadership concerning relations with Russia in the winter of 1887–88. Russian military preparations in the second half of 1887 caused widespread alarm. Count Waldersee, Vice-Chief of the General Staff, was only the most outspoken among a number of advocates of preventive war with Russia at this time. The sense of urgency in some cases was heightened by alarm at the reviving confidence of the French army. Time, it was said, was not on the side of Germany. In Vienna the German military attaché urged Franz Joseph to seize the initiative against Russia. Kalnóky, the Austrian Foreign Minister, agreed that a war must ultimately be fought to decide whether 'Slavic Russia will dominate Europe or not'.[9] The question was when. Was time on the side of the Dual Alliance, or would Slav propaganda increase divisions within the Habsburg Empire? Yet the more the Austrians looked into the matter the more obvious was their unpreparedness for war. Meanwhile in Berlin Bismarck had an ally in the old Emperor. Bismarck himself stressed the many-sidedness of the relations of the powers one with another. To weaken or eliminate the Russians would strengthen the Habsburgs, whose relations with Germany might thenceforward become less predictable. Bismarck was vindicated in the judgement, at least in the short run, in that following a temporary deterioration in Russo-German relations the worst of the shadows lifted during the years 1895–1907. The period of tension, however, had been sufficiently prolonged for France and Russia to draw together, thus removing one of the keystones to Bismarck's diplomacy since 1871, the isolation of France.

Advocates of a Russian alignment with France had become increasingly numerous and active in Russia in the 1880s. There existed, of course, much prejudice against France as a republic, but for those who could see no other way to advance Russian interests in the Balkans even a republic had its uses. However much Bismarck might try to disguise the fact, Germany was an obstacle in the Near East if only because in the last resort Berlin could not allow the Habsburg Empire to be seriously weakened. Russia and Germany were also being driven apart by economic issues. Since the 1870s both had been raising tariffs to protect special economic interests – infant industries in Russia and grain producers in Germany. Bismarck, hard though he tried to preserve power politics as an arcane science for diplomats and strategists, had to take some account of economic interests, just as he could not ignore the force of German nationalist feeling against the Slavs. Russia's effort to exclude foreigners from landholding in vulnerable border territories prompted Bismarck to try a little economic leverage at the end of 1887. But when the Russians found themselves denied loans in Berlin they could always turn to Paris. Thus the current in favour of an alignment with France gained a little more in strength, though not enough for Giers, the Russian Foreign Minister, to lose interest in the Reinsurance Treaty with Germany. Originally signed on 18 June 1887, this was due for renewal in 1890. While the treaty imposed no restraints on Germany if Russia attacked Austria, Russia was equally free to act as she chose if Germany attacked France. It also promised Russia Germany's moral support for her interests in Bulgaria, at the Straits and in Constantinople. Giers was not pro-German, but he believed that a renewal of the treaty might do something to limit or control Russo-German friction.

Bismarck, however, had fallen from office in March 1890, and his successors were anxious to do nothing to disturb the Austrians, or indeed the British with whom they were now seeking a closer relationship. Bismarck himself had been putting out feelers to the British in 1888–89. His specific proposal for an alliance in January 1889 perhaps suggests he was no longer content with the tenuous link between Britain and his partners in the Triple Alliance (of 20 May 1882, Germany, Austria and Italy) provided by the Mediterranean Agreements of 1887. Salisbury refused the offer, but the two powers continued to be drawn closer by colonial conversations which resulted in the treaty of 1 July 1890. Bismarck's successors hoped that this agreement would be followed in due course by a more far-reaching arrangement with the British. The latter, however, intended to compromise their freedom of action no more than was absolutely necessary. All that Berlin had succeeded in doing under its post-Bismarckian management was to sacrifice one admittedly tenuous tie – with Russia – without the assurance of substituting something better – or indeed as good. In fact the Russians were not merely disturbed by the non-renewal of the Reinsurance Treaty but were frightened by the spectre of an Anglo-German alliance, all of which made the case of the pro-French parties in Russia appear that much stronger. Tsar Alexander III had already treated the pro-French faction and critics of his Foreign Minister with more indulgence than Giers himself would have preferred. Similarly the interests of his father and Gorchakov in the security of France had been demonstrated as far back as 1874–75. It was the strategic argument which Alexander III himself used in March 1892: 'We really must come to an agreement with the French, and, in the event of a war between France and Germany, throw ourselves immediately upon the Germans so as not to give them time to beat the French first and then turn on us.'[10]

Here again one sees a firm acknowledgement of the strategic revolution that had been effected in 1870–71; the fear not only that France could be destroyed as a great power, but in so short a space of time as to give other powers no time to influence the outcome save by quick military action.

Yet the Franco-Russian military convention of 4 January 1894 does not represent a deep divide in the relations of the powers. It formalized what was already possible – Russian intervention against Germany to preserve the balance of power in Europe. Nor did it mean that henceforth Europe would be divided into two armed camps. Ironically it was followed by one of the quieter periods in the relations of the powers in so far as these concerned the continent of Europe. The French continued to brood over the lost provinces of Alsace and Lorraine, but knew that no power would support them in a war arising over that issue. In any case rivalries outside Europe, especially with Britain, were more pressing. Even the situation in the Balkans began to seem more manageable. Although crises occurred over Crete and the Armenians, both the regional and great-power balances worked in favour of a settlement. The Turks were able to defeat the Greeks in the war of 1897, but the powers were sufficiently united to turn Crete into an autonomous province under Prince George of Greece in 1898. The Armenians were less fortunate: they were left to their fate under the Turks as the powers probed each other's intentions, and gradually settled on a policy of *quieta non movere*. At first Rosebery and later Salisbury in 1894–95, under pressure from public opinion in Britain, tried to find ways to stop the Armenian massacres. But the Russians had Armenian subjects of their own. Reforms on behalf of Armenians in the Ottoman Empire might encourage unrest within Russia's own borders. The Russians also feared that the British might try to use the Armenian crisis as an excuse to push their fleet into the Black Sea. They contemplated the seizure of Constantinople, however, only as a defensive measure – to be employed as a last resort if the British began to move. In July and August 1895 the German ambassador in London caused a stir in Berlin with his reports that Salisbury might be considering a partition of the Ottoman Empire in certain circumstances. What Salisbury said or intended remains obscure – a misunderstanding or misinterpretation of some kind obviously occurred. Clearly nerves were on edge for a time in all the interested capitals. At one time the Germans had hopes of a new understanding with the British: at another Holstein was describing Salisbury as a trouble-maker, who was trying to excite dissension among the powers for the benefit of Britain. Salisbury himself feared a Russian dash for Constantinople.

In fact no one wished to play for high stakes. Instead the years 1895–97 brought a clarification in the policy of Britain, Austria-Hungary and Russia, this clarification in each instance making for a more restrained approach to the problems in the Near East. Salisbury, whatever he might have said to the German ambassador, had continued to show interest in the survival of the Ottoman Empire. He had done this despite warnings from the Admiralty that it would be unsafe to send the British fleet to defend the Straits against the Russians so long as it might be threatened by the French from the western Mediterranean. From 1896 Salisbury was forced to bend in the face of a reiteration of these arguments in the Cabinet. He was also driven to acknowledge that Turkish atrocities in Armenia had so outraged the British public that it was improbable that a British government would be allowed to support Turkey in the foreseeable future in any case. Constantinople could thus no longer be the key to British strategy in the Near East. Egypt, it seemed, would have to be used as the alternative. But this change in British priorities meant that Salisbury could no longer honour the limited promises he had made to the Austrians in the Mediterranean Agreements of 1887 to help contain Russian influence. With Berlin's relations with St Petersburg also undergoing an improvement, Vienna had no option but to take the road to St Petersburg itself. The internal problems of the Habsburg Empire were discouraging foreign adventures in any case. It was thus with no small relief that the Austrians discovered that the Russians, too, had their problems, both at home and in the Far East, and that they were willing to conclude an agreement in 1897 for the maintenance of the status quo in the Near East. A region whose instability had appeared to threaten the peace of Europe off and on since 1875 suddenly ceased to hold a top place on the great powers' lists of priorities.

It is true that by the turn of the century speculation was beginning to develop as to the future of the Austro-Hungarian Empire – whether, for instance, it would survive the death of Franz Joseph (in fact he was to live on until 1916). But in general by the later 1890s, despite the continuation of the arms race and the existence of the various alliances, a war between the powers over primarily European issues seemed less likely than at almost any time during the past half-century. Some historians have argued that the scramble for territory and influence outside Europe acted as a safety-valve, but the situation was probably more complicated than that. The powers both responded to the opportunities outside Europe, and were perhaps encouraged to act with more caution inside Europe in consequence, and at the same time were reassured by the relative calm in Europe so that they felt free to pursue their ambitions in the wider world. This was particularly the case with Germany. The adoption of *Weltpolitik* from the mid-1890s would hardly have been possible had Berlin been so neurotically obsessed with the Russian threat as in 1887–88, or if the fear of a two-front war with France and Russia had been so pronounced as it later became. It is true that

Germany welcomed the opportunity to divert Russian and French attention away from the heart of Europe, and looked forward hopefully to the outbreak of war between Britain and one or both of these powers. But Germany could not compel Russia and France to behave in this fashion. She could only try to exploit her new freedom of movement, and encourage the other powers to continue to turn their backs on Europe. But clearly a global dimension had been added to the European balance between the powers. Some contemporaries believed that the global dimension had become or was about to become all important. Certainly the relations between the European powers were about to be profoundly influenced by events outside Europe. This is an appropriate moment at which to begin a study of the origins of the great imperial scramble.

THE GLOBAL SETTING

The label, 'the new imperialism', is often attached to the great European colonial expansion of the later nineteenth century. The gains were impressive by any crude quantitative test. Ten million square miles and a tenth of the world's population quickly found themselves under new ownership. Many Europeans were intoxicated by the achievement and expected the advance to continue at the expense of the Ottoman and even the Chinese empires. Yet this was only the final phase of a process of European expansion which had been going on since the fifteenth century. Europeans became increasingly aware of the brittleness of most non-white societies. Anglo-French colonial rivalry reached its first climax in the mid-eighteenth century. Its renewal on a major scale seemed possible at times in the Napoleonic era. But thereafter, until the 1870s, though competition continued, a major Anglo-French colonial crisis seemed improbable.

Rather more serious was the Anglo-Russian rivalry in parts of Asia – the so-called 'great game'. This was waged from the late 1820s in Persia, Afghanistan and central Asia – though by means which stopped short of a direct collision of arms. It was the peoples of Asia who were the victims of the 'great game'. The supposed Russian threat to India led to British interventions in Persia and Afghanistan, though it probably served as an excuse more often than a cause of much of the British expansion in India at this time.[11] Too much difficult terrain lay between the British and Russian Asiatic empires until the later nineteenth century and the coming of railways, for their rivalry to advance beyond the elaborate game of intrigue and skirmishing. As the Crimean War demonstrated, the British and Russians had difficulties in coming to grips with each other even in

Europe. From the 1860s into the early 1870s the British even favoured a policy of 'masterly inactivity' concerning their strategic frontiers and interests in India. The Russians, however, did not reciprocate, but continued with a massive territorial expansion of their own at the expense of one central Asian khanate after another. Local needs of security and trade, the ambition of military and political agents on the spot, as with the British in India, explain this steady advance in part. But Alexander II and his advisers in St Petersburg were also anxious after the Crimean War to build up whatever positions of strength they could against their great enemy, the British. The advance into central Asia might be slow, but in the end it was hoped that even a vague threat to the British in India might prove of some political or military value. Not surprisingly, Anglo-Russian differences in the Near East in 1875–78 soon had repercussions in Afghanistan. Salisbury, the British Secretary of State for India, thought a Russian advance into the sub-continent 'a chimera', but he was still anxious to exclude Russian influence from Afghanistan. Lord Lytton, the new Viceroy, was ordered to make sure. Lytton, however, from 1876, acted more vigorously than Salisbury intended. Efforts to promote British influence in Kabul naturally prompted the Emir to lean towards Russia. British countermoves then produced the Second Afghan War of 1878–79.

Such was the confusion and uncertainty by 1879 that Salisbury, now Foreign Secretary, gave some thought to a possible partition of Afghanistan by Britain and Russia in the hope this would produce a solid frontier. In fact, neither power was anxious to destroy Afghanistan as a buffer state: the dispute centred on the degree of influence which each desired to exercise within its borders. The crisis was resolved for the time being by the emergence of an unexpectedly strong ruler in Kabul. In addition, from 1880, a new Gladstone ministry ruled in London, a ministry which was only too eager to disengage and which seized the opportunity to negotiate a new treaty with the Afghans. Nevertheless a war between Russia and Britain – over the Near East or central Asia – ranked high in the calculations of those who were trying to divine the future in the 1880s. The Gladstone ministry itself seemed close to war with Russia in 1885 as a result of frontier disputes and incidents between Russia and the Afghans. The British War Office concluded that in the event of conflict it lacked the forces and means to fight the Russians in Afghanistan. It hoped instead to be able to strike by way of the Black Sea. From Batum, with help from Caucasian rebels, it hoped to be able to draw off Russian forces and fight the critical campaign in a region where the main advantages would lie with the British. But in 1885 the British found the Turkish Straits closed against them. Germany and Austria-Hungary ranged themselves beside Russia, and together their influence was paramount at Constantinople. This was a great disappointment to British strategists. Worse was to follow as France and Russia drew together, so that from 1896 the British had to view Egypt and not the Straits as the key to their strategy in this region. But this also meant that, denied the chance to strike at Russia in the Black Sea, the British would have to try to meet any Russian challenge from central Asia by action from the Persian Gulf and the North-West frontier of India.

The Russian position is well described by Firuz Kazemzadeh[12]:

> The gentry and the army, twin pillars of the Tsarist regime, were bitter over the results of the Congress of Berlin. . . . The ruling class called upon the Tsar to embark on new conquests, to compensate in Asia for failure in Europe. The military saw England as Russia's principal enemy and believed she could be dealt a serious blow through India.

Even Shuvalov, ambassador in London in 1878, and reputedly pro-British, favoured a decisive advance against Afghanistan. 'We shall trade England blow for blow . . .' The importance of Asia is similarly reflected in the comment of a British diplomat in 1885 that he expected Constantinople, St Petersburg and Peking to prove the key diplomatic posts in the future. Russian railway building in central Asia increased British fears. Larger Russian armies could be more easily deployed and supplied to threaten British interests. India seemed to grow more vulnerable every year. As David Gillard observes: 'This was Britain's basic international problem after 1885, and it remained so until the German naval threat took priority in the time of Grey.'[13] The greatest fear was not so much an actual Russian invasion of India, but rather that, if the Russians threatened Afghanistan or Persia, the British would be forced to move so many troops from India as to facilitate a rising of Indian nationalists against the Raj. The British would be caught between two fires. For twenty years British strategists grappled with this problem without producing a solution. In addition they continued to fear a Russian drive for Constantinople, and, as the century wore on, they feared a Russian challenge to their interests in China. Thus Anglo-Russian rivalry ran around much of the periphery of Asia. Usually it posed a much greater threat to peace than the greatly publicized scramble for territory by the powers in Africa. It was also a rivalry whose origins predated the much-discussed imperialist rivalries of the late nineteenth century.

Other anticipations of the so-called 'new imperialism' are not difficult to find. From the French entry into Algeria in the 1830s, much of North Africa began to appear highly vulnerable. The British were soon making it plain that the French would not be allowed to walk into Tunis. There were fears, too, for Tripoli and Morocco. The British similarly kept a jealous watch on Spanish activities in Morocco. Although the 1860s found both Britain and France working

17

for the maintenance of the status quo in Morocco, the Near Eastern crisis of 1875–78 speedily reawakened concern over the brittleness of most of the Muslim societies bordering the Mediterranean. The possibility of a general partition was touched upon by Bismarck, and the matter attracted a lot of notice in the Spanish press in July and August 1876. The British had earlier approached Berlin in April 1876 to review the possibility of a joint approach to prevent 'an uncalled for attack on Morocco' by Spain.[14] From 1878 it was the turn of France to arouse British and Spanish fears that she might try to take advantage of the confusion that prevailed in Morocco. The Madrid Conference of 1880 produced a fair measure of agreement among the powers concerning the regulation of their relations with the Moors: it could not, however, put an end to speculation about the future of Morocco, especially with the French occupation of Tunis in 1881 and that of Egypt by the British in 1882. The 1870s brought a similar quickening of interest in many parts of the world. The Japanese began to fear European intrusions in Korea as early as 1873. The French, already established in parts of Indo-China, were troubled throughout the 1870s by insecure frontiers and by rebels in Saigon and Cambodia. In September 1881 they were easily persuaded that the British were about to move eastward and threaten the independence of Siam. The British were equally suspicious. Not surprisingly, by 1885 the British had taken Upper Burma and the French the rest of Indo-China. If Disraeli had no great imperial design beyond the defence of India and the routes to the east, his Colonial Secretary, Lord Carnarvon, was talking in 1876 of the need for something like a British Monroe Doctrine in Africa. The French were on the move again in West Africa by 1879. There was nothing especially momentous about the British occupation of Egypt in 1882, at least in the general history of imperialism.[15]

Indeed the British intervened in Egypt with some reluctance to protect their financial and still more their strategic interests as a result of the collapse of Khedival authority. The original plan was to act with the French. Once there the British talked of evacuation, but found it impossible to create a stable, pro-British regime. They feared the intervention of other powers if they pulled out. The Suez Canal grew dramatically in importance in the 1880s. The sailing ship was at last being eclipsed by the steamship (the triple expansion engine was producing dramatic savings in fuel costs), and steam, unlike sail, could make full use of the Suez–Red Sea route. Thus the British felt compelled to stay in Egypt, even at the cost of worsening relations with the French. They also missed an opportunity to increase their control of Egyptian finances in 1885. An important loan was guaranteed by all the European powers. To combat French and Russian influence on the commission of the debt the British thereafter were heavily dependent on the Triple Alliance, and in particular on Germany. Understandably Berlin expected to be paid for its support.

Meanwhile Egypt's strategic importance continued to grow as the British came to doubt their ability to challenge Russia at the Turkish Straits. By 1895–96, therefore, Salisbury was persuaded that for Britain to be assured of her position in Egypt, she must also control the Upper Nile. The conquest of the Sudan led to a dramatic confrontation with the French expedition under Marchand at Fashoda in 1898, and (apart from the crises over Morocco of 1905 and 1911) to the most serious war scare between the powers over the partition of Africa. But it was the place of Egypt in Britain's overall imperial and strategic interests which made Salisbury and his colleagues so determined to fight if necessary. Interestingly enough, in 1898, Salisbury was anxious to conciliate the French if possible. There could, however, be no question of concessions over Egypt and the Sudan. The compensation Salisbury had in mind lay in West Africa, not on or near the Nile. Nothing could more clearly indicate his imperial priorities, or the fact that for him British interest in the Nile and Suez followed naturally from the development of Britain as a world power (and one with very special interests in the East) from the eighteenth century.

A similar history lay behind British interest and involvement in southern Africa. Notwithstanding the growing economic importance of this region in the 1880s and 1890s, notably with the gold and diamond discoveries in the Boer states, and despite the empire-building led and inspired by Cecil Rhodes, the British government was more influenced by broader considerations. The Suez Canal did not put an end to the importance of the Cape route – it was always possible that Britain might lose control of the Mediterranean in a war. Thus British ministers jealously sought to preserve their nation's paramountcy in the region against any significant external or internal threat. The new-found wealth of the Boer republics did not merely excite the greed of British capitalists: it threatened to upset the local balance of power in southern Africa against the British-controlled Cape Colony. The British might have coexisted with the Boer republics so long as they were relatively poor, essentially agrarian societies. But with their new wealth there was no telling what influence they might wield, or what interest and support they might attract from other powers. As Salisbury himself insisted, Britain must be 'Boss'. This was the main reasoning which lay behind the British government's contribution to the outbreak of the Boer War in 1899. This, too, was a region where Britain was determined to oppose the intervention of another power – if necessary by force of arms. As it happened, no Fashoda accompanied the Boer War – though some European statesmen noted the attractions of a continental coalition to try to bring pressure to bear upon the British, a possibility which caused some headaches and alarm in London. It was finally decided in Berlin, however, that Russia and France would be the main beneficiaries from any weakening of the British Empire. Indeed, Germany might emerge as a net loser from a change in the overall balance of power.

German enthusiasm for *Weltpolitik* from the mid-1890s did not cause the leadership to forget the precept of Bismarck in the previous decade: that Germany lay between France and Russia, and would continue to do so whatever changes were made to the map of Africa. His immediate successors gave up some territory in Africa for Heligoland and the hope of a closer relationship with Britain. Bismarck himself in February 1882 rejected a suggestion that he should take a prominent part in the Egyptian question with the remark: 'The consciousness of being a Great Power must not seduce us into pursuing a policy based on prestige in the French fashion.'[16] Nor did French activity in the colonial field pass unchallenged in their own country. The 1880s witnessed some fierce parliamentary debates. Many deputies asked how some of the new territories could ever repay the heavy costs incurred in their acquisition. Indo-China alone had devoured over 30 million francs in 1888. Clemenceau insisted that the policy of overseas expansion weakened France against Germany in Europe. Jules Ferry replied for the government that France could not remain a great power without colonies. He also made use of the economic argument that France needed colonies in an increasingly protectionist world and in view of restricted economic opportunities at home. The France colonial party as a whole made much of economic arguments, and many businessmen were enthusiastic supporters of the French Empire. But historians have tended to become more impressed by the force of political and other non-economic considerations in recent years.[17] Ferry seemed genuinely convinced that without a world role France would be doomed to 'decadence'. On the Left, Louis Blanc and, for a time, Jean Jaurès enthused over France's civilizing role in North Africa. French missionaries did much to promote French expansion.

In the later nineteenth century the belief spread rapidly that great changes were afoot in the world, that in the not too distant future most of the globe would be dominated by a few huge empires, and that an ambitious people could easily be left behind in the race for territory and influence. Max Weber's inaugural lecture at the University of Freiburg in 1895 was typical. He claimed that German unification would prove but a 'youthful fòlly' unless it were followed by *Weltmachtpolitik*. But it is also worth noting that John Ruskin was lecturing on similar lines in Britain as early as 1870. Admittedly he was concerned with the foundation of white colonies when he argued that Britain should seize 'every piece of waste land she can set her foot on', but definitions of 'waste land' could prove extraordinarily elastic. 'This is what England must either do or perish: she must found colonies as fast and as far as she is able, formed of her most energetic and worthiest men . . .' was his conclusion.[18] At least one listener, Cecil Rhodes, took him literally. Not long afterwards the historian, J. A. Froude, portrayed a world in which only the territorial giants would count, and in which Britain with her 'puny' home territory must stand doomed beside the United States, Russia and even Germany – without her colonies. As early as 1881 he feared it was too late for Britain: the future of the Anglo-Saxon race lay with the Americans. 'We *cannot* assimilate our colonies, and without them we can now be nothing but a considerable commercial state. As an Imperial Power, our end is formidably near.'[19] Only two years later Seeley uttered the famous words:

> If the United States and Russia hold together for another half century, they will at the end of that time completely dwarf the old European states such as France and Germany, and depress them into a second class, They will do the same to England, if at the end of that time England still thinks of herself as simply a European state.[20]

Similarly in France a professor, Leroy Beaulieu, had insisted in 1874 that his country would become a secondary power without a great African empire.

Examples can easily be multiplied. Lord Esher, an influential figure behind the scenes in Edwardian Britain, as a young man in 1878 favoured the conquest of Afghanistan. The days of buffer states were over: the future lay with great 'agglomerations'. Théophile Delcassé, a notable French Foreign Secretary in the early 1900s, argued in 1885 that Europe was stifling within her present boundaries. While he spoke of the value of colonial markets, he was still more interested in French power and prestige. He made much of the threat from the 'expansive empires', such as China as well as Britain in Asia, and given his concern for the overall balance between the powers he welcomed German aid against Britain in Egypt.[21] Many others spoke of a contracting world, especially in the 1890s. There was a lack of elbow room. Only the fittest would survive as the dynamic powers competed to fill the available space. Gustav Schmoller, a German economist, argued in 1890: 'the course of world history in the twentieth century will be determined by the competition between the Russian, English, American, and perhaps the Chinese world empires, and by their aspirations to reduce all other, smaller states to dependence on them'.[22] George Bernard Shaw concluded in 1900: 'The partition of the greater part of the globe among such Powers is . . . now only a question of time.' Salisbury himself spoke of a world of living and dying nations, in which the former were likely to encroach upon the latter.

These expectations concerning the future did not centre purely on power and prestige, or on the need of virile peoples for ample territory in which to realize their potential. The rapid industrial growth of Europe in the later nineteenth century reinforced existing economic motives for empire. Recessions, periods of low profitability, and much pessimism as to long-term economic prospects added to the sense of urgency. Over-production not only threatened the profits of the wealthy: it caused unemployment among the masses. Without assured markets and sources of raw materials, a great power might find itself undermined from within by revolutionary forces. Empire, it could be argued, was needed not only for survival in the world as a great power, but also for the survival of the existing political and social order at home. Much more was at stake than the profits and dividends of the rich – perhaps even a whole way of life. Nevertheless this did not mean, as we shall see later (pp. 31–2, 36–8, 46–7), that all people of wealth and position were in agreement either on the need for overseas expansion or the form it should take. These divisions meant that politicians, diplomats and strategists often had scope for manoeuvre and choices of their own even in the face of considerable pressure for economic reasons. Bismarck's motivation concerning colonies in the 1880s was clearly complex, so complex that historians are still in disagreement as to the main determinants in his policy. It might be argued, for instance, that part of his responsiveness to the demands of the colonial activists arose from his need for allies in the Reichstag to offset the support he had lost when Germany's swing to protectionism resulted in higher food prices. Colonies were used to buy parliamentary supporters. The growth of protectionism in Europe from the 1870s, with the exception of Britain, fed the appetite for colonies in any case. The Germans in particular began to ask how long Britain herself would cling to free trade in such circumstances. Salisbury in turn reproached a Frenchman in January 1897: 'If you were not such rabid protectionists, we should not be such gluttons for territory.'[23] Nevertheless Salisbury, like Bismarck before him, continued to weigh each individual demand against his perception of the national interest as a whole. In 1888 Sir Harry Johnston, the great colonial activist in East Africa, and brim-full of ideas for the partition of Africa to Britain's advantage, had found Salisbury preoccupied with Egypt and anxious to conciliate the other powers elsewhere in Africa.[24] This does not mean that Salisbury was not a tenacious defender of British interests in Africa. His differences with Joseph Chamberlain over the 1898 settlement of West Africa with France have probably been exaggerated. But he was more successful than most in evaluating individual issues within their global context.[25]

Finally it must not be forgotten that it was relatively easy for Europe to expand at this time, partly because no crisis, domestic or foreign, concentrated the attention of the powers in Europe to the exclusion of all else. In addition, relatively little effort was required to effect major transformations in Asia and Africa. Only a small increase in European involvement was often sufficient to set off a chain reaction. However limited the initial intent, the effect could be so disruptive as to facilitate, encourage or even necessitate further action. Rivals were attracted to the scene, or sought compensation elsewhere. The process, once started, was difficult to reverse, as the British found in Egypt. Once committed, the new overlord was not easily put off even by unexpected and rapidly rising costs. It took defeat at the hands of Japan and revolution at home to persuade the Russian government to revise but not radically alter its Asiatic ambitions. The British were a little sobered but not daunted by the unexpectedly expensive Boer War. In general the charges imposed by the imperial race were tolerable when they were not ridiculously small. While it was fuelled in part by rivalry among the powers, even that rivalry rarely carried with it a grave risk of war. When all is said and done it is doubtful if – in the later nineteenth century – there were more than two occasions when the European powers were close to war over imperial questions – Penj-deh in 1885 and Fashoda in 1898. Britain then believed, rightly or wrongly in both cases, that major imperial interests were at stake. Any significant setbacks were expected to have far-reaching effects on Britain's position in India or the routes to the East. It was as if, in a world of competing European empires, there existed major fault-lines, one running, for instance, from Constantinople to Afghanistan. The Suez–Red Sea route formed another: the Nile a third. Southern Africa might have made a fourth, but the British were fortunate at the turn of the century when the other powers failed to combine against them. The British themselves had also begun to retire from the Central American–Caribbean area in the second half of the century, and thus avoided a collision – though not a few alarms – with the rising power of the United States.

THE FAR EASTERN QUESTION TO 1896

One other major fault-line lay outside Europe. This began in Korea and spread later to Manchuria. A war between China and Japan in 1894–95 resulted in an unexpected victory for the Japanese, a victory of so decisive a character as to excite the interest of the European powers and, even, some Americans. The vulnerability of the great Chinese Empire had been demonstrated in the 1840s and 1850s, but thereafter there had been sufficient signs of vigour for some of the question marks against its future to be removed. Indeed, the possi-

bility of China as one of the world's great powers had been
canvassed. Its defeat in 1895, however, now excited speculation of
a contrary nature. Might not China join the extensive territories
being partitioned by the imperialist nations? At the turn of the
century two Americans, A. T. Mahan and Brooks Adams, were
among those who believed that a world war might be waged to
determine the future of China. They expected the 'sea powers' to be
ranged against the 'land powers' – a war above all of Russia against
Britain, with Germany as an unknown quantity which might join
either side. This proved too cataclysmic a view, but contemporaries
certainly had much reason to give thought to the future of China,
particularly in the area where Russia and Japan seemed likely to
come into conflict. Furthermore, from the mid-1890s to 1907 the
relations of all the great powers were profoundly influenced, directly
or indirectly, by events in the Far East.

The origins of the Far Eastern question reach back many years.
In the eighteenth century most Europeans stood in awe of the
Chinese civilization, a people who held the Europeans at arm's
length, and an empire which had emerged time and time again from
internal and external crises since the second century BC with its basic
character unchanged. It is true that Lord Macartney, on his mission
to China in 1793–94, had detected much internal decay, and twice
between 1839 and 1860 the Chinese suffered humiliating defeats at
the hands of the Europeans. The country was also ravaged by the
Taiping rebellion. The Europeans and Americans secured privileged
positions in many Chinese ports, while Russia took possession of
much Chinese territory – to the north of the Amur River – and
founded the city and port of Vladivostok in the 1860s. But the
Russians lacked the means and incentive to press further. The
British, satisfied with the protection accorded their trade, had no
wish to weaken China further. They were not eager, in the 1860s, to
embark upon a repetition of their experiences in India since the mid-
eighteenth century. The recent Indian Mutiny had dispelled some
illusions: there was more awareness of the difficulties of trying to run
a sub-continent. More efforts to increase British influence in China
were likely to encourage other powers to do the same. British interests would be adequately and more cheaply served by the maintenance of the status quo. Neither France nor the United States could
afford to act to any effect on their own. Consequently, when the
Manchu rulers of China finally suppressed the Taipings, the empire
could look forward to a period of relative tranquillity in which to put
its house in order.

By the 1880s the Chinese appeared to have achieved a measure
of success. They had acquired some western arms and other mechanical aids. They were trying to assert themselves once more in
traditional spheres of influence. Although defeated by the French in

Indo-China, they were not discredited. Further north the Russians, worried by the vulnerability and undeveloped state of the 400,000 square miles they had earlier acquired from the Chinese, viewed their neighbour with some apprehension. They feared China's enormous land-hungry, job-seeking multitudes – their own handfuls of colonists in the east could easily be swamped. Russia's eastern territories were an economic liability, and were separated from European Russia by 4,000 miles of inhospitable terrain. In the absence of a railway it might take eighteen months to send an army to the east. Apart from the possible threat from China herself, the Russians were troubled by their own lack of economic success. The British were responsible for over 60 per cent of the foreign trade and investment in China, though this represented only 2½ per cent of Britain's total commerce, and only 5 per cent of her foreign investment

For Russia to have any chance of asserting herself in the Far East – perhaps even retaining what she already held – a railway was essential. Minor incidents with the Chinese in 1886, the Penj-deh war scare with Britain in 1885 (which had minor repercussions in the Far East), and a Sino-Japanese crisis over Korea all reminded the Russians of the need for action. A ministerial conference discussed the problem in St Petersburg on 18 June 1887. It concluded that a railway was a strategic necessity while accepting that there would be few commercial returns in the foreseeable future. A decision to build was taken in principle, and over the next four years resources for the Trans-Siberian Railway gradually became available. A crisis in the Balkans passed away without a war; from 1890 Russia had a veto over railway building in Persia and thus had no cause to fear that a rival (the British) would steal a march on her there. French capital began to ease Russia's financial problems. Meanwhile Russian interest in the railway was increased by the sense of impotence in Korean affairs (foreign intervention was beginning to awaken that kingdom from its long slumber), and by the fear that the British might soon extend their railway building in China to Manchuria. For some time the so-called *Vostochniki* (the 'Easterners') had formed a pressure group inside Russia, proclaiming their country's special mission in Asia. Prominent among them was Prince Ukhtomskii, a leading socialite and editor of the *St Petersburg News*. 'This great and mysterious Orient is ready to become ours', he claimed. Dostoevsky had been another enthusiast. Asia, unlike Europe, should prove responsive to Russian leadership, and especially to her spiritual influence: Russia would not be treated as an inferior by Asians. The start of the railway in 1891 intensified aspirations and beliefs of this kind: Social Darwinism mingled freely with Russian messianism.

From 1892 this drive to the east became, for some years, very much the preserve of the new Minister of Finance, Sergei Witte. A self-made man of immense vanity, he was nevertheless one of the few outstanding leaders thrown up by Tsarist Russia in its last years. An American engineer was sufficiently impressed to liken him to Cecil Rhodes, the British empire-builder in southern Africa. Given the scale on which Witte operated, a reverse comparison would have been more appropriate. Witte was a late convert to the Oriental programme, but from 1892 he saw exciting connections between the new railway and the development of heavy industry in Russia. He hoped to stimulate the Russian economy both by opening up Siberia and by the readier access to China which the line would make possible. Witte was very conscious of Russian backwardness. Russia, he warned, could share the fate of eastern peoples at the hands of Europe unless she effectively modernized herself. In fact foreign estimates of Russian strength varied wildly at this time. Many British military experts thought primarily of the size of the armies they believed the Russians might be able to mass in central Asia. Henry Adams, in contrast, contended in 1891 that Russia was so rotten she could disintegrate in a generation leaving the United States to Americanize Siberia if it were so minded. H. G. Wells once remarked that Russia might become a 'vaster Ireland'. Witte himself believed it vital for Russia to avoid war at this time, and to concentrate on economic growth. Hence his opposition to Balkan adventures, his support of the first Hague Peace Conference of 1899 (Russia would benefit enormously from a deceleration in the arms race), and his efforts to increase Russian influence in the Far East by economic penetration. Land-grabbing would only encourage other powers to do the same, and Russia was likely to emerge the loser against such competition. Thus, although in July 1903 he described 'the essence' of the Far Eastern problem to be the take-over of all Asiatic states save such as Japan which adopted western technology and skills, his real concern was to avoid a premature division of China.

Despite his apparent caution, even Witte's policies imposed a crippling strain on the Russian economy. The Chinese had still less success in accommodating themselves to the realities of the new industrial world. Very different was the situation in Japan. More isolated from the rest of the world than China before the arrival of an American naval squadron under Commodore Perry in 1853, the Japanese in less than two generations effected one of the most remarkable transformations of both government and economy which the world has ever seen. Whereas China acquired some of the appearance of a modern state – mostly in the form of western arms – Japan developed the substance. Why the Japanese should have been the first non-white people to achieve this breakthrough, and then in so dramatic and comprehensive a manner, may always in the last resort defy a satisfactory explanation. Perhaps the size of China would have thwarted the most dedicated of reformers in the late nineteenth century. Japan was more manageable in this respect, yet smaller countries had stagnated. Frances Moulder argues that the key difference between China and Japan was the greater freedom of the latter from western interference, both political and economic. In particular the Japanese government was able to spend proportionately more of its income on modernization than the Chinese.[26] But this fails to explain the contrast between the thoroughness and clarity of purpose demonstrated by the Japanese and the divided and hesitant response of the Chinese élite. Irrespective of the conduct and influence of the imperialist powers, the Japanese could still have hesitated or mismanaged their opportunity. It is necessary to take account of the discipline and flexibility of the Japanese, their open-mindedness and respect for tradition, their pragmatism and artistic feeling.

In contrast, the prime concern of the majority of the Chinese élite, irrespective of the opportunities and obstacles, appeared to be the preservation of as much of the existing order as possible. It failed to see that western armaments and technology could not be entirely abstracted from the society which produced them. Thus, whereas Japanese entrepreneurs received positive encouragement from their government and were given scope to develop and prosper, their Chinese counterparts were inhibited by the restraints imposed by central and provincial authorities. This subordination of the merchant and entrepreneur to the political order had been the norm in Chinese affairs for 2,000 years. In the past this might have made for stability or ordered progress. But by the late nineteenth century something more dynamic was required, and this the Chinese mandarins could not supply, nor would they give others the opportunity to try to supply it. The attitude of the conservative Chinese mandarin is well exemplified in a meeting in London of one of their number with a Japanese Minister of Finance. The mandarin was shocked by the degree to which the other was immersing himself in the detail of western finance. Such craft skills should be left to mere technicians: the traditional 'way' in government should not be sullied by such menial work.[27] This episode occurred in the early 1870s, and foreshadowed the outcome of the war of 1894. Unfortunately for the Chinese of the late nineteenth century they were the heirs to one of the greatest success stories in history. For 2,000 years the Chinese had been able to see themselves as the centre of the world, surrounded by peoples of greater or lesser degrees of barbarism. Even when conquered, China had ultimately assimilated her conquerors, Mongul or Manchu. It was tempting, therefore, for the Chinese leaders to believe that while China might have to acquire certain western skills and tools, the core of Chinese life and civilization could go on as before. The Japanese saw that this was not enough.

The Japanese were fortunate that a period of political confusion gave way in 1868 to a strong central government (the Meiji Restoration), which was able to direct the energies of the nation into a programme of drastic modernization which left little untouched outside the private lives and homes of the people. Tax and legal reform backed up the new army, navy, factories and administration. The aim of a strong Japan to resist and ultimately compete with the great powers was coolly and systematically pursued. At the same time it was inspiriting, and could be used to justify measures which demanded discipline and heavy sacrifices. The obedience of the mass of the population to the will of the reforming élite was impressive. Those who opposed change, or who tried to engage in adventures abroad before Japan was strong enough to act, were defeated. Japan's progress was extraordinarily rapid, but still the leadership feared that other powers might initiate the scramble for territory and influence in the Far East before Japan herself was ready to take part. They feared in particular for Korea, a country whose strategic importance to Japan was akin to that of the Low Countries to Britain. Even the shadowy Chinese influence over that hermit kingdom was suspect. Japan could tolerate no influence there but her own.

Sino-Japanese rivalry in the weak and divided kingdom of Korea had been temporarily eased by the Treaty of Tientsin in April 1885. But a new political crisis in Korea soon led to war between China and Japan in 1894–95. The Japanese won a series of decisive victories on land and sea, and in the resultant Treaty of Shimonoseki of April 1895 secured the island of Formosa, the Liaotung peninsula, and a surrender by the Chinese of their claims to tutelage over Korea. These gains, however, were grossly in excess of what some powers, and Russia in particular, could stomach. The significance of the Japanese victory is reflected in the belief of Marschall, State Secretary of the German Foreign Ministry, that 'the continued existence of China' was now in question.[28] Holstein later noted how rapidly from 1895 the idea began to spread through Europe that China's days might be numbered – that she too might be ripe for partition.[29] Tsar Nicholas II began to talk of the seizure of an ice-free port. He was restrained by Witte and his Foreign Minister. But they too were disturbed by Japan's possession of the Liaotung peninsula. This commanded the Gulf of Pohai and the seaward approaches to Peking, as well as serving as an admirable point of access to southern Manchuria. As it happened, both Germany and France were willing to join with Russia in putting pressure on the Japanese to relinquish the peninsula to China. Russia soon had other opportunities to make her presence felt. Korea remained politically unstable, a situation the Russians were able to exploit from October 1895. Japan had to acknowledge this fact, and by the Yamagata–Lobanov agreement of 6 June 1896 Korea was subjected to what was virtually a joint Russo-Japanese protectorate.

For Witte, however, Korea was one of Russia's more expendable interests in the Far East. Much more important were the opportunities presented by China's palpable weakness following her defeat in 1895. In 1895, with the help of French capital, Witte was able to set up a Russo-Chinese Bank, an invaluable political and economic instrument. He followed this a year later with a fifteen-year defensive alliance with China directed against Japan. Witte's railway interests also prospered in that the Chinese agreed to the construction of a line through the centre of Manchuria (the Chinese Eastern Railway) to provide a direct route for the Trans-Siberian to Vladivostok. This avoided the long detour to the north through Russian territory on the Amur River. Russian troops were to guard the Chinese Eastern, and many tangible advantages were expected to flow from this agreement. These Russian gains naturally whetted the appetites of the other powers, though only France secured concessions at once (far away in the south). Salisbury, as usual, showed rather less alarm than his colleagues. He reached a reciprocity agreement to soften the effect of the French gains, and philosophically reflected that this increased Russian involvement in China might lessen their activities in Persia. It would be a different matter if the Russians began to push further south in China to where Britain's main interests lay – on the Yangtze. Nor, realistically, did he have much choice. Britain had much to demand her attention in other parts of the world – the question of the future of the Upper Nile was coming to a head – and she could find no ally with which to make a stand against the Russians in China. Fortunately the British were not as yet too seriously threatened by foreign competition in the region of the Yangtze and Hong Kong.

GERMAN WELTPOLITIK

In the discussion of imperial rivalries so far not much mention has been made of Germany. This was a deliberate omission. Some historians have exaggerated the impact of German *Weltpolitik* on great-power rivalries. This has occurred particularly among scholars who have centred their studies too narrowly on Germany, and who consequently have underestimated the importance of the actions of other powers – in some case these actions being totally unrelated to Germany herself. One must be wary of such assertions as German *Weltpolitik* 'made world war almost inevitable', or that it drove Russia, France and Britain into each other's arms.[30] One should qualify the claims of Eckart Kehr who, in his anxiety to uphold the primacy of domestic over outside influences on German foreign policy, asserted that 'the fundamental lines of foreign policy were set much more by anonymous social pressures from within than by ephemeral diplomatic manoeuvres'. The state of opinion within Germany was undoubtedly important, and is crucial to understanding why the German leadership so often chose the more provocative of the courses of action open to it. But the fact remains that *Weltpolitik*, as practised by Britain, Russia, France and Japan had more effect on the relations of the powers between 1897 and 1904, and that even in the years 1905–7 Germany was but one actor among several.

It was in January 1896 that Kaiser Wilhelm II officially proclaimed Germany's pursuit of *Weltpolitik*. Historians have offered varied explanations for this renewed and greatly enlarged interest in imperialism. Golo Mann, for instance, sees imperialism as a temporary international 'fashion'. 'Nothing that passed through the minds of the German "world politicians" at that time was specifically German.' He concludes: 'My thesis then would be that German Imperialism was irrational, governed by politics and psychology, not by rational economic interest.'[31] But historians have recently given more weight to the idea that the German leadership saw imperialism mainly in the context of domestic politics, and resorted to it as an instrument with which to decrease internal tension and disunity. They hoped through success in foreign and colonial policies to excite the patriotism of the people – especially of the middle classes; to maximize support for the regime, and to weaken the socialists. Success abroad might divert attention from grievances at home. It has also been argued that the nationalist leagues and other patriotic bodies of the 1890s were largely spontaneous creations: they were not merely tools in the hands of government for the promotion of social imperialism. They were expressions of popular discontent, and were directed against the new trends in German life. Many of the lower middle classes and skilled artisans were adversely affected by the great economic upheaval which Germany experienced in the later nineteenth century. Rural areas were transformed as well as the cities. Many felt threatened on two sides by big business and trade unions, and turned to radical conservative organizations for protection and comfort. Woodruff D. Smith, for instance, has demonstrated the appeal of colonies to such people, especially settlement colonies whether overseas or even in eastern Europe. The anti- or pre-industrial outlook of these people made the idea of settlement colonies an attractive form of escapism. These radical conservative movements were sufficiently powerful for their support to be worth courting by other groups. The east German landowners, the Junkers, in the battle to protect their own position, wooed these forces, expressing an interest in overseas ventures they did not really feel. Governments and big business similarly courted them for reasons of their own. Interest in and enthusiasm for *Weltpolitik* thus sprang from many sources.[32]

The approach of big business to colonies is interesting. Their involvement with such territories was usually marginal. The German colonial empire down to 1914 was too small to be of much interest to such concerns. Even in the 1890s, when hopes of Germany's colonial future were perhaps higher, leading industrialists and financiers seemed more anxious to use colonies to demonstrate their patriotism, and to persuade the government to support German economic interests as a whole outside Europe. Woodruff D. Smith argues that this form of imperialism – what he has chosen to call 'economic imperialism' – should be distinguished from the much more limited question of settlement colonialism. The former was the true *Weltpolitik*. In time, too, Admiral Tirpitz saw that interest in colonies, as well as *Weltpolitik*, could be used to increase popular support for the great German navy which he wished to create. The same weapons also appeared in the armouries of successive German chancellors as they struggled to find ways to create and preserve majorities in the Reichstag, and to win a sufficient following among the many interest groups in Germany. Much of the rhetoric concerning *Weltpolitik* must therefore be scrutinized with care, and certainly not interpreted literally.

One can indeed find a number of different interpretations as to Germany's future prospects in the mid-1890s. Philipp zu Eulenburg, German ambassador in Vienna, noted on 3 May 1895 that Russia was turning eastward, Austria-Hungary was talking nostalgically about the *Dreikaiserbund*, whereas Germany's interest in world trade was making Britain her deadliest rival. Admiral von Müller saw the situation a little differently. He too noted the depth of German feeling against Britain. He feared that although Germany might find temporary satisfaction in the pursuit of a purely continental policy, this would end as international economic competition intensified. As German exports declined, so domestic stability would be threatened by social unrest. He concluded: 'world history is now dominated by the economic struggle'. Nevertheless, in 1896, he believed that Germany must find security in the first place on the Continent – against Russia and France. Only then would it be expedient to test whether Britain and Germany could coexist as satiated empires, or whether war must ensue. Holstein, within the Wilhelmstrasse, was rather more optimistic. In contrast to his fears in 1887–88, he now believed that Germany's international position was improving. Peace was likely to prove more rewarding than war. Germany's prime object must be to ensure that she was courted by all the other powers – that hers should be the friendship that the others most desired. From this central position Germany would derive many benefits. She would be able to manoeuvre between Britain and Russia as seemed most appropriate. In so far as he feared Britain it was because she might regain the initiative, and ensure that in any European war it

31

was Germany, and not Britain, who fired the first shot.[33] The enthusiastic supporters of *Weltpolitik*, he complained, might rob Germany of this valuable position at the centre of the balance of power by precipitating unnecessary quarrels with Britain. Some German industrialists and financiers agreed that a major crisis with Britain would be a disaster. But like the leading shipowner, Albert Ballin, they hoped to win concessions from the British through a strategy of controlled firmness and pressure. They hoped that a display of German economic competitiveness and naval potential, backed by popular support for a policy of *Weltpolitik*, would persuade the British that a grand mutual accommodation of interests outside Europe had become necessary. Competition short of war would achieve their objectives.

These were not necessarily vain hopes. Britain and France in 1904 and Britain and Russia in 1907 were to achieve something of this kind. The idea was not dead even in 1914, while Ballin himself procured a microcosm of this grand compromise in his dealings with the British Cunard shipping company. The French, Russians and Ballin (on a smaller scale), however, all had something to trade and good reasons to do so. But Germany and Britain in their dealings from 1898 to 1901 found a broad settlement or agreement unattainable, not because they were more sharply divided than say the British and the Russians (the differences between Russia and Britain in 1900 seemed much more serious and fundamental), but because neither could or would offer what the other really wanted. Bülow as Foreign Minister from 1897 and Chancellor from 1900 was as attached to the 'free hand' as Salisbury. Generally he was content to wait for major concessions from Britain – concessions which he believed Britain's rivalry with France and Russia would ultimately compel her to make. Even then the price might not necessarily be acceptable if agreement with Britain left Germany more exposed to the wrath of France and Russia. In what circumstances, if any other than prior British involvement in a war with France and Russia, would Britain interest herself in the protection of German territory from her two powerful neighbours in the east and west? Even for those British politicians who questioned Salisbury's faith in the 'free hand' the problem was the same. In so far as Britain needed an ally against France and Russia, that ally was needed to protect British interests outside Europe. The price of German aid, in the unlikely event of it being forthcoming, would be a British commitment on the continent of Europe. A major threat to the European balance of power might ultimately compel Britain to intervene, but Salisbury was only more emphatic than his colleagues in his refusal to contemplate or commit himself on so hypothetical a contingency at the turn of the century. German *Weltpolitik* was thus a cause of friction and much bad feeling with the British, but it was not the decisive reason why Britain and Germany failed to narrow their differences in the later 1890s. Although even a German moderate, such as Professor Delbrück, might argue in 1896 that the nation which failed to make large gains in the forthcoming redistribution of much of the world's territory would lose its place among the powers which would 'coin the human spirit',[34] Germany had a smaller impact in the next few years on the global balance of power than her imperial rivals.

NOTES AND REFERENCES

(*Full bibliographical details are given in the Bibliography, pp. 366–81*)
1. Bridge [1] p. 164; see also p. 188
2. Howard [1] p. 456
3. Howard [1] p. 455
4. Westlake, pp. 233–73
5. Ritter, ii, 205
6. Koch, Ch. 9
7. The British Foreign Office archives contain a number of reports of Russian concern in 1874; see e.g. Lytton to Derby, 20 October 1874, FO 27/2060. See also Hohenlohe-Schillingsfurst ii, 122–7
8. Medlicott [1] pp. 163, 173
9. Bridge [1] pp. 172–5. See also Ritter, i, 229–35, and Rich, i, 216–20.
10. Gillard, p. 151
11. But note Yapp, who argues that British policy in India, etc. was less influenced by fear of Russia than is commonly claimed.
12. Kazemzadeh, p. 58
13. See Bourne and Watt, p. 242
14. Bartlett, pp. 172–5
15. Eldridge, pp. 107 ff., 153, 165–6; H. M. Wright, p. 194
16. Rich and Fisher, iii, 59–60. See also Woodruff D. Smith, pp. 27–39
17. See e.g. Brunschwig, *passim*, and Cooke, *passim*
18. Lockhart, pp. 62–3
19. Dunn, pp. 351–60, 482
20. Seeley, p. 75
21. Andrew, pp. 14, 17–19, 27–8
22. Fischer [1] p. 9
23. Marsden, p. 204
24. Oliver, pp. 133 ff.
25. Uzoigwe, pp. 137–42
26. Moulder, pp. 199 ff.
27. See Frodsham for diverse Chinese views of the western world in the 1870s.
28. Steinberg, p. 75
29. Rich and Fisher, i, 178–9.
30. Kehr [2] pp. 37–8, 43–8. See also Geiss [1] p. viii

31. Mann, p. 263, and see his chapter in Feuchtwanger, especially p. 42
32. See Eley, *passim*
33. Rich and Fisher, iii, 511–12, 528, 550–6; iv, 9–12, 22–5. See also Röhl, pp. 162–4
34. Koch, p. 80

Chapter 2

RIVALRIES AND REALIGNMENTS, 1897–1907

CHINA AND THE POWERS, 1897–1900

The relations between the powers between 1897 and 1907 were determined to a remarkable extent by events in the Far East. It was the Germans who set off a new train of incidents with their seizure of Kiaochow in November 1897. The German government had been under some pressure from commercial and banking interests to pursue a more active policy, but this particular episode appears to have been the work essentially of the Kaiser and a few naval officers. Even Admiral Tirpitz thought the move premature. The Foreign Ministry favoured the status quo, arguing that exclusive spheres of influence in China might diminish Germany's trading opportunities in the longer run and work to the advantage of those powers, such as Great Britain, which were better placed to extend their influence. The Foreign Ministry would have preferred a carefully arranged trade-off with Britain – perhaps less support for the Boers in the Transvaal by Germany in return for a Chinese port. Instead Kiaochow produced a knock-on effect. The Tsar wanted compensation. Some of his ministers were less certain. But nerves were on edge. A British naval demonstration off the north China coast was perhaps misinterpreted. The Russians were also growing impatient with Chinese opposition to the building of a branch from the Chinese Eastern Railway to the Liaotung peninsula. Finally the Tsar and his Foreign Minister, Muraviev, were able to push through the occupation of Port Arthur at the tip of the peninsula against the objections of Witte. There were demands in Britain for compensation. Salisbury would have preferred to dampen down the excitement and discourage the scramble for concessions and spheres of influence. Only when diplomacy had failed did he agree that British prestige demanded that he take the not very satisfactory harbour of Wei-hai-wei to give Britain the appearance of a footing in the north.

Salisbury was not so much troubled by the specific Russian gains of 1898 as by the expectation that the long-term Russian purpose was political dominance in north China, to be followed by the acquisition of exclusive economic advantages. Not that the British were inactive. As far back as 1885–86 a general Foreign Office directive had authorized British diplomats to intervene on behalf of British business interests in countries where other powers were using political weapons on behalf of their traders and bankers. By the later 1890s the immediate needs of British business in China were being more than met by enthusiastic British diplomats and consuls. As in Turkey and Persia down to 1914, their aim was to make ample provision for the future. In so competitive an environment there was soon ample speculation about a possible partition of China, and the form that future struggles between the powers might take. A budding British expert on the Far East, the newspaper correspondent G. E. Morrison, anticipating great Russian advances throughout Asia, thought a war with both Russia and France probable. Britain should choose to fight at a moment most favourable to herself. *The Edinburgh Review* commented in July 1899[1]:

> When we fence with Russia or France, China has to stand between the points of the foils. Each lunge is made, as it were, through the body of the Tsungli-Yamen [the Chinese Foreign Ministry].

Nevertheless, once the initial excitement generated by the events of 1897–98 had died down, it became evident that many European political and commercial circles were not too dissatisfied with the existing status quo. The Russians, in April 1898 by the Nishi–Rosen agreement, chose to ease tension with Japan over Korea, recognizing Japan's special economic interests there. Japan, it is true, continued to arm in expectation of further crises with Russia, but neither state was in any condition to fight in 1898. Kuropatkin, the Russian Minister of War from 1898, feared that if Manchuria were annexed, Chinese migrants would overwhelm the Russians there. He believed the new railways would give Russia all the influence she needed.[2]

An agreement of a kind was even possible between Russia and Britain. In April 1899 the British agreed to refrain from railway building north of the Great Wall: the Russians agreed to keep out of the Yangtze. Britain, of course, had good cause to be conciliatory. Having weathered the Fashoda crisis, she was now drifting towards war in South Africa. Britain was the focus of widespread European hostility and suspicion. Only with the United States had a small plus been recorded. During America's war with Spain in 1898 Britain gained a not wholly deserved reputation, compared with the other European powers, of sympathizing with the Americans. But such credit, however acquired, was not usable in the Far East. True, the United States was beginning to take a little interest in world politics by this time. With the expansion of her fleet it was evident that she might soon begin to exercise some influence in the Pacific. She acquired Hawaii and the Philippines in 1898. Sections of American businessmen were becoming more outward-looking, troubled by the depression of the 1890s. Only foreign markets, it seemed, could absorb the latest increases in America's phenomenally productive economy. Given the belief in the 'closing of the frontier' (there was no longer an abundance of land to absorb America's expanding population), urban and therefore industrial growth seemed inevitable, and with them the fear of further surplus production, recession and more social discontent. New solutions would have to be found.

A handful of politicians and writers, reflecting upon America's domestic problems and the imperialist currents which were sweeping the world, provided the first sketches of a global policy for their country. Like many Europeans before them, they became infected with the fear that if the United States failed to act, this would be 'tantamount to choosing atrophy and decline instead of progress and power'.[3] A. T. Mahan's *The Problem of Asia* appeared in 1900. The author insisted that China must be saved from absorption into a Slav land empire by Anglo-Saxon intervention. Charles Conant, an economist, Brooks Adams and Theodore Roosevelt pleaded the economic and political case for an active foreign policy. It seems that President McKinley himself had hopes of using the war with Spain in 1898 to increase the interest of the American people as a whole in foreign affairs, notably in the Far East, and to strengthen the government's hand in a highly competitive world.[4] The results, however, were very limited. Some businessmen did indeed complain that America was being left behind in the scramble for concessions in China, but there was insufficient support in the country at large for a real change of policy. American missionaries in China excited some attention, and some American historians later persuaded themselves that the Open Door Notes 1899–1900 had done much to restrain great-power rivalries in the Far East – perhaps even to prevent the partition of China. Secretary of State John Hay had no illusions at the time. As he commented in September 1900:

> We do not want to rob China ourselves, and our public opinion will not permit us to interfere with an army to prevent others from robbing her. Besides, we have no army.

He dismissed press talk of America's 'pre-eminent moral position giving us authority to dictate to the world' as mere 'flap-doodle'. For the time being the United States had to rely on the balance between the other powers to prevent partition.[5] Valentine Chirol of the *The Times* on a visit to Washington at the end of 1904 was struck by the ignorance of most politicians on foreign affairs, a view which was heartily seconded by President Roosevelt. Chirol could only conclude that American policy, of all the powers, was the most difficult to forecast.[6]

The Boxer rising in China, which reached a climax in 1900 with the siege of the western legations in Peking, while it prompted a unique, co-operative relief expedition by the great powers and severe punishment of China for injuries to imperialist interests, also demonstrated that the powers were not looking for an opportunity to 'slice the Chinese melon'. Only the Russians seemed inclined to dig in, having moved in force into southern Manchuria. The indemnity exacted by the powers from China doubtless helped to slow Chinese economic development in the new century, but the powers continued to be interested only in trading and investment opportunities, and wary of the cost and unpredictability of any deeper involvement. Indeed, the difficulty of operating successfully in China began to encourage foreign co-operative ventures, to spread the risks. There were a number of Anglo-German moves of this kind in particular. China continued to be viewed with a mixture of contempt and apprehension. Where George Bernard Shaw antici- pated the forced westernization of China if it continued to stagnate, J. A. Hobson (whose anti-imperialist writings influenced Lenin) described China as 'a vast repository of incalculable forces'.Only in Manchuria was the picture different. There the Russians seemed in no hurry to retire to the north, and in Britain, Japan and the United States there were growing fears as to the ultimate intentions of St Petersburg. Manchuria might become a Russian province.

The initial Russian response to the Boxer rising had been cautious. By 1900 the Russian economy was feeling the strain of the costly Far Eastern policy which had been pursued since 1891. Efforts to accel- erate Russian industrialization in the same decade had added to the burdens borne by the peasantry and industrial workers. Worse, at the turn of the century, Russia was in the grip of a recession. Business interests which had supported the drive to the east now began to have doubts. Witte's policies had stimulated sections of the economy, and for a time many had shared the dream of China as a land of economic opportunity for Russia. But in 1900 the rail links with the east were still incomplete, Russia was having to buy from other industrial powers to meet some of her needs in Manchuria, and it was not difficult to argue that much of the huge state expenditure upon ventures in the east might more profitably be redirected to European Russia. Even before the Russo-Japanese War of 1904, Russia's Far Eastern policy was an issue on which many were eager to unite in criticism of the government. Discontent was growing among the masses. Where there had been 19 strikes in 1893, there were 522 in 1902. Russia was borrowing heavily from abroad, and foreign confi- dence could be maintained only by a balanced budget and large exports (to earn hard currency with which to service the loans). The living standards of the masses suffered. Lionel Kochan concludes concerning Witte: his policy 'of robbing the present for the sake of the future, of guns before butter, of establishing Russian greatness by impoverishing the peasantry and exploiting the proletariat was most intimately linked to the progress of the Russian revolution'.[7] Russia, it seemed, could not tackle her internal problems and remain a great power at the same time.

Some have suggested that Russia should have opted out of the imperial race for a generation or two. But no great power, once it is caught up in the great game, can easily pull out. In any case, down to the Boxer rising, Russia's international position had not seemed too exposed. A crisis had been avoided in the Near East, and relations were improving with Germany and Austria-Hungary. Britain was distracted first by problems in the Sudan and later in South Africa. The Boer War even tempted Muraviev to explore the prospects for a continental coalition against Britain. Germany, however, feared that any weakening of Britain was likely to work to the advantage of Russia and France rather than herself. Muraviev concluded in January 1900 that Russia must continue to stand on the defensive in the Near East and in Persia. Nevertheless a new loan agreement with the Persians in 1900 forbade Tehran to borrow from another power for ten years. The advantage secured by the establishment of a Russian Loan and Discount Bank in Persia from 1894 was thus confirmed, whereas British diplomats were constrained by the lack of interest displayed by British investors in so unstable a country unless their investments were protected by some sort of a guarantee from the British government. Parliament would not agree to such a measure, and therefore the Russians continued to make the running in Persia. Russia was further assisted by French resentment against Britain, especially following Fashoda, so that French capital now assisted Russian railway building in central Asia. At the turn of the century the Franco-Russian alliance was taking a decidedly anti-British turn.[8]

But if Russia's position among the powers did not seem too unsatisfactory in 1900, some ministers were beginning to have second thoughts about the extent of their activities in the Far East. That theatre was absorbing perhaps one-eighth of the government's total expenditure, and would continue to do so for little obvious return for some time to come. A larger Far Eastern fleet was needed to complement the railway network, which was itself incomplete. Communication between Russia's two main naval bases, Port Arthur and Vladivostok, was dependent on the ability to use the narrow straits between Korea and Japan. As it was, foreign workers, contractors and suppliers were the main beneficiaries from much of the Russian expenditure in Manchuria. As with Russian enterprises in Persia, some Soviet historians have been forced to describe

Russian imperialism in this era as essentially feudal–military in character – far removed from Lenin's model of monopoly capitalism with its problems of surplus goods and funds.[9] Russian ministers were thus divided between a policy of more selective advance in the east, or one of seizing the opportunity presented by their current occupation of southern Manchuria to secure more preferential or exclusive concessions from the Chinese in the hope of earlier economic returns. St Petersburg at first opted for the second strategy, though at the cost of deteriorating relations with the Chinese, Japanese, British and Americans. The debate between the Russian ministers intensified, with the result that policy became increasingly hesitant and confused. But in the absence of a firm decision in favour of retrenchment Russia was soon on a collision course with Japan. A thorough reappraisal of policy took place only after defeat abroad and revolution at home.

BRITAIN AND THE END OF THE 'FREE HAND'

Britain, too, seemed to be at a crossroads at the turn of the century. The nation's nervousness and aggressiveness reached a peak in the late 1890s. Emile Zola wondered if the imperialist fever was driving the British towards a bid for world domination. Kipling and Beatrice Webb were among those to express dismay at the intensity of British jingoist feeling. G. N. Sanderson has argued that Britain pushed further in the conquest of the Upper Nile than was strictly necessary for security in 1898: this was done to satisfy public opinion and to overawe foreign rivals. At the same time public opinion was also stirred up and led by ministers, notably by Joseph Chamberlain who feared that a democratic society might not respond adequately to the new challenges posed by foreign powers to Britain's position in the world. If Britain declined as a world power, so too would the nation's prosperity, with damaging consequences for social and political stability at home. Chamberlain was particularly active in the education of public opinion concerning the importance of southern Africa. If he hoped that an impressive display of national unanimity might overawe the Boers, he also realized that the nation could not risk war until sufficient support had been built up at home.[10]

The Boers, however, not only decided to defy the might of the British Empire in 1899, but fought with such skill and determination as to damage British prestige and confidence. The war lasted until 1902, and forced Britain to commit so many troops that ministerial fears of British vulnerability elsewhere in the world – notably in India – were uncomfortably strengthened. Even when the war was finally won the long-term costs of imperial defence provided much food for thought. The Chancellor of the Exchequer was dismayed by the demands of the services. In his view such expenditure threatened to deprive Britain of one of her greatest assets – the reserve financial power she could mobilize in time of war. The British economy must not be crippled by high taxes in peacetime. The biggest threats were presented by the navies of France and Russia, and by the Russian railways pushing down into central Asia – notably the Orenberg – Tashkent line which menaced Afghanistan. An alliance with Germany or conscription seemed the only answers. Even after the Boer War it was not easy to see how Britain could raise even 50,000 reinforcements for India, a mere half or one-third of the number which it was widely estimated would be required to meet the Russian threat from central Asia. In 1901 the Cabinet tried to meet the threat at sea from Russia and France by assuming that all the other leading naval powers – Germany, the United States, Italy and Japan – would remain friendly, and cut the projected plans of the Admiralty accordingly.

Understandably many in the Cabinet began to question Salisbury's preference for a foreign policy based on the 'free hand'. Salisbury fought back by asking how likely it was that a European coalition would be formed against Britain. He also argued that Britain would have to pay heavily for an alliance. He contended in his classic memorandum of 29 May 1901: 'The liability [for Britain] of having to defend the German and Austrian frontiers against Russia is heavier than that of having to defend the British Isles against France.' Britain had no historical justification for believing in the dangers of 'isolation'. In any case no British government could pledge itself to a European power given the vagaries of public opinion. It is true that Salisbury had no answer to Britain's Asiatic problems, other than his sarcasm at the expense of strategists who frightened themselves by using too many small-scale maps. But it was difficult to see how Germany, for instance, could be persuaded to assist in the defence of the British Empire at the price of renewed danger to herself from Russia in Europe, and equally difficult to see what Britain could, or would be able to offer her in return for such a service. In any case Germany under Bülow, as we have seen, was content to wait for the apparently inevitable war between the British and the Franco-Russian alliance. Bülow himself may never have been tempted by the idea of an alliance with Britain. On the other hand he did not want to provoke the British in case they decided on a pre-emptive war before Tirpitz's navy was ready to act as a deterrent: he was consequently anxious to control German Anglophobia. Bülow envied the British their island position and long history of political stability. Clearly with his own worries in mind he wrote late in 1899 after a visit to Britain: 'One observes that the people have never seen an enemy in their land, and do not believe that anything could ever really go wrong, either at home or abroad.'[11] Even when, as a result of the Boer War, the British evidently felt less secure, this did not remove the basic obstacles to a closer Anglo-German relationship. The price that each would have to pay was still too high.

An Anglo-German agreement of 16 October 1900 to uphold China's territorial integrity and the 'Open Door' soon revealed that the Germans had no intention of burning their fingers in Manchuria on behalf of the British. Lansdowne, who had succeeded Salisbury as Foreign Secretary in November 1900, tried to draw Germany into a Far Eastern agreement to localize any war between Japan and Russia. But Berlin replied in March and April 1901 with proposals for a general defensive alliance or British inclusion in the Triple Alliance. Most of the Cabinet followed Salisbury in rejecting these proposals, but in November 1901 Lansdowne was still showing interest in a more limited understanding with Germany. Balfour, on 12 December 1901, argued strongly that in a choice between Japan and the Triple Alliance, he believed that Britain's interests would be better served by joining the latter. France and Russia were Britain's chief rivals. Although a quarrel with them might begin in the Far East[12]:

> . . . the theatre of war so far as we are concerned would be the
> Channel, the Mediterranean, the frontier of India, and our great lines
> of commercial communication. . . . It is a matter of supreme moment
> to us that Italy should not be crushed, that Austria should not be
> dismembered, and, as I think, that Germany should not be squeezed to
> death between the hammer of Russia and the anvil of France.

In 1902 the British service chiefs welcomed the German project for a railway from Berlin to Baghdad via the Ottoman Empire: this would be an obstacle to Russian ambitions in the Near East. It was in the same year, however, that the Admiralty first began to express serious alarm about the rise of the German navy. As the First Lord wrote on 10 October 1902: 'The more the composition of the new German fleet is examined the clearer it becomes that it is designed for a possible conflict with the British fleet.' The German government itself did not seem 'really unfriendly', but one could not 'safely ignore the malignant hatred of the German people or the manifest design of the German Navy'.[13]

Meanwhile Lansdowne had been trying, unsuccessfully, to interest the Russians in some sort of compromise over Persia. But his greater sense of urgency, compared with that of Salisbury, produced at least a negative gain in the New World. He accelerated British disengagement from Central America, and in particular through the Hay–Pauncefote treaty of November 1901 he left to the United States a virtual free hand in the construction of any future trans-isthmian canal. Concessions soon followed on the disputed Alaskan boundary – at the expense of the Canadians. Anglo-American relations were improved by such gestures, though not in the sense that Britain could look for any material help from the United States against Russia in the Far East. But at least the British were spared the danger of crises of the type they had experienced with the Americans over Venezuela in 1895. It was also a matter of some importance that Washington now viewed the Russians as the main threat to American interests in the Pacific whereas in the previous century they had usually viewed the British in that light.

Despite the considerable diplomatic activity detailed above, the British still found themselves in the autumn of 1901 in a relatively isolated position in the Far East. Of necessity they became interested in a new alignment with Japan. The idea had already been canvassed in a number of quarters. It had also attracted attention in Japan, where interest waxed and waned in relation to the prospects of an 'exchange' agreement with Russia. This envisaged mutual recognition of the claims of the two powers in Korea and Manchuria. Count Ito was the leading Japanese figure in the search for this compromise. Ito, although replaced by the pro-British Katsura, was able to visit Russia in the autumn of 1901 and continued to take soundings. Witte, for one, would have been happy to make concessions over Korea. He wished to avoid a costly arms race with Japan, and to concentrate on Manchuria and the completion of his great railway projects. But Witte's influence in St Petersburg was slowly declining: the competition for the favour of Nicholas II was intense, and ministers whose views on the Far East were close to Witte's were not willing to make a united stand with him. The government in any case was essentially a cluster of ministers, each one individually responsible to the Tsar. Nicholas II, though full of ambition for himself and his country, was not an effective first minister, and at this time there was no one minister or group of ministers to fill the vacuum. Those who might have compromised with Japan could not therefore enforce their will. On the other hand, those who were responsible for Ito going away empty-handed had no agreed policy of expansion. Great things were simply expected to follow the completion of the Trans-Siberian Railway.

The confusion in St Petersburg played into the hands of those Japanese who doubted the feasibility of a compromise with Russia. Ito's visit also added to Lansdowne's sense of urgency, whereas had the true state of feeling in Russia been known to British ministers it might have strengthened Salisbury who was by no means enraptured with the idea of an alliance with Japan. But Lansdowne was powerfully backed by the First Lord of the Admiralty, whose advisers insisted that Britain needed the assistance of Japan if she were to protect her interests properly in the Far East against pressure from Russia and France. An alliance, argued the First Lord, would reduce the risk of war. Even so, the Cabinet entered the alliance on 30 January 1902 with some reservations. Great care was taken to emphasize its defensive character. It provided for the benevolent neutrality of one member if the other became involved in war with a third party. Only when one party was at war with two opponents would the alliance come into full operation. The Japanese, however, were assured of a British naval presence in Chinese waters and could expect to strengthen their position in Korea.

The British undoubtedly hoped by means of the alliance to reduce the risk of war in the Far East. The effect may well have been the opposite: the Japanese may have been given just enough confidence to risk war in 1904. Yet by and large the decision seemed reasonable enough in London in 1902 – Lord Salisbury's doubts apart. To most ministers a continuance of the policy of the 'free hand' seemed too risky. Contemporary fears are well illustrated in a letter from Lord George Hamilton to Lord Curzon on 2 April 1902[14]:

> . . . it will require men of exceptional capacity, resolution and tenacity to bridge over the time in which we shall pass from the old position we occupied in the nineteenth century to that which . . . the British Empire ought to occupy in the twentieth . . .

The Anglo-Japanese alliance did not solve all Britain's worries. In October 1902 the naval estimates were increased by £3 million to maintain the two-power standard against France and Russia, while the German navy was causing growing concern. As the Cabinet surveyed the world's trouble spots and the many threats to British interests it still seemed imperative to seek compromises with other powers whenever possible. It was the deteriorating situation in Morocco which gave the British the opening they were seeking.

The improvement in Anglo-French relations was sudden – and took everyone, especially the Germans, by surprise. Salisbury, though he had often tried to ease relations with France, had hoped for nothing better than 'a mutual temper of apathetic tolerance'. The Committee of Imperial Defence took France very seriously as a potential foe in 1902, and continued to do so down to the spring of 1904. Among British moves considered in the event of war was the incitement of Muslim revolts in Tunis and Algeria. French thinking on foreign affairs at this time was very fluid. Disappointment with Russia over the Fashoda crisis was balanced by a more intimate anti-British military relationship at the turn of the century. The possible disintegration of the Austro-Hungarian Empire prompted some anticipatory Franco-Russian negotiations, but there were also fears in Paris of a Russo-German plot to partition the empire without reference to France. Instability in other areas from the Ottoman Empire to China similarly exercised the French. The latter, for their part, suggested to Berlin that the French Empire in Indo-China might be offered for the return of Alsace and Lorraine. It so happened that the issue which came to a head first, and therefore which did so much to shape later events, was Morocco.[15]

Internal disorders had long threatened Morocco with foreign intervention. By 1902–3 it seemed that the moment had come. But the French ministers, before they acted, wished to be assured of the support of another power. Britain seemed a more suitable partner than Germany, even though her price would be a formal promise of French disinterest in Egypt. The influential French colonial activist, Eugène Etienne, had already been urging such an exchange for some years, but the French Foreign Minister, Delcassé, only took up the idea in 1903 when the Moroccan issue clearly demanded attention. Delcassé still saw this as only one move among many possible ones as he strove to increase French influence in the world – especially in Europe and the Mediterranean. Even in Morocco he desired French military and economic penetration to proceed at a pace that would not embarrass other French interests elsewhere. Delcassé's broad approach is reflected in the veto placed on French financial participation in the Berlin–Baghdad Railway lest Russia should be offended, while France continued to help finance the Orenberg–Tashkent Railway despite an improvement in her relations with Britain.[16]

Motivation was equally mixed on the British side. Britain had been impeding French ambitions in Morocco for a generation, but by 1902 it was evident that the internal decay in Morocco had gone so far that French intervention was imminent. Britain's international position left her no option but to acquiesce, or, better still, to try to arrange a deal. A free hand in Egypt was a major inducement. There were other possible side-effects. Chamberlain hoped an agreement might improve Britain's position against Germany: Balfour thought the same with respect to Russia. Lansdowne hoped for easier relations with Russia by way of Paris. Furthermore, as relations deteriorated between Russia and Japan later in 1903, Lansdowne and Balfour seemed anxious to hasten the talks with the French in the hope that this might localize any war in the Far East. Delcassé, in contrast, remained strangely optimistic about the possibility of a compromise in the Far East until the last minute.[17] British fears of a Japanese defeat doubtless increased the attractions of an *entente* with France.

British uncertainties are reflected in the nation's war planning. The army continued to pay little attention to Germany before 1905. The navy viewed Germany as only one of three possible foes. The redistribution of the fleet in the winter of 1904–5 had this in mind, many ships being stationed at Gibraltar to move into the Mediterranean or back into home waters according to the situation. Even Fisher's talk of 'Copenhagening' the German navy late in 1904 was related to the Russo-Japanese War and the fear that Germany might become an ally of Russia. Some on the British side displayed a belligerence reminiscent of Germany in 1887, with the Army Council early in 1904 remarking that a Russo-Japanese War would be the best time for Britain to fight Russia, and perhaps France as well. Earlier in 1897–98 there had been British press talk of preventive action against menacing European navies. Now, in 1904, both Lord Wolseley and G. E. Morrison argued that Japan would be wise to fight Russia before the Trans-Siberian Railway was complete.[18] In the war itself, as Japan won victory, so the British eagerly counted up the advantages that accrued to them from Japan's success. *The Times* acclaimed the Japanese attack on Port Arthur (before the declaration of war) as deserving of 'a place of honour in naval annals'.

THE RUSSO-JAPANESE WAR

The immediate origins of the Russo-Japanese War illustrate the importance of strategic considerations. Modern research suggests that in both countries policy was made by a politico-military élite with little regard for outside pressures, popular or economic. Admittedly Russophobia was rampant in Japan: policies of expansion and even war elicited widespread support. Most of the Japanese press was in favour of war by the end of 1903. The larger industrialists had at first been confident that they could export to Manchuria despite or even because of the Russian presence, but increasingly in 1903 they became troubled by Russian obduracy over Korea, and found the growing uncertainty bad for business. They therefore drifted towards the war party. Nevertheless Shumpei Okamoto convincingly argues that by and large the Japanese government, with its top military advisers, was free to decide on war or peace. An oligarchy of less than twenty men debated the pros and cons. The elder statesmen tended to favour further efforts to reach a compromise with Russia. The war party gained strength only as Russian policy excited more and more distrust, and as the fear grew that time was not on the side of Japan.

Meanwhile, in Russia, so far as outside opinion could express itself, the mood was generally opposed to an active Far Eastern policy – certainly from 1900. Nor was the notorious adventurer, Bezobrazov, so influential by the time the fatal decisions – or non-decisions – were being taken in St Petersburg from the autumn of 1903. Policy was determined by the Tsar and his ministers, and the newly created Viceroy in the Far East. The debate among these men centred mainly on how many of Russia's existing interests in the Far East should be defended, and by what means – not on their extension. To a great extent Russia was disengaging from Korea – contrary to the fears of the Japanese. The Russians did, however, wish to minimize Japan's strategic advantages in the peninsula – here there was a real conflict of interest. But above all ministers were divided as to how Russian interests should be pursued in Manchuria: whether Russia should concentrate in the north and on her railway leases: whether Chinese migrant labour was a useful tool in Russia's eastern spheres of influence or a threat to her influence. Many ministers favoured at least a temporary agreement with Japan, but were unable to agree on the terms.[19]

Naturally the government in Tokyo was unaware of the confusion in St Petersburg. Russian policy seemed more threatening and coherent than it actually was. By 1903–4, however, there was also some reluctance on the part of the Japanese to give the Russians an entirely free hand in Manchuria. Tokyo's ambitions were beginning to outgrow the earlier 'exchange' policy. Most important in determining the date of war was the argument of the Japanese military leaders that if there was to be a war it should be fought as soon as possible. At the moment they gave Japan a fifty-fifty chance of victory – each delay would lengthen the odds against Japan. What might have been a genuine inability on the part of the Russians to make up their minds concerning a clear answer to Tokyo by the beginning of 1904 was readily and understandably interpreted by the Japanese as deliberate procrastination. Time would enable the Russians to draw more benefit from the Trans-Siberian Railway. The remorseless logic of power politics was thus pushing Japan towards war so long as she had some hope of victory. The alliance with Britain offered security against France, while the Japanese knew that they also enjoyed the sympathy of the American President, Theodore Roosevelt. Tokyo was careful to keep its contacts with Washington in good order. In general the Japanese oligarchy proved itself adept practitioners of *realpolitik* at this time – more so than on many subsequent occasions leading to Pearl Harbor.[20]

The Japanese began the war in February 1904. Their military and naval successes took most observers by surprise. Even so the strain on the nation's resources was immense. British and American loans gave some relief, but it was fortunate that revolution broke out in Russia in 1905. Japan was greatly helped by the relatively poor performance of the Russian armed forces, and by the Russian decision not to fight a defensive war of attrition in Manchuria. Russian contempt for the Japanese contributed both to the outbreak of the war and their subsequent defeats. Russia was still able to fight a tenacious diplomatic battle in the peace talks conducted under American auspices in Portsmouth, New Hampshire. By the treaty of

5 September 1905 the Japanese were denied a war indemnity, but their claims in Korea were now recognized, and they inherited the Russian concessions in southern Manchuria. Russia also ceded the southern half of the island of Sakhalien. There had been no comparable Oriental success over the Europeans since the Turkish victories in the sixteenth century. Indeed some Europeans put new emphasis on the 'Yellow Peril', and spoke of the emergence of Japan as the leader of Asia against the West, or prophesied an equally dangerous partnership between Japan and China. European radicals, however, tended to welcome this blow against Russian autocracy. Japan's victory gave encouragement to some Chinese and Indian nationalists. But for the time being the main results of the war were at work elsewhere. China remained internally weak and divided. Japan was chronically short of capital. Indeed some Japanese would have welcomed the capital of other nations to assist in the development of southern Manchuria. This was not to the liking of the Japanese military and the extreme patriots. In time, as we shall see, Russia and Japan began to co-operate against rival powers in defence of the new status quo created by the war of 1904–5. Indeed America began to replace Russia as Japan's main opponent.

But of more immediate consequence was the effect of the war on the relations of the European powers. Some of the effects must obviously be the subject of some speculation, such as the degree to which the Anglo-French *entente* was influenced, or at least hastened by the outbreak of war in the Far East. Suddenly, as Lansdowne noted, the talks 'began to travel at the speed of an express train'.[21] The *entente* was signed on 8 April 1904. The Germans were naturally dismayed, but they were in any case tempted by the war in the east to look for ways in which it might be turned to their advantage. Better relations with Russia, even an alliance, seemed one possibility. Progress here might either force France and Russia apart, or compel France to associate with this new combination. On the other hand, some of the German ministers, and above all Tirpitz, were afraid that an alignment with Russia might increase the danger of war with Britain at a time when the German navy still seemed all too vulnerable to a pre-emptive British strike. The uncertainty in Berlin was not helped by the impetuosity of the Kaiser. At one time he was all in favour of a cautious foreign policy in case the revolutionary troubles in Russia began to spread westward. In July 1905, on the other hand, he met Tsar Nicholas II at Bjorko and for a time seemed to have a treaty with Russia within his grasp. In the end the Tsar was coaxed from the German alignment by Russian ministers who feared that such a treaty would weaken Russia's relations with France and in consequence leave Russia too dependent upon an over-mighty Germany. Again the logic of power politics was overwhelming. Nevertheless Germany gave some assistance to the Russian Baltic fleet on its fatal semi-circumnavigation of the world to destruction at the hands of the Japanese navy at Tsushima on 27 May 1905.

If German policy was inconclusive with respect to Russia, the Far Eastern war undoubtedly encouraged the Germans to test both the nerve of the French in Morocco and the solidity of the Anglo-French *entente*. A German move over Morocco was always possible, but Berlin might well have proceeded with caution had France's ally not been fully engaged by war and revolution. No serious thought seems to have been given to a preventive war against France, but the German General Staff were well satisfied with the military situation. Although Germany had trading interests in Morocco, she was also anxious to find a test case which would strengthen her claims against the colonial powers elsewhere in the world. Ostensibly the situation favoured Germany, but Berlin miscalculated the reaction of the British. The latter chose not to see this as a private quarrel between France and Germany, but as a bid by Berlin to wreck the *entente*. Unless Britain stood by France the *entente* might collapse; France might even move closer to Berlin. In the event it was the French who proved less resolute at the start of the affair. Delcassé, the tough-minded Foreign Minister, was quickly sacrificed to appease Germany, and some concessions were offered on Morocco. The Germans would have been well advised to pause and consolidate at this point, not least because they had feared that Delcassé was about to try to exploit the Russian defeat at Tsushima to persuade his ally to make peace and switch its attention back to Europe.[22]

But the Germans had tasted blood, and now insisted on an international conference to discuss the Moroccan question. They expected that the French and British would find themselves in a minority over the future of Morocco, not least because Berlin was counting on American support. But Theodore Roosevelt did not see French policy in Morocco as a test of the 'Open Door'. Rather he saw the crisis as one manufactured by Germany to test the European balance of power. Thus it was the Germans who found themselves in a minority at the Algeciras Conference early in 1906 – even the Austrians gave them only half-hearted support. Berlin was denied the political success it had been seeking, and worse it had driven France and Britain into a much closer relationship. As early as 28 June 1905 Lansdowne had warned the German ambassador to London that if France were attacked British public opinion might insist on aid to France. The new Liberal ministry from the winter of 1905–6 went further, and began staff talks with the French which, however non-committal, gave the *entente* a positive anti-German content which had hitherto been lacking. In Germany there was a dramatic realization that the favourable diplomatic position which the country had enjoyed from the mid-1890s had been jeopardized. Holstein again began to talk of the inevitability of war. One of his correspondents spoke of the formation of a 'frightful syndicate' against Germany. 'This will block any further possibility of our development in the wide open spaces. And we are only 'relatively' satisfied.'[23] Yet if Germany had made errors between 1904 and 1906, she clearly had not been the sole maker of events. Nowhere was this more evident than in the origins of the Anglo-Russian *entente* of 1907.

It is true that by January 1906 the British army was energetically preparing itself for war in Europe – really for the first time since 1815. It was envisaged that as many as 100,000 troops might be sent at short notice to fight Germany in France or Belgium. But at the same time fears of the Russian threat to India persisted, tempered only by the realization that the Bear would require a few years to recover from the disasters at home and abroad of 1904–5. The British navy had been greatly strengthened by the Russian defeat at Tsushima, but given time a fleet could be rebuilt. Admiral Fisher, for all his vehemence against the Germans, did not ignore France and Russia, or indeed the Americans and the 'Yellow man'. If Germany had become the prime concern from 1905, Fisher insisted in October 1906 that the navy must think in terms of the next twenty-five years. Who could tell what enemies Britain might then face? The two-power standard was still necessary.[24] Within the Foreign Office, however, a strong and consistently anti-German group was emerging, and one that was strengthened by the appointment of Grey as Foreign Secretary. The prime causes of Germanophobia in Britain were Germany's rapid industrial growth, the expansion of her navy, the recurrent outbursts of anti-British feeling in Germany (which many in Britain were not slow to reciprocate) and her erratic conduct. All were strong inducements to ease relations with Russia, and these could have operated to some extent, irrespective of the outcome of the Russo-Japanese War. British efforts to ease relations with Russia in fact predated both the intensified rivalry with Germany and the Russo-Japanese conflict. But what one can conclude is that without the setbacks experienced by the Russians in 1904–5 the British would have found St Petersburg much less willing to negotiate – indeed they might well have found it impossible to conclude a deal at all.

Most of the Russian leadership was in no mood to compromise with the British over outstanding differences in Asia before 1905. The Tsar himself was bitterly anti-British, ranking them in the order of his dislikes with the despised Jews. In 1905 there was vague talk of stirring up a rising of 'Blacks' in South Africa to embarrass the British. A vain attempt was made by the Russian bank in Persia to organize a run on its British rival, the Imperial Bank, in 1906. It is true that some Russian ministers, even before the Russo-Japanese War, were aware of the strain imposed by the current policies on

Russia's finances. But Lamsdorff, the Foreign Minister, in October 1904 certainly hoped to 'preserve for ourselves the large Persian market for a free application of Russian labour and capital'.[25] Persia might retain her integrity, but the aim was that the country should fall increasingly under Russian direction. Beyond Persia itself the Persian Gulf beckoned. In reply, although British ministers in London dissented from the hardline policies recommended by the Viceroy in India, Lord Curzon (largely on the ground that they were too costly and impractical), they were determined to exclude Russia from the Persian Gulf, and hoped that through the discouragement of railway and economic development in southern Persia, Russia would find it increasingly difficult to push south.

The prospect of an Anglo-Russian agreement on central Asia was thus not good until defeat in the east and revolution at home in 1905 forced the Russians to reappraise their priorities. As it was, the debate in St Petersburg was prolonged and stormy. Many at court, in the military and conservative circles, favoured co-operation with Germany and perhaps Austria-Hungary. Witte, however, argued that Russia's choice of friends must turn on their readiness to provide loans. The conservatives were forced to admit that only with foreign loans could the Russian armed forces be built up again after the defeats, and the Russian government itself be given the opportunity to lessen the influence which the constitutional parties had won as a result of the revolution. It was necessary to give first place in Russian foreign policy to the restoration of the empire's finances. When money was not forthcoming from Germany, the French were able to retain their position as Russia's chief creditor. They used the financial lever to their advantage at Algeciras, and to encourage the Russians to give the British a favourable hearing. Both Witte and Lamsdorff thawed a little towards the British in 1906. The first Duma was dominated by the pro-British Cadets. The reforming groups as a whole tended to be anti-German, a point noted by Holstein in Berlin with growing concern.

Negotiations between the Russians and British began in June 1906. Three months later the Russian Minister of Finance, Kokovtsov, came out strongly in favour of a compromise, insisting that Russia must devise a cheaper foreign policy. He estimated that in recent years, for instance, Russia had invested thirty-five times as much as the British in Persia, but had not benefited proportionately from this larger expenditure. In any case only about 3 per cent of Russia's total trade was with Persia. Stolypin as Prime Minister and Izvolsky in the Foreign Ministry shared this desire to act with more discrimination in Asia. A second war with Japan seemed possible, and this time the British might not remain neutral.[26] Political instability was growing in Persia, and the Russians could not be sure how much influence they would be able to exercise in a crisis, or at what cost. German railway and commercial activities in the Middle East were also causing concern. Meanwhile mutinies at home reduced confidence in Russia's armed forces still further. In these circumstances the arguments in favour of a period of cautious consolidation in Asia were becoming overwhelming, and this could only be done in agreement with the British. Furthermore, in so far as Izvolsky wished to give more attention to the Near East, he believed this to be possible without a crisis with Germany and Austria-Hungary.

A *rapprochement* with the most autocratic and reactionary of the great powers dismayed much progressive opinion in Britain. The government of India feared for British influence in Persia and the Gulf. But otherwise there was widespread recognition of the likely advantages. Despite Japan's victory over Russia, and the extension (on paper) of the Anglo-Japanese alliance to include India, the War Office remained pessimistic. Though Russia might not attack India, so long as relations remained unsettled the existence of her central Asian railways threatened to impose the burden of virtually a continental army on Britain. This seemed the only adequate yet unthinkable answer to the defence of the North-West frontier. Such additional defence preparations as might prove feasible seemed likely only to provoke a Russian reply in kind, leaving the problem much as before. Account had to be taken of other calls on British government spending – from the desire of the Liberal Party to spend more on social reform at home to the continuing challenge of the German navy. Furthermore, Germany was now viewed as a rival in the Near and Middle East, the Berlin–Baghdad Railway no longer being welcomed as a constraint on Russia. On the contrary, if Russo-British differences could be settled, Grey had hopes of a partnership which might also include the French, a partnership which should be able to exert more influence than any other great power. British commercial gains were among the hoped-for advantages. Rivalry with Germany thus formed part of the motivation behind British interest in an *entente* with Russia. Oddly enough when, a few years later, Russia again appeared to be the main threat to British interests in the Middle East, the Anglo-Russian *entente* was then seen as the best instrument with which to try to restrain Russian activities. In fact there was never unanimous support for the Russian *entente* in Britain, and there was even less enthusiasm for the arrangement in Russia. For most Russians it was a matter of regrettable necessity, forced on them by the events of 1905.

The Anglo-Russian agreement of August 1907 divided Persia into three spheres – the Russians in the north, the British in the south, with a neutral zone between. Russia also recognized British interests in the Gulf, and to a lesser extent in Afghanistan and Tibet. To Grey the *entente* seemed eminently reasonable and rewarding, precarious though its existence remained right down to 1914. With hindsight, however, one can see that any easing of Anglo-Russian relations was likely to worsen the relations of the two powers with Germany and Austria. Worst of all, if collisions of interest between the powers once more began to occur in south-eastern Europe, this was a region where intensifying national feeling would make compromises increasingly difficult to negotiate. Russia's current unpreparedness for war might provide a temporary relief, but in the longer run the prospects of peace between the powers – or at least the avoidance of general and total war – might have been improved had Asia remained a higher priority in Russian foreign policy.

THE FAR EAST, 1905–11

It was a very reluctant Russia which began to pursue a policy of compromise with Japan in Manchuria after 1905. In time, however, both powers began to discover a common interest in the defence of their positions in northern and southern Manchuria against intruders, notably the United States. Both Russia and Japan were hard put to develop their spheres of influence in the east, given their financial problems. Some Japanese politicians and businessmen even favoured the acceptance of American capital to speed up the development of their mainland empire. But others, notably the military, opposed any step that might weaken their influence in southern Manchuria. Interestingly, so long as Theodore Roosevelt was President of the United States, he was able to exercise a useful moderating influence on American–Japanese relations. He appreciated that the 'Open Door' could not be interpreted literally, or applied equally in all circumstances. He saw that each power expected preferential treatment in certain areas, and for Japan these now included southern Manchuria as well as Korea. It was necessary to bargain realistically in the knowledge that some regions might become less open to competition than others.

It is true that the anti-American trend in Japanese policy after 1905 might appear to vindicate those Americans who criticized Roosevelt's efforts to mediate between Russia and Japan at Portsmouth. Russia and Japan, it was said, should have been left to fight themselves to a standstill. Roosevelt, however, preferred to try to establish an equilibrium in Manchuria rather than leave matters to chance. He hoped to prevent 'the creation of either a yellow or a Slav peril'.[27] He could not foresee that Russia and Japan would sink their differences. American influence, in any case, was very limited. Congress gave only grudging support to his naval programme, and would strengthen neither the army nor defences in the Philippines. Roosevelt even came to regret America's possession of those islands. They could not be defended at the start of a possible war with Japan, but once lost American national pride would demand their recovery. Roosevelt was also troubled by the current expectation of many Europeans that Japan might well prove victorious in a war with the United States. Such an impression might make the Japanese over-confident in some dispute with America, and a chapter of accidents or miscalculations might result in a war which neither power wanted.

Roosevelt, therefore, sought both to reassure the Japanese and to impress them with America's potential strength. Agreement was reached on Japan's claims in Korea and southern Manchuria in return for assurances from Tokyo over the Philippines. Japanese migration to California was exciting great concern among west-coast Americans, but again Roosevelt worked – with some success – to defuse the tension without loss of face on either side. But if he spoke softly he did not forget the 'big stick'. The navy was expanded and put on show – with a round the world cruise. Its utility in the Pacific, however, was much reduced until the opening of the Panama Canal, and the building of an adequate naval base in Hawaii. It has been suggested that Roosevelt might have gone further and backed the new patriotic and reformist groups that were beginning to emerge in China: the Chinese should have been supported against the imperialists. Such a move would have been unthinkable to Roosevelt, steeped as he was in the prejudices of his age. As it was, he could rarely summon up enough support and interest in America for the more limited policies he was trying to pursue. Furthermore, Chinese politics and society were far too unstable and unpredictable for intervention of the kind suggested to be attempted with any prospect of success.[28]

What the Chinese could do (over and above the mass boycotts of foreign goods which sometimes occurred) was to try – as in the past – to play off the powers against each other. Thus the Chinese hoped to use British and American financiers to check the advance of Japan in southern Manchuria. But in 1907 British capital was frightened off – the British government gave priority to the alliance with Japan over business adventures in Manchuria. On the American side there were several false starts until in 1909 there came hints that both Russia and Japan might be willing to accept the help of others in the development of the Chinese Eastern and South Manchurian railways. Any chance of success was wrecked by the heavy-handed approach of the new American administration (Taft succeeding Roosevelt in 1909). Secretary of State Knox supported an ambitious scheme for an international syndicate to put up money which Peking could use to buy out the Russian and Japanese railway interests. The Manchurian railways would then have been neutralized, and internationally administered for the period of the loan. The British, sensing trouble, refused to co-operate. The Russians and Japanese finally allowed political and strategic considerations to prevail over the economic arguments that more capital was required. Russo-Japanese co-operation against the Americans intensified, the understanding of 1907 being reinforced by extra conventions in 1910. By these agreements Russia and Japan would keep to their respective spheres, and co-operate against intruders. 'Open Door' principles were ignored, and no reference was made to the integrity of China.

This stabilization of Russo-Japanese relations had broader implications. It made it easier for Russia to become more active in the Near East from 1908, and to resume its competition with the British in Persia. It also meant that the United States tended to replace Russia as Japan's main rival – at least in emotional terms. For Britain the Anglo-Japanese alliance was losing much of its original purpose. Instead it was becoming an insurance policy with respect to Japan herself. The British wished to concentrate the bulk of their fleet against Germany. Without the alliance Britain could have less confidence in Japanese conduct – already economic competition was growing with the Japanese in China – and in its absence the British expected either to have to increase their naval forces in the Far East or risk a possible decline in their influence. The alliance was now of much less specific value to the Japanese, but most of the leadership were reluctant to abandon a link which had served them well in the recent past. Russian conduct in the long term was unpredictable. The alliance perhaps still helped to enhance Japan's standing among the powers. If Britain was unlikely to assist Japan in any conflict with the United States, the alliance perhaps decreased the likelihood of British assistance to American 'dollar diplomacy' in the Far East. Some Japanese clearly hoped the alliance might have its uses in the maelstrom of Chinese politics. Japan, in any case, suffered from many financial weaknesses at this time, and was not in a position to embark upon a bold policy. Indeed, down to 1914 no power was well placed to seize the initiative in the Far East, or to exploit the dissolution of China into revolution and civil war from 1911. In this uneasy equilibrium some strange alignments were possible. Thus Britain and France could welcome German co-operation in a Yangtze railway venture – the Chinese were not proving so malleable as the western powers wished. There were even occasions when the British were finding it easier to deal with the Germans on economic issues in the Far East than with the Japanese, French and – naturally – the Russians.[29]

NOTES AND REFERENCES

1. Morrison, I, 62, 82
2. Clubb, p. 125
3. Iriye, p. 144
4. Iriye, pp. 133–49
5. M. B. Young, p. 186
6. Morrison, I, 284
7. Kochan, p. 26
8. Kazemzadeh, pp. 334–7
9. Kazemzadeh, pp. 171–2
10. Sanderson, pp. 396–403. For the origins of the South African War, see A. N. Porter, *passim*
11. Dugdale, III, 113–14
12. Bourne, p. 472
13. Bourne, pp. 478–9; Monger, pp. 119–21
14. Grenville [1] p. 322
15. Cooke, pp. 111–12; Andrew, pp. 121–35
16. Andrew, p. 214
17. Andrew, pp. 211, 229
18. Mackay, pp. 319–20; Spinner, p. 206; Morrison, I, 128
19. Clubb, pp. 125–33; Malozemoff, pp. 244–5
20. See Okamoto, *passim*
21. Bourne, p. 182
22. Andrew, pp. 289–99. See also Kennedy [2] pp. 207–10 and Laves, p. 158
23. Rich and Fisher, IV, 469
24. Mackay, pp. 314–28, 403; Marder, I, 125. For the reactions of the British army, see J. Gooch, Ch. 5
25. Abramsky, p. 103
26. Abramsky, pp. 118 ff. See also Kazemzadeh, pp. 482 ff.
27. Minger, p. 141
28. Beale (pp. 208, 289) takes too critical a view of Roosevelt's policies
29. Hinsley [1] pp. 357–8

Chapter 3

TOWARDS THE FIRST WORLD WAR

ANGLO-GERMAN RIVALRY, 1907–9

As is sometimes the case, a conference held to discuss arms limitation (in this instance at The Hague in 1907) had the effect, as one British delegate commented, of stimulating interest in armaments rather than the converse. Indeed, some on the British side saw the conference as a necessary preliminary if British opinion was to be persuaded that an increase in naval expenditure was unavoidable. Germany's conduct at the conference was expected to reconcile the British public to a naval race. An arms limitation agreement would have been welcome, but only if it ensured the continuance of British naval supremacy. Germany, however, still hoped to narrow the gap between the two fleets: neither power was feeling the strain of naval competition sufficiently for either to consider a compromise. The atmosphere at the conference was often belligerent: no power wished to give an appearance of weakness. Theodore Roosevelt put aside his early thoughts on some sort of naval limitation agreement in case other powers took this as a sign of American faint-heartedness. Suspicion was rife. The British feared German plots to lure Russia and France away from themselves. The Austrians thought the main British objective was to cause Germany the maximum of embarrassment. A year later the Austrian Foreign Minister was suggesting that Britain might be trying to manoeuvre Europe into a war so that she could smash Germany![1] Clive Parry concludes that there existed only the faintest signs that 'the utility of the exclusion of war by legal means was beginning to be appreciated, . . . To this extent Grey was no doubt on the side of the Angells.'[2]

The question of Anglo-German relations had been the subject of analysis by Eyre Crowe in his famous Foreign Office memorandum of 1 January 1907. He saw Germany as a new and rising nation which understandably wished to make further progress as a world power. The question was how much would she demand and with what consequences or implications for Britain. If one could agree on her legitimate demands – and Crowe did not define what he meant by legitimate – would their satisfaction make Germany a satisfied and co-operative power, or would this merely stimulate an acquisitive appetite? Crowe had no difficulty in answering these questions. Major concessions, he insisted, would endanger British interests. Germany, like Russia and France before her, could not be trusted. Crowe concluded that Britain and Germany were the victims of 'the form of a law of nations' in international affairs. He went further, even doubting if Germany were following a deliberate expansionist policy: it seemed to be mainly 'the expression of a vague, confused and unpractical statesmanship, not fully realising its own drift'.

There were indeed to be tantalizing moments during the next few years when parties in both governments seemed ready to explore the possibility of better relations – and not simply for limited tactical purposes. Wilhelm Solf, for instance, as Germany's Colonial Minister before the war, represented those who would have been content – at least for a time – to co-operate as Britain's junior partner in colonial or semi-colonial undertakings overseas, an approach akin to that pursued by the American banker, J. P. Morgan, with respect to Britain's vast international banking network. German financiers themselves often seemed interested in international co-operation, especially with Britain. Many Germans and Britons by 1914 were reassured by the complementary nature of their trading interests. In practice, as we shall see, Britain's concessions before August 1914 were too small to create a new atmosphere. The Solfs and the Ballins were unlikely to make serious headway against the neo-mercantilists, the navalists, the agrarians, the radical nationalists and all their other opponents in Germany. Nevertheless, as we shall see, Anglo-German differences were not an immediate cause of the war – or not in any direct way. If there was little promise of better things in Anglo-German relations in 1914, the years between 1905 and 1911 were the more overtly competitive. But in any analysis of the immediate origins of the First World War it is essential not to exaggerate the importance of Anglo-German rivalry.

Anglo-German naval rivalry, serious though it was, must be seen in this context. The British professed to be unable to understand why Germany needed a large fleet. Churchill once spoke of it as a 'luxury' for Germany. And on the German side there were those like Holstein who believed that Tirpitz's huge battle-fleet was a mistake: that it needlessly provoked the British when Germany should have concentrated her energies against the Russians and French. The German navalists, however, continued to prevail. Just why, for what motives, and with what effect on international rivalries must now be considered.

As recently as April 1897 the German navy had been built against Russia and France alone. The aim had been a navy that was half the size of the combined Russian and French fleets, with superiority for Germany in the Baltic. War with Britain was considered likely only if Germany were part of an alliance. From January 1894 the government had been trying to mobilize popular support for naval expansion. *Weltpolitik* necessitated a larger fleet, while a number of incidents in the scramble for colonies and concessions made it plain that Germany could never earn proper respect from imperial rivals – especially the British and Americans – without an adequate navy. The government in its turn used episodes such as the Jameson Raid to rouse German feeling against Britain in the hope of more support in the Reichstag for warship building. German businessmen with overseas interests often became naval enthusiasts, though usually for cruiser squadrons rather than battle-fleets. Some sections of heavy industry began to wake up to the profits that might be made from the manufacture of armour plate and other naval equipment. By 1912 the navy was absorbing about 12 per cent of Krupp's production. On the other hand, the navy required only about 2 per cent of Germany's total iron and steel production. The demands of the navy threatened to raise the cost of merchant shipbuilding in Germany. Some German shipping interests foresaw disaster in the event of war with Britain – German shipping would be swept from the seas to the benefit of Britain herself and the neutrals. Albert Ballin, an early naval enthusiast, had by 1908 become an ardent advocate of a naval compromise with Britain. His Hamburg Amerika line worked closely with the British Cunard company: the North German Lloyd was his main rival. Other German businessmen feared the effects of a war with Britain. Emil Rathenau insisted that industrial efficiency, not war, was the key to German export success.

The creation of a majority in the Reichstag for the passage of the famous 1898 Navy Bill was not easy. The agrarians were anti-British rather than pro-navy: they expected and received high tariffs as a reward for their votes. On the whole popular enthusiasm for the navy followed rather than preceded the bill, though by 1914 the German Navy League had perhaps 1 million supporters. Middle-class support for the navy grew dramatically: its officer corps, unlike the army, provided many openings for those of non-aristocratic birth. Tirpitz himself assiduously cultivated support, especially among big business where his ardour sometimes dismayed his naval colleagues. The German navy was thus a product of political and professional ambition, personified in Wilhelm II and Tirpitz; of certain commercial and business interests; of middle-class aspirations and patriotic pride; and of complicated wheeling and dealing within the élite. But it was also a reflection of imperial and naval enthusiasms in other countries. It would have been surprising had Germany not caught the infection, especially when, with the diversion of Russia to Asia between the late 1890s and 1905 (and her subsequent period of recovery from defeat and revolution), Germany found it possible to expand the navy without serious injury to the army and her security in Europe.

Tirpitz's minimum aim was the creation of a fleet which, while not the equal of the British, would deter an attack. Britain would be able to fight Germany only by risking her world position, given the threat from other navies. Tirpitz's great fear was that the British might choose to attack before his fleet had attained this position of security and leverage. His thinking was greatly influenced by the global struggle and balance at the turn of the century. Many have argued that his strategy made no sense once Britain transformed her world position by the alliance and *ententes* of 1902–7. This is true only up to a point. No alliance or *entente* is necessarily permanent. In the event of another diplomatic turn-round the German fleet had to be ready – it could not be improvised. Much of the criticism of Tirpitz's fleet is based on knowledge of what happened between 1907 and 1918. Where Tirpitz was at fault was in his reluctance to make any concessions to the British. In practice, as the British showed down to 1914, they could maintain a lead of about one-third in capital ships. Tirpitz could not narrow this gap, and his efforts to do so, and his refusals to negotiate, merely served to heighten British fears and their determination to stay ahead. So long as Tirpitz was dependent on a rift between Britain and France or Russia, he had no need to push the naval race to the limit: he could have settled for a smaller and less conspicuously provocative fleet. As it was, in any crisis with Britain before 1914, he could only advocate delay – his fleet was not equal to his hopes. What he would have recommended had he had the ships must remain a matter for speculation.

There were people in both Germany and Britain after 1907 who regretted the upsurge of hostility. As late as August 1914 the British historian, G. M. Trevelyan, while acknowledging the need to destroy certain 'barbarian' elements in Germany, saw much in that country which served as a barrier to the more comprehensively barbaric character of Tsarist Russia.[3] Lloyd George was impressed by Germany's record in social reform, and only after a personal visit in August 1908 was he struck by the fanatical patriotism and restlessness of many of its people. Even then, with others, he expected many of the great economic interests to work for peace. While he was willing to spend whatever might be necessary to maintain an adequate British lead at sea, he often sided with those in the Cabinet who advocated a naval agreement with Germany, and who hoped to divert spending from the wasteful arms race to social reform at home.[4] But the German naval programme was expanded from the end of 1907, and two years later Britain was gripped by a fierce debate as to whether the Germans were attempting a secret acceleration to their building of capital ships. This was probably not the case, but judicious leaks by Admiral Fisher and Lord Esher to sympathetic newspapers produced a national furore. The popular cry became 'we want eight, and we won't wait'. As Churchill aptly put it, the Cabinet split over the building of four or six dreadnoughts and compromised by ordering eight. The failure of Germany to respond to tentative soundings by Grey in the summer of 1908 on the possibility of naval talks had not been entirely unwelcome (Grey feared an unfavourable French reaction if talks got under way), but Berlin's silence helped to confirm the suspicions of the Foreign Office.

Much else was working against better Anglo-German relations at this time. Late in October 1908 an injudicious interview by Wilhelm II appeared in *The Daily Telegraph*. The Kaiser claimed he was standing alone against a widespread German desire for war against Britain. An outcry followed in both countries. Lord Roberts launched a campaign for compulsory military service in Britain. There was renewed discussion about the vulnerability of Britain to invasion. The year 1909 found Jellicoe, the future commander of the Grand Fleet, speculating concerning the threat of German submarines to British battleships in the North Sea in perhaps as few as eight years' time. But he consoled himself with the thought: 'I don't imagine we shall wait eight years for the war.'[5] Britain and Germany continued to drift apart over the question of the Berlin–Baghdad Railway. Lord Minto, Viceroy of India, commented uneasily in March 1908[6]:

> Given paramount German influence in Turkey, Asia Minor, Mesopotamia and Southern Persia our position in India would be seriously threatened and . . . we should be blind not to recognise the possibility of some future alliance between Russia and Germany.

An attempt from August 1909 by a new German Chancellor, Bethmann Hollweg, to ease relations not surprisingly failed. Tirpitz himself was adamant that the naval programme should be undisturbed. Bethmann in any case wanted a 'political formula' to accompany any naval agreement, and this the British rightly saw as a threat to their *ententes* with Russia and France. No progress was possible. Rivalries there were in plenty in international relations at this time, but there was also much of what Herbert Butterfield has so admirably described as the 'absolute predicament' in human relations, the 'Hobbesian fear', that is the insurmountable obstacle to trust in international affairs.[7]

THE BOSNIAN CRISIS OF 1908–9 AND ITS AFTERMATH

The Bosnian crisis of 1908–9 is a good example of the ease with which intentions can be misread, limited moves produce not so limited consequences, and events acquire a dynamic of their own. It is interesting that a new Austrian Foreign Minister, Aehrenthal, who was responsible for so much of what happened in 1908, should have taken office in 1906 with some interest in a revival of the Three Emperors Alliance.[8] Such an alignment would, he believed, strengthen the forces of conservatism against revolution. It would have made Austria less dependent on Germany. Austria and Germany were not the most intimate or contented of partners. There were no military talks between the two from 1896 to 1909. In April 1905 Berlin even tentatively touched on the possibility of Russo-German co-operation in the event of the break-up of the Habsburg Empire. As it was, the narrow nationalism of Germany – and it was becoming narrower – could prove an embarrassment to the government of the polyglot Habsburg Empire, especially when migrant Austro-Hungarian workers were maltreated in Germany. Austrian interests also suffered from German tariffs, from Germany's aggressive pursuit of trade and concessions in the Balkans, and from Berlin's assiduous courting of the Turks. The Austrians tried to follow a middle road at the Algeciras Conference, and were embarrassed when the Germans acclaimed them as a 'brilliant second'. On the other hand the Dual Alliance of 1879 still had some meaning, if only because neither Germany nor Austria could find a better partner. Nevertheless it made sense for Aehrenthal to try to broaden his options. Even the Serbs were not excluded despite the current trade (or 'pig') war. It made sense to try to conciliate the Slavs at home and abroad. Aehrenthal was not so much a trouble-maker by intent as from wishful thinking and impatience.

The need for caution should have been evident following the popular outcry in Russia in February 1908 when the Austrians attempted to make use of their railway rights in the Sanjak of Novibazar (between Serbia and Montenegro). But on 2 July 1908 Izvolsky made the tempting suggestion that in return for some improvement in Russia's position at the Straits, Russia herself would not oppose Austria's annexation of Bosnia and Herzegovina, Turkish provinces which had been under her administration (though still nominally Turkish) since 1878. Aehrenthal thus appeared to have a splendid opportunity to tidy up the southern borders of the Habsburg Empire. He personally believed that there could be no satisfactory solution to the Slav question until the 'seat of gravity' of the Serbo-Croat peoples lay firmly within the monarchy, with Serbia pacified or neutralized. The summer of 1908 appeared an appropriate time as the Ottoman Empire was currently paralysed by the Young Turk revolution. Austria's relations were even improving with the British. Indeed, Grey was having to resist some suggestions from within the Foreign Office that this was the time to try to woo Austria away from Germany. Grey argued that to intensify Germany's sense of isolation might increase the risk of a mad-dog act.

Izvolsky, meanwhile, hoped for British support at the Straits. Here he failed to understand that while the British were happy to see Russia as an obstacle to German expansion in the Near East, they did not want any real change to the status quo. Indeed, the British hoped that with the rise of the Young Turks their influence might rise in the Ottoman Empire at the expense of the Germans. Izvolsky, having miscalculated here, suffered a worse setback on 5 October 1908 when the Bulgarians decided to exploit the confusion in Constantinople to free themselves from the last vestiges of Turkish overlordship. A few days later Vienna announced the formal annexation of Bosnia and Herzegovina. Izvolsky, as a result of his meeting with Aehrenthal at Buchlau on 1 September, had expected the Austrian moves to be co-ordinated with his own. Now he found that Vienna had not only stolen a march on him but had engaged in what many Russians saw as an act of aggression against the Slav cause. In desperation he tried to organize a Balkan League, and supported Serbia's demand for territorial compensation.

The Bosnian crisis in the winter of 1908–9, however, found Russia in a very weak position. This was not an issue on which she could expect strong backing from other powers. Russia was still recovering from the events of 1904–5: she was in no condition to fight. Austria was strongly and confidently backed by Germany, though the German General Staff were still mainly preoccupied with the speedy defeat of France in the event of a European war. Nevertheless when, in March 1909, matters between Serbia and Austria appeared to be coming to a head, Berlin sent a virtual ultimatum to St Petersburg. The Austrian annexation of Bosnia and Herzegovina must be recognized, or Germany would not restrain Vienna in its quarrel with the Serbs. Izvolsky capitulated. Severe damage, however, had been inflicted on the relations of the Central Powers with Russia. With hindsight one may feel that mounting nationalist feeling in eastern Europe was remorselessly undermining the efforts of monarchs and diplomats to behave as if they were free to pick and choose friends and enemies in the old way without regard for public opinion. They had been living in a world of illusions since the mid-1890s, encouraged by a temporary cessation of their rivalries in the Balkans. They could coexist only so long as they agreed to uphold the status quo, and only so long as the status quo itself was tenable. Aehrenthal and Izvolsky by their clumsy diplomacy had merely made explicit what was already implicit. Indeed, the very existence of this Balkan crisis – and its character – owed much to the defeat of the Russian autocracy abroad and at home in 1904–5. Yet Slav nationalism might still have suffered a grave setback in 1909 had the government in Vienna succumbed to the proponents of a preventive war against Serbia. As it was, the Austrians were close to mobilization at the end of March. This is a tantalizing moment in European history, for Austria might have been allowed to destroy Serbia without precipitating a European war. Whether the Central Powers could then have established a position of such dominance in the Near East as to overawe local and outside opposition cannot of course be known. Indeed, at the time, once the initial shock from the crisis had passed, there seemed little reason to suppose that the relations of the powers had been significantly worsened by the Bosnian affair. An agreement over certain economic issues in Morocco was even concluded by the French and Germans in February 1909 – that is, during the crisis itself. If German businessmen benefited less than they had hoped, the British suffered some setbacks in Morocco, and still more so in the Ottoman Empire where French and German collaboration was also taking place.

The main reason for this Franco-German co-operation was Germany's shortage of capital for foreign investment.[9] George von Siemens of the Deutsche Bank had been troubled ten years earlier by the financial (and technical) difficulties Germany would face in trying to build the Berlin–Baghdad Railway, and he had been anxious to attract foreign partners to share the risks. German financiers, however, could not ignore the wishes of their government, so that they had sometimes to look to France and sometimes to Britain in accordance with the political situation. Hard-headed businessmen such as Siemens and Emil Rathenau were often troubled by the weight given to political and strategic considerations. Nevertheless Germany was able to resume talks with the British at the end of 1910 on the future of the Berlin–Baghdad Railway. The British were now inclined to accept this as a *fait accompli* and to seek the best terms they could. In their turn, both the British and French were troubled by a visit of Nicholas II and his Foreign Minister, Sazonov, to Potsdam in November 1910. There the Russians traded assent to the Baghdad Railway for German recognition of their special interest in northern Persia. This tendency of each power to try to run with the hare (at least on lesser issues) as well hunt with the hounds was also at work in the Far East where Britain, France and Germany, and the United States, together pioneered an international consortium, initially against the objections of Russia and Japan.

By 1911 Anglo-Russian relations were once more seriously deteriorating in Persia. It is true that there was no great risk, as some feared, of a Russo-German alignment in the Middle East. The

Russians were too fearful of German competition in Persia, and Sazonov's talks with Berlin were primarily designed to buy time so that Russia could consolidate economically in the north, and ensure that any link between Persia and the Baghdad Railway was built in accordance with Russian interests. Sazonov made good use of the second Moroccan crisis in 1911 (when Germany was preoccupied in the west) to obtain good terms in the agreement of 19 August, and by then it was evident that there would be no political corollaries. But any improvement in Russia's position in Persia simply added to Britain's worries. Persia itself was in a state of growing political collapse. This encouraged and facilitated foreign intervention. Late in 1911 the Russians forced the dismissal of an American who was employed to try to bring some order to Persia's finances, and also occupied some Persian territory. Russian consuls and troops controlled the north of the country. The British feebly protested, but had usually to advise the Persians to submit lest worse befell them. Perhaps their best card was Sazonov's fear that excessive Russian gains might force Grey's resignation and place the *entente* of 1907 in jeopardy. The ending of the Moroccan crisis late in 1911 also aided the British, not least because the Russians did not rule out the possibility of an Anglo-German *rapprochement*. Feeling was certainly running strongly against the Russians in London, and it was only with difficulty that Grey secured acceptance of the argument that it was better to concede Russian demands in northern Persia than upset the *entente*. Nevertheless here was a problem that was likely to recur. As Russia recovered her strength and confidence so she would try to break out in Asia or in eastern Europe. In the first case Britain would be in the front line: in the second she might be dragged into an unwanted war. British naval and military preparations against Germany in these years must not be allowed to obscure the very real problems the nation faced outside Europe.

AGADIR, 1911

On 24 July 1909 the British Committee of Imperial Defence concluded that any future European war would be short, that the first battles would be decisive, and that these, so far as Britain was concerned, would be fought in France and perhaps Belgium. Plans were drawn up for the speedy dispatch of five divisions to join the French left flank or to cover Antwerp. With Germany no progress was made towards a naval agreement. In any case in March 1911 the Cabinet accepted Grey's argument that any agreement must not weaken the *ententes* with France and Russia. The German question

also influenced relations with Japan. Some British commercial interests were complaining of Japanese competition in the Far East: the
Australian government joined those who opposed the continuance
of the Anglo-Japanese alliance. Grey, however, insisted that to
abandon the alliance would simply increase Britain's difficulties. The
alliance might not be a wholly effective restraint on Japan, but it was
better than nothing. Without it, Britain would need more naval
forces in the Far East, and these could be sent only if the fleet was
weakened in the North Sea (to the advantage of Germany) or as a
result of yet more increases in naval expenditure. The critics were
overborne, though the alliance was renewed in 1911 with provisos
which made it clear that it could not be invoked by Japan against the
United States. Given this degree of concern over Germany it is not
surprising that the Agadir incident prompted so firm a response from
London.

Several motives lay behind the dispatch of the German gunboat,
Panther, to Agadir on 1 July 1911. The Germans were dismayed to
find that despite the agreement of 1909 the French were securing the
main economic advantages in Morocco. French action in Morocco
was being stepped up in 1911 as the internal political situation
worsened. A German move of some kind was necessary to secure
compensation in Morocco itself or, more probably, in the French
Congo which bordered the German colony in the Cameroons. Some
German business interests were exerting pressure, and the German
Foreign Office under Kiderlen-Wächter was also eager to act,
conscious that Russia might be bought off with concessions in the
Middle East, and perhaps also swayed by the hope that the Anglo-
French *entente* might be weakened. Certainly his tactics finally
persuaded the British and French that this was indeed his objective,
and it seems that a more restrained approach might well have secured
concessions from Paris without a major crisis. By 21 June the British
Cabinet was thoroughly alarmed, and Lloyd George's speech at the
Mansion House was designed to show that Britain could not be
ignored, a warning perhaps directed a little at the French as well as
the main target, Germany. The violence of the reaction in Berlin
confirmed Grey's worst fears. There was a special meeting of the
Committee of Imperial Defence on 23 August to discuss British
strategy in the event of war. It was then that the War Office's plan
to send an expeditionary force to support the French left flank was
approved – despite objections from the Admiralty. The Cabinet, of
course, was still free to decide whether to support France in the event
of war: the question discussed on the 23rd was only how this was to
be done.

The crisis was in fact slowly defused over the following months. In
November 1911 the Germans secured part of the French Congo for
recognition of a French protectorate in Morocco. But profound fears

and strong feelings had been excited. As one correspondent wrote from London on 19 September 1911[10]:

> If this is decided on [further German naval expansion] the feeling in England will become dangerous. There is no alternative: either we shall have to spend £20,000,000 straight away in augmenting the fleet, or we must pick a quarrel at once with Germany. That is the universal opinion amongst the people I meet and I think it fairly represents the average of instructed opinion in the United Kingdom.

From the Foreign Office, early in 1912, Sir Arthur Nicolson commented that the world scene had never seemed so troubled. Lloyd George was arguing that it was necessary to put an end to German bullying and for this a clear British naval lead was vital. But he also hoped that once Germany 'thoroughly realised these two things' a more constructive relationship might be possible. He saw two types of imperialism developing in the world – the narrow, militarist and exclusive type, and that which was based on co-operation and consent. He hoped that Germany would choose the second type. Her activity in the Middle East might then benefit all, and help to contain Russia.[11]

There were mixed reactions inside Germany. Widespread indignation over British and French policy coexisted with relief that war had been averted. This was true of both Wilhelm II and Bethmann Hollweg. The Social Democrats opposed war. Among German big business many were fearful of war, especially with Britain. Ballin redoubled his efforts to improve Anglo-German relations. High finance was troubled by the withdrawal of short-term French loans which depressed the stock market. The German navy was unprepared for war. Germany's ally Austria-Hungary was unsympathetic, though Aehrenthal expected an Anglo-German war in two or three years.[12] Certainly the Agadir crisis and its relatively disappointing outcome enraged many German nationalists. It prompted General Friedrich von Bernhardi to produce his widely read *Germany and the Next War* which appeared in 1912, quickly running through six editions, plus an English translation. This vehement work is well known for its arguments concerning the German need to expand, the probability of an early war between Britain and France and Germany (war with Russia was not considered quite so likely). Conflict was portrayed as necessary, right and salutary: it was the key to success and advancement.

But Bernhardi's book also contained many criticisms of Germany. The patriotic fervour displayed in 1911 had not persuaded Bernhardi that the German people as a whole were yet ready to bear the burdens of a long and costly war. There was too much haggling in the Reichstag over arms expenditure, there were too many particularist and class divisions in Germany, the government was too cautious and many strata of society were becoming too pacific. Employers and employees alike in trade and industry were too interested in commerce, too ready to believe that peace would bring permanent prosperity. The book is in fact full of complaints concerning German unpreparedness for war, and the reluctance of many people to accept that Germany could find her rightful place in the world only as a result of war. Germany must fight for world status, or decline as a great power. Undoubtedly Bernhardi was representative of much opinion in Germany, but enthusiastic reviews of his book by the Right-wing press were offset by attacks from Liberals and the Left. Many in government were critical of Bernhardi, and a group of German imperialists replied in a pamphlet interestingly entitled *Deutsche Weltpolitik and kein Krieg* (German *Weltpolitik* and no war). They favoured a switch in the emphasis of German activities from eastern Europe and the Near East to Africa where they evidently hoped to achieve an accommodation with Britain in colonial matters.[13]

To what extent there was a genuine relaxation in the tension between Britain and Germany over the next two years is still a matter of debate among historians. Certainly on the vexed question of naval rivalry they could only agree to differ. Only a British promise of neutrality in a European war might have led to an agreement. Even so the naval race was not so prominent an issue as it had been. Here Britain was indebted to German fears of the reviving threat by land from Russia and France. As Germany expanded her army, even Tirpitz could not secure what he wanted for the navy. The German naval planners were also discouraged by the Anglo-French naval agreement of 1912 which led to the concentration of British ships in the North Sea. The British were adopting a strategy of distant blockade – thereby reducing the North Sea to a 'dead sea'. They were unlikely to risk valuable ships in waters where the Germans might hope to win a campaign of attrition. Unless Britain could be deprived of one or other of her *entente* partners, Tirpitz's fleet appeared likely to lose rather than gain ground in the foreseeable future. Nothing in politics and strategy is, of course, final. Given time the German admirals might have been driven to an early appreciation of the value of submarine and commerce warfare – the naval race could have taken a new twist in peacetime as it was to do in war. But as matters stood early in 1914 the British had, thanks to the French and Russian armies, a little less cause to be hysterical about the German navy.[14] Anglo-German talks on the future of the Portuguese colonies and the Berlin–Baghdad Railway by 1914 were also troubling the stauncher Germanophobes in London, and causing some concern in Paris. Could Anglo-German relations be about to take a turn for the better?

Naturally in the doldrum periods between crises the powers were sometimes inclined to drift or to experiment in the hope of finding some unsuspected current or a favourable puff of wind. This is well illustrated by Austrian efforts to decrease their dependence upon Germany. But approaches to Britain for a loan, for instance, were spurned, the British fearing that the money would be used to strengthen the Austro-Hungarian navy. It is tempting to argue that this was a moment when a strong, self-confident Britain might have made a contribution to the stability of Europe by the pursuit of more disinterested policies. But this is to exaggerate British strength and influence. In 1912–13 the British did not merely fear Germany: they feared the loss of French and Russian 'friendship'. The *ententes* were intended to restrain France and Russia, especially Russia, as well as Germany. They were designed to protect Britain's world position, as well as to maintain the balance of power in Europe to her liking. It is true that the British did show some interest in the possibility of Austro-Russian co-operation in the Balkans, but when they spoke of this the French took fright in case this should lead to a revival of the *Dreikaiserbund*. Some flexibility was, of course, possible when the stakes were not too high. This applied to some extent in the Balkan Wars of 1912–13, but these wars were also a warning as to how near some of the powers were coming to the borders of tolerance.

TRIPOLI AND THE BALKAN WARS

Although there had been talk of a Balkan League or confederation from the time of the Bosnian crisis, Russian ministers had remained divided over its form, membership and purpose. The idea in any case was academic so long as Bulgars, Serbs and Greeks quarrelled so uncompromisingly over the future of Macedonia. It was the Italian bid to conquer Tripoli in September 1911 which brought matters to a head.[15] Even so, while the Balkan states saw this as an opportunity to engage in territorial revision at the expense of the Turks, the Russians initially hoped that the war might persuade the Turks to be more amenable over the future of the Straits. It was only when Russian overtures to Constantinople in October 1911 elicited no response that the Balkan states began to make the running.

Their relationship with Russia was an interesting one. They required Russia as a shield against the other great powers. They also looked to Russia to help resolve their many local rivalries – though at best Russia could only mediate, not arbitrate. On the other hand the Balkan states possessed some leverage over the cautious Russian government, given the Slav sympathies of some educated and well-to-do Russians – especially among the more liberal elements. They could also exploit Russian state interests as Sazonov, the Russian Foreign Minister, disappointed by the failure of the October approach to Turkey and fearful of the long-term trends in Austrian policy, believed that Russia needed a Bulgar-Serb alliance to help maintain Russian prestige and influence in the Balkans. But the Russians also required assurances from Bulgaria and Serbia that they would not provoke a war with Turkey without Russian approval. Tiny Montenegro was initially excluded from the Balkan League of March 1912 as being too adventurous. The Greeks were admitted two months later. The Russians then joined with the French in an effort to persuade the Turks to carry out reforms in their remaining European territories. But they could not prevent the initiation of a war against Turkey by the Balkan states in October 1912. The latter feared that further delay might give the great powers time to intervene effectively. The opposition parties in Bulgaria were chiding the government with cowardice. Russian diplomats in St Petersburg suddenly found that they had lost control of the situation. Vienna and Berlin were taken by surprise, and were following independent and even in some cases rival policies in the Balkans. Thus the Austrians could only watch the succession of Turkish defeats with growing dismay. Some military preparations were made, and Conrad was recalled. But these were precautionary moves only: it was hoped they might impress the Balkan states. Armed intervention was a different matter: it was agreed in Vienna that this would be financially ruinous. The Austrians hoped that the unity of the Balkan League would prove short-lived, and looked to the formation of a new Albanian state as the best security against an enlarged Serbia.

The Turks in Macedonia and Albania were under attack from all sides. Their position was hopeless. At one time Constantinople itself appeared to be under threat from a Bulgarian army. Nevertheless the Turks managed to retain a toehold in Europe, and an armistice was arranged on 3 December 1912. Agreement, however, had yet to be reached on the share-out of the spoils among the victors, and how far the results of the war would prove compatible with the interests of the great powers. There had already been a threatening ministerial conference in St Petersburg on 23 November 1912 which had discussed the growing differences between Serbia and Austria. The Russian military had talked of partial mobilization, but had been headed off by Sazonov and other ministers.[16] Nevertheless this disposition of even a few persons not to rule out war was ominous. The mood in Berlin was for a time even less restrained. Germany promised on 2 December to support Austria in the event of a Russian attack. A few days later news reached Berlin that Britain would not tolerate a French defeat in the event of a European war arising out of a Balkan crisis. This prompted the Kaiser's 'War

Council' of 8 December at which Moltke argued that Germany was having difficulty in keeping pace with French and Russian military expansion and that therefore the sooner war came the better. Tirpitz, however, asked for a delay of at least eighteen months as the German navy was not ready. Admiral Müller commented after the meeting: 'The result amounted almost to nothing.'[17] Wilhelm himself soon became less bellicose. The New Year found him averse to war over Balkan issues in which Germany had little interest, and he spoke of working for peace through his contacts with Nicholas II and George V. The 'War Council' settled nothing, but it is highly revealing as to the atmosphere in Berlin – in some circles at least. What should be stressed is the sense of growing competition, and the fear that time was not on Germany's side.

The attitudes of the British and French governments also require a little attention. Although some in Britain welcomed the weakening of Turkey as just retribution for oppression and misgovernment, others feared that the many Muslim subjects of the British Crown might be outraged by the defeat of a Muslim power. There were British investments in the Ottoman Empire to consider. Finally, while it was of little direct interest to the British how much of the territory in the Balkans was shared out, it mattered a great deal if territorial disputes in south-eastern Europe should threaten the peace of the Continent as a whole. Britain, the Foreign Office believed, could not stand aloof from a general war, however caused. She could not let Germany win, nor France and Russia win without her. As the British ambassador in Berlin, horrified by the thought of British involvement in a war arising from distant quarrels in the Balkans, wrote in November 1912: 'What friends should we have left? And what figure should we cut?'[18] The Foreign Office even hesitated at first to take the lead in the interest of peace in case this should offend the Russians and so weaken the *entente*. Only in 1913 was there real confidence in London that it could safely adopt a mediatory role. Meanwhile the French were still more determined to stand by the Russians. Relations with Germany had been seriously injured by Agadir. It is true that the Russians had shown little sympathy during the crisis, but a new French government led by Poincaré from January 1912 set out to put substance into what had often been only an alliance in name since 1894. Poincaré, a Lorrainer, was famous even among his countrymen for his coldness and 'systematic intransigence'.[19] He argued that conciliation merely encouraged the Germans to ask for more. He feared the French caution might cause Britain or Russia to move towards Germany. In his visit to Russia in August 1912 he made plain his desire to co-operate against Germany. His was not a war policy, but in September he told the Russian ambassador in Paris that even in an eastern European crisis, if Germany became involved, France would stand by Russia. A more assertive mood was also to be detected among the French General Staff. The French public, however, did not share this new interest in the Balkans, while French financial interests were well content with the status quo in that region.[20] French policy was thus guided primarily by political and military considerations. The new approach weakened the pro-German factions in Russia, though for the time being most of the Tsar's ministers were still too worried by the country's internal discontents and military weakness to favour an adventurous foreign policy. But the balance of opinion was beginning to shift in favour of the militants.

In the winter of 1912–13, however, all the powers, save Austria, began to see an ambassadorial conference in London as the best forum at which to try to create a new territorial settlement in the Balkans. While Sazonov warned of the strength of pro-Slav feeling in Russia, and the difficulties that would follow any serious setbacks to Slav hopes, the Austrians struggled to create a viable Albanian state to limit the expansion of the Serbs. A very stiff stand on their part was necessary before the presumptuous Montenegrins were persuaded to relinquish Scutari to the Albanians. Even so, Slav gains as recognized by the Treaty of London of 30 May 1913 caused considerable dismay in Vienna. And the situation was soon made worse when festering differences between the Bulgarians and their former allies produced another explosion. The Bulgarians were not prepared to leave the port of Salonika in Greek hands or certain parts of Macedonia to the Serbs. Russian mediation was apparently leading nowhere, while those in possession of the disputed territory in effect defied the Bulgars to throw them out. Sofia's appeal to arms at the end of June 1913, however, badly misfired. Encouraged by Greek and Serb victories, the Rumanians and Turks also intervened against the luckless Bulgarians: the latter were forced to make major concessions by the Treaty of Bucharest of 10 August 1913. This time the great powers were driven to the sidelines. Russia could not prevent the Turkish recovery of Adrianople, while the Austrians watched helplessly as the Serbs gained further territory and self-confidence.

The next Balkan League, it seemed, must be directed against Austria-Hungary. The economy of the empire had been damaged by the recent wars, and by continuing German competition. Towards the end of 1913 the Austrians even began to explore the possibility of a French loan. Politically the Austrians were at loggerheads with Rumania, the nominal ally of the Central Powers. Bulgaria, despite its recent defeats, still looked mainly to Russia for support. The Austrian and German foreign offices disagreed on many Balkan issues, and only among the military was there a growing sense of solidarity. Moltke was convinced that a war between Teutons and Slavs was inevitable.[21] In contrast, Bethmann Hollweg had protested in June 1913: 'I have had enough of war and bellicose talks and of eternal armaments. It is high time that the great nations settle down and pursue peaceful work.'[22] An attempt must now be made to sum up the relations of the powers on the eve of the Great War.

THE RELATIONS OF THE POWERS ON THE EVE OF WAR

At the end of 1913 the powers received another warning that their rivalries in south-eastern Europe now posed the gravest threats to peace. A German general, Liman von Sanders, was given an active command in the Turkish army. The Russians protested violently in November 1913. An ingenious face-saving solution was found by the appointment of von Sanders to the post of Inspector-General to the Turkish army, but the episode had highlighted the degree to which Russo-German relations had deteriorated. Time would soon demonstrate that this relationship was the most important factor making for peace or war in Europe.

Yet, strangely enough, in the early months of 1914 a major crisis seemed almost as likely between Russia and Britain as one involving Russia and the Central Powers. In April 1912 Nicolson had commented that Germany was less of a threat to British interests than an unfriendly France or Russia.[23] Much of the care lavished on the *ententes* down to 1914, especially that with Russia, was obviously designed not only for security against Germany, but against the perils of isolation in general. Not for nothing did a report from the Committee of Imperial Defence in July 1920 conclude that the 'dominant impulse' in imperial defence for 100 years had been India.[24] In the Near East by the winter of 1913–14 the British were rather more hopeful of reaching agreement with Germany over their respective interests and more worried by the revival of Russian power and activity. The revival of the Turkish navy was now seen more in the context of the containment of Russia than – as it had been in 1909 – as an anti-German measure. The Russians hoped to achieve naval supremacy in the Black Sea by 1916–17: the British were looking for some counterweight but by means which would not jeopardize their own relationship with Russia.[25]

Meanwhile there were new Anglo-Russian disputes in Tibet and Afghanistan. More serious still was the rivalry in Persia. Each power was increasingly active in its own sphere, with the Russians fearing an advance of British oil interests to the north, and the British fearing a Russian trans-Persian railway that would menace India. By June 1914 matters had come to such a pass that only a partition of the country seemed likely to save the *entente*. While there were groups in Britain, Russia and France who were all working to preserve the *entente*, it still seemed possible that a pro-German government might be established in Russia, perhaps as part of the battle to defeat the revolutionary threat in Russia, and that such a government might, to complement a policy of monarchical solidarity and the status quo in eastern Europe, redouble Russian efforts to gain influence in Asia. Early in 1914 the British ambassador in St Petersburg warned that without more support from Britain Russia might turn to Germany.[26] Grey knew that opinion in Britain would not stomach major concessions to Russia, but agreed that something must be done to strengthen the present Foreign Minister, Sazonov, who favoured the *entente*. By 14 May 1914 he had persuaded the British Cabinet that naval talks with Russia were the answer. These would signify little or nothing in reality, yet they might strengthen the pro-British faction in Russia. Unfortunately when news of these talks reached Berlin they were seized upon by Bethmann's critics as evidence that his efforts to neutralize the British were leading nowhere. The British had unintentionally contributed to the growing belief in Berlin that time was running out for Germany.

It is not easy, as we have seen, to evaluate Anglo-German relations at this time. The British ambassador in Berlin was moderately optimistic. In Westminister and Whitehall Ireland absorbed much attention: the situation in Europe, apart from the arms race, did not seem unusually menacing.[27] An Anglo-German compromise was reached over oil in Mesopotamia in March 1914. The Berlin–Baghdad Railway question was being resolved, but the agreement on the Portuguese colonies would take effect only if the Portuguese agreed to relinquish them. Grey was also arguing in private that in any partition of the Ottoman Empire Germany must be generously treated. But those in Germany who were impatient for success could always claim that the British, like the White Queen, were only offering jam tomorrow, never jam today. There were contradictory pressures. Germany's shortage of capital contributed to the settlement of the Berlin–Baghdad question. On the other hand, this sense of financial weakness also fed German fears that they were falling behind in the race for world power: that military power was their chief asset. Thus Germany was unable to raise the funds which were needed to tie Rumania securely to the Central Powers: she had none to encourage the desire of the Greeks to lessen their dependence on France. It was only with difficulty that Bulgaria was persuaded not to take an *entente* loan. There was a keen struggle among major German interest groups for such funds as were available. Businessmen in search of assured profits did not always see eye to eye with the military and their strategic obsessions in Turkey. The German government, to please the British for political reasons, held back German bidders for a lucrative Turkish contract late in 1913.

The shortage of funds became acute in the spring of 1914 as French capital made inroads into Turkey. Krupp arms sales to the Turks were threatened by the latter's difficulties in raising a loan on the Berlin market. The Deutsche Bank feared such a loan would starve it of funds needed for its own projects, notably the Berlin–Baghdad Railway. Although a solution was found, fears continued to mount that German exports to the Near East, and therefore German influence, would decline given the difficulty of raising capital for foreign loans and investment. A shortage, not a surplus of capital was a determining force in Germany's *Drang nach Osten*.[28]

This shortage had been worsened by the Agadir crisis, when frightened French investors had begun to pull their money out of Germany, and to show less interest in co-operative ventures. The confidence of some German businessmen was being shaken by the current recession. Again there were fears of new barriers being erected against German exports by other states. It was feared, for instance, that as Russia recovered her strength, so St Petersburg would make difficulties when it came time in 1917 to renew trade treaties negotiated when Germany enjoyed the stronger bargaining hand. It is true that in 1911 Hugo Stinnes boasted: 'Give me three or four years of peace and I shall silently secure Germany's European predominance.' He was then busily looking for ways round French legislation designed to prevent foreign ownership of the major iron-ore mines in Briey, Longwy and Nancy. But it is interesting that once war broke out certain German industrialists began to clamour for annexation of this region.[29] Before 1914 Walter Rathenau, and sometimes the Kaiser himself, advocated some form of central European customs union (the precursor of the wartime *Mitteleuropa* programme) to try to guarantee German prosperity – and thus also the country's political and social stability. Rathenau described his programme as Germany's last chance to catch up with the world leaders: this was a necessary and legitimate aspiration to be achieved with or without the willing co-operation of other European states. Germany, he argued, should not have to depend on 'the charity of the world market. We need territory on the globe.'[30] Not all German economic interests, however, saw this as a solution to their problems (farmers would have been menaced by cheaper producers in a European customs union). The majority of German businessmen by 1914 were not pressing for drastic new policies. What did matter, however, by 1914 was that, with other Germans, they were easily persuaded that Germany was so menaced by her neighbours, militarily and economically, that war was a legitimate choice. A German banker, faced by the argument of the American ambassador that a further generation of peace would have Germany invulnerable because of her economic strength, replied that the strategic arguments were paramount – Germany dared not delay in an international crisis.[31] The weakness of the barriers to war among influential German opinion in 1914 was more important than the aggressive demands and tone of the most vociferous groups.

Fear of Russia among the German people at large was particularly important in 1914. It is true that many in military and political circles were anxious to capitalize on and intensify these fears (Russophobia among the Social Democrats was especially welcome and was the best guarantee of national unity in the event of war, especially if any war could be attributed to Tsarist and Slav aggression). But it would be naive to see this Russophobia as merely the fabrication of a manipulated press – government policy was not consistent on this point, while the manipulators themselves were often genuinely fearful of Russia. The Russians entered whole-heartedly into a press war in the spring of 1914. German fears were shared by others. Shortly before the war Sir Edward Grey himself showed some sympathy for Germany as she became exposed to the reviving power of her two neighbours. A British general, Sir Henry Wilson, admittedly prone to hyperbole, even remarked that Germany would be wise to attack Russia before the latter became too strong: the Germans could feel it was a case of 'now or never'. In a reference to Russia's military strength Nicolson minuted apprehensively in July 1914: 'Let us hope our relations with her will continue to be friendly.'[32] Back in January 1913 the British ambassador in Vienna had reported on Austria's growing impatience with Serbia. He noted some similarities with Britain's relations with the Transvaal before the Boer War, even down to the point of Russia playing the part of Germany as the outside *agent provocateur*. It was perhaps a pity that an American special envoy, Colonel House, on a peace mission to Europe in the early summer of 1914, confined himself to the western capitals, and was thus struck by the militant atmosphere in Berlin compared with Paris and London. His impressions of St Petersburg, Vienna and Belgrade would have been interesting. But House's attention was centred on the less explosive question of Anglo-German naval rivalry, not the most dangerous powder barrel in Europe, the tensions and conflicts in the east and south-east.

These rivalries, it is true, need not have erupted into a general European war, and it was Germany, more than any other power, which brought this about. Nevertheless, before July 1914 there is little evidence to suggest that the Kaiser and his ministers were convinced that war was the *only* answer to Germany's problems, or that they were bound to succumb to pressure from the Pan-German League and other civilian militants, or even from the General Staff. Certainly they were determined to advance German interests by any means they thought appropriate. They were fearful of being thought weak by their critics at home, though the Chancellor firmly rejected the argument that a successful war would be the best answer to the domestic challenge posed by the Social Democrats. They did not see Germany as a champion of the status quo, but their revisionism was qualitatively and quantitatively different from that pursued by Hitler and his acolytes. They were less single-minded, less ruthless, less impatient, too rooted in their own conservative order and that of Europe as a whole to think in the same radical, nihilistic terms, or to be prepared to run the same risks. Ambitious they may have been, but they required the spur of fear that Germany's current strength and advantages were wasting assets to persuade them to act; that is, to run the risk of a general war. A Hitler, one suspects, would have acted more decisively in 1905–6, 1909 or 1911–13. He moved almost before the opportunities had revealed themselves. In 1914 the German leadership staked its all only when it seemed further delay would deny it hope of further advancement by piecemeal methods. Above all one is struck by the fear that the superb German army might no longer be assured of victory in the event of war with France and Russia. Already some time had passed since the German Chief of Staff had been able to share the confidence of Schlieffen during the first Moroccan crisis: 'the time was very suitable for the inevitable war, since Russia was out, and it was not the English fleet, but the battles in France that would decide the war'.[33]

The German generals had been seeking the answer to the problem of a two-front war since the 1870s. In the 1880s and early 1890s they had usually given priority to the defeat of Russia. Schlieffen, however, had come to the conclusion that Germany's best hope of victory lay in the speedy defeat of France, and from 1897 this was accompanied by plans for an advance through Belgium to accelerate the campaign still further. Although the Russian army was not rated so highly as the French, it was feared that Russia's size might rob Germany of a quick and decisive victory. Schlieffen was not merely influenced by military considerations. He was convinced that a long war would be ruinous to a modern, industrialized state: factory wheels would soon stop turning – the economy and therefore the political and social order would collapse. He saw the Russo-Japanese War as a warning.[34] His successor shared these fears, and added some of his own. By 1912 the size of the French and Russian armies demanded a considerable expansion of the German forces, so much so that the essentially aristocratic officer corps was threatened with dilution by middle-class officers who alone could make up the necessary numbers. It also became necessary to raise more soldiers from urban areas, with the resultant risk of adding to socialist influences within the army. As late as 1911 nearly two-thirds of the soldiers were drawn from the rural population, although more than half of the German people now lived in towns. The War Ministry was even more reluctant than the General Staff to undertake this expansion which might have such serious effects on the outlook and character of the army. Worrying, too, was the problem of financing these increases. Germany already stood in need of tax reform, but the government feared the wrath of Right or Left if it attempted any significant changes. Thus although Germany in theory possessed the resources to continue the arms race with Russia and France, the domestic costs threatened to prove unacceptable. The German army was expanded from 1912, but to an accompaniment of doubts as to how often this process could be repeated in the future. Thus worries mounted concerning the costs of a long armed peace as well as of a long, inconclusive war.

The French replied to the expansion of the German army with the introduction of three-year service for their conscripts. By 1914 this left Germany's relative military position much as it had been in 1911. Her one real gain shortly before the war was the growth in her reserves. These included thirteen corps which, unknown to the French, could be committed to the western front from the outset of hostilities. Thus for the time being the Germans possessed a sufficient superiority of numbers over the French to attempt to carry out the Schlieffen Plan. But the General Staff feared this advantage would prove short-lived. The great Moltke's nephew was now Chief of the General Staff (he had succeeded Schlieffen in 1906). But the new commander was no man of iron. He had more of the pessimist and fatalist about him than a spirit of ruthless ambition. He suffered from cardiac irregularities from 1913. From 1912 he spoke increasingly of the desirability of a preventive war mainly, it would seem, from the belief unless Germany acted soon she would not be assured of victory in the event of war. Moltke was astute enough to see that even in 1914 a quick victory was not certain: a war might drag on for up to two years. He saw that popular support for and understanding of the issues of a war were vital. In November 1908 the feckless Crown Prince argued that a war could solve Germany's internal problems. Moltke replied that the people might revolt against such a 'cabinet' war.[35] He would also have welcomed British neutrality. Like most generals, he had no time for *Weltpolitik*, or felt at least that its pursuit was premature while the threat from Russia and France remained. On the other hand he could not be persuaded that French and Russian preparations were less menacing in intent than they appeared. It was their capabilities, not their intentions which counted. Railway building in Russia's western regions was clearly strategic in intent, and threatened to speed Russian mobilization to such an extent as to frustrate the Schlieffen Plan. In 1913 Moltke argued that since his uncle's day both the French and Russian armies had been so much improved that the French could not be met defensively, while the Russian was too strong to be defeated quickly.[36]

The obsessive nature of the thinking of the General Staff by this time is reflected in their refusal to listen to suggestions from the Foreign Ministry that their military plans should be revised to try to secure British neutrality. Instead, in April 1913, the General Staff even ceased to update a contingency plan whereby it was possible for Germany to stand on the defensive in the west and throw her main weight against Russia. Yet it was of the inevitability of a war between Teuton and Slav that Moltke repeatedly spoke, and not simply, one suspects, because he appreciated that the German people would most readily support a war against Russia. Admittedly in February 1913 he warned his Austrian colleague, Conrad, that the Slavs must be seen to be the aggressor. By April 1914 he was complaining to Conrad of the continuing efforts of the politicians in Berlin to woo the British. Time was running out.[37] Yet down to July 1914 the German Foreign Minister, Jagow, for instance, appeared unimpressed by Moltke's arguments in favour of a preventive war. The Chancellor, Bethmann Hollweg, however, was possibly becoming more responsive. He frequently spoke in gloomy terms of Germany's weakening international position. He was troubled by the growing burden of war preparations, and asked how these could be sustained in the future. A recent visit to Russia had left him dismayed by the awesome potential of the country: opinion in that country, he feared, was becoming more militant. Only a Russian revolution might relieve Germany of her present anxieties. More likely was an upsurge of popular opinion, even in such a state as Russia, so that government control of foreign policy would be lessened and the future made less predictable. His own difficulties with public feeling in Germany made him determined to put the onus for war squarely on Russia – in this way would support from German socialists most easily be won.

The fears of the German leadership concerning the future were thus almost certainly more important than their ambitions, unless ambition be interpreted to mean a refusal to countenance a contraction in German security and future freedom of choice as they were then perceived. War seemed a usable option. It might, in certain circumstances, seem the least unsatisfactory way forward. And while the Germans believed they retained this hope of victory, albeit a diminishing one, the Russians and the French were, for the first time for many years, determined to stand together – perhaps even to fight on an appropriate issue. By them, too, war was seen as not necessarily the worst of available options. This was not the first time there had been so much talk of an inevitable war, but given the circumstances the mood was ominous. Still more dangerous was the obsession with a short war, for a short war was not only politically more acceptable but carried with it the necessary belief that the first battles would be decisive. Everyone had to be ready to strike with all his force at the outset. Delay might be fatal. Thus once war seemed likely, it seemed criminal not to give priority to the needs of mobilization over those of diplomacy. As Paul Kennedy comments:

'Militarism, and military planning, had set up the European states like a row of dominoes; . . .' If one fell, all fell.[38] The greatest danger lay not so much in militarism itself – a highly nebulous label in any case – but in a particular type of military calculation and preparation. A malign military genius was not at work. The general staffs were producing seemingly logical responses to contemporary technology and international alignments.

NOTES AND REFERENCES

1. Bridge [2] pp. 51–3, 119
2. Hinsley [1] p. 110
3. Moorman, pp. 125–9
4. Fry, pp. 103, 128–9
5. Mackay, p. 419
6. Lowe and Dockrill, I, 87
7. Butterfield, p. 80
8. Bridge [1] p. 287. For this section, see Bridge [1] Chs 4–6
9. Laves, pp. 98–113
10. Morrison, I, 629
11. Fry, pp. 128–52
12. Bridge [2] p. 188
13. Woodruff D. Smith, p. 220
14. Ritter, II, 152–6, 190
15. See Bosworth, *passim*
16. Kennedy [2] p. 255
17. L. C. F. Turner, p. 49n
18. Goschen, pp. 58–9
19. Gordon Wright, p. 24
20. Thaden pp. 118–19. See also Gordon Wright, pp. 26–30; L. C. F. Turner, pp. 35–7, and D. N. Collins, pp. 777 ff. For a Russian view of the Franco-Russian alliance see Bovykin, pp. 20ff.
21. L. C. F. Turner, p. 49. See also Ritter, II, 243, and Bridge [1] p. 364
22. Wayne C. Thompson, p. 43
23. Dilks [1] I, 38–9
24. Orde, p. 156
25. Hinsley [1] p. 270
26. Steiner, p. 121. See also Gooch and Temperley, XI, pp. x–xii
27. Goschen, pp. 38, 60–1; Steiner, pp. 215–17
28. Koch, pp. 93–121
29. Gatzke, pp. 33–4
30. Koch, pp. 123–4
31. Sheehan, p. 230; Koch, p. 205
32. Gooch and Temperley, XI, 53; see also p. 55. Koch, p. 150
33. Kitchen [1] p. 105
34. Gerd Hardach, p. 55

35. Zedlitz-Trützschler, p. 225
36. Ritter, ii, 216–17, 226, 249–53. See Dupuy, pp. 140 ff. for argument that the Elder Moltke's defensive–offensive strategy carried with it a greater danger of stalemate than the Schlieffen Plan as implemented in 1914. Note also that the German generals before July 1914 were watching Russian railway building with growing apprehension: the faster the Russians could mobilize and move, the graver the threat to the Schlieffen Plan. The German ambassador in St Petersburg might argue that Russia was not systematically preparing for war: the German generals read Russian preparations very differently
37. Kitchen [1] pp. 110–12
38. Kennedy [2] p. 4, and see generally pp. 1–19

Chapter 4

THE FIRST WORLD WAR

THE OUTBREAK OF WAR

A Russian diplomat who visited Vienna in the winter of 1913–14 was struck by the atmosphere of pessimism. Some great financiers pronounced war preferable to the deplorable effects of the current uncertainty on business.[1] Austro-Russian relations were deteriorating, with each empire stepping up its arms preparations. Conrad was torn between the risks of a general war and a belief in its inevitability. If the empire's internal divisions continued to increase the imperial army itself might cease to be an effective force. Perhaps Austria-Hungary already faced only the prospect of an honourable defeat. Conrad's dismay deepened in the spring of 1914 as Rumania edged closer to the enemies of the Central Powers. This development also troubled Moltke, but he failed to impress the German Foreign Minister, Jagow, with the argument that the time had come 'to orientate our policy to the early provocation of a war'.[2] Similarly the ministers in Vienna were not yet prepared to recommend war. Instead, in June 1914, they drafted a memorandum which simply urged the creation of a joint Austro-German approach to Balkan questions: in particular they wanted a concerted drive with Berlin to cultivate friends in the Near East.

Nor was the Serbian government looking for a crisis with Austria at this time. True it was tolerating or was unable to stop anti-Habsburg propaganda and terrorism. The plot to assassinate the Archduke Franz Ferdinand was hatched on its soil, and duly took place in Sarajevo on 28 June 1914. Most Habsburg ministers now agreed that their earlier plan had been overtaken by events: Austria-Hungary, it seemed, would have no better opportunity to cripple Serbia. The powerful Hungarian Prime Minister, Stephan Tisza, vainly argued that the international situation might yet improve. His objections to war were still important, but could be overridden if Berlin supported

Vienna. As it was, the Habsburg appeal to Berlin was based on the conviction that Austria would forfeit her credibility as a great power unless she acted. Time was working in favour of Russia and the Slavs, while no incident was likely to evoke so much sympathy for Austria as the Archduke's assassination. Berchtold later, on 21 July, insisted that the empire would suffer more harm by doing nothing. Delay would only increase the internal and external threat.[3]

Austria-Hungary, however, dared not act without a blank cheque from Germany. The Austrian appeal for support was considered in Berlin on 5 July. On the face of it the Kaiser and Bethmann Hollweg gave their approval without much deliberation – as if they had already made up their minds. It is clear that they wanted Austria to act as quickly as possible against Serbia – though this insistence on speed may have been mainly motivated by the belief that this gave the best chance that the crisis would be localized – the 'crime' of Sarajevo would be fresh in the minds of the European cabinets. At the same time Berlin was clearly anxious to weaken the alignment between Russia, France and Britain – at the risk of a general war if necessary. This does not indicate a preference for war, only a readiness to wage it based on a belief that the position of the Central Powers was deteriorating and had to be improved. Such at least would appear to have been the thinking in Berlin. But one must also ask why there was no apparent consideration of alternatives – why, in particular, there was no recourse to diplomacy at this stage? Was it simply that the international situation of the Central Powers appeared so desperate that nothing short of a major triumph over the *ententes* would suffice? Were considerations of *Aussenpolitik* all-important?

Much has been, and can be made of the character of German society before 1914 – its illiberalism, its divisions and insecurity, the undue respect for authority and the military, an unhealthy mixture which in the years immediately preceding 1914 was creating a widespread belief in the inevitability of war. In some cases this even extended to a belief in the desirability of war to purge German society of its many weaknesses and impurities.[4] But the German élite has also been described at this time as 'a cartel of anxiety', and if Bethmann was fearful of the German chauvinists he seemed still more fearful of Russia. As he commented to his faithful servant, Riezler: 'The future belongs to Russia which is growing and growing and is becoming an ever-increasing nightmare to us.'[5] Soon after his decision to aid Austria he remarked: 'If we urge them [the Austrians] ahead, then they will say we pushed them in; if we dissuade them, then it will become a matter of our leaving them in the lurch. Then they will turn to the Western Powers, ...'[6] Such a reversal of alliances might seem improbable, yet it is entirely compatible with Bethmann's general pessimism. Interesting too is his later confession, in

February 1918, that in 'a certain sense it was a preventive war'; from Germany's point of view the best time for war had passed; July 1914 was only 'the least unfavourable time'.[7] Historians must face the fact that Germany's belligerence increased as Russia recovered her strength and France her confidence. They must also ask themselves whether Bethmann would have acted as he did in July 1914 had Austria-Hungary been stronger or Russia weaker. Historians must note German ambition and aggressiveness, but they must also acknowledge that the dynamic of the European state system tended to work against the strongest power. Even the rivalry between Russia and Britain, as we have already noted, tended to work to Germany's disadvantage![8]

Bethmann early in July 1914 foresaw several possibilities. The Austrians might lack the nerve to fight. The Russians might give way. The French and British might refuse to back Russia.[9] As it was, the Austrians acted much more slowly than he had hoped. Their army, it was said, could not be mobilized for war against Serbia before 12 August. Only on 23 July was the Austrian ultimatum presented in Belgrade. It included terms no self-respecting state could accept. Yet the Serb reply impressed Wilhelm II when he saw it on 28 July. Unfortunately this was not the general view in Vienna or Berlin. Serbia had to be crushed or reduced to a Habsburg protectorate. Germany and Austria-Hungary stuck to their chosen course and only a Russian abandonment of Serbia would have saved the peace. In July 1914 there was little possibility of this. Weakness had forced the Russians to back down several times between 1909 and 1913. It is true that their military programme was still far from complete in 1914, but with French support it could be argued that victory was possible.

Some mystery still surrounds the visit of Poincaré and Viviani to St Petersburg on 20–23 July. Viviani, the Socialist–Republican Premier, represented that portion of French opinion which favoured *détente* with Germany. Some progress had been recorded in 1914. But Viviani stood in the shadow of the President when it came to foreign policy. One cannot be sure what Poincaré said in Russia, and while it was not necessarily designed to increase Russian belligerence, equally one suspects that there was little to encourage flexibility. Sazonov acted after the visit as if he were sure of French support. Meanwhile the peace party in Russia had been weakened by the resignation of Kokovtzov early in 1914. The recent strikes had increased the fear of revolution in Russia, and it was a matter of dispute within the government as to whether a choice of war or peace was the more likely to lead to renewed internal turmoil. As it happened, those in power were more inclined to argue that a failure to take up the Teutonic challenge would increase the risk of revolution – the government would be discredited in the eyes of all patriots.[10]

The Russians began some military preparations on the 26th, partly because of their growing alarm about the general European situation, but also to try to warn the Austrians to moderate their conduct. They quickly found that partial mobilization threatened to slow general mobilization, should that become necessary a little later. Austria-Hungary, confident of German support, declared war on Serbia on the 28th, although her armies would not be ready to move until 12 August. Nevertheless, Belgrade was bombarded on the 29th. The Russians became increasingly pessimistic. They felt their options were narrowing. As for Bethmann Hollweg, his conduct at this time remains a matter of controversy. Impressed by Russian conduct and British warnings he perhaps tried to restrain Vienna. Alternatively his tactics were simply designed to ensure that the blame for war appeared to fall on the Russians.[11] This, at any rate, was the moment (29–30 July) when, had there been sufficient fear of general war in Europe, the diplomats had their last chance to pull back from the brink. But in Vienna, St Petersburg and Berlin it seemed less dangerous to risk general war rather than give way. The influence rapidly increased of those who believed war to be inevitable. A point had been reached where they could argue that delays in mobilization would diminish their countries' prospects of victory. By the end of July the German military had but one aim – to mobilize as quickly as possible to gain the maximum advantages from the opening of a war in accordance with the needs of the Schlieffen Plan. Not surprisingly some of the political leaders felt they had lost control. Bethmann himself remarked that 'the situation had got out of hand and the stone has started rolling'.

General mobilization was ordered in Berlin on 31 July. War was declared on Russia on 1 August and inquiries made as to French intentions. German demands on France were such as to preclude agreement – though it is doubtful if France would have stood aside in any case. The ultimatum to Belgium, demanding passage for German armies, was sent on the 2nd, and war declared on France on the 3rd. Britain joined the war on 4 August when Germany refused to respect Belgian neutrality. Belgium was the issue around which opinion in Britain could unite most easily in favour of war. The Cabinet itself had been divided until the last minute. Indeed, on 29 July, when Grey had warned the German ambassador that Berlin could not rely on British neutrality, a majority of the Cabinet still opposed war. Despite the many Anglo-French military conversations since 1905–6, Britain had given a firm promise only to defend the northern coasts of France from German naval attack by the agreements of 1912. As the crisis deepened so opinion began to move in favour of Grey within the Cabinet. But the City of London, the Liberal press, many Liberals and those to the left of that party opposed war. Grey himself was so impressed at one point by the threat of financial chaos that even he wondered if Britain could risk war.[12] In the end he decided that financially it would not matter much either way. Politically and strategically he believed that British interests demanded that she stand by her *entente* partners. But it was the German threat to Belgium which produced the national consensus which he required.

Given the diversity of opinion in Britain it is easier to see how the nation was driven to war than why. Certainly there were important elements in the Foreign Office and the armed services which believed an Anglo-German war to be inevitable. Some indeed saw the crisis of 1914 as Britain's best opportunity to fight Germany.[13] But as at earlier times there were those who thought more in terms of Britain's position within the global balance of power. The *ententes* to them were more than anti-German instruments: they were designed to protect and promote Britain's influence as a world power. Thus Eyre Crowe minuted on 25 July that it was already too late to use France to restrain Russia: if there was a war Britain must join, otherwise the outcome would find her isolated and friendless whichever side won. The British ambassador in St Petersburg warned of a Russian threat to India if Germany were defeated without British assistance. Arguments of this type could of course be used by those who were primarily anti-German in July 1914, but the fact that they were used suggests that those at whom they were directed were expected to be influenced by such considerations. British fears of Russian and French policy in the event of a collapse of the *ententes* have already been noted, and will be again. This does not mean that Britain went to war in 1914 to protect the British Empire against Russia and France, or that she had no quarrel with Germany. Nor was sophisticated calculation on the global balance of power by Foreign Office and other experts the decisive influence on British policy. It could be but one among many influences in a parliamentary state. But such calculation throws light on the general character of international rivalries and Britain's place within them at this time. Special circumstances, however, simplified the situation in August 1914, and made it possible for a British public, suddenly brought face to face with war, to enter it in the patriotic faith that it was a just war.

The enthusiasm with which war was greeted in most countries surprised those who feared serious opposition from dissident subject peoples and from urban workers indoctrinated with socialism. Jaurès, Bebel and Brailsford, however, had all pointed out before the war that when peoples, irrespective of class, felt themselves part of a country and that country believed itself the victim of aggression, they would fight. There were exceptions, but these were unimportant in the atmosphere of patriotic fervour which prevailed in August 1914. These nationalist passions did much to ensure that the war, once started, would become 'total' in its aims and conduct, whatever its original causes. The latter have sometimes been described unhelpfully as imperialist. If by this is meant the struggle for territory and influence outside Europe, it does not take one very far towards an understanding of the causes. Lenin called it an imperialist war partly because he saw it as a struggle for a general redivision of *all* territory among the powers – that is, in Europe as well as overseas. But his stress on the responsibility of monopoly capitalism is less meaningful, and has little relevance in two of the three front runners in the descent to war – Russia and Austria-Hungary. Capitalism was not a united force in Germany, France or Britain. Businessmen pulled in different directions according to their interests, and often found themselves out of step with their own governments on specific questions. British businessmen, with others, contributed to the overall sense of international competition, but they had little to do with the decisions which led London to conclude understandings with France and Russia rather than with Germany. Furthermore, capitalist activity could also transcend national boundaries. In June 1914 the Second International gave high marks to many business interests for their promotion of international co-operativeness.[14] Colonies, trade and foreign investments had little to do with the immediate origins of the war compared with fears of national stagnation, frustration, decline or disruption, with all their internal and external implications unless the challenge of war was accepted.

EUROPE AT WAR

It was widely believed in 1914 that any war between the great powers must be a relatively short affair – a matter of months if not weeks. In the later nineteenth century, as weapons became more expensive and formidable, so consolation was found in the belief that as war became more horrific, devastating and costly, the speedier must be the outcome. One of the great worries of British military planners before August 1914 was whether their expeditionary force could be transported in time to its assigned place on the French left to take part in the decisive battles. It is true that not all were of this opinion. Kitchener forecast a three-year war in 1914. Most prophetic of all had been a Polish banker, Jan Bloch. In his six-volume study, *The Future of War*, published in 1898, he had correctly predicted that modern weaponry would favour the defensive. This could lead to wars of attrition which, if persisted in, could lead to economic collapse and revolution. The young Winston Churchill warned the House of Commons on 13 May 1901 of the passing of limited war:

> But now, when mighty populations are impelled on each other, each individual severally embittered and inflamed, when the resources of science and civilization sweep away everything that might mitigate their fury, a European war can only end in the ruin of the vanquished and scarcely less fatal dislocation and exhaustion of the conquerors. Democracy is more vindictive than Cabinets. The war of peoples will be more terrible than those of kings.

Critics of the short-war philosophy and the obsession with the offensive, however, had little influence before 1914. If the Schlieffen Plan is usually cited as the epitome of military thinking in 1914, the French offensives further south should not be forgotten. In the controversy over the reasons for the failure of the Schlieffen Plan, insufficient attention is usually paid to the fact that such success as the Germans enjoyed owed much to the French preoccupation with their own offensive. Even then the French, helped by railways, the growing logistic problems of the Germans and a number of other factors, were still able to make a stand on the Marne, and force their opponents back. The ensuing weeks underlined the advantages which lay with the defending army – the fire-power of well-entrenched infantry, the limited battlefield mobility of the attackers. They also demonstrated how all the belligerents had underestimated the intensity of modern warfare. Thus the Germans ran short of shells after only six weeks of campaigning although they had provided five times as much ammunition for each artillery piece as in 1870–71.

Military stalemate at the end of 1914 might, in some circumstances, have persuaded the powers to attempt to negotiate a compromise peace. As it happened, in the winter of 1914–15 they not only possessed the motivation and will to continue the conflict, but also the means. The ability of modern economies to sustain long wars came as a surprise. If Britain alone made a serious effort to increase direct taxes, the credit-worthiness of governments – even the Austrian – proved astonishing, as did the public tolerance of inflation. Another expectation had been unemployment and general economic dislocation, but not until 1917 did the strains of war begin to have major economic, and then political, consequences. Before that, given time for adjustment, even a country such as Russia was able to provide the equipment for ever larger armies and longer battles. Given such resources there seemed no necessity to adjust war aims. The growth in the size, power and skill of government bureaucracies made it possible for the state to tap and use resources as never before. It is true that Austria-Hungary and Turkey had to lean on Germany, and France and Russia on Britain. Even the British war effort was being subsidized by the United States long before 1917. But clearly industrial strength, the enhanced powers of governments aided by the receptivity of the peoples to patriotic appeals of all kinds, meant that war could be waged on an unprecedented scale.

From the outset the powers viewed the war as an opportunity to turn the balance of power in Europe – in some cases, the global balance – to their advantage. The continuity between war aims and pre-war aspirations – notably with respect to Germany – may be revealing. But it must be remembered that aspirations do not necessarily result in action, and action when it comes may introduce new imperatives of its own. In practice the war aims of the powers were usually a matter of continuing debate within each state. Differences between the members of the two alliances were a further complication, and this was extended as each side went in search of new allies. War aims thus became more than a projection of pre-war hopes and grievances: they grew and fluctuated according to the circumstances of the moment. At the same time, at bottom, each power sought the maximum security for the foreseeable future. The status quo ante which had existed with only minimal changes between the powers since 1871 became unacceptable once hostilities commenced. Any outcome short of a decisive victory suggested not a return to stability but merely a breathing space while the powers gathered their strength for a second round to determine who should prevail. Furthermore, as the conflict lengthened and the casualties mounted, so governments believed that conclusive results were essential in order to justify to their peoples the sacrifices they had required of them.

Initially for many Germans the war in the west was only a necessary preliminary to the advance of German interests in the east. If, for Tirpitz, Britain was always the main enemy, for others such as Bethmann and Riezler it was Britain which transformed a European struggle into a global conflict. It was the war itself which made Britain into the prime enemy of Germany, so great was the dependence of Russia and France upon her economic strength. Thus Riezler in August 1916 portrayed the war as one of defence against France, prevention against Russia, but a struggle for world supremacy with Britain.[15] This global dimension had not formed part of the calculations of the German leadership in July 1914. It is true that in September 1914, in his first summary of Germany's war aims, Bethmann had insisted that Belgium must be reduced to the level of a vassal state in order to provide security against Britain, and he also envisaged colonial gains for Germany in central Africa. But his prime concern was with German security in Europe for the foreseeable future, to be achieved mainly through a permanent weakening of France and by thrusting Russia bodily eastward. Of course, had Britain remained neutral in 1914, and had Germany then achieved her objectives in Europe, it seems reasonable to surmise that in due course the oft-discussed struggle for global power between Britain and Germany would have followed. A sequence of events and decisions in the decade before August 1914 had simply fused into one what some Germans had seen as two separate struggles. Historians, however, must deal with history as it happened, and on that basis they must note the degree to which other powers besides Germany determined the course of events, whether on the causes of the war, war aims, or why no compromise peace proved possible.

On the question of a compromise peace, it is tempting to ask whether Germany might have achieved by diplomacy what she failed to achieve by military means – that is, a separate peace with one of her opponents in such a way as to open the door to victory over the others (the 1918 peace with Russia came too late as Germany had already provoked the United States to join the war). In the continuous debate within the German leadership on war aims and on the methods, military and diplomatic, by which these could be attained, many have been impressed by the flexibility and subtlety of Bethmann Hollweg compared with, say, Hindenburg and Ludendorff. L. L. Farrar, however, has persuasively argued such divisions have 'concealed the fundamental agreement among the German leaders . . . on the general goal of world power'.[16] If Germany was to free herself from the two-front threat from France and Russia, if some form of European customs union (*Mitteleuropa*) was to be established to enable Germany to compete with 'the great closed economic bodies of the United States, the British and Russian Empires', if Germany was to create the foundations of a Reich that would put her on a par with the Americans, British and Russians, all with their vast tracts of territory, then compromise with any one of her three main enemies was almost impossible. The German navy, for instance, began to dream of a chain of world-wide naval bases from which to challenge the financial hegemony of the British and the Americans.[17] In the years of peace before 1914 the German leadership had sometimes shown itself capable of pursuing a limited number of objectives at a time (even then it had not been infallible): once at war it became a matter of all or nothing. And so it was with their opponents. They agreed on 5 September 1914 to continue the war until each had achieved its basic aims.

Not that Britain, France and Russia were in entire accord with each other. Britain was determined to expel the Germans from Belgium, but did not fully share France's determination to deprive Germany of Alsace and Lorraine. Both Britain and France could feel uneasy over Russia's ambitions in eastern Europe and the Middle East. Reflection over what was needed to give them security against or superiority over Germany led inevitably to an uncomfortable awareness of the probability of new rivalries and sources of friction among the victors themselves. Nor was it easy to maintain a consensus within each government. The British, for instance, were agreed that they required security against Germany on land and sea, but found it harder to settle what this meant in real terms, or how far Germany should be weakened without regard for the balance of power in the long run. Thus demands for the seizure of German colonies as early as August 1914, or the later insistence of most politicians that only the purging of Germany of its authoritarian and militaristic tendencies would provide an adequate guarantee of peace in the future, should be contrasted with the view sometimes expressed that Germany might yet have a part to play in the equilibrium of Europe (and Asia), especially if Russia emerged much strengthened from the war. British generals, such as Kitchener and Robertson, were often of this opinion.[18] Grey, Haldane and Robert Cecil agreed that a drastic transformation of the balance of power would store up trouble for the future: consequently they were interested in some form of institutionalized international co-operation. Grey himself hoped some kind of Anglo-American partnership would develop after the war.[19] For the French the chief imperative was much clearer: Germany must be deprived of the means to attempt yet another invasion of their country. The Russians wished to safeguard their position against Germany by the creation of an autonomous (in name at least) Poland within their empire, thus squeezing Germany in the east. They also held out hopes of some form of liberation to the various Slav peoples of central Europe.

Although there existed some vociferous supporters in Britain of the subject peoples of the Austro-Hungarian Empire, official thinking was more cautious. True some of Austria's territory on the Adriatic was offered to Italy in 1915 to win her as an ally against the Central Powers, but down to 1918 there was much interest in the preservation of most of the Habsburg Empire as an essential component of the balance of power. There was even talk at times of a union of Austria with a weakened Germany to assist in the containment of Russia. Early in the war Grey even had hopes of preserving the Ottoman Empire as a buffer against Russia. The French also feared Russian advances in this quarter. These allied differences, however, were dwarfed by the determination to deprive the Central Powers not merely of the gains they had made in the opening stages of the war, but of the power to take the initiative for war a second time. Germany in her turn was intent on the creation of at least an unassailable position in the heart of Europe. Given these aims, compromise was impossible. Each belligerent would fight until its strength or will-power gave out. Possibly a faint opportunity existed for a separate peace between Germany and Russia late in 1916, but this was lost when the German generals in particular insisted that Poland must be drawn unquestionably into the German orbit.

No description of the war will be given in this book, but among the aspects which require attention are the hopes and disappointments which attended the allied efforts to weaken the Central Powers in the Mediterranean and the Near East. These are important, not simply because they represent an interesting attempt to shorten the war, but for the light they throw on the long-term differences between Britain, Russia, Italy and France. They include hints of the continuing global struggle, and evidence of the working of the balance of power as a whole.

Initially the British would have preferred the Near Eastern question to lie dormant, despite Turkey's alliance with Germany. But on 2 November 1914 Russia declared war on Turkey. Such a conflict, the British feared, could easily spill over into Transcaucasia and involve Persia. The British were disturbed by a Russian proposal that Persia be induced to join the war with a promise of the Shiite Holy Places in Mesopotamia. Such a development would offend Sunnite Muslims from Egypt to India – with damaging consequences for the British Empire. Grey warned that any threat to British interests could rebound against Russian hopes of acquiring Constantinople and the Straits. He thought it far better for Russia and Britain to stand on the defensive in the Middle East, reacting only if Turkey herself violated Persian territory. One should worry about the break-up of the Turkish Empire only after the defeat of Germany. Within Russia, however, Sazonov was under pressure from groups who were far more interested in gains at the expense of the Turks than in the war with Germany. An influential committee favoured the annexation of Constantinople, driving Sazonov to remark that 'the pressure of public opinion and strategic necessity . . . always overrules all other considerations'.[20] Further inquiry, nevertheless, indicated that the Russians had no forces to spare from the struggle in Europe, and that they would be wise to wait for a more appropriate time, a time too when the British and French would be unable to impede Russia's advance. As it was, Russia herself was soon in need of their aid against the Turks.

Controversy still rages over the wisdom of the British attempt, largely inspired by Churchill, to knock Turkey out of the war, first by a naval attack at the Straits and then by landings at Gallipoli. It was the Russian appeal for aid against Turkey at the end of 1914 which did much to tip the balance in London in favour of the operation. Hopes were also developing that a decisive blow here might swing the neutral Balkan states to the side of the allies. A British attack on the Straits, however, was not at all what the Russians had had in mind – they would have preferred an attack much further south. They were also dismayed to find that the British were assiduously courting the Greeks. A plot to place Constantinople in Greek hands was suspected, or at worst a strengthening of the Greeks in the Aegean. But with no means of deploying force themselves in this region, the Russians had to rely on diplomacy. Sazonov warned the French ambassador on 5 March 1915 that the failure of Russia's allies to consider her interests and aspirations could lead to his resignation and to a new Foreign Minister who might be more interested in a revival of the 'old system of the *Dreikaiserbund*'.[21] This seemed an improbable development, but the British and French could not afford to get out of step with Russia. In any case the Greeks were too divided to fight. Thus on 12 March 1915 the British and French finally agreed that Constantinople and the Straits should fall to Russia after the war. The British, however, secured the neutral zone in Persia. Russia promised to treat Constantinople as a free port, with free passage for merchant ships through the Straits. Even so the British continued to agitate for Greek intervention, with Smyrna as the probable reward. Allied distrust and rivalries were far from over.

Sazonov wrote in some alarm on 12 March 1916 concerning the eastward drive of French ambition in Syria:[22]

> . . . the appearance on the great extent of our Asiatic frontier, in localities of a mixed and turbulent population, of a great European power, although at the present time allied to us, and its intrusion towards a corner of the Russo-Persian frontier, must be recognized as undesirable.

Although this particular problem was resolved in April 1916, Anglo-French rivalries over the future of the Turkish Empire were still more extensive. The famous Sykes–Picot agreement of 16 May 1916, as we shall see, provided only temporary relief. Some in London feared that a great allied victory would result in increased French and Russian competition with the British in the Mediterranean as well as the Middle East. Although Churchill and Haldane argued that a German defeat should enable the Royal Navy to reassert its supremacy in the Mediterranean, it was tempting for the British to look to a strengthened Italy as an additional makeweight. British and Italian interests seemed far more compatible than those of either state with Russia or France.

Italy had been too weak in August 1914, and too divided internally to risk war. Nominally she was allied with Germany and Austria-Hungary, yet her main territorial ambitions could only be satisfied at the expense of Austria. But if Austria were too much weakened this could leave Italy exposed to Slav and perhaps Russian influence in south-eastern Europe. There was thus no self-evident path for the Italian government to follow. Ideally it needed to join the winning combination at the moment when that side was prepared to pay most generously for Italian help. Italy could easily enter the war too early or too late: she could easily pick the wrong alliance or be left with no worthwhile gains. Salandra, the Italian Premier, and Sonnino, the Foreign Minister, reviewed the problem in the winter of 1914–15.

Apart from the *irredentist* claims concerning Italian communities still outside the motherland, they concluded that Italy could not become a truly independent power until she had control of the Adriatic, with security against Russia, Austria and the Slavs,

The possibility of an allied victory at the Straits in the spring of 1915 did much to force a decision on the wavering leadership. Italy dared not let Greece and Bulgaria join the allies ahead of her. Fortunately the British were prepared to pay handsomely for Italian entry into the war. Furthermore, a strong Italy in the Adriatic was expected to serve as a useful postwar counterpoise to Russia. The problem was to reconcile Italian aspirations with those of the Slav peoples of the western Balkans, and to overcome Russian objections to certain Italian demands. The Italians wanted Dalmatia, and were determined to prevent the creation of a naval power on the rest of the eastern shoreline of the Adriatic. They insisted that they would not fight merely 'to substitute Slav for Austrian predominance' in that sea.[23] The British and French were impressed: Italian fears of the Slavs might yet prompt them to side with the Central Powers. On the other hand, with Italian support, Greece and Bulgaria might be driven off the fence, and with their backing a great allied victory in south-eastern Europe assured. Russian objections were finally overborne, and the Treaty of London of 26 April 1915 met most of the Italian demands. Unfortunately Italian entry into the war a month later was to coincide with a turn for the worse in the fortunes of the allies. Frustration at Gallipoli was soon followed by Russian defeats. Warsaw was lost in August, and the eastern front was not stabilized until September. Not surprisingly the allies failed to recruit further supporters. Indeed Bulgaria threw in her lot with the Central Powers in October, thus guaranteeing the defeat of the Serbs early in 1916. By then the allies had also abandoned their toeholds on Gallipoli. It was for the allies a grim end to a year which at times had promised so much. In particular the setbacks of 1915 robbed Tsarist Russia of its best chance of survival. Furthermore, by the beginning of 1916 there was no obvious alternative to the horrific struggle of attrition on the two main battlefronts. There were no short cuts to victory. Nothing but the physical and moral exhaustion of an opponent would suffice.

Major signs of this began to appear only in 1917. War-weariness was evident in Austria-Hungary. The rash French offensives under Nivelle led to mutinies later in the year. But it was Russia which experienced a progressive and finally decisive collapse, two revolutions in 1917 leading ultimately to the Bolshevik take-over, and to the conclusion of peace with the Central Powers at Brest-Litovsk in March 1918. This might have been the turning-point of the war. But what should have provided the Germans with the basis for a skilful political and military campaign against the British and French –

leading to an advantageous though improbably a dictated peace – had already been undermined by earlier German decisions which had forced the United States into the First World War. The Germans, who might otherwise in the spring of 1918 have been able to review their options and plan with some time at their disposal, found themselves confronted with the prospect of an enormous build-up in American strength in Europe from the summer of 1918. The Ludendorff offensives were simultaneously an imaginative and desperate attempt to win the war in the west before the Americans could intervene with overwhelming effect. Thus a war which had been sparked off by primarily European causes, and fought almost exclusively in Europe, was to be largely resolved in its final stage by a non-European power.

THE UNITED STATES AND THE WAR IN EUROPE, 1914–17

The war had already had serious and political repercussions in other parts of the world before 1917. The Japanese, for instance, made significant gains in the Far East. There was speculation in Tokyo and Washington as to the implications for the global balance of power if the war in Europe resulted in an all-out victory for one side or the other rather than in a settlement approximating to the status quo ante. There were even a few Americans who, early in the war, deemed a German defeat an important American interest. German activities in Latin America and the Caribbean had been causing some concern from the beginning of the century. Theodore Roosevelt's interest in the global balance of power has already been noted. He was increasingly disturbed both by Germany and Britain – the former for her strength, ambition and erratic temper; the latter because she no longer seemed so strong or so self-confident as in the past.[24]

American planning before 1914 was influenced by rivalry with Germany as well as with Japan. In the case of Germany a great campaign was anticipated in American and West Indian waters (all rather reminiscent of European naval operations in the New World before the nineteenth century!). A great naval battle off Puerto Rico was expected to form the climax. Security was sought in absolute terms (the General Board wanted a fleet of no less than forty-eight battleships by 1919), with no regard being shown for Germany's problems in Europe, and on the assumption that Britain might, if neutral, even sympathize with Germany in view of Anglo-American trade rivalry. The American navalists were, of course, well aware of the need to catch the eye of the American public: the latter might be expected to understand trade rivalry but not global power politics.

Nor was the economic issue wholly irrelevant. It was not ignored by the British, some of whom in 1916 feared that the American navy might be used to try to break the British blockade of the Central Powers. On general grounds, too, during the war, even so pro-British a figure as Colonel House, Woodrow Wilson's close adviser on foreign affairs, warned that a total German defeat would leave the British and their navy in too powerful a position in the postwar world. The great expansion of the American navy which began in 1916 was intended to secure American interests against whichever powers emerged victorious from the war. Once more America's overseas economic interests were heavily stressed.

Woodrow Wilson's foreign policy from 1913 was itself marked by a deep concern for America's material interests – for all the idealistic rhetoric. Americans and Europeans feared each other as trade rivals. Wilson himself shared the fear that America's growing productive power might swamp the home market: social unrest would follow wage cuts and job losses. It was thus essential to promote American exports as much as possible. Wilson wished to avoid the cruder aspects of dollar diplomacy as practised by his predecessor: he recognized the interdependence of the world's economies. The United States had to buy from abroad if it were to sell. Powerful interest groups at home limited the amount of tariff cutting which the administration might hope to achieve, but Wilson was determined to work for the liberalization of international trade. Among the possibilities he wished to explore was that of great-power economic co-operation in the less developed parts of the world. Such a policy was obviously to the advantage of the United States, it being neither a colonial power nor likely to become one. But through co-operation Wilson also hoped to lessen international rivalries, and perhaps provide new economic openings for Germany in Latin America in a way that might prevent political and strategic complications. On the other hand, the First World War prompted in his mind the thought that it had diverted Germany from an ultimate clash with the United States in Latin America. He and Colonel House agreed in August 1914 that a German victory in Europe would necessitate the militarization of the United States. The two men went further, and began to speculate as to the final distribution of world power a few centuries hence. America, Russia and perhaps China emerged as their favoured candidates.[25] But in the shorter run the fear of Germany was very real. Whatever the faults of British imperialism, and they were many, Germany was seen as a more overt practitioner of *Machtpolitik*, and far more likely to pursue neo-mercantilist policies.

The First World War speedily demonstrated the immaturity of American capitalism outside its own territory. Internationally the American economy was heavily dependent upon the services of others (in finance, insurance and shipping). This was true even with respect to Latin America despite American pretensions on that continent. Not until 1916 was the United States able to take full advantage of the economic openings created by the war. It was from immediate necessities as well as earlier ambition that the Americans became more active in the fields of finance and insurance. Even so businessmen were still tempted by short-term profits rather than longer-term consolidation.[26] The banker, J. P. Morgan, argued that it was wiser and more profitable to co-operate with experienced British concerns, rather than to start from scratch. But some government officials, notably in the Department of Commerce, foresaw serious competition from Europe after the war. If the Germans talked of a *Mitteleuropa* and *Mittelafrika* in the event of their triumph, it also seemed likely that the allies, if victorious, would seek special advantages for themselves at the expense of the vanquished – and of neutrals. An allied meeting in Paris in the summer of 1916 caused particular concern: assurances that there would be no discrimination against neutrals failed to satisfy.[27] On the other hand there existed no consensus in the United States as to the nation's economic needs. The internationalist emphasis provided by the Wilson administration was not acceptable to all interests. But what matters here, as B. I. Kaufman concludes, is that no previous American administration had worked so hard to promote American economic interests abroad. Among its achievements were the modifications to the anti-trust laws in 1918–19 to enable American banks and firms operating abroad to co-operate closely in order to meet foreign and especially British competition.

The most immediate threat to Anglo-American relations during the war arose from the blockade waged by Britain against Germany, with the consequent infringement of neutral rights. Friction on this issue, however, until the summer of 1916, was diluted by the greater American indignation aroused by the German use of submarines. The strength of anti-German feeling varied from time to time, reaching peaks over such episodes as the sinking of the *Lusitania*. Wilson himself sometimes complained of German 'frightfulness' and 'deception', and even wondered if their 'militaristic' ideas would not finally drive the United States to war.[28] Support for American neutrality was rarely less than overwhelming, but in so far as Americans took sides pro-allied sentiment was clearly in the lead. This was encouraged in the early stages of the war by the efforts of the British Foreign Office to temper the British blockade so that certain major American economic interests were not antagonized. Thus cotton was not added to the contraband list until the summer of 1915 when Britain was able to keep up the price by additional purchases to offset lost sales to Germany. In general the allies, and Britain in particular, were soon boosting American exports far beyond their pre-war levels. American farmers as well as industrialists benefited from this boom, and without conscious choice many Americans found themselves involved in the allied cause. Any major interruption to this trade threatened to precipitate a crisis in the American economy. As early as October 1914 some American bankers began to provide short-term credits for the allies. By the summer of 1915 allied purchases from the United States were seriously depleting their gold reserves, so much so that considerable sales of British securities in America seemed possible. Such sales, however, would have depressed the American stock market, and American government and bankers alike thought it better that the allies should be allowed to raise large loans in the United States. Thus America continued to prosper while allied financial problems were eased. Meanwhile the interruption of American trade with the Central Powers tended to hurt the pride of Americans – not their purses.

American ill will against British infringements of the 'freedom of the seas' was further diminished by German submarine activity from February 1915. While Tirpitz's great battle-fleet lay idly at anchor for most of the war, the German navy found in the U-boat a weapon of immense potential. Unfortunately operational experience soon showed that for submarines to be used to maximum effect, especially given their extreme vulnerability, merchant ships had usually to be sunk without warning – contrary to all the tenets of contemporary international law. In such circumstances, as was most dramatically illustrated in the sinking of the British liner, the *Lusitania*, in 1915, the lives of neutrals were bound to be lost. Woodrow Wilson and most leading opinion in the United States chose to argue that the loss of American lives was a more serious matter than British interference with American trade. Secretary of State Bryan protested that Wilson was not following an even-handed policy in his responses to the British blockade and the German submarine campaign. But his resignation had no effect on the administration. Priority continued to be given to the diplomatic battle with Germany, and further incidents in the spring of 1916 carried Washington to the brink of a break in diplomatic relations with Germany. Berlin was forced to accept the American interpretation of international law concerning the treatment of belligerent merchant shipping, and its curtailment of submarine activities was, for some months, of considerable value to the allies. But the United States, having taken so strong a stand, could hardly do less in the event of another crisis.

For the time being, however, Wilson had a chance to demonstrate that his defence of American neutral rights did not only apply to Germany. In the second half of 1916 relations deteriorated with Britain as Wilson sought concessions in the enforcement of the blockade. In addition Wilson was anxious to find ways to put pressure on the British in the interest of a compromise peace. Although

German conduct sometimes drove him closer to the allies, he clung to the hope – and he admitted that it was no more than a hope – that the belligerents might ultimately be edged towards a compromise in a peace without victors. The German submarine crises generated a greater sense of urgency in that these carried with them a real risk of war for the United States. In the winter of 1915–16 Wilson hoped that at an opportune moment Britain might co-operate with the United States in launching negotiations for a compromise peace, reinforced by disarmament and an international league of some kind with the United States as a member. The British, however, saw such ideas as very much second-best alternatives to an all-out victory. Only the latter, they insisted, would ensure that Germany would be unable to make a second bid for hegemony in Europe in ten or twenty years time. The Anglo-American conversations tended to promote misunderstanding rather than mutual comprehension, with the British seeing Wilson as a woolly idealist, and with Wilson himself later in 1916 having growing doubts about the depth of British liberalism.[29] The President was intent on the creation of a liberal capitalist world order, an objective which sprang both from his idealism and his interpretation of America's material interests. For the British a compromise peace, whatever the thinking behind it, was something they were prepared to consider in 1916 only as a last resort.

By the autumn of 1916, however, some influential figures in Britain feared that the United States might soon possess sufficient economic leverage to force Britain to the negotiating table. Wilson was beginning to equip himself with powers to limit loans and to restrict exports to Britain and her allies. The Treasury was impressed by this threat to British policies, but the Foreign Office argued that too many American jobs and profits hung on sales to the allies for Wilson to exert a great deal of leverage. It also saw his moves in the context of the forthcoming presidential election. The Treasury was not reassured. It claimed that of the £5 million which it had to find 'daily for the prosecution of the war, almost £2 million' had to be found in North America. France had already exhausted her gold and dollar reserves, while British borrowing was beginning to outstrip the capacity of even the great American banks. It was becoming necessary to raise money from the American public, a more difficult and politically sensitive affair. McKenna, the Chancellor of the Exchequer, concluded bleakly on 24 October 1916 that by June 1917, or earlier, Wilson might be in a position 'to dictate his own terms to us'. These fears seemed to receive some confirmation in November when Morgan tried to float a short-term unsecured loan on behalf of the British. The Federal Reserve Board warned American banks against involvement, a warning which Wilson supported in order to increase the pressure on Britain for a compromise peace. The feeling was even developing in the United States that some degree of economic downturn was preferable to the continuance of almost indiscriminate loans to Britain. The British replied with a cut in purchases from America to test Wilson's nerve, only to experience a serious run on their reserves. As a result, the British Treasury was driven to all kinds of improvisation to meet the payments on imports from America. Britain had perhaps no more than a month's funds in hand for transatlantic dealings by April 1917. Nor did American entry into the war in that month put an immediate end to the Treasury's worries.[30]

It is one of the great paradoxes of the First World War that the relations of the United States with Britain should have reached their lowest point shortly before American entry into the war on the side of the allies. Wilson's thoughts, from his re-election as President in November 1916, had been concentrated on the search for a compromise peace. His aim, he said, was to create 'not a balance of power, but a community of power; not organized rivalries, but an organized common peace'.He spoke of a peace of equals; of peace without victory. His tactics dismayed his own Secretary of State as well as a number of leading Republicans. They feared his actions might prevent an allied victory over the Central Powers, a victory which they believed American national interests demanded.[31] Peace, however, was far from the thoughts of most of the European belligerents. The British and French generals were hopefully planning new offensives for 1917. It is true that the German leaders were troubled by the British blockade, by the strains imposed by the ceaseless struggles on the Western Front, and by the growing weakness and war-weariness of Austria-Hungary. But these worries only drove the majority to accept more desperate policies. Bethmann Hollweg could no longer hold out against the demand for the introduction of unrestricted submarine warfare even if this led to American involvement in the war. An unrestricted submarine campaign, it was hoped, would starve Britain into submission in six months. Britain's allies could not fight on without her. The United States, if she declared war, could not prevent a German victory if the above calculations proved correct. This fateful German decision destroyed Wilson's illusion that he might yet be able to manoeuvre the belligerents to the conference table. It also brought him face to face with the consequences of his earlier moves against the unrestricted use of submarines by Germany. Confronted by Germany's proclamation that from 1 February 1917 a war zone would exist around the British Isles into which all ships (including those flying neutral flags) would venture at their peril, Washington had no option but to break off diplomatic relations with Germany on 3 February.

A diplomatic breach, however, was no more than a gesture. For two months Americans deliberated. In March four American ships were sunk. Many stayed in port, their owners waiting for a lead from the government. Armed neutrality was considered, but those who advocated war gradually carried the day. It is interesting that those, like Theodore Roosevelt and Henry Cabot Lodge, who wished to see Germany defeated as soon as possible, concluded that appeals to American pride and emphasis upon the defence of neutral rights would have most effect upon public opinion. Americans certainly sensed no direct threat from Germany, while among the knowledgeable it was broadly assumed that the odds still favoured an allied victory. Lodge himself on 15 February 1917 was fairly hopeful that the British could defeat the submarine threat. There was no conspiracy among sections of the American business community to rush to the aid of the allies to save the latter from military defeat and themselves from economic loss. The crisis was not seen in those terms. At most those who favoured intervention on behalf of the allies saw that the Germans had played into their hands. Material interests were at stake in the question of neutral rights, but above all it was a question of America's pride and her position as a great power. Lodge added that the credibility of the Wilson administration was at stake. The advocates of war received further aid on 1 March when the notorious Zimmermann telegram was published. This revealed that Germany was trying to incite Mexico against the United States — once again not in itself a serious threat to American security, but an emotive issue, and a move that helped to confirm the growing American belief in German perfidy. Opinion within Wilson's Cabinet swung strongly in favour of war, but again it is interesting to note that this was largely a product of the pressures of the moment. Robert Lansing, the Secretary of State, was unusual in his advocacy from 1915 of the defeat of Germany as an American national interest, and in his effort as early as 24 August 1915 to persuade Wilson that American influence was likely to decline the longer the war lasted.[32]

Wilson had rejected Lansing's argument in August 1915. February and March 1917 still found him reluctant to countenance war. But one policy was in ruins, and armed neutrality promised no long-term advantages. As his options narrowed, so he began to discover reasons that might make war acceptable to himself. He was increasingly persuaded that by any moral test Germany had put herself more emphatically in the wrong than any other belligerent. Wilhelmine Germany, he told himself, was too aggressive, authoritarian and perfidious to become a reliable member of the postwar comity of nations which Wilson hoped to see emerge from the current bloodshed. The submarine campaign and the Zimmermann telegram provided the main, but not the only proof of German culpability. Wilson's inner turmoil was also eased by the overthrow of the Tsarist regime in Russia in March 1917. There was the promise now that a liberal order would replace one of the world's worst examples of autocracy. Russia, he declared, could now become a 'fit partner for a League of Honor'. By the end of March the pieces were falling into shape. Wilson began to argue that his aims could most quickly and effectually be attained by American entry into the war. Not only would this hasten Germany's defeat, but through direct participation in the conflict American influence over the peace settlement would be enhanced. Wilson was thus able to establish a continuity in policy despite a drastic change in the means to the desired end. But while Wilson was guided by this vision, and made ample use of idealistic rhetoric to promote popular support for the war in America, it is doubtful if many Americans shared his hopes. Some fought like Lansing, Roosevelt and Lodge to hasten the defeat of Germany. Most fought out of a sense of patriotic duty and for American prestige and rights.[33] But whatever the motivation, the American decision to fight was to guarantee the defeat of Germany.

THE WAR, 1917–18

The United States entered the war on 6 April 1917 not as an ally but as an 'associated power'. A British diplomat, Sir William Wiseman, noted in August 1917 how remote Americans were from the realities of war. Few felt menaced by Germany: many were suspicious of 'Tory England'.[34] Colonel House commented at the end of the year: 'None of them [the allies] at heart likes each other, and I doubt whether any of them like us. It is the thought of "hanging together or separately" that keeps them going.'[35] Wilson, once a German defeat seemed assured, began to worry about British commercial greed after the war, though he hoped to counterbalance this through the financial dependence of the allies on the United States. The British, in their turn, feared that the longer the war lasted the greater would be the influence of the Americans. The initial expectation that the American contribution to the defeat of Germany would be primarily economic and (to a lesser extent) naval was speedily undermined by events in 1917. The need for a large American expeditionary force to fight on the Western Front steadily became apparent. Fortunately there were some on the allied side, especially in Britain, who wished to make a virtue out of necessity. Grey, though no longer in office, was an important spokesman for those who believed that a postwar Anglo-American partnership was desirable. Others hoped that the United States would play a prominent part in any postwar international organization to promote peace. It is interesting that Russia as well as Germany was seen as a possible disturber of the world's tranquillity.[36]

Fear of Russia contributed to the continuing British interest in the preservation of the Habsburg Empire in 1917. British references to a peace of nationalities and to self-determination earlier in the year had been prompted essentially by the desire to impress opinion in the United States when Wilson was still anxious to mediate between the belligerents. Hopes of a separate peace with the Habsburgs, however, gradually faded as it became apparent that the Austrians had become too dependent upon Germany to make a break. The new Emperor, Charles, and his ministers found themselves in an impossible situation. They were threatened by German domination in the event of victory, but they were equally dubious concerning the empire's ability to survive a defeat. Only a compromise peace which embraced all the belligerents appeared to offer any hope for the future. Thus when Count Mensdorff met General Smuts in Geneva in December 1917 the former tried desperately to demonstrate the compatibility of British and German interests. Smuts, however, bleakly replied that German military power must be destroyed: the British Empire meant to continue the war until 'either victory had been achieved or the dark forces of revolution had done their work in Germany as they had already done in Russia'.[37]

The Anglo-Austrian talks not surprisingly led nowhere, and by the spring of 1918 the British government was losing interest in the Habsburg Empire. But these exploratory peace moves had been part and parcel of the uncertainty which existed in the minds of some of the British leadership by the winter of 1917–18 as to the wisdom of continuing to fight for an all-out victory over Germany. Indeed, as Russian resistance weakened and the Bolsheviks seized power in the October Revolution, so the feasibility of such a victory had to be considered. The Chief of the Imperial General Staff doubted if Germany could be defeated without Russian assistance. Even before the revolution Hankey, Secretary to the War Cabinet, recorded on 22 September that if Germany's current peace moves developed along satisfactory lines the Russians should be told that they must either fight effectively or 'we should have to agree to a peace at their expense'. He thought Lloyd George agreed with him, but Hankey was obliged to note several changes of opinion by Lloyd George over the next few months, especially concerning Britain's dealings with the Bolsheviks.[38] The British leadership reflected on possibilities which ranged from a peace with Germany at Russia's expense (Haig, commanding British forces in France, thought another year of war would reduce Britain to a dependency of the United States, and wished to see Germany diverted to the east) to an agreement with the Bolsheviks which accepted that Russia could not continue the war. The French vigorously opposed the last idea, and dismayed the British Foreign Secretary, Balfour, by suggesting Japanese and American intervention in Russia. Although the British later became strong advocates of this strategy, at the end of 1917 they were content to aid those areas and groups in Russia which were still firmly on the side of the allies.[39] Even this move was controversial, given British and French competition for influence in Russia. It was agreed by the convention of 23 December 1917 that France should take responsibility for the organization of pro-allied forces in the Ukraine, while the British did so elsewhere. The convention was not a sinister plot to divide Russia into spheres of influence with longer-term aims in view. Indeed it was a reflection of Anglo-French rivalry rather than the extent of their ambitions in Russia.

Richard Ullman rightly stresses 'the sheer desperation' that lay behind British policy in the winter of 1917–18.[40] London was haunted by the fear that Germany would be able to secure resources from Russia which would nullify the effects of the blockade. Germany might become invincible. At worst, it seemed, the war must be prolonged. The British in fact underestimated the time and effort needed to move significant supplies of coal, corn and oil from southern Russia, but it must be remembered that in 1918 the speed of the German collapse was not foreseen. It was generally assumed that the war would not end until 1919 at the earliest. The French were equally concerned, and at first were more ready than the British to risk a breach with the Bolsheviks in the search for some effective counter to German influence in the east. Indeed, all allied hopes of co-operation with the Bolsheviks did not end with the conclusion of the peace of Brest-Litovsk on 15 March 1918. The Germans imposed such harsh terms that an early renewal of Russian resistance did not seem impossible. But the allied desire to make use of the Czech legion – made up from former Austro-Hungarian prisoners of war in Russia – brought matters to a head. Again the British and French were divided – this time as to whether the Czechs should be used in Russia or shipped back to Europe via Vladivostok – but the question was resolved when the Czechs became embroiled with Bolshevik forces in the heart of Russia. The Czechs quickly seized control of a long stretch of the Trans-Siberian Railway. The allies were determined to 'rescue' the legion. Wilson, who had hitherto opposed all the Anglo-French schemes for the use of allied (mainly Japanese) troops in Siberia, agreed to the dispatch of some American troops on 6 July. This precipitated a much larger Japanese intervention in eastern Siberia. Tokyo had been reluctant to act without the approval of Washington. The ensuing Japanese operations, however, were directed to the promotion of Japanese interests in east Asia; not, as the British and French had hoped, to the establishment of a line against German influence at least as far west as the Ural mountains. For this and other reasons, allied intervention in Siberia did not develop into a powerful anti-German movement as had originally been intended by London and Paris. Instead the limited allied involvement with anti-Bolshevik forces in Russia was turned into something much more formidable. In July 1918 Balfour himself acknowledged the danger of conflict with the Bolsheviks. On 29 July Lenin warned that a new war was developing – a war caused by Anglo-French imperialism. Paradoxically the French had not wanted the Czechs to fight in Russia at all (they wanted them as reinforcements in the west); the British had hoped that the Czechs could be used against Germans in Russia without precipitating a conflict with the Bolsheviks; while from July 1918 neither the Americans nor the Japanese supported British plans for large-scale operations against Germany in Russia. Thus the allies became involved in a new conflict just as the First World War turned dramatically in their favour.

The belligerents, having so often been mistaken concerning the prospects for victory since 1914, were taken by surprise by the speed of events in the autumn of 1918. It was now that the strain of four years of war finally told on the Central Powers. Allied offensives in the west and in the Balkans suddenly began, by the standards of the First World War, to make rapid progress. The position in Austria-Hungary had long been critical. Semi-starvation in many parts of the empire was increasing the threat of revolutionary disruption from within. Inside Germany many of the leadership believed that only a successful war could prevent revolution, and made much of this argument to oppose moderates who favoured a compromise peace. But with the failure of the Ludendorff offensives in the first half of 1918, and with allied strength in France being continually reinforced by more and more American troops, German morale, even among the General Staff, was becoming very brittle. Towards the end of September 1918 Ludendorff himself began to despair. He urged the speedy conclusion of an armistice before the discipline and cohesion of the army itself were lost. The first Geman peace note was sent to Woodrow Wilson on 3 October. All fighting ceased on 11 November as the armistice took effect.

NOTES AND REFERENCES

1. Nekludoff, p. 236. Nekludoff thought that, with a few notable exceptions, the mood was more optimistic in St Petersburg, pp. 236–7, 241–4, 285
2. Koch, p. 71. See also Ritter, ɪɪ, 227–36, and Fischer [2] pp. 395–8
3. Bridge [1] pp. 448–9
4. Berghahn and Kitchen, Ch. 2 (W. J. Mommsen, 'The topos of inevitable war in Germany before 1914.')

5. Berghahn, pp. 191–2. See also Stern, p. 101, for Bethmann's objection late in 1914 to a possible compromise peace with Russia – he claimed this would mean another war with Russia ten years later
6. Craig, p. 335
7. Koch, pp. 162, 261. See also Moses, pp. 31 ff.
8. See e.g. Stern, p. xxv
9. Wayne C. Thompson, pp. 70–94
10. Gordon Wright, pp. 138 ff.; Kennedy [2] pp. 258 ff.; Kochan, pp. 167–8. For a strong plea from the Russian peace party, in February 1914, see Vernadsky, iii, xvii, 24
11. Langhorne, p. 117; see also pp. 115–20, and Geiss [2] pp. 268–9, 291–3, 302–3
12. Hinsley [1] p. 406
13. Fry, p. 190n
14. Howard [3] pp. 71–2
15. Hunt and Preston, p. 123. See aso Stern, pp. 101–5, for Bethmann and Riezler feeling that to some extent Britain had forced a global struggle on Germany
16. Farrar [2] pp. 103–4
17. Woodruff D. Smith, pp. 223–5. See also Hunt and Preston, pp. 119–22, and Herwig, pp. 135–9, 151
18. Hunt and Preston, pp. 22–37; Hinsley [1] p. 483
19. Hinsley [1] pp. 482–5
20. C. Jay Smith, p. 115
21. C. Jay Smith, p. 216
22. C. Jay Smith, p. 365
23. C. Jay Smith, pp. 253, 264
24. Beale, p. 382
25. Link [1] xxx, 461–2; xxxi, 355
26. Kaufman, *passim*; Parrini, pp. 1–48, 101 ff.; Levin, pp. 14–18, 23–4
27. Link [1] xxxvii, 287–8
28. Link [1] xxxiv, 506
29. Link [2] pp. 100–5, 119–20. See also Link [1] xxxiii, 279–84; xxxiv, 8–10, 140, 514
30. Burk, *passim*
31. Widenor, pp. 252–3
32. D. M. Smith, pp. 18–19, 74–81; Link [1] xxxiv, 151, 319. See also Harbaugh, pp. 447, 465
33. Widenor, pp. 277 ff.
34. Fowler, pp. 211–14, 248–53
35. Trask, p. 181
36. Hinsley [1] pp. 479–85
37. Zeman, pp. 152–9
38. Roskill [1] i, 437, 471, 474, 493
39. Lowe and Dockrill, ii, 260 ff., 271–2, 307. For French policy, see pp. 318–19
40. Ullman, i, 95n

Chapter 5
PEACEMAKING, 1919–1922

THE GERMAN PROBLEM

In November 1918 four empires lay in ruins. Paradoxically Germany, the power against whom the main struggle had been conducted, was the least damaged. Indeed Germany proper, territorially, was largely intact. It forfeited the trappings of empire – the colonies, the navy, the imperial dynasty – but not its real sources of power – the homeland, its industrial base, the vast majority of its people (the most numerous in Europe apart from the Russians, and in many respects the most skilled). The efforts of the victors to grapple with this potential imbalance were damaging to Germany in the short run but ineffectual in the longer term. As it happened, however, the defeat of imperial Germany did contribute to the early restoration of another empire, the Russian, if under a new name and in another guise. For had it been otherwise in 1918 it is hard to conceive of the speedy re-emergence of a broadly reunited Russia, given the power of an undefeated Germany to prop up a successor state such as the Ukraine. A German alliance with Georgia and the Cossacks had been another possibility. Some had even spoken of Russia as Germany's 'India'. Indeed, given peace with the rest of Europe, one wonders how long the Germans would have coexisted with the Bolsheviks. An undefeated Germany would have posed a greater military threat than the half-hearted allied intervention, or the invading Poles in 1920. Thus both Germany and Russia remained potential great powers. But for the Ottoman and Habsburg empires, the defeat was final. The Turks at least had the satisfaction of freeing their Anatolian homeland from intruding forces, whereas the Austrians were denied even the satisfaction of developing into a stable, prosperous minor state until the 1950s.

As has already been noted, only Russia and Italy among the great powers had been seriously interested in the redistribution of Habsburg lands before 1918. President Wilson himself, in his Fourteen Points in January 1918, had referred only to autonomy for the subject nationalities. It was only with the allied military setbacks early in 1918 and the end of hopes of a separate peace with Austria-Hungary that the western powers began to lose interest in the empire's place in the balance of power, whether as a partial counterpoise to Germany or Russia. Only then did they begin to welcome Slav and Czech disaffection within the empire, and to give support to exiles and refugees. On 9 August 1918 Britain recognized the Czech national council in Paris as the 'present trustee of the future Czechoslovak Government'. On 3 September the United States accepted the same body as the *de facto* Czech government, and recognized the Czechs as belligerents. Even then the allies were not wholly clear as to their aims in central Europe, and they were quite unprepared for the rapid and total disintegration of the Habsburg Empire in the closing stages of the war. Of great significance, for example, was the return of 1.5 million Austro-Hungarian prisoners of war from Russia. Revolts broke out in several parts of the empire in the second half of October 1918. The victorious great powers did not so much create the successor states as try to settle their final boundaries. They were also anxious to find the best and quickest ways to bring order and stability to a Europe which seemed dangerously vulnerable to the Bolshevik infection. If Austria-Hungary could not be saved, the strongest possible lines of states had to be found to assist in the containment of Bolshevik Russia – and in the longer term, of Germany. In a world full of unknowns, the powers worked with such tools as came readily to hand.

The defeat of the Central Powers and the turbulent condition of Russia made possible the re-emergence of Poland in 1918–19. Indeed, so weakened were the former rulers of Poland that the Poles believed they had the opportunity to turn themselves into a formidable power in eastern Europe. Polish aspirations began to attract French interest from the Treaty of Brest-Litovsk. A strong Poland, it was often argued, was needed to act as a barrier against Russo-German collusion, or to replace Russia as a counterweight to Germany in the east. The British were less certain. They feared that an assertive Poland would generate conflict rather than stability in the region. The British General Staff continued to think that a strong Russia would most effectively check any future German ambitions in the east.[1] Woodrow Wilson found the Poles too ambitious and aggressive. They quarrelled with Germans, Russians, Ukrainians and Czechs, yet he was not convinced they were strong enough in the long run to hold back Bolshevik Russia. At the Versailles Peace Conference it was Lloyd George who was most anxious to limit Polish territorial gains at the expense of Germany, insisting that each German loss would increase the risk of future conflict. The British also opposed Polish ambitions further east which could only be satisfied at the expense of peoples of mostly non-Polish stock. The final Polish frontier, however, ran well east of the line favoured by Britain. Even the French were sometimes troubled by the appetite and conduct of the Poles. But for them Poland existed, Russia was not an alternative option, nor seemed likely to become one. Strategic logic suggested that France must make a friend of Poland or risk a possible *rapprochement* between Warsaw and Berlin.

The acute French sense of insecurity after 1918 was not readily appreciated in Britain and the United States. On the contrary, it was not long before some in Britain began to take an exaggerated view of French power and ambition. By 1922 American military intelligence was also commenting unfavourably on French activities and pretensions in Europe and the Near East as a whole.[2] Yet French power at this time was largely illusory – especially so long as Germany suffered no major amputations of territory. Even the French recovery of Alsace and Lorraine did little to lessen the overall disparity. In the long run Germany could expect to mobilize twice the number of men for war: her heavy industrial potential was about four times that of France.[3] Many Frenchmen were aware that if and when Germany recovered her strength the new Poland would be a poor substitute for the Russia of 1914. Clemenceau, Prime Minister of France until January 1920, was convinced that no peace settlement was likely to give France a permanent advantage over Germany – certainly no peace settlement that would be approved by the British and Americans. He therefore argued that France's best hope of security lay in the continuance of the *entente* with Britain and in co-operation with the United States. In Britain, Lloyd George, Balfour, Austen Chamberlain and Milner were equally convinced that permanent American involvement in the affairs of Europe would provide the best safeguard for the future. Indeed the British, having less at stake in Europe than the French, could only welcome any American commitment so that their own responsibilities would be shared. Unfortunately whatever gap was beginning to open up between the French and British as to their respective interests was likely to be widened several times over, with the passage of time, between the British and the Americans.

It is true that America was not drifting rapidly towards isolationism immediately at the end of the war. Certainly she was bound to become more inward-looking, but far more important was the division in the ranks of the internationalists. A great variety of views abounded on such questions as the treatment of the vanquished, the character of the overall peace settlement, the League of Nations and other means whereby the peace and prosperity of the postwar world might be assured. Some wished to undermine imperialism in general: others concentrated on the containment of

Germany or Bolshevism. Some approached peacemaking from an idealistic standpoint: for others American national interests (narrowly interpreted) were paramount. Thus internationalists could range in approach from a radical restructuring of international politics to a policy of limited, though precise commitments – notably, some sort of guarantee to France. Wilson was not one of the more extreme idealists. His major biographer, A. S. Link, describes him as a proponent of 'higher realism'. His thinking was reformist rather than radical. He did not neglect material factors. But he suffered from rigidities in thought and manner which separated him from Clemenceau, to a rather lesser degree from Lloyd George, and worst of all from certain key American senators.

Wilson in 1918 became the focus of many unrealistic radical and liberal hopes. Yet the fostering of those hopes had done much to revitalize allied morale after the setbacks of 1917, especially among the Centre and moderate Left. The Fourteen Points had helped to lessen the appeal of Lenin's arguments in favour of peace and revolution. They had made it easier for the Germans to sign the armistice of 1918 in the hope that this might lead to a generous peace dispensed by the American President. The eleventh of November, to repeat a remark made by John F. Kennedy after the Cuban missile crisis, was a good night for the President to go to the theatre. Yet Wilson remained extraordinarily confident as he prepared for the peace conference. He expected the allies' dependence on American economic aid to work strongly in his favour.[4] At the same time much of his thinking was less radical than many of his admirers imagined. His approach to the problem of Germany, for instance, was ambiguous: he wished to see both the ultimate integration of Germany into a liberal world order (based on the 'Open Door' and the League of Nations) and some fairly severe measure of punishment. The Treaty of Brest-Litovsk had hardened Wilson's attitudes against Germany. He spoke more and more of the need for Germany to prove herself a reformed character, worthy of admission to the comity of nations.[5] He feared the continuing influence in Germany of the militarists and imperialists. On the other hand he feared that if Germany were too harshly treated she might turn to revolution and socialism. She must be prosperous enough to allay her domestic discontents – and indeed in order to pay the reparations which Wilson was convinced must be demanded of her.

The views of his advisers varied. Lansing, for instance, favoured the admission of a liberalized Germany to the League of Nations as soon as possible to strengthen the barriers against Bolshevism. The debate as to whether the main enemy was now Germany or Bolshevism is interestingly reflected in the recently published intelligence summaries prepared by the intelligence division of the American General Staff. In the course of 1919 it produced several different assessments of the strength of the various groups in Germany, and the influence of outside forces. Initial fear of Bolshevism in Germany had been replaced in the summer of 1919 by fears of renewed German activity in Russia – at least in the future. An intelligence summary for the week ending 12 July 1919 also concluded pessimistically: 'The *Deutsche Allgemeine Zeitung* probably voices the general German sentiment: "Germany will toil tirelessly and recapture the position due to her. Then she will revenge herself".'[6] A little later, however, concern was being expressed at French rapacity towards Germany. This was seen as a threat to the German moderates: it could be exploited by the extreme German nationalists as proof that Germany had no future save by a return to the policies of expansion.

But while Americans might debate the merits of harsh or lenient treatment of Germany, the final decision did not lie solely in their hands. American influence in Europe in 1919 was much less than Wilson had expected. Although many countries were dependent on American food and money, they were not without leverage of their own. A withholding of American supplies could not guarantee success. Such a step, it was feared, might also facilitate the spread of Bolshevism. It was as if Wilson and his European associates were congregated in one leaky lifeboat in which, although Wilson controlled many of the supplies, he was dependent on the ability and readiness of the others to keep rowing and bailing. Furthermore, given the importance Wilson attached to the formation of the League of Nations, the Europeans could also trade support here for American concessions on other issues. Indeed, the sort of world order that Wilson desired could not be imposed by a *diktat*. He needed broad-based and reasonably willing support for a liberal capitalist international system. On the American side there was also an important constraint. Wilson's use of America's economic power was limited by his own desire, and that of the American people as a whole, to cut government spending. Taxation, it was said, was running at an intolerable level. Foreign loans, it was argued, were best left to bankers and businessmen. The government could still hope to influence private transactions abroad, but it recoiled from policies which required long-term public funding.

It is pointless to speculate as to what might have been achieved had the American government been able and willing to respond to British and French interest in continuing postwar economic co-operation. But it seems that the French, for instance, might have been less insistent on huge reparations had American policy on financial questions been less negative.[7] On the British side John Maynard Keynes, inventive as usual, produced a grand scheme for the economic recovery of Europe which might have provided the basis for some reciprocal reduction of reparations and war debts. From a narrow economic point of view, however, only the Europeans stood to gain at first from such a project. The American government would have borne the cost of some at least of the allied war debts. Great imagination and magnanimity would have been required of the Americans. Understandably they were more concerned with tax cuts and other policies which appealed to the American electorate. Keynes's ideas were foreign to their own beliefs and practices. Thus on 3 May 1919 Washington merely promised to help individual European states on a short-term basis as it saw fit. In any case a scaling down of allied war debts and reparations would have been only a start. Success would have depended upon mutual confidence and restraint in Franco-German relations. As we shall see later (pp. 138–42), although reparations were at the heart of the Ruhr crisis between France and Germany in 1923, French policy was influenced by concern at the speed of Germany's economic revival and fear of an early return to the old imbalance between the two countries.

The French had made strenous efforts to find permanent security against Germany early in 1919. Reparations, disarmament and the League of Nations all seemed inadequate. Consequently there was much talk of the separation of the Rhineland form Germany. Clemenceau, however, found first Lloyd George and later Woodrow Wilson adamant on this point. It was in an attempt to break this impasse that Lloyd George suggested an Anglo-American guarantee of immediate aid against a German attack in March 1919. The British were anxious to share their European responsibilities with the Americans. Much hard bargaining lay ahead, but Clemenceau was strongly attracted by the guarantee, especially from Britain. He was finally able to insist on an allied occupation of the Rhineland for fifteen years, or even longer if the Germans failed to honour the peace treaty. Even so he was able to prevail only with difficulty over the objections of Foch and Poincaré who looked for ways to weaken Germany permanently rather than put so much faith in the intervention of others on behalf of France.[8] The treaty of guarantee, however, never a strong instrument, evaporated the following year when the American Senate refused to ratify it. The occupation of the Rhineland remained a source of contention with Germany in the next decade. But French advocates of a separate Rhineland buffer state might nevertheless have found in practice that this, too, was not a solution – only that they had committed themselves to a wearing and perhaps unwinnable struggle. Much damage would have been done to Anglo-French relations in the process. Several times between March and the German signature of the Treaty of Versailles on 28 June 1919 Lloyd George proposed concessions to Germany, concessions which were not so much a product of British goodwill towards Germany as of dismay at the cost of coercing or trying to control a Germany which refused to sign a peace treaty.[9] British policy cannot yet be described as consistent, notably on reparations, but an underlying tendency, if not a trend, is detectable. As the fierce emotions generated by the war began to cool, so the British became rather less committed to a punitive peace and decidedly more conscious of the discomforts that such a peace might entail. The 20 miles of sea between Dover and Calais was already beginning to influence the British and French perceptions of the German problem.

The story of Versailles is very much the story of allied differences. But the Congress of Vienna had been similarly plagued by allied rivalries. These, however, had not prevented effective allied co-operation, not merely against Napoleon after his return from Elba in 1815, but on several occasions down to 1853 whenever they were confronted with the possibility of French revisionism. In contrast, the victors of 1918 not only imposed a harsh peace on Germany, but then failed to combine in its enforcement thereafter. Efforts to revise the treaty in the 1920s were similarly marked by a lack of allied harmony. The allies were failing either to crush or to conciliate the Germans. They lacked the united will to attempt either. Given their differing interests and priorities it is not surprising that this should have been so. Nor, of course, does it follow that a policy of leniency, had it been practicable, would necessarily have succeeded. Neither France nor Austria had been appeased by the settlements of 1815 or 1866 respectively: they were restrained by the subsequent lack of revisionist opportunities. Nevertheless, it is to be regretted that the allies from 1919 did not lend more support to the moderate revisionist elements in Germany. There were, for instance, Germans of the Left and Centre who, early in 1919, seemed anxious to make a new start. Albert Ballin and the banker, Max Warburg, argued that Germany could only prosper if she found her rightful place in the international economy. This implied relatively free trade, a diversified German economy, and co-operation at home between the ruling élite, the middle classes and the Social democrats. Germany had to become a liberal democratic state in a world order of the type portrayed by Woodrow Wilson in the Fourteen Points. The Treaty of Versailles was a great blow to such hopes. Warburg was among those to defect to the revisionists.[10]

Naturally the allies, and especially the French, feared that if and when Germany recovered her strength so even the moderates would be infected in some degree with revisionism. As it was, when Germany was most under the control of the allies and was subject to heavy reparations in the early 1920s, many German industrialists were skilfully and ruthlessly restoring their fortunes. Some Frenchmen soon began to fear that Germay was recovering from the war more rapidly than France, a nominal victor. Not surprisingly there occurred a prolongation of the emotions which had made the Versailles peace what it was. The chances of imaginative revision in later years were thus diminished from the outset.

THE LEAGUE OF NATIONS

Woodrow Wilson believed that the treatment of Germany under the terms of the Treaty of Versailles was firm but just. He acknowledged that time might reveal certain defects, but he looked to the League of Nations to carry through any necessary amendments. With respect to the League itself, he had not been among the first to propose such an agency. His intense devotion to the League idea had come later. The League was the product of many minds. Unfortunately in 1919, at governmental level in the United States, Britain and France, interest in and enthusiasm for some kind of international authority differed sharply. For the French it was primarily another instrument to enhance their security against Germany. Official British interest owed much to public support for the League, and to the efforts of Lord Robert Cecil.[11] At best it was seen as a new diplomatic tool – a body which might sometimes have a mediatory role in international affairs when both sides were anxious to escape from a crisis. For those who entertained hopes of postwar Anglo-American co-operation, the League was seen as perhaps the most appropriate body where this might take place, given American prejudice against, and suspicion of, traditional European diplomatic methods and procedures. But if the League was a forum through which Britain might hope to mobilize some American support, the British government had no desire to undertake additional responsibilities as a result of membership. Already in 1919 the British were feeling the strain of their world-wide interests, the recent war having generated new commitments from an occupation force in Germany to an enlarged military presence in the Middle East. For the British the League was not much more than an updated version of the nineteenth-century Concert of Europe. Woodrow Wilson, however, set his sights much higher, if not so high as the most extreme Anglo-American supporters of the League. Early disappointment, for instance, with the terms of the Treaty of Versailles led many, especially with the passage of time, to see the League as a league of victors, intended to protect the spoils acquired as a result of the war. As early as May 1919 the liberal American journal, *The New Republic*, complained that the League was an instrument of 'competitive imperialist nationalism'.

The great debate on the League in the United States in 1919–20 was primarily about the nature of American involvement in European affairs – not whether there should be such involvement. Popular American feeling swung against the League essentially under the influence of this debate in the Senate and as a result of the party battle in the country. Naturally interest in foreign affairs declined with the defeat of Germany. Many problems at home clamoured for attention. But the fate of the League was and could be settled by the politicians. The Senate was the crucial battlefield, and there fewer than twenty senators were outright opponents of American membership of some form of league. A two-thirds majority was theoretically attainable. It is also interesting to note that in the case of Wilson's most formidable opponent, Henry Cabot Lodge, the latter was anxious that America should make some contribution to the containment of Germany. It has recently been argued that Lodge 'was too successful for his own good'.[12] He was successful in his campaign against the President, but in the process he made it impossible for the United States to make the more limited but rather more specific commitments which he believed necessary to uphold American interests in Europe.

To understand what happened in the Senate in 1919–20 one must see the struggle as more than a personal vendetta between Wilson and Lodge. Even American participation in the war had only tempered the party battle. Wilson deeply distrusted the Republicans: he was too ambitious for himself and for his party to broaden his government (Franklin D. Roosevelt was to learn from his mistakes in 1940). Admittedly one detects little bipartisan potential on the other side. From the autumn elections of 1918 party strife was resumed in earnest. Whether the Democrats achieved a great success or not in their foreign policy was believed to be of the utmost electoral importance. At the same time both parties were divided internally over the League, and the degree to which America should involve herself in European affairs. Genuine differences of principles and interest existed between the various schools of thought, and the same was true of Lodge and Wilson. Nevertheless this remained a situation in which compromise might have been possible across party lines. The issues did not cleave the Senate on strictly party lines. It is tempting to suggest that a more astute and flexible President might have forced Lodge to play his cards differently. Support for the League with Senate reservations was not impossible. As it happened, no two-thirds majority could be engineered for Wilson's League or any other variant.

The League was undoubtedly weakened by America's failure to join. But having said this one cannot tell how much stronger it would have been with American membership. One may surmise that the mere fact of American membership would have been of more significance than the terms on which the United States entered. It is thus difficult to avoid the conclusion that Wilson was often fighting over words and not matters of real substance as to the future of the League. The crucial article in the Covenant was the tenth, by which states pledged themselves to uphold each other's teritorial integrity and political independence. But the League Council was empowered only to *advise* upon the means by which this obligation should be fulfilled. As early as 1923 the League Council could not decide whether its advice was binding. Perhaps this owed something to the American failure to join: more probably had Wilson carried the United States into the League his successors would have insisted on the narrower interpretation. Indeed, when Wilson was pressed by critics at home in 1919 as to what he understood by article X, and how far it impinged on the nation's sovereignty, he replied that while it was 'the very backbone of the whole Covenant', and represented 'a very grave and solemn moral obligation', it was only 'a moral, not a legal obligation'. It left 'our Congress absolutely free to put its own interpretation upon it in all cases that call for action. It is binding in conscience only, not in law.' But having said this, Wilson insisted on the acceptance of Article X as it stood. Doubtless there were several reasons for his stand. Among them, however, must have been the reluctance to make concessions to Congress after his recent struggles in Paris to secure some allied support for the League. In so far as he recognized the weaknesses of the League, he had to look to a *moral* commitment to the Covenant as the real hope for the future. Dilution of Article X was thus unthinkable.

Lodge's approach was very different. In addition to his personal and party battle with Woodrow Wilson, he was moved by a different interpretation of international relations. He distrusted Wilson's moralizing and search for overall solutions. Like Theodore Roosevelt he was close to European thinking on the nature of power politics. A determined aggressor could not be restrained by talk and international law alone. Indeed, he recoiled from the open-ended, if nebulous commitments which made up the Covenant of the League of Nations. He thought it far wiser for the United States to give limited and more specific pledges – promises it was more likely to fulfil. He wanted, for instance to protect Europe and the United States from a German militarist revival.[13] But the Anglo-American guarantee of France sank with the American failure to ratify the Versailles settlement and the League. Lodge's approach would have been understood by many in Europe. Much of the apparent interest in the League of Nations was generated by the hope that its establishment would lead to continuing American involvement in the affairs of Europe. True, some like Curzon were as sceptical of the United States as of the League itself, but most British ministers agreed with the Canadian Prime Minister, Borden, that the Empire was more likely to find security in good relations with the United

States than in any number of extra strategic bases or new territory.[14] The French were troubled by Wilson's obduracy in the final stages of the League debate in the United States, especially over Article X. The hardening of French policy towards Germany owed something to doubts concerning America's future role.[15]

American non-ratification of the League of Nations and Treaty of Versailles was not quite the end of the story. American membership of some sort of League attracted some discussion during the 1920 presidential election, and it was only after they had secured office that the Republican leadership decided that party feeling ruled out a new initiative. The Republicans thereafter attempted to influence developments in Europe by other means.

THE ALLIES AND BOLSHEVISM

While the allies were trying to settle the affairs of Europe their policies were often influenced by the fear of Bolshevism in Russia, and by the spread of the infection westward. As early as 9 November 1918 the Chief of the Imperial General Staff, when asked by Lloyd George whether he preferred an armistice or a prolongation of the war to weaken Germany, had replied, 'Our real danger now is not the Boches but Bolshevism.'[16] But there was little agreement within or between the various allied governments as to how the Bolsheviks should be handled. Opinions differed from time to time as to the seriousness of the threat. When Lloyd George spoke in the spring of 1919 of the danger of Bolshevism spreading to Germany if the latter were too harshly treated, Clemenceau retorted that concessions to Germany would work to the benefit of Bolshevism in Germany's neighbours. Clearly tactical use was being made of the Bolshevik 'threat' in these talks. Earlier in the year Lloyd George and Wilson had even displayed a momentary interest in the negotiation of a truce between the warring factions in Russia in the hope that a compromise government might follow. The White opponents of the Bolsheviks refused to co-operate, while the Communist International, set up on 24 January 1919, further discouraged Anglo-American interest in negotiations with Lenin. Wilson had already declared on 10 January 1919[17]

> Food relief is now the key to the whole European situation and to the solution of peace. Bolshevism is steadily advancing westward . . . and is poisoning Germany. It cannot be stopped by force but it can be stopped by food.

The French, though fearful of Bolshevism in central Europe, put more faith in the Poles.

Hungary was under Bolshevik control from March to August 1919 until Czech and Rumanian intervention contributed to Béla Kun's overthrow, and fears of a revolutionary advance deep into Europe began to recede. Allied policy towards Russia, however, remained confused. More was at stake than a Bolshevik take-over of the old Russian Empire. Whether weak or strong, under Red or White (that is, anti-Bolshevik) rule, Russia was expected to have a profound influence on the global balance of power. Winston Churchill, for instance, was not so obsessed with Boshevism as to rule out other possible developments. On 21 February 1919 he warned that Russia might ultimately be revived with German and Japanese aid. A strong Russia would threaten India. The League of Nations would be ineffectual without Russian help. The final balance might find Germany in an even stronger position than ever before. Churchill did not want simply to use Germany to hold back the revolutionary tide. He wanted to be sure that no Russo-German axis would develop. He therefore wished in April 1919 to 'feed Germany; fight Bolshevism; make Germany fight Bolshevism'.[18] Lloyd George noted in May 1919 that although Russia had been torn to pieces by rival factions and the formation of new states, nevertheless 'in five years time who could tell what it would be'. The Slavs, he thought, would remain 'an incalculable factor' whether under the rule of the Bosheviks or a White dictator. But he also stuck to his earlier argument that British intervention against Bolshevism would prove the surest road 'to bankruptcy and Bolshevism in these islands'.[19] He warned of the intense hostility that would be provoked among the British working classes if intervention were attempted on a large scale. At the same time, as Prime Minister of a coalition largely made up of Conservatives, he had to make some allowance for strong anti-Bolshevik prejudices and fears. He found Churchill a constant critic.

Churchill agreed that a large British army could not be sent to Russia, but otherwise wished to give all possible aid and encouragement to the Whites. The worst policy, he believed, was the one being pursued in 1919 – that of half-hearted aid to the anti-Bolshevik forces. Better not to intervene at all! Lloyd George dismissed both Churchill's policies as undesirable and impractical, given opinion at home and the international situation. Massive allied intervention was ruled out. Lloyd George cited the relative ineffectiveness of 1 million Austrian and German troops in Russia in 1918. Basically he believed that the Russians must be left to determine their own fate. He was, however, ready to give the Whites sufficient backing to see if they could win real popular support in Russia. At the same time both Lloyd George and the Americans continued to worry about the sort of White Russian regime that was likely to emerge following a Bolshevik defeat. A White Russia was likely to be autocratic, militarist and expansionist: in short, it could mean a return to the troublesome Russia of the Tsars minus the Romanov dynasty. A White Russia which followed illiberal trading and domestic policies, which was anxious to recover the European Russian frontiers of 1914, and which was once more active in central Asia and the Far East, would not only menace British interests but would also remove a large slice of the world from the liberal capitalist order which Woodrow Wilson hoped to create.

It was true that a strong Russia might once again prove a useful partner against Germany, but it was also possible that as a result of the Treaty of Versailles Russia and Germany might find that they had more in common as revisionist powers, notably at the expense of Poland. A strong Russia might also be expected to act against Finland and the Baltic, countries which had all been under Russian rule in 1914. In the Far East a revival of Russo-Japanese co-operation in Manchuria – and even further afield – could not be ruled out. Diplomats and strategists could even begin to frighten themselves with the spectre of a grand revisionist alliance made up of Germany, Russia and Japan. Thus the policy of the western powers towards Russia was guided by more than anti-Bolshevik considerations. While the British gave some help to the Whites, they also tried to moderate the home and foreign policies of the White leaders. For instance, the British wished to postpone recognition of the Kolchak regime not merely because they were uncertain of its future prospects, but in the not very realistic hope that it would pay more attention to British interests to secure recognition. The British faced a dilemma in May 1919 when Kolchak, briefly, seemed close to victory in Russia. It was then feared that to delay recognition would propel Kolchak into the arms of the Germans and Japanese.[20] Kolchak was defeated before the British had committed themselves, but the problem returned in October 1919 when another White leader, Denikin, menaced Moscow from the south, and it persisted until his defeat. American reactions in 1919 were similar. They could agree that Bolshevism was worse than its alternatives, past and present, but they wished both to help and liberalize the Whites. Colonel House, indeed, thought a restored Russian Empire, whatever the character of its rulers, too large for the health of the world. Wilson disagreed, but some in Britain, especially those concerned with the safety of British India, wished to preserve Georgia and Armenia as independent states. The weaker Russia, the more influence Britain could hope to exert in Persia, and around the Caspian Sea. Lord Curzon, for one, campaigned vigorously on these lines. Other members of the Cabinet, however, speedily became impressed by the prohibitive costs of continuing British activity in these regions on the scale envisaged by Curzon. Nor did the Secretary of State for India agree that British rule in India would be helped by such adventures.

The British were perhaps most successful in the Baltic – at least until the postwar settlement was upset by the outbreak of the Second World War in 1939. There both Finland and the Baltic states were able to establish themselves. A small British naval force helped to check both Bolshevik and German influence, though the British often found themselves in the embarrassing position that any help or encouragement given to the Finns and Baltic states might injure their relations with the Whites who were anxious to recover the frontiers of 1914. The British spent some £100 million on aid to the Whites, not a little of this, one feels, being a form of insurance against a White victory. The French approach under Clemenceau was very different. Despite the pleas of Marshall Foch, who rivalled Churchill as an advocate of intervention, French forces were pulled out of Odessa in April 1919. Little interest was shown in Siberia, save in so far as interest was displayed in the White cause as a form of insurance to anticipate its possible victory. French support for Denikin in southern Russia later in 1919 owed something to jealousy of British interference in what had been the French zone under the agreement concluded in December 1917. Clemenceau frequently referred to the danger of German influence in Russia, arguing that Russia herself would not count for much for many years to come. France's great need was to build up the states of eastern Europe, especially Poland, to contain Germany – not Bolshevism. But it was only under his successor in 1920 that the Poles received some encouragement from France to expand eastward.[21] By that time most other allied aid to the Whites had come to an end.

White resistance in Siberia west of Lake Baikal collapsed early in 1920. In European Russia the anti-Bolshevik forces were confined to the Crimea and the rump of the Ukrainian state. The Poles, now confident that the Whites would not be the beneficiaries from their intervention, and in the belief that they enjoyed at least a temporary military advantage over the Bolsheviks, decided to act. In March they proposed a Russian renunciation of territory that had been Polish before the first partition (in 1772) and recognition of the states which had broken away from the old Tsarist Empire since 1917. Against British advice the Poles attacked on 26 April. Lloyd George was convinced that in the long run the Russians must win, but Churchill thought the Poles correct to attack before the Red armies were strong enough to menace Polish security. In June the Whites in the Crimea seized the opportunity provided by the Polish invasion to go on to the offensive themselves. This gave the British an excuse to stop aid to the Whites.

As the Polish attack began to falter in June, the British (and to a lesser extent the French) tried to exploit these setbacks to achieve agreement on a realistic Russo-Polish frontier. It was at this point that the so-called 'Curzon Line' was devised (credit for its delineation is now given to Lloyd George's private secretary, Philip Kerr, or to the future historian, Lewis Namier). British peace overtures encountered a mixed reception in Russia. Trotsky, on this occasion, was one of the less 'hawkish'. He did not share Lenin's view that the British were bent on the destruction of Bolshevism, using the Poles and Crimean Whites as their agents. He believed that the British Cabinet was divided, and that peace was both possible and desirable. The prospects for revolution in Europe and Asia were not good. He wished to accept the 'Curzon Line'.But his colleagues were soon carried away by Russian military successes over the Poles. When the Russian advance caused the British to talk of intervention, this was rightly interpreted by the Kremlin as a bluff. Indeed, neither the British nor French had troops with which to act: nor was the Chief of the Imperial General Staff dismayed by the possible extinction of Poland – he welcomed direct contact between Russia and Germany as this was likely to result in 'constant friction and enmity'. At this very moment difficulties between Germany and the western powers over reparations were again provoking fears of Russo-German collaboration.[22]

Nevertheless the rapid Russian advance deep into Poland in August 1920, with the growing threat to Warsaw, caused considerable alarm in western capitals. Even in the United States, where the mood was increasingly introspective (if not isolationist), the Russo-Polish War was followed with immense interest by military intelligence. There were dire predictions of further Bolshevik advances if the Polish barrier broke. Given the Bolshevik 'declaration of war against the United States ... success ... in Europe has an immediate military import for the United States'. There were fears of repercussions in Mexico. American military intelligence regretted American non-membership of the League where it was felt useful interchanges with the other great powers should have been possible. French hostility to Germany was criticized as divisive at a time when unity was needed among the opponents of Bolshevism. Great faith was placed in the British Empire as 'the great stabilizing element in the world today'. It was important that the British retained India.[23] If much of this was naive and unnecessarily alarmist, it is interesting that the British General Staff was also arguing that the German people should no longer be treated as 'outcasts and pariahs'. Germany should have sufficient arms to defend itself against Bolshevism at home and in the east. There was some talk of an Anglo-French defensive alliance. Even Lloyd George sounded alarmed in public, though privately he hoped that matters could be peacefully resolved between Germany and Russia in the event of Poland being overrun.[24] The French were appalled by this calculation. The situation, however, was dramatically transformed from the middle of August 1920 by a successful Polish counter-attack. Soon the extent and speed of the Polish advance was troubling the French, as well as those who were less interested in the establishment of a strong Polish state. But on 12 October a preliminary peace was agreed at Riga. The new Poland now stretched some 200 kilometres beyond the 'Curzon Line' and included about 3 million people of non-Polish stock.

The war in the east had interrupted Lloyd George's efforts to establish some sort of working relationship with the Bolsheviks. These caused much controversy in the government, while the Chief of the Imperial General Staff feared that negotiations would encourage subversive elements inside Britain. But Lloyd George insisted one must face facts. Bolshevism would not go away in Russia, despite all the huffing and puffing in some parts of the Conservative Party. In any case the real threat to domestic peace in Britain stemmed not from the existence of Bolshevism in Russia and any intrigues that might be inspired by Moscow, but from the overall decline in trade and employment. Perhaps Lloyd George exaggerated, or deceived himself concerning the potential of the Russian market – certainly his trade treaty of 1921 did not greatly increase British exports to Russia. But he was correct in his diagnosis of the problem. It was wiser, both from the point of view of the domestic political situation and Anglo-Russian relations, to negotiate with the Bolsheviks rather than to treat them as untouchables as the Conservative diehards advocated. In 1921 Britain gave the new regime *de facto* recognition, and it is interesting that when the succeeding Conservative government adopted a more hostile stance towards the USSR, British businessmen should have been numbered among its critics. It was left to a Labour government to establish full diplomatic relations with Russia in 1924.[25]

THE MIDDLE EAST AFTER THE FIRST WORLD WAR

The problem of Russia and Bolshevism loomed large in British policy with respect to Turkey, Persia and Afghanistan. The British before 1914 had sought various solutions to the threat posed by Russia to the routes to India and even to India herself. The ideal solution was the maintenance of buffer states between the two empires. But the fact that in the early 1920s Turkey, Persia and Afghanistan were all showing signs of promise in the performance of this role was not something for which British policy-makers from 1918 could be given as much credit as might be expected. British policy-makers were often pulling in different directions, and those who had their way were often wrong in their courses of action. The British were saved from important errors partly by their lack of resources, sometimes by the good judgement of men in or nearer the areas of crisis, and above all by the nationalism or the strength of local feeling in the three countries in question.

At times it seemed as if Moscow would have the advantage in these three states, in that each had more reason to quarrel with the British than with the Russians. Zinoviev, at the First Congress of the Peoples of the East, held in Baku in September 1920, proclaimed a 'holy war' against British imperialism. But in Afghanistan, for instance, the Russians soon found that the new nationalist leader, Amanullah, could be almost as much of an embarrassment to them as he had proved to the British from 1919. In 1922 he was threatening to march to the support of rebels in Ferghana and Bukhara until warned off by the Russians. Meanwhile the British were gradually learning to live with the emergent nationalist forces in Persia. At first, under the guidance of Lord Curzon as Foreign Secretary, the British had tried to reduce Persia to the level of a vassal state. But the treaty of August 1919 was unworkable, with no Persian government daring to submit so humiliating an instrument to the Majlis for ratification. Curzon continued to press for a strong British policy in this region, arguing that with the collapse of White forces in southern Russia in 1920 Bolshevism would continue to advance southward – with India as its final target. The government in India, however, was much less apprehensive, while the War Office, troubled by unrest in Ireland, India, Mesopotamia (and fearful of major disturbances even in Britain), had no troops it could willingly spare to continue to play the 'great game' in central Asia in accordance with the wishes of Lord Curzon. Fortunately for the British a strong leader was emerging in Persia in 1921. This was Reza Khan who, four years later, was to found the Pahlavi imperial dynasty. Although the Chiefs of Staff in 1926–28 could still discuss the Russian threat to India in terms reminiscent of pre-war days,[26] the government of India had shown itself much less alarmist.[27] In 1921 even Curzon himself acknowledged that Persia must be left to her own devices.[28]

Elsewhere in the Middle East the defeat of the Ottoman Empire in 1918 had left a great many territorial questions unresolved among the great powers and among the former subjects of the Porte. Over the period of the war and its immediate aftermath Ottoman lands had been freely drawn upon by the opponents of Germany to satisfy their own ambitions and to try to win new allies. So much had been promised that disputes naturally arose as to precisely who was entitled to what. Britain, France, Italy and Greece, Arabs and Zionists were all making claims to parts of the empire.[29]

Contrary to the hopes of some in Britain, the Americans refused to become directly involved. Some British ministers hoped that an American mandate somewhere in the Middle East might lead to more American participation in world affairs and to more American understanding of Britain's problems as an imperial power. But the Americans were not to be caught in this way. In so far as they were interested in the Middle East, it was in limiting the influence of British oil companies. Rivalry here, however, was gradually brought under control, with the Foreign Office by the mid-1920s preferring to make concessions to Jersey Oil rather than give encouragement to the Bolsheviks through the continuance of 'capitalist contradictions'.[30] Circumstances were also forcing the British to view French claims in the Levant with more sympathy. Economic pressures were obliging the British to reduce their garrisons in the Middle East, while contrary to their original hopes the Arabs were proving less grateful, less co-operative and docile following the removal of their Ottoman overlords. The Arabs were upset by British concessions to the Zionists in Palestine. Restlessness under western rule soon began to spread throughout the region, especially against the French in Syria. Britain and France agreed at San Remo in April 1920 that Syria and the Lebanon should become French mandates, while Iraq (Mesopotamia) and Palestine fell to Britain. Revolts had to be suppressed in both Syria (1920) and Iraq (1920–21) before the situation became reasonably stable in the Middle East.

Further north allied plans were also being drastically altered. Much of the periphery of the coastline and hinterland of Turkey in a great arc from Constantinople along the shore of the Aegean and the Mediterranean, and so eastward to Cilicia, seemed destined to fall under the influence of Greece, Italy and France – if the allies could but agree among themselves. Agree, however, they could not, for when in April 1919 the Italians moved to secure the 'equitable' share of the region around Adalia promised under the Treaty of London of 26 April 1915, Britain and France responded by encouraging the Greeks to occupy Smyrna to limit the Italian advance. The future of the Straits and Constantinople was also causing concern, at different times an American mandate, a Greek mandate and an international regime all being suggested. Not surprisingly the Secretary of State for India warned that the threatened disruption of Turkey would transform the Turks into allies of Bolshevism, and would also inflame Muslim opinion against Britain. The slighting of the Sultan and Caliph must stop. In any case, he argued, it would not be possible for the British to use Indian troops if they wished to coerce the Turks.

The Turks still received harsh treatment under the terms of the Treaty of Sèvres of 10 August 1920, although the Sultan was allowed to retain Constantinople. Sèvres, however, was soon consigned to the waste bin as the Turkish nationalists began to assert themselves in the heart of Anatolia under their new President, Mustapha Kemal. Lloyd George, against the advice of many in London, chose to rely on the Greeks to contain this new Turkish challenge. Others expected a Turkish victory and the emergence of a new Turkey which would prove an effective barrier to Bolshevik Russia. Thus a Greek advance into Anatolia received only half-hearted support from a divided British government. In contrast, the French and Italians were perceptive enough to negotiate with the Turkish nationalists, and to content themselves with economic concessions in Adalia and Cilicia instead of territorial influence. The nationalists, indeed, were proving equally skilled in the arts of diplomacy and war. A treaty of 16 March 1921 secured their rear against the Russians. Then, in a great counter-offensive in the summer of 1922, they were able to sweep the Greeks from Asia Minor. By the end of September the national-ists were advancing on Constantinople and the Straits, and were threatening to overrun the British garrison at Chanak. For a time a major collision between the British and the Turks seemed possible. Fortunately much good sense was displayed by the men on the spot, and war was averted. But the crisis contributed to the overthrow of the Lloyd George coalition government in Britain, and its replace-ment by a Conservative ministry under Bonar Law.

A new peace settlement with Turkey was now necessary and possible. At the Lausanne Conference (November 1922–July 1923) many concessions were made to the Turks. The British and Turks were even able to draw together in the face of a Russian demand for the closure of the Straits. Had this been conceded, the Russians would have become the dominant naval power in the Black Sea. In general the British emerged with many undeserved advantages, given their policy towards Turkey since 1919. They had good reason in 1923 to expect that Turkey would remain an effective barrier to Soviet influence in much of the Middle East. No other great power had made gains which seemed likely to embarrass British interests in the foreseeable future. The heaviest price for the new status quo was paid by the Armenians, their hopes of independence being extin-guished by a Russo-Turkish agreement of March 1921, and their very survival put at risk by the ferocity with which the Turks restored their power thereafter. Professors Grant and Temperley have commented on the 'singular' fact that these 'horrors' failed to awaken public opinion to the same extent as many 'lesser tragedies'.[31] By 1923 the British, however, had had their fill of postwar crises. The government in particular, given its new treaty relationship with Turkey, was not disposed to look a gift-horse in the mouth.

British adjustments to nationalist unrest were also taking place in Egypt and Iraq. The 1914 protectorate over the former was ended in 1922. The British between 1922 and 1930 relaxed the close control they had originally sought to exercise over the affairs of Iraq: by 1930 they were content with a close military alliance. Even in India the British were beginning to temper repression with political reform.

But nationalist challenges to British imperial rule varied sharply from country to country: in some parts of the empire the challenges were negligible. Even in the Middle East, where the British made the most adjustments and concessions within many, though not all of their spheres of influence, over a number of years the British enjoyed a fair measure of success in upholding their most important interests against local challenges. Indeed it has been argued with respect to Britain's imperial position as a whole in the inter-war period that the British were less troubled by internal disruptive tendencies than by fears of the 'irruption of . . . imperial rivals into their ill-defended empire'.[32] Notwithstanding the growth of nationalism in some parts of Asia, and the Bolshevik challenge, it had not been necessary to revise pre-war perceptions of the empire in its international setting to any radical extent. Concessions to various peoples on the running of their internal affairs did not necessarily involve significant changes in the strategic and economic relationships. In particular the British between the wars could continue to hope to retain control of the foreign policies of India, Iraq and Egypt for many years to come. The substance of power appeared to be changing less than the form. This could also be the view of observers on the Left. Thus John Strachey in 1932, as he looked forward to the triumph of socialism in his book, *The Coming Struggle for Power*, expected the British Empire to survive in a revised form just as the old Tsarist Empire had re-emerged under Soviet rule in Russia. Britain would play much the same role in a socialist British Empire or Commonwealth as European Russia in the USSR. As for imperialism itself, Strachey believed that the age of real exploitation had yet to develop as the partition of the world had only just been completed.

Emphasis upon the importance of the great powers – with the rest nowhere – was equally prominent among those who took a reformist view of the future of international relations. Lloyd George's private secretary, Philip Kerr, argued after the war that Britain and the United States must co-operate through the League of Nations to clean up 'the stagnant pools of humanity' in Africa and Asia before they infected the rest of the world.[33] He wrote to Lloyd George on 15 November 1919: 'We have all been running on the assumption that the great powers, including America, were going to stand together and more or less run world affairs.'[34] Bertrand Russell also thought in terms of power blocs. If he then saw America as 'the chief enemy of the human race', he added that, given time, 'Japan, after absorbing China will be. I believe that the conflict between the white and yellow races will come one day.'[35] The leaders of the Soviet Union were also coming to acknowledge the importance of conventional diplomacy and traditional power politics – their rhetoric concerning revolution and counter-revolution must not be allowed to obscure the speed with which they adapted to the world as it was.

After 1920 most of the Soviet leadership expected slow progress towards world revolution. It was agreed at the Third Comintern Congress of 1921 that any policy 'which is a necessity from the standpoint of Soviet Russia is also a necessity from the standpoint of world revolution'. Could any Russian leader ask for more? As the USSR showed in many of its dealings with the Weimar Republic, and in its recovery in 1929 of the Chinese Eastern Railway from a Manchurian warlord, its leaders were no longer novices in the conduct of foreign policy. Although both the Russian and British leaderships had had to come to terms with the strength of the nationalists in some parts of the Middle East in the early 1920s, this had not entailed a major revision of expectations as to the future roles of the great powers.

THE FAR EAST AND THE WASHINGTON CONFERENCE

Shortly after the defeat of Germany the influential South African and Commonwealth politician, General Smuts, forecast a generation of peace in Europe, and warned that the next great war might be fought in the Far East between the United States and Japan. There were indeed many unresolved problems in the Far East at the end of the war. Both the British and Americans were disturbed by the way Japan had extended her influence while their attention had been distracted by events in Europe. Japan's activities had strengthened and inflamed Chinese nationalism. The Russian civil war had provided Japan with new opportunities, and for a time the political future of much of north-east Asia was in doubt. The international tension was also reflected in the continuance of American and Japanese naval construction on a large scale despite the ending of the war in Europe. By 1921 this had become sufficiently ominous for the British to take some steps towards the modernization of their own battle-fleet, despite the earlier assumption that there would be no war for ten years.

The United States and Japan had been drifting apart since 1905 to the growing embarrassment of the British. The alliance had made it easier for Britain to concentrate her navy against Germany, but it had not prevented the development of some friction with the Japanese over trade in the Far East and the future of China even before the outbreak of the First World War. In China the Manchu dynasty was overthrown in the revolution of 1911, and thereafter the country was normally in the grip of a major political crisis of some kind or other. For a time it seemed as if a strong central government might be emerging under the direction of Yüan Shih-k'ai, but his failure seemed assured even before his death in June 1916. Apart from internal enemies, he was under much pressure from the Japanese, and this increased when the First World War distracted the attention of the other powers in Europe. Japan, as the ally of Britain, was able to seize the German concessions in Shantung – as well as the German-held islands in the north Pacific. The war also removed Japan's main economic rivals, so that her trade flourished, and she became the main source of loans to money-hungry Chinese politicians. Realists in Britain such as Grey and Eyre Crowe consoled themselves with the thought that Japan could not be stopped and it was better that she seek advantages in China rather than elsewhere. The British were also helped by the fact that the Japanese leadership was divided over policy. The Elder Statesmen had already opposed young Pan-Asian enthusiasts in Japan who wished to support the republican groups led by Sun Yat-sen. Japanese conservatives feared that a strong Chinese republic might damage the position of the Japanese Emperor. The Elder Statesmen would have welcomed the restoration of the Manchus as constitutional monarchs, and were also interested in co-operation with the British. The latter were averse to great-power intervention, and on the whole welcomed the rise of Yüan Shih-k'ai as the man most likely to protect British interests. The Japanese disliked him initially as a republican, and later, when he aspired to found his own dynasty, as a potentially strong leader who would oppose Japanese interests. The Japanese were also tempted by the situation in China early in 1915, and by the preoccupations of the other powers, to confront Yüan with the so-called Twenty-One Demands, demands which if conceded in full would have left China almost in the position of a Japanese protectorate. China received little diplomatic support from Britain or the United States, but there was perhaps enough Anglo-American criticism to disturb and strengthen the influence of those among the Japanese leadership who already regarded the Twenty-One Demands as too extreme and provocative. The final outcome was thus a victory for the moderates in Tokyo. The fifth group of the Demands (which included proposals for Japanese political influence in China) were dropped. Japanese interference in the affairs of China nevertheless persisted after 1915, despite this compromise.

Japanese divisions over policy also continued after 1915. Anti-western and Pan-Asian groups were active. There were some advocates of an alliance with Germany. But the Japanese government clung to the British alliance, content for the time being to turn it to modest advantage. In addition, many of the Japanese leaders were impressed by the growing power of the United States, especially after her entry into the war in 1917. Japan drew much of her steel and other key imports from America. In August 1917 Tokyo bowed to the American wish that China should be allowed to join the war against Germany. The Lansing – Ishii agreement in November 1917 attempted to paper over the differences between the two powers. Japan acknowledged America's interest in the 'Open Door' in return for American recognition of Japan's special interests in China, given the last two countries' close proximity to each other. By a secret protocol Japan agreed that she would not 'take advantage of present conditions to seek special rights and privileges in China which would abridge the rights of citizens or subjects of other friendly states'. The leadership in Tokyo was divided when the question of allied intervention in Russia arose in 1918. The British were pressing hard for Japanese action to exclude Germany from Siberia, but many in Tokyo believed that Japan should move only with American assent and co-operation. This did not come until July 1918. It was only then that the Japanese military had the opportunity to take policy in eastern Siberia largely into their own hands, and to engage in what was in many ways a private exercise in empire-building. By the time of Germany's defeat in November 1918 special circumstances had combined with Japan's own varied activities to renew fears in Washington, soon to be followed by some alarm in London, concerning the postwar character of the balance between the powers in the Far East.

The Versailles Peace Conference in 1919 touched upon a number of east Asian issues. The Japanese vainly tried to raise the question of racial equality. They were allowed to retain the German concessions in Shantung which they had seized in 1914, but only after an acknowledgement of Chinese sovereignty. This concession failed to satisfy Chinese nationalist sentiment, which erupted in what has become known as the May 4th movement. A widespread boycott of Japanese goods followed, and China refused to sign the peace treaty. Woodrow Wilson's (reluctant) recognition of Japan's claims in Shantung also produced an outcry in the United States. Tokyo was troubled by these Chinese and American reactions. The Japanese government was also disturbed by the resumption of battleship building in the United States (anti-submarine escorts had been given priority from 1917 to 1918) and in renewed American interest in an international banking consortium to handle loans with China. The Japanese were particularly anxious to exclude Manchuria and eastern Inner Mongolia from the operations of the consortium – whatever other concessions might prove necessary.

The British followed events in the Far East with mixed feelings. There was, for instance, as late as September 1919 some discussion within the Foreign Office on the question of temporary Japanese control of the Chinese Eastern Railway to increase the efficacy of anti-Bolshevik operations in the east. This was viewed with horror by the British diplomats in China who were anxious to win the sympathy of the growing nationalist forces.[36] The Foreign Office as a whole was soon taking a very pessimistic view of Japan's ambitions in the Far East, and was apprehensively considering a number of possibilities. Was Japan, it was asked, about to become a Far Eastern Prussia, intent on domination in China, and threatening British control of India with a Pan-Asian programme? Alternatively, might Japan try to achieve her aims by economic means, gradually undermining the 'Open Door', and subtly drawing China and other eastern states within her orbit? It was accepted that Japan had been denied true equality in many parts of the world, and that she needed new outlets. It was still tempting to see eastern Siberia as a place where Japan might safely be allowed to satisfy her ambitions. On the other hand, a strong Russia might suit British interests better.[37] These inconclusive deliberations certainly underline British weaknesses in the Far East at this time. Admiral Jellicoe led a naval mission to the Dominions and India in 1919–20. His report highlighted the prohibitive cost if Britain tried to provide permanent naval protection for her eastern empire against Japan.

There were those in London who hoped to escape from the defence dilemma by close co-operation with the United States. But few Americans were thinking in such terms in 1920. Indeed, for many American navalists, the British navy was as serious a rival as that of Japan. Much use was made of British naval power and the Anglo-Japanese alliance to justify American naval expansion. Parity with Britain was the minimal objective: some argued the case for a two-ocean fleet. America, it was said, might have to use her navy to uphold neutral rights and to protect American trade against some future British blockade. Freedom of the Seas had been the second of Woodrow Wilson's Fourteen Points. Both Wilson and his Republican successors were prepared to use America's potential ability to outbuild the British in a naval race to exert leverage over British policy, and in particular to put an end to the Anglo-Japanese alliance. It was hoped that without the alliance Japanese policy in the Far East would be much less assertive and self-confident. At the same time it must be recognized that in the first years following the war American policy, like that of Great Britain, was exposed to many cross-currents. The Bolshevik advance deep into Poland in the summer of 1920 was one such distraction. Apart from the 'Red Scare' at home, Latin America was also being closely watched for signs of revolutionary influences. The weekly summary from the military intelligence department, dated 31 July 1920, spoke melodramatically of three groups battling for control of the world: 'the Proletarian dominion, approximately the old Russian Empire; the dominion of Autocracy, approximately the Empire of Japan; the dominion of Liberalism, Western Europe and the Western Hemisphere'.[38] For the time being the rest of the world was the vassal of the Liberal dominion, but this was war-weary and on the defensive. Proletarianism was on the offensive, aiming at control of Europe and the disruption of the British Empire. Japan was pursuing an opportunist foreign policy, exploiting the weaknesses and divisions of other states. The intelligence department, dismayed by the possibility that Bolshevism was about to sweep across Europe to the Atlantic, described the British Empire as 'the great stabilizing element in the world today'.[39] Unlike the American navy, the army was more inclined to view Britain as America's natural ally against Bolshevism and Japan. Reports that some Japanese favoured an alliance with Russia and Germany were anxiously scrutinized. Great attention was paid to the influence and ambitions of the Japanese armed forces. On the other hand, some consolation was drawn from an estimate that in the event of a war between America and China on the one hand and Japan on the other, Japan would lose about 80 per cent of her trade. Furthermore, by 1920 it was increasingly evident that many groups in Japan were turning against the expensive military adventures on the Asiatic mainland. These were proving a burden – not an asset – on the Japanese economy.[40]

Meanwhile the British continued to deliberate over Anglo-American relations. One school of thought, in which Curzon was prominent, insisted that the strength of isolationist sentiment in the United States ruled out any long-term relationship between the two countries. It was accepted that the alliance with Japan was defective, but it at least served as a brake on Japan's ambition, and in its absence Japan might well turn to Russia or Germany – or both. But there were others in the Foreign Office and elsewhere whose distrust of Japan was such that the alliance no longer served Britain's interests in the Far East. It was a barrier to Anglo-American co-operation, the only force which might impose some restraint on Japanese conduct, and build up China as the regional defender of the 'Open Door'. Alternatively, a tripartite agreement might be reached with both Japan and the United States. In June 1921 the British ambassador in Washington described the Anglo-Japanese alliance as a threat to Britain's relations with the United States. At the end of the month, at the Imperial Conference in London, the Canadians expressed their opposition to any policy that might harm relations with the United States. Up to that point the British Cabinet, under the influence of Lloyd George and Curzon, had been inclined to renew the Japanese alliance in tandem with an exploration of Far Eastern and related issues with the United States which might or might not lead to concrete results. Under Canadian prompting, however, and with mounting signs of American interest, the Cabinet now decided that a conference on the Far East should precede the renewal of the alliance. On July 8 Washington proposed a conference on naval limitation, conscious that opinion in Congress and among the general public would not support the existing naval programme without some prior attempt to negotiate an international disarmament treaty.

By 1921, at least on paper, the Japanese and American naval construction programmes were approaching the scale of the Anglo-German naval race before 1914. The British Admiralty was working on the assumption that the United States would soon have twelve battleships of post-Jutland design, Japan eight, and Britain no more than one – the inadequately armoured *Hood*. Four super battle-cruisers were therefore authorized, and the British also began to draw up war plans against Japan. But the Cabinet evidently hoped that the projected ships would be used only for bargaining purposes in arms limitation talks. The British government was anxious to economize on naval expenditure, and from 8 July 1921 preparations for a conference began to make rapid progress. The proposed conference, however, if it were to be a success, had to tackle a number of problems more or less simultaneously. Apart from naval limitation, agreement was necessary on the future of the Anglo-Japanese alliance, security in the western Pacific and the treatment of China. Nor could the naval issue be isolated from rivalries in Europe. British naval policy was much influenced by French submarine construction, while the French in turn were fearful of Italian naval pretensions in the Mediterranean.

The British delegates proceeded to Washington (the conference opened on 12 November 1921) in the expectation that the Anglo-Japanese alliance would be renewed, though probably in a revised form. The Japanese approached the conference with mixed feelings. Fortunately by 1921 control of foreign policy lay primarily with those who believed that Japan was spending too much on her armed forces and adventures on the mainland. The country's economy was crying out for relief. They argued that it was necessary to make a pragmatic and objective reassessment of the balance of forces in the Far East and in the world as a whole. Military chauvinism might prove a false god in the new age. But in the initial critique of current policies, the majority of the élite still favoured the continuance of the Anglo-Japanese alliance. This was especially popular among the politicians and the navy. The army, however, was split on the question of the alliance, and there was growing anti-British feeling among the radical nationalists whether they thought in ultra-patriotic or Pan-Asian terms. This was also a period of growing unrest and strikes at home. It was not an auspicious environment in which to experiment with the most parliamentary form of government that Japan had yet tried – the Prime Minister himself was assassinated in November 1921. Nevertheless the political moderates remained in the ascendant throughout the period of the Washington Conference, and they were able to ensure that at the end of the day Japan was a signatory to the treaties.

The government had much business support for its policy of reducing military expenditures, easing the tax burden and relying more on diplomacy and economic weapons to promote Japan's interests on the mainland. The War Minister, Tanaka, was successfully cultivated by the civilian ministers, and was persuaded to restrain the activities of the military in Siberia and China. Fortunately, too, the more sophisticated of the naval leaders, such as Admiral Kato, recognized that in any long-drawn-out arms race with the Americans the latter must prevail, given their vastly superior resources. Indeed, among many of the Japanese élite there was growing interest in the United States and its ways, and a readiness to acknowledge that Japan must learn to live with the world's richest power. If Japan was interested in trade with China, that with America was also important. As for China, neither strong-arm methods, nor the efforts to work through sympathetic warlords and the pro-Japanese Anfu regime in Peking (this had fallen in July 1920) had been particularly effective. Despite its inner confusion, Chinese nationalism was now a sufficiently strong force to dispel any Japanese hopes of a relatively simple military solution. Russian influence was reviving in the Far East. Some Chinese were already looking with interest towards Moscow. Anti-Bolshevik forces were collapsing in Siberia, leaving the Japanese army in an isolated position. Thus many Japanese were alive to the possibility of change even before the Washington Conference began its work.

Once at Washington the British and Japanese delegates speedily recognized that real progress was dependent on the abolition of the Anglo-Japanese alliance. Any regrets on the Japanese side did not mean that reactions to some new arrangement that would include the United States were wholly negative. Indeed, Baron Shidehara, the Japanese ambassador in Washington, helped to draft the new instrument. In the end it was a four-power treaty (France being included on American insistence), signed on 13 December 1921, which replaced the alliance. This treaty was of necessity a somewhat nebulous affair. The Americans had bluntly stated before the conference that they 'could enter into no alliance or make any commitment to the use of arms'. Hence the new treaty provided only for mutual respect for the rights of each signatory in their respective 'insular possessions and insular dominions in the region of the Pacific Ocean'. The four powers agreed to hold joint conferences to discuss future disputes over such rights, and they pledged themselves to full and frank discussion in the event of any threat to peace. Although the treaty was not of a character to engender much enthusiasm, it opened the way to a respectable burial for the Anglo-Japanese alliance, and provided a reasonable basis from which the powers could build, were they so minded.

Rather more substantial progress was achieved with the Five-

Power Treaty on Naval Limitation of 6 February 1922, an agreement which was concluded only after highly complex negotiations. Success was founded on the underlying anxiety of all the powers to economize on arms expenditure. Though arms limitation had been the subject of occasional discussion in the nineteenth century, and still more so with reference to the Anglo-German naval race before 1914, the only tangible achievement before 1922 had been the Anglo-American agreements concerning the Canadian frontier and Great Lakes. At Washington, in contrast, a significant number of warships were scrapped, including a number of formidable ships already on the stocks or about to be laid down. In practice, of course, the powers were largely agreeing not to do what they were not anxious to do in any case. The discussions were prolonged by the understandable desire of each party to secure the best possible bargain, and by many very real practical problems. It was not easy to compare one battle-fleet with another, Britain for instance having many older ships than the Americans. Britain, unlike the United States and Japan, had also to take account of the French and Italian fleets. It was the French strength in submarines, above all, which prevented any limitation to the numbers of cruisers and smaller warships, though some restrictions in tonnage and armament proved possible. But among capital ships it was possible to reach broad agreement on the basis of the following ratios – ten each for Britain and the United States, six for Japan, and three and a half for Italy and France. A ten-year building moratorium (with some small exceptions) was also approved, and limits placed on the tonnage and armament of any ship completed within that period. The ratios were based on the current strength of the battle-fleets of each signatory. Britain had already conceded parity to the American navy in principle. Japan initially tried to argue for a larger ratio, but was finally compensated with a non-fortification agreement covering the western Pacific. This meant in practice that Britain and the United States would possess no major bases nearer than Singapore (which had yet to be developed) and Hawaii. Japan's main islands were thus protected by some 3,000 miles of sea. All the clauses taken together gave Japan very considerable security – and certainly much more than she would have attained had she become involved in a serious arms race with the United States.

The limitation agreements have been criticized for doing too little and too much – the latter on the basis that the British and Americans should never have relaxed their guard against Japan. This argument rests too much on hindsight. Both London and Washington by 1922, given their interests and priorities, had reason to feel some confidence in Japan's future conduct in the Far East. It seemed wise to encourage and strengthen the 'moderates' in Tokyo. Furthermore, it is important to note that in 1921–2 neither the British nor American government was well placed to spend heavily on defence.

America's riches were offset by the popular demand for disarmament, while Theodore Roosevelt had already noted (before the First World War) that Congress was unlikely to vote funds for the development of American bases west of Hawaii – notably in the Philippines. As for greater arms cuts in 1922, these would have demanded more drastic changes in policy than any power was prepared to contemplate in the current circumstances.

The Nine-Power Treaty of 6 February 1922 was a less impressive achievement, yet it developed naturally out of a situation in which the Americans, with the British in tow, were more anxious to elaborate principles on paper than to put physical pressure on the Japanese. The Chinese were indeed allowed to recover the Shantung concessions (though the Japanese remained active in the region), and were given a larger return from their tariffs – though they were not granted tariff autonomy. The nine powers also promised to respect the sovereignty, independence and territorial integrity of China, to facilitate the development of an effective and stable government, to work for equal opportunity for all foreign commerce and investment in China, and to refrain from the pursuit of special privileges detrimental to the rights of the citizens of other states. There was talk of the establishment of a Board of Reference to which appeal could be made against violation of 'Open Door' principles. In fact, observance of the principles continued to rest upon the good faith of the powers, and, as Professor Vinacke has concluded, China gained little from the conference. The advantages, such as they were, were essentially negative mainly 'because she did not lose more than had already been lost, and because the Powers did not take advantage of the internal situation to promote their own interests'.[41] Western governments had already used the international consortium and other instruments to exert influence over the Chinese economy, and any vague British or American interest in a reformed China came to nothing, or was frustrated – for example – by the influence of financial interests such as the House of Morgan which co-operated with British groups to control investment in China to its advantage. American official activity soon died away, and the Foreign Office also despaired of progress. By 1927 the latter was pinning such hopes as it had of stability in China on Chiang Kai-shek, the leader of the increasingly influential Kuomintang party. Chiang, it was believed, might find it in his interest to protect British investments. Morgan, meanwhile, was also co-operating with the Japanese, having large holdings in the South Manchurian Railway – a relationship which continued even after the outbreak of the Sino-Japanese War in 1937.[42]

Overall the Washington treaties can only be regarded as an interim solution. Yet tensions had been lessened by the early months of 1922, and a useful base laid on which others might subsequently have built

– had they chosen and the situation been propitious. British confidence with respect to Japan is reflected in the specific application of the Ten-Year Rule on defence preparations to Japan in 1926–28, the only power which was causing real concern in Asia at this time being Russia, mainly with reference to India.[43] Under the Ten-Year Rule the British armed forces were ordered to plan on the assumption that there would be no war for ten years.

NOTES AND REFERENCES

1. Nelson, p. 51
2. USMI, xxi, 9252–3, 9269, 9287, 9310–12, 9452
3. Néré, p. 12; Hunt and Preston, pp. 48–50
4. FRUS, Paris Peace Conference, i, 285
5. Elcock, p. 20
6. USMI, viii, 1321
7. See Trachtenberg, *passim*, who argues that French policy on reparations became extreme only when all else seemed to have failed, and when France felt badly let down by the Anglo-Saxon powers. See also Silverman, *passim*
8. Watson, pp. 344 ff. See also Stevenson, *passim*
9. Dockrill and Goold, pp. 69 ff.
10. Haupts, *passim*
11. Dockrill and Goold, pp. 57–63
12. Widenor, p. 348, and see generally pp. 336–48
13. Widenor, pp. 222 f., 253 ff., 293 ff., 331–48
14. Nelson, pp. 51–2
15. Leffler, pp. 14–17, 31
16. Ash, p. 254. See also Roskill [1] ii, 70–2, for the inclination of Hankey, Secretary to the Cabinet, to subordinate the question of peace terms with Germany to the containment of Bolshevism early in 1919
17. J. Thompson, p. 223. See also FRUS, Paris Peace Conference, ii, 88 ff.
18. Gilbert [1] iv, 253–4, 277
19. FRUS, Paris Peace Conference, vi, 212; Gilbert [1] iv, 251
20. Elcock, p, 261
21. Watson, pp. 374–9
22. Ullman, iii, 141, 155, 173, etc.
23. USMI, xii, 3456–8; xiv, pp. v–viii, 5085, 5175, 5215, 5271, 5298, etc.
24. Ullman, iii, 203, 211
25. See White, *passim*. French recognition was granted in October 1924, that of the United States not until November 1933
26. Bond [1] pp. 82–4, 103–8, 110–11. On the Soviet Union and Amanullah, see Ullman, iii, 347, and for the Viceroy's views, see iii, 345
27. Ullman, iii, 328–9
28. Ullman, iii, 326 ff., 394 ff., etc.

29. See Hinsley [1] pp. 445 ff.; Kedourie, pp. 97–101, 125–6, 141. Note also for Britain and the Middle East in general the two studies by Briton C. Busch
30. Hogan, pp. 159–83. See also Nelson, pp. 138–40
31. Grant and Temperley, p. 569
32. Darwin [1] p. 679. See also Bond [1] pp. 82–4
33. Egerton, p. 889
34. Dockrill and Goold, pp. 204–5
35. Gilbert [4] p. 103
36. BD, 1st series, iii, 538, 550–1
37. BD, 1st series, iii, 700–32, 735–8
38. USMI, xiv, 5122
39. USMI, xii, 3456–8
40. USMI, xii, 3542–3
41. Vinacke, pp. 427–8. On the Washington Conference in general, see Roskill [2] i, 204 ff., 300 ff.; Vinson, *passim*; Buckley, *passim*
42. Dayer, *passim*
43. Bond [1] p. 82

Chapter 6

FROM THE RUHR
OCCUPATION TO MANCHURIA

EUROPE, 1921–24

George Kennan once remarked that it was in the quieter periods of
international rivalries that the crucial mistakes were made: much less
so in the periods when the options were narrower. In the light of
events from 1931 or 1933 it is tempting to see the 1920s as a time of
missed opportunities when, with more imagination and generosity,
the foundations might have been laid for a lengthy European peace.
Alternatively, one may conclude that it is all too easy to be critical
of the French obsession with security, of the failure of the British
and the Americans to guarantee European frontiers against forcible
(though not negotiated) change, of allied conduct on the question of
reparations, of blinkered American views on war debts and tariffs,
of the errors in economic policy of so many governments which
contributed to the Great Depression, of the mutual distrust which
divided the Soviet Union from most capitalist states, of the usually
fruitless talks on disarmament, and of the limitations of the League
of Nations. For if the period is viewed as contemporaries saw it, at
least from 1924 to 1928, they might be forgiven a modest sense of
achievement. For the time being the critics could be dismissed as
hopeless idealists. It was only with the Depression that affairs
obviously began to get out of hand.

Winston Churchill was on the right lines when, at the Imperial
Conference in July 1921, he declared that if Britain could become the
'Ally of France and the friend of Germany' she would then be able
to 'mitigate the frightful rancour and fear and hatred which exist
between France and Germany'. What was needed was 'an appeasement of the fearful hatreds and antagonisms'.[1] Earlier, on 24 March
1920, he had suggested to Lloyd George that Britain should offer
France a defensive alliance in return for a more conciliatory policy

towards Germany.[2] Put like that it seemed so obvious and simple. And, indeed, very late in the day, the offspring of the Locarno Conference of 1925 may be seen as the sickly, anaemic child of such ideas. Unfortunately much had happened in the interval. The French occupation of the Ruhr in 1923 completed the financial ruin of many Germans, especially among the middle classes. This disaster, preceded by the traumas of 1918–21 and with the Great Depression to come – all crammed into a mere fifteen years – combined to make moderation seem a mockery to Germans who might otherwise have opted less readily for extreme policies. These same events confirmed, and, if that were possible, strengthened the prejudices of the hypernationalists, traditional and radical. The three crises interacted with grievances, ambition and the belief that Germany could yet be strong to make – what still seemed improbable in 1929 – Hitler a front runner for office.

The state of party politics in Britain, France and the United States in the early 1920s did not make for clear, far-sighted policy-making. A Talleyrand would have been hard put to escape from the consequences of political instability in France, and the deep-rooted suspicions of Germany. No British minister from 1918 could hope to possess the relative freedom from domestic influences that Castlereagh enjoyed after the defeat of Napoleon. No country had the resources *and* the will to repeat the British role at Vienna in 1815. Within the United States party dissension had knocked away the first two important props to the postwar structure – American participation in the League and the Anglo-American treaty of guarantee to France. On the question of American inflexibility over war debts, recent studies suggest that successive administrations were as influential as public opinion, if not more so.[3] To Americans a reduction in these debts seemed neither necessary nor desirable. A reduction also implied higher taxation in the United States. Instead successive Republican administrations believed it sufficient to try to encourage the conditions in which private investment from the United States might flourish in Europe. Rapid results were not expected, but there was no great sense of urgency. Given time, the workings of the free market and democratic politics were expected to restore the Atlantic world to some sort of equilibrium. Such thinking was superficial and self-interested. Before the French occupation of the Ruhr in 1923, for instance, American loans to Germany were doing little more than help German governments pursue basically inflationary policies while American financiers put up the money in the hope that the German mark would appreciate! Apart from the economic issues, Americans felt little reason to interest themselves in the affairs of Europe until the French occupation of the Ruhr occasioned a crisis of more than usual importance – with financial implications for Americans.[4]

Given the overall American attitude, the British were unable to make any progress with their suggestions for a reciprocal reduction of war debts among the victors. When the United States continued to insist on payment in full, the British replied that they would collect from their debtors only so much as they needed to satisfy their creditors. The Europeans as a whole argued that the scale of reparation payments must be linked to war debts. Poincaré claimed in 1922 that France was being ruined by the burden of her debts to Britain and the United States, and that only reparations from Germany were keeping the economy afloat. Not only did he find the British and Americans unhelpful on the question of war debts, but unwilling to put pressure on a Germany that was increasingly failing to meet its reparation payments. Historians in recent years have begun to show much more understanding of French policy. It was by no means so consistently narrow-minded or vindictive as has so often been assumed by Anglo-Saxon scholars. If domestic political considerations imposed some constraints, the toughest anti-German policies were adopted only when it appeared that other alternatives had been exhausted. In particular French policy hardened as German industrialists aggressively exploited the advantages to be derived from a depreciating mark in export markets. Germany appeared to be recovering from the war more quickly than France. The Right in Germany seemed as ambitious as ever. Hard-headed Frenchmen appreciated that Germany could not be held down indefinitely, but they hoped for at least a breathing space during which France herself might regain her strength and confidence, and thus be able to face the future with some assurance.[5] Instead the year 1922 was proving one of growing disappointment.

The question of some sort of British guarantee to France had been reopened in January 1922. But British interest was confined to western Europe, and there was the further hope that such an agreement would enable London to seek a settlement with Germany without incurring a French charge of desertion. A new French ministry under Poincaré, however, wanted British support in eastern as well as western Europe. Lloyd George, therefore, concentrated his attention on the forthcoming conference at Genoa where he hoped to achieve a comprehensive European agreement which would embrace even the Soviet Union. His hastily devised plans stood little chance of success in the most favourable circumstances, but with the Americans boycotting Genoa, the French in an uncooperative mood, and the Russians and Germans reaching an understanding of their own at Rapallo the conference was an unqualified failure. Unfortunately, too, every setback of this kind was increasing British prejudice against European entanglements. The Dominions were even more hostile to such imbroglios, and there was no shortage of imperial problems to distract British attention. Lloyd George himself fell from power in October 1922, and his successor, Bonar Law, fought and won an election on the promise of 'tranquillity and freedom from adventures and commitments both at home and abroad'. Britain could not be the world's policeman. In so far as British policy appears dull and unimaginative under the Conservatives compared with the Coalition, it was closely in accord with the mood and resources of the country.

By the end of 1922 Poincaré was dismayed by France's worsening prospects. Germany was falling behind on reparation deliveries. The United States was merely offering to participate in an inquiry into Germany's capacity to pay: no concessions were being offered on war debts. The British would not meet France's demands for 'productive guarantees' from Germany. French experts feared that while the economy of their own country was faltering that of Germany was gaining rapidly in strength. Germany seemed well on the way to economic ascendancy in Europe. It was thus in a mood of desperation that the French began the occupation of the Ruhr on 11 January 1923. The object was to improve French bargaining power not merely with Germany but also with Britain and the United States. The French hoped the Anglo-Saxon powers would intervene in favour of a new, effective reparations agreement, with some increase in international control over Germany. Unfortunately the Anglo-American response was slow in coming. The extent of German passive resistance also took the French by surprise, and Germany persisted in this policy despite the ruinous inflation that followed. The German currency was destroyed. There were also attempts at revolt by the Right and the Communists. German offers from 2 May 1923 to abide by the decision of an expert international commission on their ability to pay met only a blank French insistence that passive resistance must end before talks could begin. By the time of a significant British initiative, on 11 August, German marks were being exchanged at the rate of a million to the pound, with more noughts to follow. The forces of moderation in Germany were gravely injured. Progress was slow even from the end of September 1923 when a new German government under Stresemann abandoned passive resistance. Although the crisis was injuring their own economy, the French continued to take a tough line. Temporarily in the autumn of 1923 they were encouraged by signs of separatism in the Palatinate. Above all Poincaré feared that any relaxation of the pressure would leave France with gains which were apparent rather than real. Only in November 1923 did the French agree to the establishment of an expert committee to inquire into German finances, and other concessions followed slowly in 1924. The situation was perhaps helped by the fall of Poincaré in June 1924, and by the formation earlier in the year in Britain of the first Labour government – under Ramsay MacDonald.

The committee of experts, chaired by the American delegate, General Dawes, provided for a reform of German finances – assisted by a foreign loan. There was some reduction in German reparation payments, but it was hoped that these would now proceed on a regular and assured basis. The Ruhr was evacuated. In September 1924 the British, with French approval, proposed German admission to the League, while in the following month a new German loan was successfully floated, mostly with American money. The United States also joined the Reparations Commission. This reduced the likelihood of any further unilateral moves by France. Nevertheless many fundamental economic problems remained. American loans were to a great extent merely postponing the day of reckoning. They were sustaining German reparations, European purchases from America, and helping to ease the payment of war debts. But they were not providing a long-term solution to European indebtedness to the United States, partly because of the uses to which they were being put in Europe, and partly because American tariffs were proving such formidable obstacles to European exporters. It was only in the context of a Second World War and the onset of the Cold War that radical innovations, which reached their climax in Marshall Aid and the European Recovery Programme, began to make for a healthier economic relationship between Europe and America, and indeed within western Europe itself.

But in the period 1924–29 the illusion existed that current policies offered some hope for the future. American governments in particular believed that, within the limited guidelines they provided, responsible private enterprise would flourish, and that Europe would gradually find peace and stability. Franco-German differences would be resolved, and Bolshevism contained. Hoover, as President from 1929, was particularly anxious to use economic influence to promote disarmament. In practice even the short-term results were disappointing. The British, for instance, believed that their efforts to create an economic *entente* with the Americans from 1923 had not been adequately rewarded. There were differences even on the question of disarmament, despite the progress made at the Washington Conference in 1921–22. The British believed that they had conceded enough in practice and in principle to meet the American desire for naval parity with Britain, only to find in 1927 at the Geneva Naval Conference that their peculiar requirements as an imperial and maritime nation for a large number of light cruisers were not being sympathetically received by the Americans. In general there were times in the 1920s when the British – and other Europeans – were troubled not so much by American isolationism as by the selective interventionism practised by the great power across the Atlantic.

THE ERA OF LOCARNO

The mid-1920s found the European states trying by various methods to increase their security. A small trading state with little to fear from invasion reacted very differently from one which saw itself as a probable battleground. The Scandinavian peoples, the Dutch and Swiss were particularly interested in disarmament. In eastern Europe there was much reliance on alliances of the traditional kind, with several of these states having ties with France for protection against Germany. The British found themselves pulled in different directions on questions of collective security and disarmament. Both had attractions in the abstract: both could have unwelcome consequences. Obligations under the League had to be weighed against the fact that as a world power Britain might find herself called upon to act almost anywhere. Indeed, enforcement of League sanctions against an 'aggressor state' might lead Britain into conflict with the United States, a non-League state, over neutral rights – America might try to break a blockade imposed by the Royal Navy. Disarmament had many attractions, but not if it increased British insecurity at sea, or threatened to interfere with the maintenance of order within or on the borders of the empire. As for collective security, especially with reference to Europe, the attitudes of the British public could not be predicted over a long period, while among the policy-makers themselves and the main political parties there were many shades of opinion – all of which, moreover, stopped short of interest in major commitments in Europe.

Two attempts to strengthen international security in 1924 both misfired. It seems likely that even if Britain had agreed to the Geneva Protocol the French would have sought other guarantees to protect their position.[6] Yet action of some kind was desirable. Austen Chamberlain as British Foreign Secretary from 1924 feared that unless the French were reassured in some way they might, in some future state of desperation, create the conditions for a new war. There could be no stability in Europe until France felt secure and until Germany was convinced that 'she cannot hope to divide the Allies or to challenge them with any hope of success for as long a time as any man can look ahead'.[7] But Chamberlain had difficulties in the Cabinet. Churchill, for instance, now believed that France would be more restrained in her conduct if she had no agreement with Britain. These divisions finally made the Cabinet receptive to a new idea. In January 1925 Stresemann had begun to press for a mutual security pact which would embrace all the western powers. By such means he hoped to head off a separate Anglo-French agreement, and enhance the prestige of the German government at home and abroad. Gradually Chamberlain began to respond so that by the end of March he had the outline of an agreement with which he hoped to reassure France, deter and conciliate Germany, separate Germany from Russia, and yet still meet the requirement of the Cabinet that there should be no onerous British commitments in Europe.[8]

The negotiations were complicated, and were prolonged in particular by the problems presented by eastern Europe. Germany was willing to guarantee the frontiers of France and Belguim, but did not want to bind her hands in the east. Nor were the British prepared to enter into commitments in eastern Europe. Yet France was determined to uphold Poland and Czechoslovakia. The French foresaw that an agreement applying to western Europe alone would leave Germany free to strike in the east. Unless Germany herself violated the western treaty, France would be placed in the invidious position of violating the treaty herself, or waiting for a League condemnation of Germany to free her from its restrictions. The problem remained even after France was allowed to reaffirm her eastern treaties, while Germany concluded arbitration treaties with her eastern neighbours. The aim behind the Locarno treaties of 1 December 1925, however, was to build international confidence, to encourage restraint and co-operation. The eastern problem, it was hoped, would be resolved by never allowing it to develop into a crisis. Much of the rhetoric which accompanied the Locarno Conference and its aftermath can now be seen in all its emptiness, yet at the time there was a case for exaggeration in the hope that opinion in all the main countries would begin to translate the appearance of harmony into something more substantial.

Clearly Locarno was only a hesitant step toward a more stable Europe – more fragile at its inception perhaps than the Washington treaties. Thus the British ambassador in Berlin feared that German extremists might assassinate Stresemann in protest at his collaboration with the western powers. In the Reichtag Communists and many on the Right opposed both Locarno and the plans for Germany to join the League. General von Seeckt, head of the German army, spoke privately of the recovery of the frontiers of 1914 by force. Stresemann himself argued that he had merely given up the unattainable, and hoped that his policy would lead to the early allied evacuation of the Rhineland, a favourable settlement of the Polish Corridor and the future of Danzig, and the return of some former German colonies as mandates.[9] More immediately he was able to exploit Soviet fears of a pro-western orientation by Germany and the formation of a grand European anti-communist coalition in order to continue Russo-German military contacts and to negotiate the Treaty of Berlin with the Russians on 24 April 1926. On the other hand, given Germany's geographical and disarmed condition, Stresemann was able to insist to London and Paris that Germany could not support any League action against Soviet 'aggression'. The French, too, were exploring their various options, and made approaches of their own to the Russians to try to limit German influence in the east. The grant to Germany – albeit only after some difficulty – of a permanent seat on the League Council was a slightly more hopeful step. Between 1926 and 1929 there were also the so-called 'Geneva tea-parties' at which Stresemann, Briand and Chamberlain met informally to exchange opinions. Even these prompted some contemporary criticism – they smacked of old-fashioned secret diplomacy. But as Jon Jacobson has demonstrated, the Locarno period represented no more than a period of limited *détente* in European politics during which the aims of the three main participants remained basically unchanged – for France, security; for Germany, revision; for Britain, peace and stability in Europe at the lowest cost to herself. It was the methods which changed, with France recognizing that the punitive approach of 1923 had on the whole been counter-productive. Thus even the allied supervision of the state of German armaments became increasingly perfunctory.

Locarno was followed by a few years of precarious prosperity in Germany. Tax cuts helped to diminish criticism from Right-wing nationalists. But revisionism was still strong, and Stresemann himself wrote to a friend in 1927: 'But I lack the material power of an army, and this, in the nature of things, despite all the pacific assurances of the peoples of the world, still remains the really decisive factor ...'[10] The German frontier with Poland was the greatest single source of revisionist complaint in the medium term, with reparations and the allied occupation of the Rhineland as the most immediate problems. The French generals were the main impediment to an early evacuation of the Rhineland, their aim being to retain a foothold there until the completion of the Maginot Line on the Franco-German frontier. It seemed improbable, however, that Germany would pose a military threat to France before the end of the 1930s, or until some time after the completion of the French defences. Thus Briand, for one, appeared more interested in assuring France of British support in a crisis than in clinging to military gages of dubious value. But he could not prevail against the French generals. A possible chance to ease Franco-German relations as early as 1927 was thus missed. This was the story of the Locarno years. The Germans appeared impatient, demanding and perhaps insatiable. Austen Chamberlain thought them 'a very disagreeable people': Stresemann, he complained, was lacking in the true spirit of give and take. Briand meanwhile made conciliatory noises, and played with a number of ideas. But his hands were usually tied by French opinion. On the British side Chamberlain seemed something of a spent force after Locarno. Admittedly he could do little without French and German co-operation: he was hampered also by British complacency. It is true that the British were distracted in 1927 by difficulties with the Soviet

Union, the United States (over naval questions) and the Kuomintang in China. But there existed in addition the widespread feeling that British policy under Chamberlain was too pro-French. Anglo-French negotiations on defence questions in 1928 strongly confirmed this belief, with the British seemingly favouring the French requirement for a large reserve of troops against Germany while the French sympathized with British cruiser needs against American objections.

Despite the fact that Britain broke off relations with Russia in May 1927, and Chamberlain once described the western powers as battling with the Soviet Union for the 'soul of Germany', Russia and Communism did not loom large enough in the calculations of the western leaders to bring about a radical alteration in policy towards Germany. Meanwhile the German elections of May 1928, although they strengthened the Social Democrats, so complicated the party balance that a 'cabinet of personalities' had to be formed under a Social Democrat, Hermann Müller. The continuing militancy of the Right made this government only too anxious to secure a success of some kind in its foreign policy. An early evacuation of the Rhineland was the obvious target, and the Germans now found the French not unresponsive provided they were given satisfaction on the still troublesome question of reparations. The British made more difficulties, as they did not want reparations to be considered in isolation from war debts. Nevertheless another committee of experts was finally assembled to try to establish what Germany could reasonably afford to pay. Again there was American participation, though with Washington insisting that the American representatives were not 'officially appointed'.

The Young committee, named after its American chairman, had no easy task. It was near failure in April 1929. This so alarmed Germany's foreign creditors that they began to reduce their holdings. The German government, though risking political defeat and disorder in the streets if it accepted the new terms, was driven to make concessions. The alternatives were heavier taxes, a further decline in its credit-worthiness abroad, a worsening recession and yet more internal unrest. The Young plan at least offered a reduction in reparation payments in the short term and the prospect of more foreign loans. Unfortunately American private capital was already being diverted to the fatal speculative boom on Wall Street. When the Great Crash occurred in the United States in October 1929 the movement of funds to Europe ended completely. Even before the Crash German unemployment had risen to 1.75 million, and there were many other unhealthy economic symptoms. Money was dear, the government was borrowing heavily, wages for those in work were high. The Social Democrats, fearful of electoral losses to the Communists, opposed the orthodox solution of government retrenchment. The Müller government was paralysed, though its collapse was delayed until March 1930. The fact that it finally secured ratification of the Young plan was meaningless. The plan became the subject of a furious debate inside Germany. In a national referendum over ratification of the Young plan, 14 per cent (6 million) voted against acceptance. Not surprisingly the Brüning ministry, which followed Müller in office, decided that foreign policy successes were vital if it was to boost its authority at home. Revisionist stances were adopted towards both the Young plan and the Versailles treaty. Even so by September 1930 the extreme nationalists had secured about one-quarter of the seats in the Reichstag.

From 1929 it was not so much that western leaders suddenly shrank in political stature to the height of pygmies but that the problems caused or aggravated by the Great Depression began to assume unprecedented and incomprehensible proportions. Agreement that the Rhineland should be evacuated not later than June 1930 and hints that the Polish – German frontier might be renegotiated at some time in the future failed to arrest the slide.[11] In March 1931 the Brüning ministry tried to negotiate a customs union with Austria, a move prompted by both political and economic considerations. Paris was hostile, and was in a position to call the tune, at least to the extent of preventing the customs union, given the financial weakness of Germany and Austria. But all this was achieved only at the cost of additional economic damage in central Europe, and at a time when the British economy was running into serious difficulties. On 20 June 1931, in the face of Europe's mounting difficulties, President Hoover proposed a one-year moratorium on all inter-governmental debts. The French refused unless they were promised some compensation over the matter of reparations. Germany was in dire need of fresh loans, but could not accept the French counter-demand that she drop the question of treaty revision until the money was repaid. Not surprisingly in these circumstances, the Nazis began to attract a vast following. Britain herself experienced a major financial crisis in the summer of 1931 which brought down the Labour government. Only a slow economic recovery was possible under a coalition ministry.

The situation in Germany, however, went from bad to worse. In 1932 both the British and French might have been prepared to write off most of their remaining reparation claims (although Washington was uncooperative on the question of war debts). But neither London nor Paris was prepared to concede the German claim for parity in armaments. Hitler came to power in January 1933, and while the Nazi triumph did not go unremarked in Britain,[12] it was not immediately apparent that his foreign policy would be very different from that of his immediate predecessors. The state of the German economy in 1933 encouraged comfortable illusions as to the future. In addition there were many other problems, both at home and abroad, to absorb the attention of the other powers. When Ramsay

MacDonald complained at the end of 1932: 'There is no doubt a great deterioration in the disarmament position . . .' he was thinking not only·of the aspirations of Germany, but also of the deadlock between France and Italy over the latter's claim to naval parity.[13] More ominous still was the sequence of crises between China and Japan in the Far East. Japan was clearly becoming dissatisfied with the naval ratio allowed her at the London Naval Conference in 1930. It was in March 1932, mainly with the Far East in mind, that the Committee of Imperial Defence accepted the recommendation of the British Chiefs of Staff that some of the restraints on defence spending should be lifted. When the first steps were taken from November 1933 to make good some of the deficiencies in Britain's armed forces which had been developing since the 1920s, priority was initially given to the Far East.[14] Japan similarly commanded the most attention among Russian military planners, and in the United States navy.

THE FAR EAST, 1922–31

It has often been said that the first shots of the Second World War were fired in Manchuria in 1931. From this date the hopes which had been placed in the League of Nations and collective security, such instruments as the Kellogg – Briand Peace Pact, and in disarmament began to recede. To the experts, of course, the League had always been less than the sum of its parts. Of the states with military and economic power, or potential, in the Far East, the Soviet Union and the United States were not members of the League. Indeed, in the event of Russian and American neutrality in any hypothetical crisis in the Far East, it is difficult, if not impossible, to see how the League could have mustered a force sufficient to impress or deter Japan. Britain was too weak by herself: France and the Netherlands possessed some forces in south-east Asia, but all these in combination represented no threat to Japan in the north-west Pacific. In the case of Manchuria in 1931, Russia alone of the great powers was directly interested, and she was too preoccupied with domestic problems to act. Furthermore, some historians have begun to change the character of the debate by arguing that events in Manchuria and China should be seen not as a life and death issue for the League but as a continuation of the small wars of the nineteenth century; that while ultimately the Sino-Japanese conflict became an essential part of the global power struggle which reached its climax in 1941–45, in its initial stage it was of only local significance.

The Washington settlement of 1921–22 had worked fairly well in the 1920s, and superficially it appeared to be reaffirmed and even extended at the London Naval Conference in 1930. From 1921 the majority of the Japanese ruling élite, with varying degrees of enthusiasm, had attempted to work broadly within Anglo-Saxon conceptions of world order.[15] Japan, the land of the rising sun, was highly sensitive to the policies of other rising or ascendant powers. In the 1920s many Japanese were greatly impressed by all things American – much to the disgust of some British diplomats. It is true that American racial policies, restrictive tariffs and continuing jealousy of Japanese naval power also caused much ill-feeling, and played into the hands of anti-western groups in Japan. There were many who burned to pursue more active and what were said to be more truly Japanese policies. Such groups saw Baron Shidehara, ambassador to Washington in 1919–22, and Foreign Minister for five of the seven years between 1924 and 1931, as the personification of the 'weak-kneed' school with its emphasis upon internationalism, commerce and peaceful expansion. Shidehara, in fact, was no less ambitious for his country's welfare and strength than his critics, but he was more sensitive to the ways of the outside world. He spoke excellent English, was popular with foreigners, whereas in Japan he was seen as a loner, a man of independent outlook who did not suffer fools gladly. He claimed that foreign policy should be a non-party matter. Significant, too, was his marriage into a family which formed part of the Mitsubishi business complex, one of the four great family holding companies (the *zaibatsu*) which prospered in the 1920s when many lesser Japanese firms failed. The Mitsubishi with their wide foreign interests believed that conciliatory policies towards the other great trading powers – and indeed towards China – best served their needs. In the early 1930s they were among the sharpest critics of those who thought that something approaching an autarkic Japanese empire or regional bloc could be created. If their arguments were self-interested, they nevertheless offered a not implausible interpretation of Japan's place in the world economy – at least in the conditions which prevailed down to 1929.

Shidehara shared the widespread fears in Japan of overpopulation, food shortage, unemployment and popular unrest. But he believed that the course of events since 1914 had demonstrated that territorial expansion was not the answer: it could be counter-productive with the growth of Chinese nationalism when even trade boycotts were important weapons. Difficulties with China could also complicate relations with the Anglo-Saxons. He therefore favoured the political conciliation of the Chinese as far as possible, coupled with an aggressive search for markets in general. In the 1920s about a quarter of Japan's exports went to China. Thus, while Shidehara was anxious to preserve Japan's special position in southern Manchuria, its importance had always to be weighed in relation to Japan's trade with China. Hence he disliked the intrigues of the Japanese military in

Manchuria, and the threat which these posed to good relations with China.

But Shidehara's policies were menaced by Chinese as well as by Japanese nationalists. Sun Yat-sen's Kuomintang, with Soviet help and advice, was steadily gaining ground in China. By 1926, the Kuomintang, now under the leadership of General Chiang Kai-shek, was strong enough to turn on the native Chinese Communist Party. Even the formidable Manchurian warlord, Chang Tso-lin, began to pay his respects to the new central government. For the first time since 1894 it did not seem fanciful to anticipate the re-emergence of China as a reasonably unified and potentially important state. Inevitably, as Chinese confidence grew, incidents multiplied with the imperial powers as the latter tried to cling to their privileged positions. The Kuomintang captured Peiping (Peking) in June 1928, and finally obtained international recognition as the government of China. But continuing rivalries within the party, and the strong anti-foreign feeling that existed among the Chinese masses, at least in coastal regions, forced Chiang to take a tougher line in negotiations with the powers than he might have chosen for himself. A number of incidents occurred in the treaty ports affecting the British in particular. This helps to explain why so many Britons in China sympathized with the Japanese in 1931. When, in 1929, the Soviet Union frustrated an attempt by Chang Tso-lin's son and successor, the 'young Marshal', to seize control of the Chinese Eastern Railway, this successful exercise of military muscle was watched with some envy by the British ambassador in China. He was saddened by Britain's reluctance or failure to act in the same decisive manner.

In fact both the British and American governments were prepared to make concessions to the Chinese, but they clearly expected there to be a long period of adjustment before all the unequal treaties were scrapped. For the Japanese the problem was more acute, given their interest in Manchuria, and their greater dependence on trade with China. In practice neither the conciliatory policy of Shidehara nor the rather tougher methods employed by Tanaka in 1927–29 provided an answer. Tanaka was a less experienced and subtle international politician than Shidehara: he was more inclined to dig in his heels, and call up troops and gunboats. He differed, too, in being so vehemently anti-communist. Shidehara had worked for increased trade with Russia, and had been anxious to prevent the creation of a firm alignment between Russia and the Kuomintang against Japan. The Tanaka ministry followed his conciliatory line towards the Anglo-Saxons, but in China it clumsily and rather ineffectively tried to limit the Kuomintang advance. Japan's trade with central China suffered, and Japan displaced Britain as the main focus of Chinese resentment. Matters were made worse in June 1928 by the assassination of the Manchurian warlord, Chang Tso-lin. This was the work of a Japanese colonel in the Kwantung army in southern Manchuria – a foretaste of much more serious independent action by the military. Although Japanese troops prevailed in a clash in Shantung, a Chinese trade boycott forced Tanaka to adopt a more conciliatory line shortly before he fell from office in July 1929. He had become the object of both military and business criticism – by the former for inconsistency, by the latter for provoking the Chinese without advantage to Japan. Shidehara, however, fared no better on his return to office as incidents multiplied on the mainland, and, worst of all, the Kuomintang proceeded with its ambitious plan to build a rival line to the Japanese-controlled South Manchurian Railway.

This possibility of a more united and formidable China was but one of the developments of the later 1920s which were causing the Japanese service chiefs to challenge the defence policy that had been followed from 1921–22. The army had lost 20 per cent of its manpower, and the provision for the remaining seventeen divisions had not been generous. The Soviet recovery of the Chinese Eastern Railway, and the proclaimed intention of the first Five Year Plan to treble production in certain key industries by 1933 persuaded many Japanese that they would soon have to take Russia seriously as a major power in the Far East. Japan should look to her security on the mainland. The admirals were also restless. The restraints imposed upon the Japanese navy by the Washington and London treaties were widely criticized. The capabilities of the latest aircraft carriers and heavy cruisers, it was argued, were extending the operational range of modern fleets, and therefore undermining those provisions of Washington which had been included to persuade Japan that the 5 : 5 : 3 ratios were not incompatible with her security. American experts agreed that an American navy at full treaty strength would be able to operate west of Hawaii. A major attempt was made at the London Naval Conference to resolve a triangular dispute between Britain, Japan and the United States over heavy cruiser construction. The Japanese Cabinet, anxious to save money and to avoid a crisis with the Anglo-Saxon powers, was not dissatisfied when, after much hard bargaining, the Americans agreed to relax the 5 : 3 ratio in cruisers a little in favour of Japan until the projected naval conference in 1936. This decision, however, was bitterly condemned by most Japanese naval officers, and they received strong support from radical and traditional nationalist groups.

The Japanese Cabinet did not enjoy the same powers and authority as that in Britain. It needed, for instance, the support of the Privy Council which was made up of a variety of court officials and advisers. The Meiji Constitution itself had become a subject of debate at this time, with some civilians disputing the claim of the two service ministers and chiefs of staff that they alone should advise the Emperor on defence questions. The distinguished authority on the constitution, Professor Minobe, and others argued that the strength of the two services could be settled by the Cabinet – that military advice was not necessarily binding. In practice, whatever the theoreticians might argue, the Cabinet could not govern without support from other key institutions of state, and the London naval treaty in particular was only approved after difficult and complex negotiations within the ruling élite of which the members of the Cabinet formed only a part.[16] It was soon clear that the Cabinet had won a pyrrhic victory. The services were determined to increase their influence within the government. The Seiyukai, the opposition party in the Diet, did its best to exploit the embarrassment of its rival in power. Extreme nationalist agitators of all kinds were becoming increasingly active. The authority of the Cabinet was in decline.

The Minseito ministry was also being undermined by the disastrous impact of the Great Depression on the Japanese economy. The collapse of the silk market in the United States was merely the most far-reaching of many damaging blows – the value of Japanese raw silk exports was halved in 1930. In this instance, with nearly half the farming population engaged in silk production (a secondary occupation which saved many farmers from acute distress or ruin), the effects can easily be imagined. Northern Japan suffered most severely (in 1932 this was followed by a rice famine). The army drew many of its recruits from this region, while a large proportion of the junior and middle-rank officers came from the smaller landowning families. An acute awareness of the suffering of their friends and relations intensified the zeal of those who were already hostile to the two main political parties whose policies, even before the Depression, had worked mainly for the benefit of big business. The parties were readily seen as agents of the rich, and as unpatriotic, given the pro-western leanings in their foreign policies. By 1930 they were widely denounced as obstacles to Japan's advance to greater power and prosperity, and as enemies of justice and fair dealing at home. Many smaller businessmen shared these beliefs. The 1920s had not been a happy time for them. The war boom had collapsed in March 1920. An overvalued currency held back exports in the 1920s. They were badly hit by the banking crisis of 1927. Both before and during the Depression the government pursued orthodox deflationary policies which hit the weaker sectors of the economy, as well as hampering the creation of employment for a labour force which was growing at the rate of about half a million a year. In response to the Depression civil service salaries were cut, and the armed forces feared that the government would look for more economies at their expense. Throughout 1930–31 the government pursued policies which hastened the drain on the nation's gold reserves, and which appeared open to the charge that they were designed to protect the *zaibatsu* and reassure the Anglo-Saxon powers, rather than protect the Japanese masses.

Thus the Minseito government would have been vulnerable in 1930–31 even if there had been a long history of party rule in Japan. But political parties were recent, fragile, superficial growths. Despite the grant of universal male suffrage in 1925, police powers against Left-wing movements had been strengthened, while the electorate continued to be largely manipulated by local community leaders and officials. Parties secured office first and were then well placed to organize electoral support. The parties were largely made up of factions based on personal loyalties: 'pork barrel' methods were used to build up followings. They thus had no real roots among the people. But during the 1920s many of the ruling élite had seen the parties as a most useful tool with which to control popular forces, especially when the electorate was widened to try to lessen popular discontents. By 1931, however, the system was under such strain as to encourage interest in new approaches to government. Party government encountered growing opposition in the bureaucracy as well as in the armed forces. There were both traditionalist and radical critics of party influence, and while the opposition groups were hopelessly divided their attitudes and actions (from non-co-operation through thoughts of a military coup to the assassination attempts of the secret societies) were steadily undermining the Minseito Cabinet despite its appearance of success in a recent election.

The Prime Minister, Hamaguchi, was shot and seriously injured in November 1930 by a Right-wing patriot. A conspiracy to over-throw the government in 1931, the so-called March Incident, was stopped by General Ugaki, the War Minister, whom the plotters had hoped to set up as the leader of a military government. But Ugaki's political stance remained highly ambiguous, and there were many like him. Shidehara's policies were not fully supported even by his own ministry. The weakness and isolation of the Minseito Cabinet was increasingly evident. Of an episode before the Mukden Incident the British ambassador reported that 'the fat was in the fire, leaving the Shidehara policy very near to melting point'. After the start of operations in Manchuria he noted the breadth of popular support for the army.[17] Even the Social Democrats were in favour, and spoke of the creation of a socialist Manchuria. Certainly many of the younger officers in the Kwantung army hoped to launch social and economic experiments in Manchuria free from the influence of Japanese big business as well as the party politicians. Business attitudes on Manchuria varied, with the Mitsubishi organization, for instance, sharing the views of Shidehara on Japan's place in the world economy. Another of the big four, Mitsui, with larger interests in Manchuria, was torn between hope and fear. In the past it had preferred the softer approaches where possible, and had been dismayed by the assassination of Chang Tso-lin. Where it shared common interests with the army, such as the future of the South Manchurian Railway, it also recognized that the army's priorities might differ.[18] By and large it was the smaller and newer business concerns which favoured the more aggressive policies.

The originators of the Manchurian crisis in September 1931 were the Kwantung army with the broad, though not unqualified, support of the General Staff in Tokyo. The Cabinet itself had heard that direct action of some kind was impending, but had been unable to restrain the army. The Kwantung forces used the Mukden Incident to seize the whole of southern Manchuria, their colleagues in Korea promptly sent reinforcements, while the General Staff in Tokyo looked on with a mixture of approval and apprehension. They feared that the over-confident troops on the mainland might precipitate some more general crisis for which the nation was not prepared. The Kwantung army moved into northern Manchuria later in the year, again on its own initiative, but its boldness was vindicated when the local Soviet forces meekly withdrew. Meanwhile the Minseito Cabinet strove to reassert some control over the army, to win support at home and at the same time reassure the other powers concerning the limited nature of Japan's ambitions. It was a vain struggle. There were divisions within the Cabinet. Britain's departure from the Gold Standard in September 1931 fortified those who were arguing that the international economic system of the 1920s had been totally discredited. At the end of November 1931 there occurred a breakdown in Shidehara's talks with the Chinese. The resignation of a civilian minister in December brought down the ministry.

JAPAN, CHINA AND THE POWERS, 1931–33

The fall of the Minseito ministry had already been preceded by suggestions that a coalition government was needed to handle the current crises. But the process of selecting a new Prime Minister centred on the last of the Elder Statesmen, Saionji, and he finally chose a moderate figure, Inukai, from the opposition Seiyukai party. His ministry duly won an election in February 1932. Inukai tried to negotiate with the Chinese, and for a time was able to frustrate the army's wish to turn Manchuria into an independent state. Inukai was prepared to leave China with a vestige of sovereignty. But his slim chances of success were already being wrecked by a new incident with China, this time at Shanghai. His own party was divided, and many people were in the grip of fervent nationalist emotions, even hysteria.

The secret societies remained active, and those terrorists which were seized received light sentences. Finally in the middle of May 1932 Inukai himself fell victim to one of these murderous gangs. His death meant the end of party government until Japan's defeat in 1945. Yet Saionji even then, in his search for a new premier, was not merely responding to terrorist threats or to pressure from the army with its refusal to provide a Minister of War for a party government. The weaknesses and demoralization of the parties ruled them out in any case, and among the ruling groups in general it was strongly held that some sort of 'all nation' government was necessary. Saionji's choice of Admiral Saito to lead such a ministry was based on the assumption that once the extremists had been brought under control and the worst of the foreign and economic problems overcome the parties would once again emerge as a force in government.[19] The new ministers were mostly cautious, realistic men, strongly representative of the bureaucracy as well as the armed forces. The autonomy of the individual ministries was very marked – more so than usual in Japan – and this was to complicate policy-making in the future. Untidy and unsatisfactory compromises became even more the order of the day, with damaging consequences, especially in all that related to the conduct of foreign policy.[20]

The army itself had acted in Manchuria from a mixture of motives. Where radical officers were often as anxious to challenge the existing order in Japan, especially the power of big business, as to ward off the danger from China, for other officers the main considerations were emphatically strategic. They were impressed by the contribution of economic warfare to Germany's defeat in 1918: Japan, they argued, must have ample raw materials under its control. They were moving towards the idea of a national defence state – Manchuria was only one small step to that end.[21] As one of the Kwantung army conspirators agreed, Manchuria was of limited economic value but it was a 'vital base'. This still left open the question as to how far Japan should prepare herself militarily against China or Russia – or both. As it happened, Russia's failure to defend northern Manchuria when the Kwantung army acted, and the offer of a non-aggression pact in December 1931 encouraged the idea that at least a temporary accommodation with the Russians might be possible. The expansionists in Tokyo were fully alive to the importance of not provoking other powers unnecessarily, a point not wholly overlooked by some of the leading figures in the Kwantung army. Although Japanese interest in a Far Eastern equivalent of the American Monroe Doctrine was growing, some still hoped for British and French co-operation against the Chinese nationalists, and their appreciation of Japan's role as the eastern bulwark against communism. Foreign capital would still be welcome in Manchuria, though under Japanese direction and control. But there was also a tendency to underestimate the United States, and to hope that the Depression would result in a lengthy American preoccupation with domestic affairs. Certainly the Japanese admirals hoped that the Depression would discourage the American administration from attempting to compete with their own planned expansion of the Japanese navy.[22] A final restraint on the United States might be the fact that its trade with Japan was far more important than its trade with China.

Nor were Japanese hopes in such matters entirely without foundation. Initially both the British and Americans believed that Manchuria would be a passing crisis. They had little interest in the region. Many felt that the Kuomintang had been guilty of much provocation, that Japan was needed as a barrier against communism in general, and against anarchy in Manchuria in particular. Secretary of State Stimson was almost alone among Americans in arguing that something other than a little tepid moralizing was called for when the Japanese upset the status quo in Manchuria. He frankly accepted that the United States might well find itself acting in parts of Latin America much as Japan was acting in the Far East, but he became increasingly insistent from mid-November 1931 that America should not forfeit its position as a power in the western Pacific or in the minds of the Chinese people.[23] In official British circles the tendency was to criticize Japanese methods rather than their aims. The Foreign Office in the winter of 1931–32 concluded that Britain was more interested in Japanese friendship than the maintenance of the status quo in Manchuria. Japan was valued as a stabilizing influence in the Far East against both Russia and China. More development was likely in Manchuria under her rule than if China took over. *The Times* took the view that China was not a genuine sovereign state.[24]

This complacency was shaken a little by the outbreak of fighting between the Japanese and Chinese in Shanghai in January 1932. Again the Japanese government was not the originator of the incident, but in time it felt obliged to intervene and send reinforcements so as not to lose face in China. The British and Americans also possessed sufficient economic interests in Shanghai to decide on a naval demonstration. About three-quarters of Britain's investments in China were concentrated in Shanghai. Apart from this, the Foreign Office feared that without a stand of some kind Britain would lose face in China and Japan, and furthermore that her credibility as an imperial power would be injured elsewhere.[25] At the same time it dreaded the consequences of a full-scale crisis with Japan. As early as 1924 Admiral Beatty had warned that, in the absence of an American fleet in the western Pacific, Britain kept her position in the Far East only on 'the sufferance of another power', Japan. On 1 February 1932 Sir Robert Vansittart, the Permanent Under-Secretary in the Foreign Office, drew a bleak picture of Britain's position[26]

. . . *We* are incapable of checking Japan in any way if she really means business . . . .

(3) Therefore we must eventually be done for in the Far East, unless

(4) The United States are eventually prepared to use force.

(5) It is universally assumed here that the United States will never use force.

(6) I do not agree that this is necessarily so. . . . The Japanese may end by kicking in the U.S. . . . if they go on long enough kicking as they are now . . .

(8) By ourselves we must eventually swallow any and every humiliation in the Far East. If there is some limit to American submissiveness, this is not necessarily so.

Baldwin, the key minister in MacDonald's Cabinet, said much the same at the end of February. Sanctions, he argued, could easily lead to war, especially when neither Russia nor America was a member of the League. 'If you enforce an economic boycott you'll have war declared by Japan and she will seize Singapore and Hong Kong, and we can't, as we are placed, stop her. You'll get nothing out of Washington but words, big words, but only words.'[27] The Chiefs of Staff on 3 March 1932 were equally pessimistic. They could not guarantee the arrival of an adequate battle-fleet in the Far East before Japan's seizure of Britain's chief bases. The Dominions could offer little help. In general British interests did not seem commensurate with the risks involved. China absorbed only about $2\frac{1}{2}$ per cent of Britain's exports and 5 per cent of her foreign investment. British businessmen in China frequently sympathized with the Japanese rather than the Chinese in view of the treatment they had often received from the latter. As for the Foreign Office, it remained torn between the fear that any show of British weakness against Japan might encourage anti-British forces elsewhere in the world, and dismay over the consequences if its policy should provoke the Japanese.[28]

All American overtures in 1932, whether over non-recognition of Japanese action in Manchuria or indeed over Shanghai, were treated with great caution lest, as Sir John Simon put it, Washington continued to sit in the stalls and ask the Christians to attack the lions.[29] The British responses were not wholly negative, but London took its time, and correctly gauged the limits of Stimson's influence in Washington. In any case the Shanghai Incident was soon closed, once the Japanese had demonstrated their power. Over Manchuria the Americans were not prepared to go beyond non-recognition. The British thought it wiser on the whole to work through the League, the hope being both that the position of the League would not be injured by the crisis, and that the two sides might find in the League a means of resolving their differences without any loss of face. In the last resort there was a tendency in both the British and American diplomatic communities to look to the sheer size of China, its embryonic nationalism, and to the damage which the Japanese economy would suffer as a result of a disruption of its trade with China to preserve some sort of balance in the Far East. Nevertheless it is worthy of note, in passing, that the American services calculated that with their current level of armaments it would take the United States up to four years to win a war against Japan: in alliance with Britain victory might be secured in two. Even the American navy was below the strength allowed by the treaties of Washington and London. But these were no more than academic assessments, and Stimson was left by his government – and public opinion – with no more than the rhetorical shadow of the policing role to which he aspired for the United States in the east.[30]

The British, meantime, were content with the resolutions of the League of 16 February and 11 March 1932 that members should not recognize changes in territorial status brought about by means contrary to the Covenant and the Kellogg – Briand Pact. The Lytton Commission was set up to inquire into the affair in the hope that some sort of compromise could be devised. Unfortunately attitudes were rapidly hardening in Japan. Western moralizing fuelled the xenophobia of the extremists and embarrassed the moderates. There was an increasing sense of isolation, which played into the hands of those who argued in favour of larger armed forces and a more active foreign policy. Japan, they declared, must become the leader of the East against the imperialist West. The romantic and fanciful ideas of writers such as Kita Ikki, with his *Plan for the Reorganization of Japan* of 1923, began to take on a more substantial form in the hands of certain bureaucrats and military personnel. The new Saito ministry, although in August 1932 it acknowledged the need to pay attention to the views of other powers, put the case for increased armaments. It spoke of increased trade with China, but also of keeping the peace in key Chinese markets and opening up others as necessary. Already there was talk of Japan leaving the League of Nations if this proved an obstacle to her ambitions. In September 1932 the Saito ministry recognized the so-called state of Manchukuo, a Japanese puppet regime already having been established in Manchuria by the Kwantung army. The Lytton Commission therefore reported vainly in October 1932 in favour of Manchurian autonomy under Chinese sovereignty. This effort to satisfy both sides was approved by a special assembly of the League early in 1933, only to be followed by Japan's resignation from the League on 27 March. Even as diplomacy floundered the Japanese army was pushing into Jehol, a mountainous area north of the Great Wall deemed vital for the security of Manchukuo. Chinese forces were soon being pursued close to Peking despite the desire of the Japanese government to avoid unnecessary escalation. A truce was negotiated with the

Chinese (Nanking) government on 31 May, and Japan secured a demilitarized zone south of the Great Wall to protect its position in Jehol.

If the Japanese army was still very much the pace-maker in these latest advances, the government following at its heels was undoubtedly encouraged by the lack of external opposition. Chinese resistance was limited. Chiang was more intent on the destruction of the enemy within – the Chinese Communist Party. Britain alone of the powers imposed a brief embargo on arms sales to the two sides. The League itself got no further than the appointment of an advisory committee to follow developments in China. Interestingly it included a non-voting American representative – the United States had yet to take its great plunge into isolationism. The Japanese, meanwhile, were offering trade openings in Manchukuo to other nations in return for recognition of the new state. Some American and British businessmen were tempted, but not their governments. Non-recognition, of course, remained a meaningless gesture. By 1933 the main restraint on Japanese expansionism was provided by the divisions among the leadership in Tokyo.

NOTES AND REFERENCES

1.   Gilbert [1] iv, 897
2.   Gilbert [1] iv, 384–5
3.   See Artaud, *passim*, and Leffler, especially pp. 359–67. On French policy, see Silverman, especially pp. 1–12, 278, 298
4.   Leffler, pp. 359–67
5.   See above, note 3
6.   Waites, p. 108
7.   Waites, p. 109
8.   Orde, pp. 87, 96–7; Jacobson, pp. 17–24; Middlemas and Barnes, pp. 349 ff.
9.   Orde, pp. 146–53
10. W. Carr [1] p. 327. For an important study of Stresemann and Germany in the later 1920s, see Grathwohl, *passim*
11. Jacobson, pp. 154–6
12. Marquand, pp. 748–51
13. Roskill [2] ii, 143
14. Roskill [2] ii, 144–6
15. See especially Nish [3] Chs 7 and 8
16. See Mayer-Oakes: the translated Saionji – Harada memoirs provide excellent insights into the problems of governing Japan at this time
17. BD, 2nd series, viii, 655, 698–700
18. Roberts, pp. 316–17; see pp. 310 ff.
19. Berger, pp. 45–53

20. Crowley, p. 180
21. Crowley, pp. 88 ff.
22. Pelz, pp. 34–40, 63
23. Thorne [1] p. 155, and see also pp. 226, 245
24. BD 2nd series, VIII, 810, 822, 827–9, 944–7; IX, 31, 262–7
25. BD 2nd series, IX, 266, 281–3
26. BD 2nd series, IX, 282–3
27. Jones, p. 30
28. Trotter, pp. 21–2
29. Thorne [1] pp. 263–4
30. Thorne [1] pp. 268, 353

Chapter 7

THE NEW EXPANSIONISTS, 1933–1937

JAPAN IN SEARCH OF A POLICY, 1933–36

In 1933 it was impossible to predict the ease and speed with which Hitler would be able to consolidate his authority in Germany and begin to turn his country into the most formidable power in Europe. Although some Japanese were soon persuaded that fascism was the wave of the future, nothing like a consensus on this matter was created in Tokyo until the summer of 1940. Thus in the mid-1930s in particular, the Japanese leadership remained far from united as to future policy. Some were anxious to reach a compromise with Britain. In the spring of 1933 the Director of the European–American Bureau within the Foreign Ministry warned that it was unrealistic to strive for hegemony in east Asia and the western Pacific. War with the United States had to be avoided, and an accommodation sought with Britain and France over the future of China.[1] Extremists, however, were emerging even inside this ministry, and its influence in any case was in decline. Yet the generals were also divided, with some favouring speedy aggressive action against China or Russia, while others wished to consolidate and build up the economy. Indeed, many in Tokyo in 1933 seemed content with an independent Manchukuo and foreign recognition of certain Japanese interests in China – interests which it was claimed would not injure Chinese integrity or exclude western trade. On the other hand the militants continued to make progress, the army on the mainland being allowed in 1933 to exclude the Kuomintang from north China and to work for the creation of autonomous regions under Japanese influence. The navy was granted a free hand on the question of future naval limitation.

Japanese expansion from 1931 has sometimes been explained in terms of economic necessity and as a response to population pressures. The Japanese themselves made use of these arguments. But these claims must be treated with caution. It is true that the Mukden crisis occurred during the Depression. Japan's great period of expansion from 1937 to 1941 coincided with mounting western barriers to Japanese trade. On the other hand it is important to remember that Japan's trade expanded considerably between 1932 and 1936 and that much of this took place outside east Asia. By 1935 exports were 10 per cent higher in value than those for 1925, the best year in the 1920s. There was a greater increase in volume. South Asia's share of Japan's exports rose from 17 to 23 per cent, and began to rival those to east Asia, the area where Japan was militarily active. Japan was able to force a cut in Indian tariffs by means of a temporary boycott of Indian cotton exports. There were export gains in other parts of the world. Japan's trading success in the mid-1930s was, in relative terms, greater than that of any other power (even if her exports represented only 4 per cent of the world's total, and no less than 40 per cent consisted of textiles). On the other hand Japan was worryingly dependent on imports from the United States (about one-third of the total) with whom she had a serious trade deficit. It is also true that after 1937 Japan's trade with the yen bloc rapidly increased, greatly to the benefit, for instance, of the Mitsui organization. Yet in 1941, as we shall see, Japan was still far from the attainment of a self-sufficient empire, and could hope to secure one only as a result of a successful war with the United States, the British and the Dutch, as well as with China. Various interpretations of Japan's economic problems are thus possible. It does not follow that territorial expansion and war were the only solutions. In so far as economic motivation was important, as it clearly was, it must be seen in a political and strategic context rather than a narrowly economic and business one.[2]

The business community itself was divided as to the best approach to economic recovery from the Depression. The hostility of the army towards the *zaibatsu* has already been noted. The soldiers from 1932 turned in the main to newer and less influential businessmen to assist in the development of Manchuria and north China. Where the military, and many politicians and bureaucrats wanted economic strength to meet the political and strategic needs of Japan, businessmen thought (primarily) in terms of the profitability of their operations. Thus increased imports of cheaper Manchurian coal were opposed by Japanese coal-owners, and a cut of 20 per cent was agreed in 1932. The Mitsubishi interest in Manchuria declined in the early 1930s in view of poor returns and the need to accept so much military control. They found new and more profitable openings, especially in Australia – trade between the two countries doubled in 1931–33. Mitsubishi remained the strongest advocate of an international approach to Japan's economic problems, and demonstrated in a 1936 research publication that a self-sufficient empire was not a practical possibility given the scale of Japanese trade with the United States and the British Empire.[3] Mitsui was more ambivalent. Unlike Mitsubishi its activities were more concentrated in the yen bloc and in east Asia. It was more sympathetic to aggressive mainland policies. But Mitsui later opposed those who favoured an alliance with Germany, and emphasized Japan's dependence on Anglo-American markets and capital (the American banking house of Morgan had large investments in Mitsui). As the historian of the company concludes: 'The last thing in the world the *zaibatsu* wanted or needed was a war against the Western powers.'[4]

Naturally, as relations deteriorated with the western powers, partly through Japanese aggression and partly because of growing western barriers to Japanese trade in the later 1930s, so the *zaibatsu* became more dependent upon military contracts and upon the openings provided by Japan's expanding empire. But the *zaibatsu* were reacting to developments rather than making policy. They continued to compete for influence with the military. They found that the new openings on the mainland could not always be fully exploited for want of sufficient capital. American exports to northern China actually increased in the period 1938–40 given the inability of Japan to meet all the needs of the area.[5] Furthermore from the mid-1930s the Japanese economy was increasingly under strain as a result of the mounting armament programmes. This adversely affected some industries engaged in non-military production. The services sought ever more control over the economy to the dismay of businessmen as the international situation worsened.

But if caution is required in any discussion of the economic motives behind Japanese expansionism, so too is it necessary in any consideration of the role of the armed forces. It is not enough to refer to the differences between the army and navy. Nor is it enough to see the army as divided into two main factions – those who wished to give priority to the subordination of China and those who wished to concentrate on preparations for what they saw to be an inevitable war with Russia. The divisions within the army were more complex than this. The abortive military coup by a group of young army radicals on 26 February 1936 did not lead to the dominance of an army faction that was intent on conquests in China. If anything the military chiefs in Tokyo by 1937 were more intent on the long-term threat from Russia. Opinions changed in the light of changing circumstances. General Ishiwara, for instance, who had been happy to use force against China in 1931 as a prelude to the unification of the East against its many enemies, had – by the mid-1930s – become an advocate of the concilation of China. As a member of the General Staff he was now impressed by the enormous and perhaps insurmountable difficulties in the way of a Japanese conquest of so vast a country as China. He was also convinced that war was likely to break out with Russia within five or six years. China's friendship would then be invaluable, provided that she would acknowledge Manchukuo, Japan's indispensable mainland base. Ishiwara also believed that Japan must prepare herself for total war against the West, in which grouping he included Russia, insisting on the likelihood of a great collision between the spiritual civilization of the East and the materialism of the West. Shigemitsu, the Japanese minister in China, was another who wished to conciliate China and divert her intense nationalist feelings against the West. Certainly as long as there existed a threat from the West he believed Sino-Japanese co-operation to be possible, with Chinese dependence upon Japan providing the latter with all the leverage and influence she needed in China proper. Manchukuo must of course remain. The Japanese navy also favoured a policy of conciliation rather than coercion on the mainland, not least because it feared that crises with China would enable the army to increase its calls on the nation's resources at the expense of the navy.

In the course of 1934, notably in the Amau statement of 18 April, Japan made several attempts to define her special role in east Asia and China, and the terms on which other nations might deal with the Chinese. Such relations were not to menace Japan in any way. But at this time China was receiving some aid from the United States in the development of an air force. A German general, Hans von Seeckt, was serving as chief military adviser in Nanking – though his services were mostly being used by Chiang Kai-shek to try to crush the Chinese Communist Party. League of Nations' experts were working on plans to help in China's economic reconstruction. The Japanese viewed most such developments with dismay. In the circumstances the extremists tended to gain in influence. More and more Japanese began to insist on the creation of regional administrations, especially in north China, which would be exposed to Japanese influence. But there were times when compromise between Tokyo and Nanking did not seem impossible. In January 1935 a Kuomintang goodwill mission arrived in Japan to offer co-operation on equal terms provided that Japan would cease to promote autonomous regimes in the north. Sufficient progress was made for ambassadors to be exchanged in May 1935. In September 1935 the Kuomintang offered *de facto* recognition of Manchukuo if it were allowed to reassert its authority in northern China.

The gap between the two governments, however, remained very wide. Chiang was temporizing in the hope that he could win an early and complete victory over Chinese communism. The Japanese leaders were divided over the degree to which they could trust the Chinese and the amount of control or influence they needed to exercise over northern China. At the end of 1935 it was agreed that Japan must possess at least a privileged economic position in north

China, though the military hardliners still pressed for and (in a number of incidents) made some progress towards their aim of a buffer zone embracing Hopei, Chahar, Suiyan, Shansi and Shantung for security against both China and the Soviet Union. The effect of these Japanese advances was to provoke fresh Chinese boycotts, and to stimulate anti-Japanese feeling. Many in China became impatient with Chiang's preference for war with communism to the formation of a united national front against the external enemy. Paradoxically, had communism posed a greater threat in China in the mid-1930s, and had the Soviet Union been stronger in the Far East, Nanking and Tokyo might have felt impelled to sink their differences. Certainly Russian policy worried Japan, but not sufficiently to unite the leadership behind a policy which gave priority to the elimination of the Soviet threat. Friction there was in Mongolia – the Russians concluded a defensive alliance with Outer Mongolia on 31 March 1936 – and the Soviet Union was making it plain that the sale of the Chinese Eastern Railway was intended to be its last act of appeasement in the east. Russian forces were being strengthened, and the Trans-Siberian Railway was being double-tracked. From 1933 the Russians were busily looking for political and material help in Washington – they were even willing to take old American lines to speed work on the Trans-Siberian.[6] But for the time being the Russians were clearly, if resolutely, on the defensive. Therefore while relations with Russia caused Tokyo to deliberate over policy towards China, they did not produce any significant reappraisal until 1937 – by which time it was too late. The Japanese continued to be tempted by the prospect of increased cotton imports from north China to reduce their dependence on India and the United States. Iron and coal reserves in north China and Inner Mongolia were much greater than those in Manchuria. Northern China, with its population of almost 100 million, was seen as a potentially valuable market for Japanese goods, and in general this region was expected to carry Japan much further towards the goal of self-sufficiency than Manchuria. There were political and strategic arguments for the advance as well. As with the British in India from the mid-eighteenth century, the security of one conquest appeared to demand yet more conquests, and so the process continued.

An army pamphlet, published in October 1934 and entitled *The Essence of National Defence and Proposals to Strengthen it*, argued that postwar efforts at reconstruction since 1919 had broken down, and that the current world emergency demanded radical policies. All aspects of national policy should be subordinated to the needs of national defence and the ability to wage a total war. It was necessary to formulate a 'great plan for our country's next hundred years'. The so-called 'co-operative' diplomacy of the Shidehara era should be replaced by 'renovationist' policies. A sympathetic group within the

Foreign Ministry produced a pamphlet on similar lines in December 1936, and called for a foreign policy based on the idea of race with Japan acting as the leader of Asia against Russia and the West.[7] The government, however, remained a coalition of competing interest groups, a fact which was only thinly disguised in a document entitled 'The fundamental principles of national policy' of August 1936, an ambitious attempt to define future foreign policy. Caution, ambition, idealism and xenophobia were freely mixed together. Only in this way could any sort of consensus be achieved. The desirability of peaceful advance was stressed, but plans were also laid to expand both of the armed forces. The latter continued to compete for scarce resources, but the need for naval hegemony in the western Pacific was underlined, not least as one of the bases for future economic penetration of the European colonies in the south seas.[8] There was much emphasis on the principle of 'co-prosperity and co-existence based on the Imperial Way' in east Asia under Japanese leadership. Much was made of the desirability of an anti-communist triple alliance uniting Japan, Manchukuo and China. This combination was vital if a successful war were to be waged against the Soviet Union. The subordination of China to Japan was assumed, contempt for the Chinese having grown apace since 1894.[9]

Nevertheless by the winter of 1936–37 a more cautious note was becoming evident. There was a growing disposition to question the wisdom of recent Japanese activities in northern China, and to ask whether economic penetration and influence might not suffice. The General Staff in Tokyo was becoming more fearful of Russia, and wished to concentrate on the modernization of the army. Indeed a war with China was seen by many in both services as an unwelcome distraction which would devour resources needed for other purposes. The goal of an autonomous national defence capability continued to beckon, but there was less certainty by the beginning of 1937 that the continued coercion and provocation of the Chinese was the best way forward.

TO THE SINO-JAPANESE WAR OF 1937

In the mid-1930s Japan was under no immediate threat from any of the great powers. The Russians had much to concern them at home, and were troubled by the rise of Nazi Germany. American moralizing was not as yet interfering with trans-Pacific trade, while the British would happily have resolved their differences with Japan had this been possible. Britain, from 1935, was distracted by Mussolini's attack on Abyssinia, by German revisionism, and from 1936 by the

Spanish Civil War. Any British hopes of co-operation with the United States were dispelled by the growing strength of isolationist feeling across the Atlantic, even if by 1936 the two naval establishments were beginning to show mutual concern at the rise of the Japanese navy, and to set aside their recent rivalries.[10] In general there was not as yet any great depth of anti-Japanese feeling in Britain. Japanese trade competition mainly affected the Lancashire textile manufacturers. In 1934 a British trade mission to Japan received a relatively friendly reception. Exporters of heavy goods feared for their trade with Japan if Britain restricted imports of Japanese cotton goods. More trade with Manchukuo seemed possible. Only in 1935 did the Japanese make it clear that trading openings would be dependent on British political concessions.

In 1934 Neville Chamberlain, the Chancellor of the Exchequer, had proposed a pact with Japan, hopeful that British rearmament could then be concentrated on the build-up of the air force as a deterrent against Germany. The idea was criticized by some both in Britain and the Dominions on the ground that Britain could not afford to antagonize the Americans. But nothing came of the move as there was no Japanese response.[11] Nevertheless the idea continued to command attention, especially in the Treasury. Chamberlain and others were convinced (rightly) that Britain could not uphold the status quo simultaneously in Europe and the Far East. The Foreign Office agreed, but thought it unlikely that Japan would make a worthwhile offer, especially over trade. Nor did it wish to offend the United States. It had, however, no positive ideas of its own to offer. The Foreign Office bleakly commented that even if means were found to help the Chinese there was no guarantee that a victorious China would be more sympathetic to British interests than a triumphant Japan. At the same time it continued to admit that any appearance of British weakness in the Far East might precipitate challenges to British authority elsewhere in the world.[12] Not surprisingly the Treasury lost patience with this negative outlook. It sought both to strengthen the Chinese economy and to discover ways of co-operating with Japan in the spirit of the Washington treaties. This was the purpose of the Leith-Ross financial mission of 1935. The mission encountered some sympathy among Japanese financial circles, but it was soon forced to recognize that the real power lay elsewhere. Leith-Ross himself remarked that the most influential person he met was a Japanese major-general, a staff officer with the army in China. Many Japanese simply saw the mission as part of an Anglo-Japanese battle for control of the Chinese economy. The Treasury, despite its inventiveness, was no more able to find a satisfactory policy than the Foreign Office.[13]

Even so the Japanese negotiations with Germany which resulted in the Anti-Comintern Pact of November 1936 must not be taken as evidence that the hardliners had gained control in Tokyo. This was a vague, if friendly understanding, intended by many Japanese to do no more than strengthen their position against Russia. Only in the army was there widespread enthusiasm for the pact with Germany. The exclusion of Italy until November 1937 was a victory for those who believed that Japan should still try to keep open a line to the western powers.[14] Differences persisted between Berlin and Tokyo over policy towards China until the end of 1937 – the Germans for a time were seriously interested in good relations with the Kuomintang, and with good reason, for an alignment with Nanking and Tokyo would have embarrassed both the British and the Russians. Within Japan itself, early in 1937, there was a strong upsurge of feeling against the army, with many civilian groups complaining about its excessive influence and the costliness of its plans. The *zaibatsu* and certain sections of the bureaucracy believed they saw an opportunity to increase their influence. The emergence of Prince Konoye as Prime Minister in June 1937 was significant. Here was an attempt to use a personage of high standing to bring about a new consensus in the leadership, and to end the existing friction and frustrations. Unfortunately Konoye's social prestige was greater than his abilities. In less troublous times he might have made a competent leader. As it was he seemed very much at the mercy of events and stronger personalities.

In so far as agreement could be reached on anything in Tokyo in the early summer of 1937, it centred on a programme to provide long-term security against Russia. To this end it was necessary for Japan to draw the greatest possible benefit from the economies of Manchukuo and north China, as well as from her own. But there was no intense feeling of urgency: only a general desire to become less dependent upon imports from the western powers. War with Russia was not expected for some years, though the army chiefs were anxious to push on with their modernization programmes. The mood in Tokyo was such that both the British and Americans momentarily hoped that the worst was over. Chamberlain eagerly reopened the question of an understanding with Japan, especially over China, which he thought 'one of the great potential markets of the world'.[15] Japan's economy was suffering from inflation, the yen was weak and nearly half the budget was being devoted to the armed forces. Doubts continued to grow about the wisdom of recent policies in China. Even some of the military on the mainland by June 1937 seemed disposed to agree that the resources of Manchuria and east Hopei (a region of north China) would meet the needs of national defence, although Tojo Hideki still had many supporters for his view that the main armies of the Kuomintang must be defeated before Japan could risk war with Russia. It was necessary to eliminate this 'menace in our rear'.[16] The General Staff in Tokyo, however, with their eyes on

Russia, were among the strongest opponents of new adventures in China. By and large the Japanese leaders in the early summer of 1937 appeared more interested in a compromise with China than a new crisis. Why then did the Marco Polo Bridge Incident near Peking on the night of 7–8 July 1937 so quickly escalate into a major war?

The incident was not the result of any deep-laid plot, even among the Japanese army leaders on the mainland. It was the sort of incident which can easily occur when two armies, in close proximity to each other, have been coexisting in a prolonged state of tension. Initially there was no reason to treat it as more than a misunderstanding, but the suspicion and hostility which had been building up between China and Japan over a long period of time soon began to dominate the negotiations. In addition, on this occasion, the Chinese were more determined to make a stand. Their financial position was improving. They had enjoyed some limited military success against Japan in northern China in 1936. Nationalist feelings were running high, and this was reflected in the extraordinary Sian episode at the end of 1936 when Chiang Kai-shek had been imprisoned by one of his own generals in protest against orders to launch new offensives against the Chinese Communists in the north-west of the country. Much of what happened at Sian remains obscure, but Chiang was subjected to pressure from various quarters (including the Soviet Union) to work for Chinese unity against Japan. A precarious united front was in process of formation when the Marco Polo Bridge Incident occurred. Chiang had little room in which to manœuvre. He was unable to approve the agreement reached by the local commanders near Peking, and in the face of this stand by Nanking the Japanese also toughened their position. Tokyo was soon convinced that it was necessary to give the Chinese a sharp reminder of Japanese power, and it exaggerated the ease with which it expected to achieve this objective. In August Tokyo once more demanded that China accept a pro-Japanese administration in the north, and the negotiation of a comprehensive treaty to unite the two governments in a common stand against communism. In so far as doubts existed as to the wisdom of this policy, they prevailed among the General Staff rather than among the civilian leaders. The General Staff had no up-to-date contingency plans for war, and wished to use no more than fifteen divisions in a quick, punitive operation (by 1940 nearly forty divisions were deployed in China).[17] The conflict rapidly escalated. The Chinese were unusually confident, and looked expectantly for western aid, perhaps in the form of League sanctions against Japan, and later from the Brussels Conference, a meeting of the Washington signatories in November 1937.

Such hopes were totally unrealistic. The British, conscious of the growing demands on their strength in Europe, would still have preferred to negotiate an accommodation with Japan. Australia and

New Zealand feared for their own security, and detected a hollow ring in British assurances that the main fleet would be sent to Singapore in the event of a crisis. The Admiralty was well aware that as matters then stood Britain might be unable to live up to all her assurances and commitments. It was known that Japan intended to build super-battleships, and that up to seventy days would elapse before a British battle-fleet could reach Singapore. Japan would possess great advantages in the initial stages of a war. If Italy intervened, 'this would at once impose conflicting demands on our fleet'.[18] As it was, the defensibility of Singapore was being exaggerated, and the forces needed for a war against Japan underestimated. Great faith was placed in economic pressure, although it was expected that two years at least would be required to defeat Japan by such means.[19] When in August 1937, Japanese military operations spilled over into Shanghai and the Yangtze valley, regions of prime interest to Britain, the Foreign Office could only inquire – not very hopefully – as to the view of the United States, and in the meantime offer its good offices to China and Japan.

Nothing came of the meeting of the Washington signatories in Brussels in November 1937. Japan became more and more exasperated with the Nanking government. The latter was insisting on a return to the status quo as it existed before the start of the conflict on 7 July 1937. Tokyo finally lost patience. On 16 January 1938 it decided to 'annihilate' the Kuomintang and to seek a new and more co-operative Chinese regime – or regimes. Again the General Staff was among those in Tokyo who were least happy with this strategy. Konoye himself later admitted that the step was 'an utter blunder' once it became evident that while Japan could seize control of the great coastal cities of China, and areas which were reasonably accessible by river, road and rail, much of China could not be subdued. Relatively poor though those regions might be, they could still sustain considerable military forces, and it was from these remoter regions that the Kuomintang, as well as the Communists, were able to offer enough resistance to embarrass the Japanese. Before the year was out Konoye was leading a new attempt to negotiate with the Kuomintang – though without success. The Japanese also tried to find other Chinese leaders and politicians with whom it might be possible to co-operate, and so persuade the bulk of the Chinese people to abandon their resistance.

Problems existed even in the areas that were firmly under Japanese control. Japanese military and business interests continued to conflict. Businessmen, though active, were often short of capital, and production in northern China in 1939 was still below its pre-war level. This accounts for the continuing interest of some Japanese businessmen in the attraction of foreign capital to China, and for the import of many American goods into Japanese-held areas. In August and September 1938, too, the Japanese General Staff produced papers in favour of peace with China. The latter, they argued, could not be turned into a second Manchukuo. Priority should be given to preparation for war with Russia. Not surprisingly there were hopes both in Britain and the United States that Japan might yet be worn down by China's powers of resistance. In Tokyo General Ishiwara warned that Japan was likely to suffer the fate of Napoleon in Spain. But try as they would, those Japanese who regretted the war could find no way to bring it to an end, while events in Europe from the later 1930s were gradually creating a situation which was to play into the hands of those Japanese who believed that the time had come to create a new balance of power in the Far East.

HITLER AND THE GERMAN PROBLEM

Historians have had more success in revising the first generation of writing on Japan's part in the origins of the Second World War than they have with respect to that of Hitler and Germany. The Japanese had no equivalent of Hitler and his party following. Their influence on the course of events was much less; their divisions over aims and methods of fulfilment much more pronounced. Admittedly historians no longer centre their attention quite so much on the extraordinary personality of Hitler, and have become more conscious of E. H. Carr's warning, written as early as September 1939, that one must not attribute any war simply to the ambition and arrogance of a handful of men: one must look for deeper causes.[20] It is necessary to take account of the forces which placed Hitler in power in 1933, and the reasons why the German people continued to welcome or acquiesce in his leadership thereafter.

By the early 1930s the traumas which Germany had experienced since 1914 had produced such an accumulation of despair, frustration and resentment that a drift to the Right, to extreme nationalism and an expansionist foreign policy seemed the most probable alternative to a decline into ungovernability. Vast numbers of Germans by 1933 were desperate for a regime which would restore national prosperity, power and pride. Under the impact of the Depression many of the industrialists had swung from faith in conventional trade policies towards autarky and other extreme remedies.[21] Fear of the Left in Germany invested with great attractions for the wealthy a party with a mass following committed to the destruction of the Left. This mass support for the Nazis came from many sources: from the young, the jobless, anti-Communists, anti-Semites, opponents of Versailles, and those who sought a total break from the past with the creation of a classless *Herrenvolk* in a more spacious Germany. There was the charisma of Hitler himself, and the appeal of a movement with its camaraderie and emotional strength. Others were attracted simply by its ruthlessness and brutality. The Nazi Party meant different things to different people, but above all it seemed to offer an escape from the failures associated with the Weimar Republic, and from the threat from the Left. Hitler and his party possessed a programme, but their conduct and policies were also 'shaped by the national and social expectations of large sectors of German society'.[22]

In time, however, the alliance of interests which destroyed Weimar came to be dominated by hard-core Nazis. Hermann Rauschning was one of the first to discover what Hitler and the Nazis were really like. Initially attracted by Nazi vitality, he was appalled to uncover what he later described as its 'will to anarchy' and its revolt against the 'higher forms of our Western civilization'.It was one thing for active young Germans of all classes to be waiting for 'the opening of the gates to a hard but varied and adventurous life as colonists', but he believed that the Nazis were leading Germany to self-destruction by their irrational and infinite aims. Rauschning, although he thought the Versailles treaty intolerable, had parted company with Nazi foreign policy by the winter of 1937–38. In 1938 many more Germans were dismayed by the risks Hitler was prepared to run over the Sudeten question. Indeed, by this time serious tension was developing between the nationalist extremists led by Hitler and those who believed the internal revolution had gone far enough, and that in foreign policy a patient, restricted revisionism was enough. Hitler feared that the regime was in danger of settling into a conservative, authoritarian groove, and he struck out against it. The Hossbach[23] meeting may be seen in part as a test of the dynamism and nerve of leading generals and ministers – some who queried his strategy were purged soon afterwards. By November 1938 Hitler was to be found insisting that the psychology of the German people had to be adjusted to accept the use of force in certain circumstances. He was determined, as Rauschning had noted, to push the revolutionary and nihilistic elements to the fore.[24]

But while many leading officers and bureaucrats differed from Hitler over timing and methods, and recoiled from his wilder dreams, many in practice were prepared – in their own time – to go a very long way with him. Just how far may be a matter for speculation. Klaus-Jürgen Müller,[25] for instance, has deployed an impressive array of evidence to suggest that a large majority of the officers supported the aim of German hegemony in Europe and were deeply moved by fear and hatred of Bolshevism. General Ludwig Beck's opposition to Hitler in 1938 was based primarily on the fear of a premature war and a German defeat. Beck believed that Germany needed colonies, living space, the destruction of Czechoslovakia –

but war demanded careful timing. Similarly Hitler's first Foreign Minister, Freiherr von Neurath, was determined to destroy Versailles, and to extinguish the Czech 'will for self-determination'.[26] Indeed, Neurath appears to have kept his head better over the Rhineland crisis than Hitler himself – once it was under way. Nevertheless it is difficult to find in any of the other potential leaders of Germany at this time the same extraordinary combination of ability, nerve and ambition that one finds in Adolf Hitler. Those who shared his eagerness to gamble on the highest stakes were usually men of straw, thrust into high places (like Ribbentrop) because of their relationship with Hitler. As for the ambitious men of ability, they rarely showed the same determination to force the pace. As Albert Speer commented later, 'what was decisive was . . . [Hitler's] reckless courage to take risks'.

It is important to note that Hitler himself from 1938 feared that time was running out for Germany; that she could not make the intended breakthrough to European hegemony, let alone the dominant position in the world if she delayed for more than a few years. Other states, notably Britain and Russia and perhaps even the United States, were mobilizing their resources for war. Germany had to strike before they were ready. Thus a more hesitant leadership might well have found war an unrealistic option, whatever their ambitions; their very caution might have given time for the formation of that equilibrium in Europe which Hitler was determined to destroy. It is, for instance, open to doubt whether Hitler's most likely successor in the later 1930s, Hermann Göring, for all his ruthlessness, would have acted with equal boldness and precipitancy. It has even been suggested that a union of all Germans under one flag, some colonies, and indirect hegemony over eastern Europe might have satisfied him.[27] As for those who argue that the strain imposed on the German economy by rearmament left Hitler little option other than war by 1939, it must be remembered that it was Hitler himself who insisted as early as 1936 that the nation must be ready for war in four years, and who dismissed economic problems as something which could always be overcome by will-power. For all the account that historians must take of Germany's political, social and economic condition in the 1930s, the war of 1939 must still be seen very much as 'Hitler's war'.

Hitler, according to A. J. P. Taylor, wished to make 'Germany the dominant power in Europe, but had no clear idea how to do it'. Many scholars have noted the vagueness in Hitler's thinking before circumstances suggested, or even propelled him into a certain course of action. In *Mein Kampf* and in many of his later statements the element of day-dreaming was certainly present. Yet it was not irrelevant. Even when it lacked coherence and substance, it was indicative of a mind eager and willing to exploit – and push to the limit –

opportunities as they presented themselves. They reveal a mind predisposed towards certain lines of action. The contrast with Bismarck is revealing. Bismarck was restrained by his commitment to a Protestant, Prussian and conservative Germany. He was also deeply rooted in the society of his age. Hitler had no such constraints. Equal or superior will and military strength alone impressed him.

The extent of Hitler's ambition is still a matter of debate among historians. Andreas Hillgruber has ascribed to him a *Stufenplan*,[28] or a programme of expansion in three stages, the first to reach its fulfilment with the conquest of *Lebensraum* in Russia, the second with the defeat of the United States, while the third would find a German Aryan élite as the controlling force in the world. As William Carr[29] has pointed out, the second and third stages await clarification for want of evidence. Carr adds that Hitler's ambitious naval plans in the winter of 1938–39 may be a possible pointer. One may see here the beginning of preparations against the United States (as well as the Royal Navy) some time before Hitler had reason to expect serious American involvement in Europe. It is obvious that Hitler initially could not be sure how much, if any of his plans would be fulfilled in his lifetime, though of his desire to complete the first stage, and to set Germany irreversibly on the road to world power there can be no doubt. He hoped to achieve this while he was in the prime of life, and while the other powers were too weak to resist. With adequate *Lebensraum* in the east he hoped to lay such solid foundations for the Third Reich that his successors could not possibly go astray. Even in the 1930s he gave hints of a preference for disaster to some lesser achievement. He vehemently rejected less revolutionary remedies to Germany's problems, remedies which had significant supporters. These he dismissed as totally inadequate. The frontiers of 1914, for instance, would mean only a return to encirclement – a Germany squeezed between France and Russia; trade and colonies, he insisted, could provide only an interim solution to Germany's economic problems, and would lead in time to a new war with Britain and the reimposition of the blockade. Germany must find space to achieve self-sufficiency and the satisfaction of all her other ambitions.

Incomplete, contradictory and impractical though they often were, and influenced too by the needs of the moment, various remarks by Hitler during his early years in power are also revealing. Taken together they underline this determination to do things beyond the norm. In 1933 and 1934 Rauschning and Germany's military chiefs were regaled with descriptions of Germany's needs and desserts, with talk of German domination of Europe, the acquisition of living space and the possibility of war in the east and west as necessary.[30] In the summer of 1936 came the specific order to prepare Germany for war in four years, while September found Hitler musing, 'If we had at our disposal the Urals, with their incalculable wealth of raw materials, and the forests of Siberia and the unending wheat-fields of the Ukraine, our country would swim in plenty.[31] Hitler was determined to learn from the errors of Wilhelmine Germany: he was also pushing to their logical conclusion all the pre-war ideas concerning a global struggle for power between the greatest peoples of the world from which no more than a few, and perhaps only one, could emerge victorious. But Hitler was both more ambitious and more cautious than his predecessors. The determination to control the Eurasian heartland is clearer and more comprehensive: the effect on the conquered territories more revolutionary in intent. But if Hitler was determined to act at the first opportune moment (Wilhelmine Germany at most steeled itself to decisive action when it feared that the window of opportunity was closing on it), he was also anxious to avoid a long and costly war of attrition like that of 1914–18. He hoped to achieve his extraordinary ambitions by means of short, decisive wars against isolated opponents – wars that would clear the ground for a new start in the east with Aryan control and colonization.

EUROPE'S EARLY REACTIONS TO NAZI GERMANY

Hitler came to power in January 1933 ostensibly in the most unpromising of circumstances, domestic and international. The country was politically divided, crippled by the Depression, and militarily weak (despite the efforts to circumvent the disarmament clauses of the Treaty of Versailles). Hitler was very conscious of German vulnerability. Of the early stages of German rearmament he had commented in 1932: 'If ever there are grounds for preventive war, there are in this case for an attack by France against Germany.'[32] In fact the French army from 1930 was mainly preoccupied with home defence. If it was reasonably confident, this was because it believed it had time to complete the Maginot Line, behind which the nation could mobilize in the event of war. In co-operation with Belgium it had hopes of holding the line of the Meuse. Aid to allies in eastern Europe, however, would be a different matter. But in Paris, as in London, there were hopes that office would tame Hitler.

In Berlin the British ambassador, Sir Horace Rumbold, was very conscious of the change of the mood in Germany since his arrival in 1928. Even before the Nazi take-over he complained that the satisfaction of one German grievance merely encouraged new demands. In 1933 he described Hitler's regime as abnormal. He was appalled by the anti-Semitism of the Nazis.[33] War would come sooner or later; perhaps in only four or five years. Nor was there total complacency in London.[34] But a militant, revisionist Germany was a daunting prospect. For Britain this would entail rearmament, deep involvement in European affairs, even war itself. Most policy-makers readily seized upon any evidence that a peaceful solution might yet be possible. In any case some saw no need to separate Nazi ambitions from German revisionism as a whole.[35] It was tempting to hope that Hitler's ambitions would not menace British interests. In so far as dangers were recognized it was difficult to settle on the timing and size of a rearmament programme, and to mobilize the necessary national support. There were widespread fears that a victorious war might prove a greater disaster to Britain than major concessions which nevertheless kept the peace. The ultimate beneficiaries might be Russia, Japan and even the United States. Naturally there were many personal, political and professional prejudices at work among those in Britain who favoured appeasement. Yet their critics were often as guilty of bias. Even good intentions could be cursed with impracticality. As early as 1933 Ernest Bevin had to remind a Labour Party Conference – when there was much talk of the value of general strikes as a preventive of war – that Britain alone of the great powers had an effective trade union movement.[36] Many in Britain blamed Versailles and the French for the current instability in Europe. Lord Lothian had no wish to maintain an 'outworn *status quo* in Europe at the dictation of Russia and France'. It was imperative to find for Germany and Japan the place 'to which they were reasonably entitled because of their power and traditions with the minimum destruction of the liberty of other people . . .'[37] There was also a strong temptation to stand aloof from Europe – what Lothian called a policy of 'armed neutrality'.[38] But those in authority were conscious that Germany in the end might push her revisionism to a point where the peace of Europe was endangered, or where British interests were directly threatened. Counteraction would then be inescapable. It seemed wiser to try to prevent the creation of such a crisis in the first place.

Many hopes continued to be centred on disarmament or arms limitation of some kind. Major talks were in progress in 1933, but in the autumn Germany withdrew from the disarmament conference. Hitler also astutely concluded a non-aggression pact with Poland early in 1934. This agreement ran counter to German prejudice and ambition with respect to Poland. But Hitler was anxious to weaken Franco-Polish ties, and was able to exploit the doubts which existed in Warsaw as to the readiness of France to assist in the defence of eastern Europe against Germany. But what Hitler gained for a time with respect to Poland he lost when it came to the question of Austria. There German-backed Nazi activities gradually pushed

Mussolini closer to Britain and France. At the time of the unsuccessful Austrian Nazi *putsch* at the end of July 1934, Mussolini ostentatiously moved 100,000 troops closer to the Brenner Pass. By 1934 negotiations on disarmament were no more than a charade. In March Hitler authorized a substantial increase in German defence spending, although he appreciated that a denunciation of the Versailles clauses on German armaments was still premature. But his moves pleased sections of German heavy industry and the service chiefs. Hitler was already informing the latter of his determination to fight for new markets or, preferably, for *Lebensraum* in the east, which was to be ruthlessly 'Germanized'. Naval planning, however, excluded war with Britain.[39]

The French response was mixed. The economy was faltering, and the lean years were at hand when the numbers of men available for conscription into the armed forces were dropping sharply. Both these circumstances encouraged the French to concentrate on the defence of their eastern frontiers.[40] Their relations with the British, the Belgians and especially the Poles were not so close as they would have liked. But in 1934 the tough-minded Louis Barthou was appointed to the Foreign Ministry, and he began to push ahead with talks with the Italians and the Russians. General Gamelin noted the need for well-equipped mobile forces to give credibility to France's commitments in eastern Europe. Barthou suggested that an eastern Locarno might be possible, but this was probably designed to reassure the British and to test the mood in Germany. It was soon evident that neither Germany nor Poland, given their hopes of territorial revision in eastern Europe, would co-operate. Barthou made more progress in Moscow and Rome. Russia was admitted to the League of Nations in September 1934. But a month later Barthou was dead, assassinated with King Alexander of Yugoslavia by a Croat fanatic. French policy thereafter seemed to lose momentum, but it is important to remember that Barthou's political base in France was weak, his ministerial future uncertain, and it was easier to open contacts with Moscow and Rome than to develop them into something solid. In any case the British would have nothing to do with eastern Europe. The most Baldwin offered was his famous remark of 30 July 1934: 'When you think of the defence of England, you no longer think of the chalk cliffs of Dover. You think of the Rhine. This is where our frontier lies.' In practice, however, the British (and the Belgians) clung to a narrow interpretation of the Locarno treaties. Admittedly the Foreign Office was becoming uneasy: it was troubled by the Cabinet's reluctance to expand the Royal Air Force. But there was also interest in the negotiation of a comprehensive agreement which would legalize German rearmament in return for German concessions on other issues.[41]

Meanwhile another power was anxiously following developments in Germany. The Russians already had plenty to occupy them at home and were under pressure from Japan in the Far East. They therefore hurriedly negotiated non-aggression pacts with neighbouring European states in 1933–34, although their Foreign Minister, Litvinov, was careful to offer an olive branch to Berlin with his assurance that these pacts 'should not by any means be regarded as an attempt to encircle any country, since every State belonging to a given region may join in these pacts'.[42] The Kremlin was similarly trying to ease relations with Britain, after the Metro-Vickers affair in 1933, and managed to secure American diplomatic recognition in November of the same year. The Soviet Union ceased to describe the League of Nations as a 'league of imperialist robbers', but was careful to project itself as a pragmatic power rather than as an enthusiast for collective security. It continued to stress its desire for better relations with Germany, and to make the occasional discreet overture.[43] At the same time talks proceeded with France, and a mutual assistance treaty was signed in May 1935. In default of evidence from the Russian archives one cannot be dogmatic about Soviet intentions, but in the light of their pressing domestic difficulties – the crisis with the peasants, and the long haul before their five-year plans could begin to pay off – as well as their international worries, it made sense for the Russians to pick up foreign agreements when and where they could. One might surmise that the Kremlin's prime concerns in Europe were to give the lie to Nazi and other portrayals of Russia as a revolutionary power, and above all to prevent the formation of a hostile coalition of all the leading capitalist powers against itself. This last fear was exaggerated. At the same time one must note the reluctance of most members of the British government to negotiate with the Russians. Indeed, Baldwin remarked on the academic attractions of a Nazi – Bolshevik conflict which would destroy both. Even Barthou supped with a long spoon in company with the Russians. On 1 April 1935 the American ambassador in Rome thought it improbable that Britain and France would co-operate seriously with Russia: this would invite communism into the heart of Europe.[44] As D. C. Watt has reminded us, much of Europe felt itself close to civil war in the 1930s.[45] Spain experienced its actuality from 1936. Many feared that a major European war would leave a badly damaged continent hopelessly exposed to Russian influence and communism. By 1936 the French Right was becoming fearful of the dangers attendant upon no more than a treaty relationship with the Russians: they feared the encouragement this would give to the Left in French domestic politics.

As for the British, nothing of consequence developed out of Eden's ostensibly successful visit to Moscow at the end of March 1935. It is true that Vansittart for a time led a group in the Foreign Office which favoured a closer relationship with Russia, the prime aim being to prevent a Russo-German *rapprochement*. But this concern could not prevail against the growing conviction that Britain's wisest course was to work for a general settlement with Germany. Hitler himself was making much of the Bolshevik 'menace' in 1935, and was doing his best to frighten the British into the belief that the Franco-Russian agreement, and any other western dealings with Russia, would wreck all prospect of a general pacification of Europe. Even in the Foreign Office interest in dealings with Moscow began to wither in the face of these tactics. By the beginning of 1936 fear of giving offence to Germany was the strongest influence on British policy towards Russia.[46]

THE ABYSSINIAN DIVERSION 1935

Meanwhile fears of German ambitions in Austria were drawing France and Italy together. But Mussolini also hoped that, following the failure of the Nazi *putsch* in Vienna in July 1934, he might have sufficient time to fulfil his ambitions at the expense of Abyssinia before a rearmed Germany forced Italy to concentrate upon European questions. He calculated, too, that French fears of Germany might persuade Paris to grant him a free hand in East Africa. A better opportunity seemed unlikely. Unfortunately for the balance of power in Europe Mussolini was intent upon a dramatic and overwhelming success in Abyssinia (Ethiopia). Italian interests might have been promoted in East Africa by more modest coercive methods, so attracting less attention in Europe, and thus perhaps making the question of aggression seem much less clear-cut. From December 1934 Mussolini frequently clashed with his professional advisers who wished to proceed in this manner. He continued to insist on a major campaign which would bring victory in the shortest possible time. In so far as Mussolini feared Germany he had a point, but one suspects that the exhibitionist in him was also at work. Be that as it may, he landed himself in a war which could not be swept under the carpet away from the notice of the League of Nations and the British public.

It is possible that the French also failed to read Mussolini's intentions aright. Both Barthou and Laval, his successor at the Foreign Ministry, offered assurances of some kind concerning Italian ambitions in Abyssinia, but not necessarily the degree of freedom which Mussolini later claimed. On the other hand the French were well satisfied with the improvement in their relations with Italy with respect to Europe. The agreement of 7 January 1935 rapidly evolved into the convention of 27 June 1935 which provided for the joint defence of Austria. A start was made to staff talks. Italian friendship had much to commend it when (otherwise) as much as one-fifth of the French army was required to defend French interests in and around the Mediterranean.[47] This provided France with some compensation for the German repudiation of the Versailles disarmament clauses in March 1935, and the reintroduction of conscription.

On 11–14 April 1935 Mussolini met with the British and French at Stresa. The British were determined to make no new commitments beyond those already contained in the Locarno treaties. They saw Germany as 'in a volcanic mood and not inclined to yield to threats'.[48] They were determined to continue to negotiate with Berlin. Equally, despite some British knowledge that trouble was stirring between Italy and Abyssinia, no effort was made to discourage Mussolini. Therefore at Stresa Abyssinia was ignored, German rearmament was condemned, and interest expressed in the continuing stability of Europe. There was no Stresa Front: only a facade. The British were critical of the completion of the Franco-Soviet Pact on 2 May 1935, although the French Foreign Minister, Laval, did not intend to follow it with staff talks. In fact he dreaded another war, feared communism, and merely hoped to use the pact to lever Germany towards a compromise. The British believed that even gentler methods were needed to conciliate Hitler.[49] The latter's speech on 21 May was full of fair promises. Germany might return to the League, sign a pact concerning military aircraft and enter into a naval agreement with Britain. The British were also considering the possible return of some German colonies as part of an overall European settlement. Hitler, however, was interested neither in colonies (save as a tactical talking point with the British) nor in a general settlement. He wanted to neutralize Britain, and with this in view offered a naval agreement. He was prepared to limit Germany's naval tonnage to 35 per cent of that of the British. But he wanted a higher percentage in submarines, and the package was presented with the brusque warning that the British must respond quickly: such generous terms would not be offered a second time. The British were surprisingly meek in the face of such tactics. The Admiralty was only too eager to accept given the evident determination of the Japanese to sign no more naval limitation treaties, and to undertake a massive expansion of their fleet. The Foreign Secretary, Sir John Simon, warned the Cabinet on 6 June that unless Britain accepted Hitler's terms immediately he might increase his demands. Talks proceeded rapidly between 3 and 22 June as the Germans simultaneously wooed and blackmailed the British. The subsequent British claim that they wished to make peace with Germany provided the latter made peace with everybody else had a hollow ring.[50] Furthermore it is doubtful if the British gained any advantage for themselves from the 1935 naval treaty.

Meanwhile concern was mounting over Italy's worsening relations with Abyssinia. Some, like Vansittart, were convinced that Italy should be bought off if possible, especially in view of suggestions that Germany might be ready for war by 1939. Abyssinia in itself could not be accounted a British interest, but in the eyes of the British public this question was rapidly becoming a test case for the League of Nations. The British Cabinet's view of the League was not wholly cynical, though its policy was undoubtedly influenced by its desire to satisfy the British public. It would have been easier for the British had the French bluntly refused to put any pressure on Italy – the government could then have argued that without French support League action was bound to fail.[51] But the French were divided on the issue. There was a deep reluctance to offend a possible ally against Germany, yet sufficient reservations existed to prevent a total abandonment of the League. Both London and Paris were thus tempted to follow two courses simultaneously – to make overtures to the Italians in the hope that a compromise would emerge, and increasingly in parallel with these to try to bring pressure to bear on Italy by way of the League. Had they been dealing with the traditional Italian élite alone their policy might well have succeeded, but Mussolini declined the advice of many of his professional advisers to compromise. With hindsight it is tempting to argue that the British would have been better advised to have opted unequivocally for a policy of appeasement or of support for the League.[52] But the first would have required the neutralization of British public opinion, while the second would have entailed a greater readiness to run major risks. The Admiralty dreaded the loss of even a few major units in a war with Italy – this would increase the threat from Japan in the Far East – while the Cabinet itself continued to hope that the policy of ambiguity might yet succeed.[53]

Mussolini's invasion of Abyssinia on 3 October 1935 evoked an uncertain response from the League and its leading members, Britain and France. The first sanctions were not introduced until 18 November. But in the same month the League invited Britain and France to make new overtures to Italy. A general election in Britain had returned Baldwin to power, but the government had created an impression of being more single-minded in its support of the League than it truly was. Indeed some ministers feared that if Mussolini suffered a major setback, his regime might be weakened or overthrown – to the advantage of the Communists in Italy. Most, however, were more troubled by the practical obstacles to effective pressure on Mussolini. The initial list of sanctions omitted oil – the most effective and also the most controversial economic weapon. American co-operation was essential if the oil sanction was to work, and American support was doubtful. Furthermore, while a comprehensive oil embargo would quickly paralyse the Italian war effort, it might also provoke Mussolini to declare war on Britain. If it came to war the British were anxious for French support, but of this there was no guarantee. Even if the French government rallied to the support of Britain some observers feared that France would be paralysed by internal divisions.[54]

There was a crucial meeting of the British Cabinet on 2 December 1935. It took a pessimistic view of American conduct, the threat from Japan, and the help to be expected from France. Hoare was about to meet Laval in Paris, and he was instructed to examine the prospects both for Anglo-French staff talks and a peace settlement with Italy. The Cabinet did not expect quick progress. Hoare was merely required to refer back if the peace talks seemed likely to fail, or if France refused to co-operate militarily.[55] The key figure on the British side in the Paris talks was Vansittart. He was influenced by rumours that Mussolini might be content with less than all of Abyssinia. A settlement with Italy would enable Britain and France to concentrate on the main threat – Germany. Alternatively, if a new approach to Mussolini failed, Vansittart then believed that France would have no choice but to follow Britain over Abyssinia. Vansittart's logic, however, was faulty on two counts. While he could not have foreseen that the new proposals to be submitted to Mussolini would be leaked almost at once to the French press, he was underestimating the difficulty of persuading opinion in Britain to reward aggression. In the second place he was assuming that Mussolini would be a reliable partner of the British and French once the Abyssinian crisis had been resolved. It is true that one may too readily assume the inevitability of the Rome–Berlin Axis. Vansittart could not forsee the impact that the Spanish Civil War would have upon the relations of the powers in Europe. But it was not enough to buy off Mussolini in East Africa. To keep Hitler and Mussolini apart in the long term it was necessary for Britain to show a more positive interest in eastern and central Europe, notably in Austria, and it is difficult to see how the necessary consensus could have been built up in the British government on this point. Nevertheless Vansittart must be given credit for positive thinking, and for his effort to weigh British interests and priorities from a realistic rather than a sentimental angle.

News of the Hoare–Laval Pact took the British Cabinet by surprise, but after some small amendments it at first tried to stand by the terms which Hoare and Laval wished to put to Mussolini. The Cabinet feared a rift with France if it did not. It was, however, speedily overwhelmed by the outcry in Britain. There were protests from many quarters, including *The Times*, some groups in the City of London, and many Conservative back-benchers. The last-named were perhaps the most influential. Mussolini, it was now agreed, could not be rewarded for his aggression with so large a part of

Abyssinia.[56] Hoare was repudiated and replaced as Foreign Secretary by Anthony Eden. In Rome the Fascist Grand Council had been willing to accept the terms prepared in Paris, but Mussolini had hesitated long enough to learn of the British change of heart. Hitler was relieved by the failure of the Hoare–Laval plan. Had it succeeded, he feared a revival of the Stresa Front and its development into a serious obstacle to his plans. But while Hitler welcomed the outcome, the Hoare–Laval Pact has been seen by many as not merely infamous but as a crucial element in the whole story of the failure of the League to stand up to Italy in 1935: Abyssinia was one of the great missed opportunities in the inter-war period when firmness might have prevented further aggression. Certainly it is difficult to see how Britain and France could have pursued a more disastrous policy than they did in December 1935 when they dismayed supporters of the League, and neither deterred nor appeased Mussolini. Hitler was the only beneficiary. Had it been possible for the British and French to co-operate and to stand firm, and had oil sanctions been effective, Mussolini might well have been driven to retreat. This would have delayed Hitler's reoccupation of the Rhineland. Yet, had Mussolini survived this setback, it is likely he would have been even readier to co-operate with Hitler. Had he fallen, the resultant political confusion in Italy might have increased the fears of the Right in France. In other words, there is no guarantee that a different outcome to the Abyssinian crisis would have had more than a marginal effect upon the advance of Hitler's Germany. It is useless to speculate further, but the historian cannot fail to be struck by the paradox that British and French policies for the most part designed to give priority to the German threat in fact played into Hitler's hands.[57]

THE RHINELAND AND THE SPANISH CIVIL WAR

The effects of the Hoare–Laval fiasco were not immediately apparent to contemporaries. Abyssinian resistance to Italy proved tougher than expected: early in 1936 it still seemed possible that Mussolini might have to compromise. In the middle of January 1936 Hitler thought his defeat possible.[58] The British did not give up all thoughts of pressure on Italy at once, but found the French no more co-operative than before. Paris did not foresee that a German move on the Rhineland was imminent, but the French government was determined to run no risks with Italy unless the British were prepared to give them more assurance against Germany. All that even the

Foreign Office had in mind was the inclusion of the Rhineland in some general package which, with German co-operation, might relieve the tension in Europe.

A keen debate was in progress in the Foreign Office as to the best course to pursue towards Germany. Even Vansittart did not rule out conversations with Germany, but the country had to be absolutely clear as to the price it was prepared to pay, and had also to recognize that Germany might prove unappeasable. It was important, in any case, to try to gain time through diplomacy, both for British rearmament and in the hope that something would turn up to improve the international scene – even a change of heart in Germany![59] Eden, in a pessimistic report to the Cabinet on 17 January 1936, agreed that Britain should still be looking for a *modus vivendi* with Germany. He was convinced that Hitler desired to unite all Germans in Europe under the German flag, but once that had been achieved it was unclear to what extent and in what ways Hitler would seek further power and influence.[60] In the early months of 1936, therefore, Eden was working on a many-sided approach – British rearmament, co-operation with France and perhaps even to a limited extent with Russia, the influence of the League, and negotiations with Berlin – by which Hitler might be coaxed and levered into a general settlement. Had Germany been ruled by a more cautious and orthodox regime such a strategy might have produced some results. But, as in Italy, Britain was not dealing with the traditional élite.

Instead Hitler was gradually persuading himself by the middle of February 1936 that the time was ripe for the remilitarization of the Rhineland at least one year ahead of his original hopes. Mussolini was making overtures to Berlin. Germany had no cause to fear either Russia or Poland. Hitler was well informed concerning the British lack of interest in the Rhineland *per se*. France, for the moment, was isolated. Nevertheless Hitler was careful to accompany the reoccupation with fair promises to London and Paris as to his future conduct. He even hinted that Germany might return to the League. If, however, the French resisted, a withdrawal of German forces was planned, though probably only to the best defensive lines.[61] The remilitarization began on 7 March 1936. The French protested, but made no military moves. General Gamelin had already asserted at a meeting of the French General Staff on 19 February that France alone could not oppose a German occupation. The French government agreed on 27 February that France could not act without the support of the other Locarno signatories. In response to the actual occupation the French generals insisted that resistance was possible only if a large part of the French army was mobilized. This would take two weeks. Intervention by France was likely to result in an early stalemate. The general mood in France was pacific, as predicted by Vansittart. Indeed, one French historian writes of 'une tornade pacifiste' sweeping through France.[62] Most of the French ministers shared this dread of a general war, and their talk of force and sanctions was mostly designed to win firmer commitments from the British as to the future safety of France. It was hoped that the Rhineland would at least alert other states to the danger from Germany. But Belgium was swinging towards neutrality (this was finally proclaimed on 14 October 1936), while eastern European states were impressed by Germany's new strategic frontier – a French offensive in the event of a German drive to the east now seemed even less likely.

In Britain Eden was disappointed that the Rhineland had been lost as a bargaining point in the negotiation of a hypothetical general settlement. He still hoped to secure an air pact, non-aggression treaties and the return of Germany to the League. His Cabinet colleagues thought on much the same lines. They were worried by French suggestions that economic pressure might be exerted on Germany. The Prime Minister, Baldwin, recalled the Ruhr crisis of 1923. In the event of war he thought a defeated Germany might turn Bolshevist. Yet for the health of the *entente* something had to be done to reassure the French. Staff talks were promised, if with no real enthusiasm. As it was the government was attacked by Lloyd George and the Labour Party for departing from its role as mediator between France and Germany.[63] Even Churchill was not yet ready for a French alliance. In fact little came of the staff talks, while the reaffirmation of Locarno was seen as an interim move until a comprehensive arrangement could be worked out with Germany. Reassurances were dispatched to Berlin. Eden informed the House of Commons on 18 June 1936 that the government's aim was 'nothing less . . . than a European settlement and appeasement'.

In Dr Schacht, Hitler's economics minister, Eden might have found a kindred spirit. Schacht wished to put a ceiling on German armaments – say a forty-division army – to keep the strain on the economy within bounds. His great aim was to boost Germany's foreign trade. The situation in eastern Europe was promising, with France and Britain unable to absorb much of the surplus of those countries, and with Italy in eclipse as a competitor as a result of the Abyssinian crisis. Schacht also hoped to regain some former German colonies, or at least new openings for Germany in Africa. The economic appeasement of Germany was exciting considerable interest in parts of the British Foreign Office, the Treasury, the United States and among the Dominions.[64] In the debate as to whether a 'lean' or a 'fat' Germany was likely to pose the greater threat to European peace, the future Lord Gladwyn, then a rising figure in the Foreign Office, believed that a prosperous, conciliated Germany should be Britain's aim. He hoped that after a peaceful union with Austria and with an advantageous economic position in eastern Europe, Germany would join with the western powers in the maintenance of peace in Europe and the prevention of further communist advances.[65] Indeed, Hitler often portrayed himself to his various foreign visitors as a bulwark against communism, and was careful to suggest that he was no more than a German nationalist with limited revisionist aims. British visitors in particular were eager to believe him. They did not have to be fascist sympathizers to react in this way, though to be fearful of communism was a help. Desire to avoid another great war was the strongest motive: prejudice against Versailles counted for something, as did bias against the Latin races. Lord Lothian, for instance, thought the Germans a better people than the French or the Italians.

The election of a Popular Front government in France in 1936 increased Right-wing fears of the Left and of the advance of communism. Although many on the Right continued to fear Germany and favour its containment, they readily shared the fear that a European war might work only to the advantage of Russia and communism in the long run. Earlier interest in a pact with Russia declined in case it strengthened the Left in France, or was used by the Russians to embroil France with Germany to the advantage of the Kremlin. Even the Popular Front ministry held Russia almost at arm's length and declined Moscow's proposals to hold military talks late in 1936, so fearful was it of adding to political dissension in France.[66] In Britain most of Eden's colleagues in the Cabinet disliked his interest in drawing a little closer to the Soviet Union: apart from anything else such moves might hamper talks with Germany. Baldwin feared a frustrated or defeated Germany might turn to communism.[67] The outbreak of the Spanish Civil War in July 1936 understandably intensified the fears and disunity in the two western powers. It also ensured that the ending of the Abyssinian War in April 1936 would not be followed by an improvement in their relations with Italy.

The Spanish Civil War began on 18 July. The rebel generals did not win the quick victory they had anticipated. This made the conduct of Germany and Italy all-important. Mussolini turned down the first rebel appeals for help on the 19th. The German Foreign Ministry also favoured a policy of non-intervention. It was a rumour of French intervention on the side of the Republicans on the 25th which caused Mussolini to change his mind. He feared a hostile Franco-Spanish combination under Leftist anti-Italian leaders if the Spanish Republicans prevailed with the help of a French Popular Front government.[68] Hitler also decided to help the Spanish generals on the night of 25–26 July, though he could not have perceived at that stage all the advantages which would flow to Germany as a result of the great struggle which was to envelop Spain for almost three years. Meanwhile the French government hesitated. Sympathies for the Spanish government and its Left-wing allies were balanced by fears that the civil war might escalate into a European conflict. The French Right also opposed aid to the Left in Spain. Given the prospect of dissension at home and the fear of a European 'religious' war, neutrality was not a difficult choice for many in the Popular Front. British advice in favour of non-intervention may have had some effect, but it was also welcomed as an excuse for French inaction.[69]

Whatever policy the British government pursued towards Spain was bound to excite controversy at home. In practice its policy was most influenced by the fear that foreign meddling in the civil war might lead to a general European war, and by the determination of many Conservatives to do nothing that might advance the cause of communism. In November 1937 Harold Nicolson commented that 'Tory opinion is almost entirely on the run and would willingly let Germany take Russia and over-run the Near East so long as she leaves us alone'.[70] Baldwin frankly confessed at the end of July 1936 that if there was any fighting to be done he preferred to see the Nazis and Bolsheviks doing it. Lord Gladwyn later claimed that he had not favoured a policy of encouraging Hitler to fall out with Russia, but had it occured the western powers should have turned it to their advantage. Eden thought the converse true of Russia. As he told the American ambassador on 1 June 1937, Russia 'wanted the British to pull its chestnuts out of the fire and would not be disturbed if Germany was at war with England and France leaving Russia with a comparatively free hand on the other side'. At the start of the civil war Baldwin warned his Foreign Secretary that on no account must Britain find herself involved in war on the side of communism. Although in August 1936 all the powers agreed to a policy of non-intervention, the British Foreign Office had no illusions as to its efficacy. German and Italian aid continued, and Russia soon followed. But the pretence of non-intervention provided, in its view, the best chance of avoiding a great-power war.[71]

Russian policy concerning the civil war was hesitant at first. The Kremlin seemed torn between its desire to prevent another fascist victory (nor could it ignore its standing among Communists and the Left in general) and fear of driving Britain and France into the arms of Germany. Its role in the civil war was always carefully calculated, with Spanish Communist strength being directed against anarchist and Trotskyite rivals as well as against Franco's armies, and with the Spanish Communists themselves being carefully controlled from Moscow. For Hitler the civil war had several uses. It was a useful testing-ground for Germany's new armaments. There were times when the prolongation of the war appeared to serve his interests better than an early victory by Franco. The war increased Italian dependence on Germany, worsened Italy's relations with Britain and France, and deepened the fear of communism in influential circles in western Europe. In the United States it strengthened isolationist feeling, especially among Catholics. Thus the Spanish Civil War limited and confused the options of all the powers save those of Germany.

FROM BALDWIN TO CHAMBERLAIN

Stanley Baldwin complained in the summer of 1936 that no one seemed able to give him reliable information about the mysterious German dictator and his real intentions. He was aware of Hitler's expansionist ideas as set out in *Mein Kampf*, and commented that if he did move east it would not break his heart. While he did not rule out some 'mad dog act' in the west, he hoped that Hitler would be deterred by the strength of the western powers. The Prime Minister agreed with his Chiefs of Staff that an alliance of Germany, Italy and Japan would prove fatal to the British Empire, but he argued that an attempt to form a counter-alliance might precipitate the very war they were all trying to avoid.[72] Nor was it easy to find the necessary components for such an alliance, given American isolation and the obstacles to any partnership with the Soviet Union. The British, for instance, raised objections in Paris when they learned of a Russian offer (of military aid in the event of war) made to the French on 17 February 1937. As it happened, the Popular Front ministry under Blum was too divided to explore the Russian offer. There were grounds for supposing it was not all that it appeared. Any dealings with Russia were bound to excite political controversy in France. The General Staff was particularly hostile. The Blum ministry had not entirely despaired of talks with Germany, and in any case in the east its strategy relied heavily on the anti-communist Poles. What it required of Russia was its neutrality in a crisis with Germany so that the Poles would be free to concentrate their forces on their western borders. This at least was the theory. In practice France's ties with eastern Europe continued to loosen: even opportunities to gain influence by economic means were being neglected. Finally, and worst of all, France's rearmament programme was plagued by internal economic and political problems. The production of aircraft was the worst affected.

Meanwhile it was only in 1937 that the British government began to tackle rearmament with a sense of urgency. Hitherto it had been proceeding with caution, both because it feared the economic consequences of heavy defence spending, and to a lesser extent because of the state of opinion in Britain. Hugh Dalton complained privately concerning his colleagues in the Labour Party: 'They won't face up to realities. There is still much anti-armament sentiment and many more are agin' our own Government than agin' Hitler.'[73] Armaments for use under the umbrella of the League were as much as many of the Left were willing to concede.

The government had also to recognize that if there were a war Britain could hope to win only in the event of a long struggle – that is, unless there was a sudden collapse of the German economy. Down to 1939, therefore, from whatever angle the questions of war and defence were examined, they could not be divorced from the health of the British economy. If Britain rearmed too precipitately she might lack the economic strength to carry a war through to a successful conclusion; she might even be struck by an economic crisis before a hypothetical war occurred, with fatal consequences to her foreign standing and to stability at home. There could be unpleasant economic consequences even if the defence programme successfully deterred Germany – thought had to be given to the implications of a larger peacetime military establishment and of surplus arms capacity. It was estimated that up to one-sixth of the relatively modest 1937 defence programme could be met only through imports: this extra burden on the balance of trade was a serious matter. The reserves would suffer unless Britain's foreign earnings increased. Indeed, if rearmament caused inflation, a decline – not an increase – in British exports had to be anticipated. Rearmament could thus adversely affect the British economy in a number of ways. Nor was it easy to be optimistic so long as the Johnson Act and the Neutrality Legislation ruled out the possibility of loans from the United States. The Chancellor of the Exchequer on 5 July 1939 described Britain's prospects in a war without American aid as 'exceedingly grim'.[74] The best that the British could hope for here was that American fears of a dramatic shift in the global balance of power might before too long effect a revolution in American legislation.

Not surprisingly British rearmament was painfully slow in its early stages. Fierce controversies raged over defence priorities. The navy wished to give special attention to Japan, but was restrained by the Treasury. The apparent strength of the French army and the Maginot Line discouraged spending on a British Expeditionary Force, and this was pushed to the bottom of the list. 'Limited liability' with respect to the defence of western Europe became official policy in December 1937. Much was made of the need for air parity with Germany, yet the high priority accorded to the Royal Air Force had disappointing results – at least in the short run. It proved impossible to create the powerful bomber force with which Chamberlain and others hoped to deter Germany from war at tolerable cost to the national Exchequer. Rather it was Britain in 1937 (and for much of 1938) which seemed to lie at the mercy of a 'knock-out' blow by the German air force. This at least was the belief. The defence of India against Russia continued to receive some attention, while on the much more serious and pressing question of the threat from Japan the Chiefs of Staff could only suggest that Japan was unlikely to attempt a direct assault on Britain's position in the Far East unless and until Britain was already engaged in a war in Europe.[75] Clearly even rearmament on a massive scale could not meet all these threats. Not surprisingly the Chiefs of Staff insisted that Britain must try to reduce the number of her potential enemies.

Very different was the situation in Germany. Hitler insisted in August 1936 that the economy had to be ready for war and the German army operational within four years. He accepted that shortages of raw materials ruled out a long war, but otherwise he pushed economic difficulties to one side – it was 'solely a question of will'.[76] Later in the year Göring declared that peace was 'desired until 1941', but thought complications might develop with Russia and Britain before then. War with Russia was inevitable.[77] In practice Germany was able to outspend both Britain and France on armaments down to 1939, although by that time only the outbreak of war and Germany's sensational victories saved Hitler from a major economic crisis. What must be stressed, however, is the fact that the character of his aims and his regime made it possible for Hitler to take a very different approach from the British in the production of armaments.

In May 1937 Neville Chamberlain succeeded Baldwin as British Prime Minister. His name has become almost synonymous with the much-abused, overworked and emotive word, 'appeasement', a word which until 1938 was used with no pejorative meaning. Chamberlain became a convenient scapegoat, being credited with more responsibility for the course of events than was properly his. Historians have sharply revised the original picture, though many differences of interpretation remain. Simon Newman goes so far as to argue that under Chamberlain Britain never made sufficient concessions to Germany to warrant the description, appeasement. Klaus Hildebrand sees Chamberlain's policy as a realistic attempt to save the British Empire from a war it could not win. Keith Middlemas is more critical of Chamberlain's policy after Munich than before, although in noting the continuity from the mid-1930s he feels that on the whole Chamberlain showed less skill and insight than his predecessors.[78] Amid all the controversies it is important to stress that Chamberlain differed in the main from colleagues and the Foreign Office (when indeed he did differ from them) over tactics rather than aims. One is also struck by his optimism, his greater susceptibility to self-delusion and his temperamental aversion to uncertainty and delay. Even an unsatisfactory solution seemed preferable to postponement in the hope that something would turn up. Thus although Chamberlain sometimes speculated as to the sanity of Hitler, he eagerly grabbed at any suggestion that Hitler was a man with whom one could do business. Though he professed to regard Nazis and Communists as equally bad, he was more ready to give Hitler the benefit of the doubt. In negotiations with Hitler and Mussolini he was far more flexible than with the French or the Americans. He clearly wished to uphold a liberal capitalist Britain and its empire against all comers – Socialists, Communists, Fascists and Americans. But until September 1939 he regarded war as probably a greater threat to British interests than some strengthening of Germany, Italy and Japan. The conversion of most of his fellow countrymen to an acceptance of the inevitability of war with Germany was also a slow and hesitant business. As Winston Churchill remarked to a Swedish diplomat in March 1937: 'Even if we win, it would cost us so much the victory would look like defeat.'[79] The same sentiment was expressed repeatedly by others well into the summer of 1939.

One must also recognize that in the first half year of Chamberlain's premiership Britain's position began to seem more exposed than had previously been imagined. Britain could find herself fighting the wrong war, at the wrong time and in the wrong place. There was a sudden deterioration in the state of the economy. Chamberlain spoke of 'ruin' for all if the 'mad armament race' were not checked.[80] By the end of 1937 it was evident that crises of some kind over Austria and Czechoslovakia could not be long delayed. Eden expressed Britain's dilemma over central Europe at a meeting of the Imperial Conference on 21 May 1937: Britain could neither fight over nor disinterest herself from this region.[81] But if it came to a war, was this the time and place to fight? Well into 1938 many in government feared British vulnerability to a 'knock-out' blow from the air – Britain might be defeated at the very start of a war. It is true that had the military situation been more favourable, Chamberlain and his closest colleagues would still have sought a compromise over the future of Czechoslovakia. But given the state of Britain's defences Chamberlain was even less disposed to take the advice of those like Vansittart who argued that Britain must try to keep the dictators guessing.

Chamberlain's self-confidence and impetuosity made an important contribution to Eden's resignation in February 1938. Eden saw the Prime Minister's efforts to conciliate Mussolini as a one-way street. Chamberlain, on the other hand, complained: 'Anthony, you have missed chance after chance. You simply cannot go on like this.' The gap between the two men was less wide than contemporaries imagined: the differences were essentially tactical and temperamental.[82] Admittedly tactics can be important. Chamberlain's efforts to woo Mussolini only aroused the latter's contempt. *Il Duce* dismissed the British leaders as decadent sons of virile fathers: Britain had lost the spirit of Drake which had made her great.[83] But there were times when Mussolini feared that Germany was becoming too powerful and ambitious and argued that Italy should follow a more independent policy. Finally, in 1940, Mussolini's course was determined not by the diplomacy of the powers but by Germany's military success against France. Given Mussolini's ambitions, and his susceptibility to military arguments, neither the Chamberlain nor the Eden approach could much affect the outcome. Mussolini's policy would be determined by the degree of success or failure enjoyed by the British and French in their relations with Germany.

Chamberlain, as we have seen, had decided that it was too dangerous by the end of 1937 to attempt to keep Germany guessing, or engage in a policy of 'cunctation'. One of his worries was that the French might do something foolhardy, but while Paris often took a toughish line in talks with the British, it was in fact losing confidence in its ability to influence events in eastern Europe. French honour and credibility as a great power were at stake given the treaty with Czechoslovakia: in the event of a German attack on Czechoslovakia France might have no option but to fight. Most French ministers viewed the prospect with dismay. Not surprisingly German diplomats and others from November 1937 were picking up hints from French as well as British sources of the desire for a peaceful solution to the Sudeten question (the ostensible cause of the deterioration in German–Czech relations). The visit of Lord Halifax to Germany in November 1937 was only the most direct of a number of efforts to persuade Hitler that a policy of restraint on his part would be rewarded by a general settlement of the problems of Europe. Some Germans seemed embarrassed by western frankness. There were those in the diplomatic corps and other parts of the government who feared that Anglo-French assurances were merely encouraging the Nazi extremists to take greater risks: the Nazis might overcall their hand and blunder into an unnecessary and perhaps disastrous war. In 1938–39 the British occasionally picked up mysterious hints that they should adopt a tougher tone towards Germany. Neurath, after Halifax's visit, argued that it proved that Germany could make advances only if she proceeded 'logically' and 'cautiously'.[84]

Hitler and his colleagues took a very different view of Germany's prospects. Earlier interest in British neutrality had evaporated. Ribbentrop believed an alliance with Japan would solve many of Germany's problems. From 1937 the German navy was being prepared for war with Britain, and on 5 November, at the famous Hossbach Conference, Hitler spoke of Britain as well as France as 'hate-inspired antagonists'. Hossbach's memorandum, taken in conjunction with Hitler's directives in June and December 1937, provides ample evidence – despite the objections of some historians – of the broad intentions of Hitler as and when opportunities presented themselves in the near future. That neither Austria nor Czechoslovakia fell within Germany's orbit in 1938 in the manner suggested in November 1937 is neither here nor there. Of particular interest is Hitler's fear by the end of 1937 that time could soon begin to run out for Germany and for himself. Germany had to achieve her basic aims before other powers were strong enough to resist. Given advances in weapon technology Germany's aircraft and tanks would soon become outdated. Finally Hitler was beginning to fear for his own health – he was determined to achieve irreversible progress towards hegemony in Europe before his own faculties began to decline. Despite the doubts of many of his professional advisers Hitler was determined to press on with all speed, in so far as the situation as he perceived it allowed.[85] Given this state of mind, he was unlikely to be impressed by diplomacy, however skilful, unless it was backed up with military power and a real readiness to fight.

NOTES AND REFERENCES

1. Thorne [1] p. 373
2. Allen, Ch. 10, especially pp. 159–60. See also Roberts, pp. 316–17, etc.
3. Mitsubishi (ERB),pp. 482, 554, 573, 591, 639, etc.
4. Roberts, p. 341
5. Boyle, p. 105
6. FRUS, USSR 1933–39, pp. 53–61, etc.
7. Morley, pp. 11–17
8. Silberman, p. 274
9. For an interesting though rather impressionistic study of the mood in Japan, 1931–45, see Ienaga, *passim*
10. Roskill [2] ɪɪ, 291, 313
11. Trotter, p. 100
12. Shai, pp. 22–7
13. Trotter, *passim*
14. Morley, pp. 5, 35, 39–41
15. AD, ɪ, 119–20
16. Crowley, p. 321
17. Coox and Conroy, pp. 299 ff.
18. Roskill [2] ɪɪ, 352
19. Roskill [2] ɪɪ, 352
20. E. H. Carr [1] p. ɪx
21. W. Carr [2] pp. 36–7
22. Broszat, p. xiii
23. See below, p. 192
24. Rauschning, pp. 279–90. See also Broszat, pp. 347–60
25. Müller, *passim*
26. Kitchen [2] pp. 285–311. See also Deist, pp. 22–6, 37–8, 50–3, and Heinemann, *passim*, especially pp. 88–9, 115–16, 187, which highlight both Neurath's ambition and his differences with Hitler

27. Hildebrand, pp. 57–9, 71
28. For reviews of the question, see Michaelis, pp. 331–60, and Hauner, pp. 15–32
29. W. Carr [2] pp. 131 ff.
30. Robertson [1] pp. 6–7; O'Neill, pp. 40–1, Ch. 10
31. Ryder, p. 348
32. Hiden, p. 65
33. Gilbert [2] pp. 316–20, 330–62, 377–81
34. Marquand, pp. 748–51, 759–60. For the debate in the British Foreign Office, see Medlicott in Dilks [1] I, 78 ft. Note Butler, p. 215, for speculation by N. Chamberlain in June 1936 as to whether any 'real bona fides in Germany' existed or not
35. See Peden, p. 138
36. Howard [3] p. 89
37. Butler, pp. 197, 208–11
38. Butler, p. 216
39. Hildebrand, p. 28
40. R. J. Young, pp. 48–63
41. Dilks [1] I, 81–6
42. Ulam, pp. 218–19
43. Weinberg [1] pp. 221–2
44. FRUS, 1935, I, 215–16, 296
45. Watt, Ch. 1
46. Manne [1] pp. 725–56
47. Robertson [2] p. 16
48. Adamthwaite [2] p. 137
49. Warner [1] pp. 60–92; Middlemas and Barnes, pp. 813–14, 818–19
50. Roskill [2] II, 302–9
51. Robertson [2] p. 157
52. Warner [1] p. 100
53. Middlemas and Barnes, pp. 877–8. Note Roskill [1] III, 187–9 for an interesting exchange between Hoare and Hankey on sanctions and the potential of the League. Hankey took the Vansittart position while the Foreign Secretary put the case for the League and public opinion
54. BD 2nd series, xv, 427–31, 444
55. BD 2nd series, xv, 360–3; Middlemas and Barnes, pp. 884–99
56. BD 2nd series, xv, 467–8, 496–7. For a recent analysis of the Hoare–Laval Pact, see Medlicott in Dilks [1] I, 118–38
57. Waley, p. 142, notes that in June 1936 Baldwin insisted that his controversial 'sealed' lips comment in Parliament during the Abyssinian crisis referred to the German threat and the desirability of retaining Italy as an ally. The Defence Requirements Committee argued late in 1935 that Britain must be ready for war by the beginning of 1939 (Dilks [1] I, 111)
58 Robertson [2] p. 186
59. BD 2nd series, xv, 713–36, 762–91
60. BD 2nd series, xv, 569–70
61. Emmerson, pp. 98–100
62. Duroselle, p. 171. See also R.J. Young, pp. 120, etc.
63. Middlemas and Barnes, p. 923

64. MacDonald, pp. 1–28. See below, pp. 205–6
65. Gladwyn, pp. 53–68
66. R.J. Young, pp. 146–9. For growing anti-communist concern in Britain and its effect on attitudes towards Nazi Germany, see Griffiths, Ch. 7
67. Middlemas and Barnes, pp. 915, 918
68. Coverdale, pp. 74–83
69. Micaud, pp. 116–17; Duroselle, pp. 304–5; Edwards, pp. 25–8
70. Nicolson, p. 313
71. See Middlemas and Barnes, pp. 948 ff., especially pp. 955, 961; FRUS, 1937, I, 318; Gladwyn, p. 296; Coverdale, pp. 90–8; Edwards, pp. 24, 30–7
72. Middlemas and Barnes, p 950
73. Middlemas and Barnes, p 948
74. Hinsley [2] p. 70. On Britain's economic problems in general, see Peden, pp. 63–96
75. Roskill [2] II, 345–6
76. DGFP, C, v, 853–62
77. Robertson [1] pp. 85–8
78. Hildebrand, pp. 54–5; Middlemas, pp. 41–58, 412–21; S. Newman, pp. 1–7
79. Hagglof, p. 103
80. MacDonald, pp. 42, 66–7. See also Gibbs, pp. 400–1
81. AD, I, 74
82. Carlton, pp. 100–33
83. Coverdale, pp. 351–3
84. DGFP, D, I, 68–71. See also DGFP, D, II, 72–4, 218–23, 246–7, 252–3, 326–8, etc. Note Seabury, pp. 93–6; Watt, pp. 128–9
85. Weinberg [2] pp. 36–45

Chapter 8

EUROPE, 1938–1940

FROM THE ANSCHLUSS TO MUNICH

The Austrian crisis of February–March 1938 was not stage-managed by Hitler alone. Anxious as he was to bring Austria firmly under his influence, the actual course of events owed something to the impatience of the Austrian Nazis, and to the last-minute efforts of Chancellor Schuschnigg to escape the net that was being prepared around him. Schuschnigg responded to the pressure exerted on him by Hitler at Berchtesgaden on 12 February by calling for a national plebiscite to be held on 13 March. Voters were to answer the question, 'Are you for a free and German, independent and social, Christian and united Austria?' Hitler was outraged. Schuschnigg was forced to call off the plebiscite and resign. His Nazi successor invited German troops into Austria to preserve order. The German occupation on 12 March had to be hastily improvised, with Göring often showing more drive and resolution than Hitler himself.

In Britain the Foreign Secretary, Lord Halifax, took the view that, much though one might regret what was happening, there was nothing to be done. Churchill, in contrast, called for the formation of a Grand Alliance. Chamberlain described this as 'a very attractive idea ... until you came to examine its practicability'. Such an alliance would not save Czechoslovakia, the country now under threat. To go to war on the Czech question, he also argued, would simply be a pretext for going to war with Germany. The Sudeten Germans had a grievance, and he refused to believe that the Sudetenland was worth a European war.[1] Halifax doubted if Britain should risk defeat on such a question, and argued that German success here would not necessarily lead to hegemony in Europe. To others in the Foreign Office, while a policy of appeasement seemed 'cowardly', it also seemed the 'least bad' of the available options.[2] On 24 March 1938, therefore, Chamberlain told the Commons that Britain would make no promises to Czechoslovakia, though if war broke out 'the inexorable pressure of facts might well prove more powerful than formal pronouncements'. Some arms increases were already contemplated, mainly for the air force. The Chiefs of Staff, however, continued to insist that Britain should risk no European war before the spring of 1939 at the earliest. They warned further that any war was likely to spread and include Italy and Japan, and it was not possible to envisage a time when Britain would be safe against such a combination. The service chiefs also argued that eastern Europe was not a British strategic interest, that eastern European states would be liabilities rather than assets so far as Britain was concerned, and that Czechoslovakia could not be defended against Germany.[3] The politicians readily added other justifications, such as the hope that Hitler would be content merely to bring all Germans under one flag in Europe, the claim that Czechoslovakia was an artificial creation of several nationalities which could not hope to endure indefinitely, or assertions that the French were weak and irresponsible, and that the Dominions would not support Britain in a European war unless they saw vital Commonwealth interests at stake.

There was thus no British welcome for Litvinov's proposal on 17 March for a great-power conference on Czechoslovakia, with perhaps some role for the League of Nations. The Foreign Office was divided on the advisability of drawing Russia into such questions. Chamberlain was not alone in his belief that Russia's aim was to cause confusion and war in Europe. Russia's interest in a deal with Germany rather than the western powers cannot be discounted.[4] One cannot assume that a Russian alliance with the western powers was there for the asking. At the same time one must acknowledge the strength of anti-Russian prejudice in the British government, and its fear that any dealings with Russia would wreck all hopes of agreement with Germany. Both attitudes betrayed a lack of imagination. A tentative probing of Russian intentions could hardly have increased the dangers facing the western powers in 1938, even if it seems improbable that any comprehensive agreement could have been negotiated at this time. At most the three governments might have tried to demonstrate to Germany that co-operation between them was not impossible in the face of continued German provocation. Hitler might still have been able to call their bluff, but as it was in the summer of 1938 he was able to act in the virtual certainty that Russia would not be involved.

Russia, less even than Britain and France, was in no condition to run risks in 1938. Her industrialization programme was still in its early stages, and she was recovering from the effects of the agricultural crisis and of the great Purges. Tension with Japan in the Far East exploded into serious border clashes in the summer of 1938, and it was the middle of August before the Russians could be sure that the Japanese were not intent on war. In the west one cannot say whether they saw a European war as a threat or an opportunity to make gains. But they must have been disturbed by Berlin's failure to respond to their tentative overtures, and by its attitude in general. The agreement with France had brought no dividends; in fact relations were cooling from 1936. The American embassy in Moscow thought it detected signs of Russian disillusionment with 'Geneva' diplomacy and other western links from the beginning of 1936, and tendencies towards isolation and self-reliance. But the embassy also stressed the difficulty of making any assessments because of the seclusion in which foreign diplomats were kept in Moscow – the normal contacts outside formal meetings with politicians and bureaucrats were missing.[5] Soviet behaviour in 1938 was ambiguous. Certainly there was talk of Russia honouring her commitments to the Czechs – though it is important to note that the Russian treaty with Czechoslovakia provided for assistance only after intervention by the French. Furthermore, even if it came to war, Russia could send aid only through or over the territory of Poland and Rumania. Resistance from these states was possible, especially from Poland. Not surprisingly German policy-makers paid relatively little attention to Russia during the Sudeten crisis. It was noted that the nearest Russian territory was 400 miles distant from what would have been the main battlefield in Czechoslovakia.[6] It is true that Russia should have had an interest in the survival of an unbroken Czechoslovakia, both to check German expansion and perhaps as a source of friction between France and Germany. A common front with the western powers in the hope that this might deter Hitler might have had some appeal, though, hardly, one suspects, if it carried with it any grave war risks. But Russia above all had cause to try to keep its options open, and to ensure that in the event of war it did not repeat the crippling experience of 1914 – that Russia, in other words, should be free to enter any conflict at a moment of its choosing.[7]

Meanwhile on 28 March 1938 Hitler had reached agreement with the leader of the Sudeten Germans, Konrad Henlein, that the latter would always demand more whatever the Czechs conceded. Hitler was determined to smash the Czech state just as soon as he believed it safe to do so. On the other hand the British were stepping up their efforts to avert a general European war over the fate of the Sudetenland. In talks at the end of April the British persuaded the French that the Czechs must be prepared to make very extensive concessions to Germany for the sake of European peace. Although a German–Czech crisis on 21 May produced a British warning to Berlin on the lines of Chamberlain's speech of 24 March, London also warned Paris at the same time that it could not expect automatic British support in the event of war. In fact this episode increased the determination of Chamberlain and his closest colleagues to try to find

a peaceful solution. In Germany it made Hitler all the more determined to act as soon as possible even though it led to more difficulties
with some of his generals. As General Jodl noted on 30 May 1938:[8]

> The whole contrast becomes more acute between the Führer's intuition
> that we *must* do it this year, and the opinion of the Army that we
> cannot do it yet, as most certainly the Western Powers will interfere,
> and we are not as yet equal to them.

What, one wonders, would have been the effect if the British and
French had played their cards closer to their chests, or if Germany
had been less confident of Russian non-involvement? Would the
professional soldiers and diplomats around Hitler have offered more
resistance than they did? As it was, the faint-hearted opposition of
the western powers produced the resignation of the army Chief of
Staff, General Beck, in the summer of 1938, and Hitler was forced
to postpone the complete disruption of Czechoslovakia for six
months.[9]

Not surprisingly controversy continues to surround the conduct of
British policy in the summer of 1938, and especially of Chamberlain's
role therein. Serious contemporary criticism, however, developed
only in the second half of September – that is when Hitler showed
his determination not merely to settle the Sudeten question but to
do so in a way most damaging to the Czechs. Of those closest to
Chamberlain Halifax was the most sensitive to shifts in public
opinion.[10] Tension built up steadily in the summer of 1938, with the
British trying to retain the initiative with the dispatch of Lord
Runciman to act as mediator between the Czech government and its
minorities. As prospects for a settlement worsened in August and
early September, so the British government again warned that no
one could be sure how far a war might spread. But in any war of
nerves the advantage lay with Hitler. He had good intelligence from
many sources on the thinking and reactions of his opponents, and it
was not difficult to fill in the gaps.[11] It was as if he could read the
appreciations by the British and French service chiefs in the late
summer of 1938 as they issued dire warnings that Czechoslovakia
could not be saved other than by the defeat of Germany in a long,
unlimited war. At this time the French were even more fearful than
the British of the threat from the air. The French had no effective
offensive plans, and intended to wait while allied strength was built
up and Germany was weakened by economic warfare. The British
Chiefs of Staff believed that after '*a long war*' this economic pressure
would be decisive.[12] Interestingly enough the German generals were
equally pessimistic. It was claimed that the Siegfried Line could not
hold out for more than three weeks – too little time in which to
overcome the Czech defences and a thirty-two division army.[13] The
German air force was not prepared to launch great air attacks on

London and Paris. But Hitler seemed unmoved by such considerations. Probably he calculated that, if he wished, he could always
avoid war with the western powers at the last minute, that he was
free to raise or lower the tension largely as he saw fit, and that the
nature of the opposition (including the potential opposition within
Germany) would normally leave him with the initiative. Above all
he could always exploit the Anglo-French desire for peace even when
they might seem on the brink of nerving themselves to fight.

For Britain and France to choose war in September 1938 they had
to believe both that it was inevitable and that this was the best time
to fight. Halifax thought it a confession of despair to regard any war
as inevitable. As he remarked to the American chargé on 24 August,
there was a moral issue at stake, but he questioned if it were more
serious than that involving Manchuria or Abyssinia. He doubted if,
assuming an allied victory, it would be wise to reconstitute Czechoslovakia in its present form. He agreed that if war were regarded as
inevitable it would be better to fight with the aid of the Czechs, but
he could not bring himself to accept that premise. Nevertheless he
admitted:[14]

> The background of this horrible situation . . . is of course the mentality
> of Nazism which 'comes from the devil', and that there might not be
> lasting peace in Europe until that spirit is killed. They were dealing
> with a man who for all practical purposes is a madman, and from that
> arises all of the uncertainty.

Chamberlain at times said much the same. Nevertheless he clung to
the hope that Hitler might be surrounded by wild men who were
isolating him from the true facts. He also feared war by accident.
Hence his desire for personal contact with Hitler to see if he was
truly a man with whom one could do business – or whether he was
indeed 'half-mad'. Unfortunately he was too eager to be persuaded
of the former.

There is no need to retell the story of Chamberlain's negotiations
with Hitler at Berchtesgaden and Godesberg between 15 and 22
September. Chamberlain rarely showed his mettle as a negotiator
during the two visits. Only his dread of war, and the feeling that
Hitler's excitable temperament might result in some irrational act if
he were pressed too hard, can explain this weakness. At first Hitler
seemed to offer a way out with talk of self-determination for the
German areas in the Sudetenland. Chamberlain, with difficulty, won
Cabinet and French support for this solution. Britain and France then
brought pressure to bear on the Czechs to accept. The French also
ignored an overture from the Russians. If Russian aid was ever a
possibility, London and Paris alike showed no real interest. Chamberlain's feelings are revealed in a comment to the American ambassador on 21 September that 'war is the end of this civilization – that

Communism or something worse is liable to follow'. Another minister remarked that a war for the balance of power might result in a balance favourable only to Bolshevism.[15] But to Chamberlain's consternation Hitler rejected his new proposals at Godesberg. Hitler demanded an unacceptably speedy transfer of territory, as well as making new claims. Nevertheless Chamberlain was prepared to comply, so anxious was he to avoid war. This time, however, he encountered growing opposition in the Cabinet, opposition which became decisive when Halifax, after some hesitation, stood out against the Prime Minister. On the 25th Halifax insisted that Britain could not press such terms on Prague. If war followed, so be it.

For the next three days Europe seemed close to war. Britain and France began to make preparations, the Royal Navy being mobilized on the 27th. On the same day the French Prime Minister gloomily commented that Hitler was risking a conflict he could not win, but from which revolutionaries and Communists alone would benefit.[16] Nevertheless the search for peace continued, with Chamberlain hoping that Britain's new stance would force Germany to the conference table. At first the signs were not hopeful, but Hitler was under pressure in Germany as well as from abroad. Göring joined the peace party, while the mass of the German people was clearly averse to war. Roosevelt addressed peace appeals to Hitler and Mussolini, and on the 28th Mussolini himself asked Hitler to think again. One cannot be sure why Hitler changed his mind, but he now conceded just enough to make possible the four-power meeting at Munich on the 29th. In fact he had to yield very little (though one should not forget his great sense of frustration – the destruction of Czechoslovakia being his real objective in September). The changes to the Godesberg terms were essentially cosmetic, and Chamberlain was mainly interested in Hitler's 'assurances' concerning his future conduct – that he would consult with Britain over future problems, and that he wished to avoid war. Some of Chamberlain's remarks about peace with honour and peace in our time on his return from Munich were doubtless those of a tired and relieved politician carried away by the excitement of the moment. But there is other evidence of his optimism concerning the future. He told Hankey on 2 October that he believed he had at last laid 'the foundations of a stable peace, though it still remains to build the superstructure'. At the end of October, at a Cabinet meeting, he failed to share the reservations of some of his colleagues, and in particular agreed to only a modest increase in the rearmament programme. It is true that within the diplomatic community as a whole expectations as to the future varied sharply. The American military attaché in Berlin thought peace possible for a decade. Geneva hummed with speculation, hopeful and otherwise, as League personnel watched impotently from the sidelines.[17] But few were so optimistic as Chamberlain.

It has been argued that Britain and France should have fought in 1938 when they would have had the assistance of thirty well-equipped Czech divisions. The French would have had an advantage of four or five to one on their own front. A German exercise earlier in 1938 had resulted in considerable 'French' successes in just such a situation.[18] Gamelin, however, foresaw another Somme if France attacked. He preferred to wait while Britain mobilized: in 1938 he could not count on even two British divisions.[19] The British defence chiefs on the whole thought a delay of six months advantageous. But for Chamberlain it was above all a question of averting war – not assessing how it could best be won. As we have seen, many shared his view that even a victorious war would be disastrous. Oliver Stanley, a British minister who was thoroughly outraged by German conduct, left Harold Nicolson with the following impressions:[20]

> At the same time any reference to Russian assistance made him wince, and at one moment he sighed deeply and said, 'You see, whether we win or lose, it will be the end of everything we stand for.' By 'we' he obviously means the capitalist classes.

Many thought Munich a 'necessary defeat', while the Permanent Under-Secretary in the Foreign Office, Sir Alexander Cadogan, reflecting on the prospect of war, commented: 'Pray God we shall never have to depend on the Soviet, or Poland or – the United States.'[21] Nevertheless historians may fairly complain of the lack of imagination and finesse displayed by British policy-makers, and criticize Chamberlain's reluctance to speed rearmament after September 1938, and to dilute his hopes of a final settlement with Germany.[22] Munich may have been unavoidable, given the state of feeling in France and Britain, but the crisis should have taught Chamberlain and others more about the nature of Hitler and his intentions.

THE UNITED STATES AND EUROPE, 1933–38

One of Hitler's basic assumptions in the 1930s was that he could largely ignore the United States. The British viewed the Americans with divided and mixed feelings. War debts, economic and naval differences had done much to injure Anglo-American relations since 1919. Even among those who felt that co-operation was desirable or (given Britain's weakened state) imperative, serious doubts existed as to whether it would be available. Others were afraid that if American help were forthcoming the cost would prove expensive, if not intolerable. The feeling was widespead in British governing circles that Americans were greedy and selfish in matters of trade and tariffs, jealous and irresponsible in their attitude towards the British Empire, and ignorant or unrealistic concerning international affairs. The great upsurge in isolationist sentiment in the United States in the mid-1930s was not the only obstacle to Anglo-American co-operation, and as historians are now increasingly revealing even when circumstances forced the two peoples to co-operate the competitive element was never absent. Nevertheless the German embassy in Washington was warning Berlin from 1938 that it could not count on permanent American neutrality in the event of a European war and a threat to the balance of power on the Continent. Unfortunately Hitler chose to believe that he could achieve European hegemony before there was any risk of American intervention.

From the outset of his presidency in 1933 Roosevelt followed international affairs closely. He encouraged American diplomats to write to him privately, and he also built up a correspondence with some non-Americans. He exposed himself to a variety of opinions. In the later 1930s supporters and opponents of appeasement wrote frankly and confidently to the President. But initially Roosevelt had to give priority to home affairs and to the alleviation of the unemployment and poverty brought about by the Depression. In the struggle to push the New Deal legislation through Congress Roosevelt picked up allies where he could, and their number included some of the strongest isolationist groups in the United States. Disarmament, however, remained a popular issue, and for a time Roosevelt hoped that a link might be forged here with neutral rights – that in return for international progress on disarmament the United States might waive its rights as a neutral should the League impose sanctions against certain aggressors. But Roosevelt's hopes that he might be entrusted with discretionary powers in the enforcement of American arms embargoes against belligerents were frustrated in the Senate: isolationist western Progressive Senators were able to trade support for Roosevelt's domestic programme for an arms embargo against all belligerents. The Abyssinian crisis in 1935, and a renewed possibility of war in Europe, wrecked all the President's efforts to find some freedom of manœuvre in the conduct of American foreign policy.

Even before Americans awoke to the possibility of a new war in Europe, hostility to involvement in transatlantic matters had been increased by the vexed question of war debts, and the final defaulting of all European states except Finland in the early 1930s. In 1934 the Johnson Act forbade loans to any state which was in default. The First World War and its distorting effects on the world economy were also seen as a major cause of the Depression. There had been early American critics of the Versailles peace, and even in the 1920s some American historians had begun to challenge orthodox interpretations of the causes of the First World War and American involvement in it. Such criticism became increasingly widespread and popular in the

1930s. In 1935 the work of the Nye Commission led many to believe that American bankers and arms manufacturers with their western European interests had dragged the United States into an unnecessary war. In this climate it is not surprising that an opinion poll of April 1937 found that nearly two-thirds believed that the United States had been wrong to enter the First World War.

The isolationists did not form a single, homogeneous body. Some were nationalists first and foremost, anxious to avoid foreign commitments and constraints. Some were genuine pacifists: others were determined not to be caught up in another European war. Few considered the implications of isolation systematically, though the historian Charles Beard did so more than most. Interestingly, as the situation worsened in Europe, even he could be found acknowledging at times that American security was bound up with the maintenance of some sort of balance of power in Europe.[23] It was the hope that America need not be seriously threatened by anything that happened in Europe (or Asia) that made the isolationist case so appealing in the 1930s. There was also a tendency to opt for selective isolationism in the belief, for instance, that trade with belligerents in non-military goods might still prove compatible with American neutrality. This desire to reconcile American trading interests with the avoidance of war did much to shape the Neutrality Legislation of 1936–37. A conscious effort was made to learn from the experience of the period between August 1914 and February 1917. American citizens were forbidden to travel in the liners of belligerents; no arms were to be sold to belligerents; other goods were to be paid for by belligerents in cash and carried away in their own ships. Even some Congressmen thought this a rather too ingenious way of having one's cake and eating it. Roosevelt in his Chautauqua speech of 14 August 1936 denounced all war profits as 'fool's gold'. He also appealed to a deep-rooted American belief when he asserted that it was the duty of American democracy to serve as an inspiration and model for others. By this many Americans meant that it was no part of their country's mission in the world to intervene on other continents: one great attempt had been made in 1917–19 to put the world to rights with a singular lack of success – America should not attempt the impossible again. Indeed, disillusionment with Versailles led many to feel that the Germans were merely rectifying legitimate grievances. It was no small step from there to see Nazi Germany and Japan as behaving in the customary manner of imperialist states and in no way as departing from the norm of power politics as practised by the European great powers. Even those who feared or disliked the Nazis might feel that Russian communism was every bit as bad. It was tempting to hope that the Nazis and Communists might destroy each other, while those whose anti-communism ran very deep argued that any attempts to form an anti-German front would simply render a service to communism. American isolationism thus sprang from a variety of motives, and expressed itself in a number of ways which were not necessarily consistent with each other. It was possible, for instance, to behave as an isolationist towards Europe without necessarily washing one's hands of the Far East.

Roosevelt made great play with the importance of American neutrality in his (successful) bid for re-election in 1936, but in private he was exploring the possibility of a more positive foreign policy. At this time, however, he was more inclined to play with ideas than give a positive lead even to his subordinates. A trade boycott of Germany was mooted. He followed the meeting at Stresa in 1935 with interest. The increase in naval construction from 1934 was an anti-Japanese as well as an anti-recessionist move. But in general Roosevelt felt as if he were groping for a door in a blank wall. Early in 1937 he described his policy as one of 'watchful waiting', adding, 'I would not dare to say this out loud because sometimes it is better to appear much wiser than one really is.'[24] He continued to follow events in Europe very closely, insisting that Germany, not communism, was at the root of the problem, and seeking information, for instance, on the ability of the Poles and Czechs to defend themselves against Germany.[25] At the same time he responded to the interest of his Secretary of State, Cordell Hull, and others in a grand programme of trade liberalization as the best road to peace. It was claimed that freer access to markets and raw materials should remove the grievances of the revisionist powers and facilitate not only economic growth, but disarmament, respect for the rule of law and even the revision of disputed clauses in Versailles and other treaties. At least such policies might strengthen the moderates in Germany, Italy and Japan.

The proposals of the State Department, however, received a tepid reception in Britain. In part the British feared that the Americans were trying to dilute imperial preference and to secure other economic advantages for themselves. But they also argued, in conjunction with the French, that German and Italian concessions should precede a policy of economic appeasement. Chamberlain insisted that Germany would not be co-operative until confronted by an effective British deterrent. To this the State Department replied in March 1937, reiterating its belief that an improvement in trade relations and economic welfare would ease existing political tensions. Roosevelt added in July that 'the British tories were still tories and in spite of Eden's denial, want peace at a great price'.[26] The British, especially under Chamberlain's guidance, preferred to negotiate with Germany in their own time and in their own way. Talks on trade and other economic issues continued well into the summer of 1939, giving rise to American fears of an Anglo-German deal at their expense. The British, in fact, had several objectives in view. They wished to protect and promote their own economic interests as far as possible, and they wished to reduce the danger of war and the burden of armaments. In certain circumstances, therefore, Britain might lean more towards Germany than the United States. Persistent British approaches to Berlin, however, brought no lasting rewards, and in 1938 Britain finally made some economic concessions to the United States in the hope, among other things, that the resultant trade treaty might serve as a reminder to Germany that the New World could not be ignored in the power balance.[27] Chamberlain, however, was determined to yield no more than the bare minimum to the United States, and well into the summer of 1939 he continued to negotiate with Germany despite his own occasional admissions (those of his advisers were more frequent) that economic issues were secondary so far as the Nazis were concerned. In November 1937 Chamberlain sadly remarked: 'Politics in international affairs govern actions at the expense of economics, and often of reason.'[28]

Meanwhile Roosevelt's approach remained tentative and experimental. From the summer of 1937 he was impressed both by Japan's belligerence in the Far East and by the failure of the German moderates to assert themselves. Economic appeasement no longer looked very promising. But his relations with Chamberlain remained distant, and isolationism strong in the United States. Historians over the years have differed sharply in their interpretation of Roosevelt's conduct and aims: whether, as MacGregor Burns argues, he failed to provide his country with a sufficiently vigorous lead: whether he exaggerated the importance to America of what was occurring in Europe and east Asia; or where exactly he stood between these two extremes.[29] Perhaps it is wisest to start by acknowledging how difficult it is to make any unqualified assertions concerning Roosevelt. He was one of the least dogmatic of politicians. On the one hand he was determined not to get seriously out of step with feeling in the United States: on the other he believed that American security and prosperity could be seriously threatened if Germany and Japan were able to dominate Eurasia. Just what should or could be done by the United States to ward off these threats would, however, be determined primarily by what seemed possible and wise at any given moment. His initial task, as he saw it, was to awaken American and foreign opinion to the danger. Doubtless he hoped that the United States would not find itself in the front line of any resistance that was offered to aggression. But his aim was to exploit opportunities as they arose to deter and obstruct the expansionist powers, hopefully at the least cost to the United States.

Roosevelt's 'quarantine' speech in Chicago in October 1937 was his first significant move, and is a classic example of his methods. The speech contained no proposals of substance: the suggestion that aggressors might be quarantined was meaningless (save in so far as Roosevelt might have envisaged a long-distance naval blockade of

Japan).[30] But his real purpose, as Roosevelt explained to the President of Columbia University, was to stir up 'world sentiment' and strengthen the forces for world peace. He tried to encourage the Roman Catholic Church to speak out on behalf of peace, and hoped that there would be some lead from the British. His aim was to try to awaken opinion (in America as well as elsewhere) to the danger of war because only then would democratic governments be in a position to take more concrete steps. He grumbled when other governments failed to respond, and feared that a British policy of appeasement would strengthen isolationist sentiment in the United States.[31] Yet Roosevelt could hardly complain when, at the Brussels Conference summoned in November 1937 to consider the conflict between China and Japan, he failed to respond to British inquiries about the possibility of a joint naval demonstration in the Far East against Japan. Doubtless the British were less confident than they pretended, and certainly Chamberlain did not share Eden's interest in Anglo-American co-operation. Roosevelt instructed his representative at the conference that the United States could not act with the League, take the lead itself or act as 'a tail to the British kite'. Independent action might be forthcoming, but Roosevelt was clearly determined not to alarm isolationist groups in the United States. He contented himself with the secret mission of Captain Ingersoll, USN, to London early in 1938 to exchange naval information with the British Admiralty. These talks included no commitments or promises, but they began to lay a basis for naval co-operation should the two powers find themselves at war against a common enemy. Roosevelt also pushed ahead with the expansion of the American navy. The search for other ways forward continued, but the sinking at this time of an American gunboat, the *Panay*, by Japanese aircraft failed to evoke a national outcry, while in January 1938 the Ludlow Amendment – a proposal that only a national referendum should permit an American government to declare war, save in response to a direct attack – was only narrowly defeated in Congress.

Within the State Department the battle intensified between those who believed that Germany and Japan could be appeased and those who did not. Early in 1938 Roosevelt agreed to float the idea for some sort of international conference to push for trade liberalization, disarmament and other steps which might reduce international tension. There was an equivocal response from Britain. Chamberlain wished to give priority to his negotiations with the Italians. Hitler's purge of 'moderate' generals and other key figures in February 1938 also discouraged Roosevelt. Eden's resignation was another disappointment, but one should not suppose that the British missed a significant opportunity to draw the United States into a more active role in world affairs in January–February 1938. Roosevelt was still preoccupied with finding ways to educate opinion: at best he hoped to persuade the dictators that they could not ignore the United States in the long run. Indeed, in the spring of 1938 he was largely content to watch and comment in private. Chamberlain's policies, for instance, prompted the following commentary on 9 March 1938:[32]

> As someone remarked to me – 'If a Chief of Police makes a deal with the leading gangsters and the deal results in no more hold-ups, that Chief of Police will be called a great man – but if the gangsters do not live up to their word the Chief of Police will go to jail.' Some people are, I think, taking very long chances.

The realist in him expected concessions to work only temporarily, and to be followed by worse trouble.

Over Czechoslovakia in the summer of 1938, Roosevelt was undoubtedly dismayed by Germany's demands and her final success. On the other hand he had received so many reports from Europe of Germany's military advantages – especially the threat which her air force posed to France – and of low French morale that when war seemed imminent at the end of September he spoke out in favour of peace. He may even have entertained some hopes that the Sudetenland was indeed Hitler's final demand. But basically his strategy remained the same – the encouragement of resistance to the dictators and such warning hints as he could manage to send to them. Thus on 15 September he informed his ambassador in Rome of his expectation of war within five years: when it came, 90 per cent of the American people would support the British and French, and he would do all he could to encourage 'their natural sympathy'. But he also added that he had no thought of sending troops to Europe.[33] The Sudeten crisis strengthened his hand a little. An opinion poll suggested that nearly two-thirds of the people now believed that an Axis victory in Europe would endanger American interests. It became a little easier to increase American defence preparations, and Roosevelt placed special emphasis upon air power. As early as November 1938 he was speculating on the possibility of loaning as well as selling warplanes to Hitler's opponents. He also passed on to Chamberlain, by way of a mutual acquaintance, some generalized assurances concerning the economic aid that Britain might expect in the event of war.[34] British and American relations, however, were not significantly closer than at the beginning of the year. Halifax remarked that Britain would be most favourably situated if she could balance between Germany and the United States (Russia's mischief-making capacity would also be curtailed). But one had to face the facts as they were. The Foreign Office therefore even favoured economic concessions to the United States if these brought some political advantages.[35]

Roosevelt, when he spoke to the Senate Military Affairs Committee on 31 January 1939 and in off-the-record remarks to the press later in the year, began to spell out the dangers to the United States from an Axis victory in Europe. He made much of the potential Axis threat in Latin America. If there was some exaggeration there was also a genuine underlying fear. The State Department suspected German involvement in an attempted coup in Brazil in May 1938. Axis domination of Europe threatened to give it great influence in Argentina, 80 per cent of whose exports went to that continent.[36] From the American embassy in London there came an estimate in March 1939 that an Axis victory might rob the United States of half its export trade and destroy 3 million jobs. America could meet such a challenge only with a drastic reordering of its economy and society. Faith in democratic ideals and methods would inevitably suffer.

> In short, America, alone in a jealous and hostile world, would find that the effort and cost of maintaining 'splendid isolation' would be such as to bring about the destruction of all those values which the isolation policy had been designed to preserve.[37]

Assistant Secretary of State Adolf Berle is a good example of one of those within the administration who moved at this time from a policy of relative aloofness towards Europe and suspicion of the British Empire to the belief that British imperialism was at least preferable to that of Germany and Italy. Indeed, in self-defence the United States itself might be driven to empire-building.[38] Given the evident movement of opinion within the United States Roosevelt attempted in 1939 to revise the Neutrality Legislation in favour of Britain and France. With American economic support he had reason to hope that the western powers might hold the military line against the Axis by themselves. Isolationist groups in Congress, however, were too strong for him until after the outbreak of war in Europe in September 1939.

TO THE POLISH GUARANTEE

The Polish Guarantee has been described as the 'culmination' of, not a revolution in, British policy, 'going back to before September 1938 . . . [with] the attempt to stem German expansion in eastern Europe by any means short of war but in the last resort by war itself'.[39] British policy, even after Munich, was hardly as clear-cut as this. For a time Halifax and Cadogan, for instance, seemed disposed to write off parts of eastern Europe. Cadogan wrote: 'German economic preponderance in certain countries of central and eastern Europe is bound to develop . . .' He also declared: 'We must cut our losses in central and eastern Europe – let Germany, if she can, find there her "lebensraum", . . .' *A Mitteleuropa* would not necessarily prove fatal to British interests. Halifax put much the same point of view to the American ambassador on 12 October 1938. This region accounted for only about 1 per cent of Britain's trade, and it was possible in any case that some mutually beneficial trading arrangement might be reached with Germany.[40] Countries bordering the Mediterranean and even the Black Sea were a different matter: real British interests were at stake there. Indeed, Halifax was soon looking for ways to increase Britain's tenuous trading influence in the Balkans.[41] As before, the difficulty was to find some way in which to make Britain's presence felt. In practice a dramatic escalation of Britain's fears of Germany had to occur before tentative economic moves were supplanted by direct political involvement in the spring of 1939. Only the growing expectation of war with Germany generated something approximating to a consensus among the British leadership on the need for eastern allies with which to wage a two-front war against Germany; and to increase the efficacy of the economic blockade.

Oddly enough Hitler himself had hoped to avoid a crisis and war with Poland. Professor Weinberg argues persuasively that after Munich his thoughts were turning more and more to the elimination of the threat posed by the western powers.[42] Staff talks with Italy at the end of 1938 envisaged a direct breach of the Maginot Line, and the exclusion of Britain from the Continent. German interest in an alliance with Japan was growing. Such an alliance, it was hoped, would divide British resources and weaken the will to resist. In the winter of 1938–39 Hitler gave much thought to the development of a huge surface navy. This Z-Plan (*Ziel* or Target) could not, however, be completed before 1944–45, a date which Hitler often described as a completion, not an opening stage in his bid for European hegemony. Apart from Hitler's worries about his own fitness to lead Germany by the later 1940s, there was the growing strain on the economy imposed by the existing armament programmes. To some it seemed that Germany would soon have no choice but to gamble on war or pursue a more modest and conciliatory foreign policy. Hitler, it seems, had ideas about the future, but no clear plan. Whatever his own inclinations, his course of action in 1939 was greatly influenced by the decisions of others. In the end he was to make his decision for war, but not in circumstances that were entirely of his own making.

One must stress, therefore, that in his negotiations with the Poles in the winter of 1938–39 Hitler was feeling his way. He wished to clear up the question of Danzig and the Polish Corridor, and at the same time establish how far the Poles were prepared to subordinate their foreign policy to German interests. Would the Poles join the

Anti-Comintern Pact and follow a common policy towards Russia?[43] The Poles, however, made it plain that they wished to follow an independent line. German pressure on Warsaw was slowly increased early in 1939, but as late as 25 March Hitler told his army commander-in-chief that he did not wish to solve the question of Danzig by force. 'He would not like to drive Poland into the arms of Great Britain by doing so . . . ' Only if there were 'exceptionally favourable political conditions' should Poland be knocked out.[44] It was the Anglo-French Guarantee of Poland which persuaded Hitler that he must eliminate the Polish threat as quickly as possible. The events and calculations which persuaded the British in particular to give this guarantee to Poland clearly deserve careful scrutiny.

In the winter of 1938–39 mysterious rumours began to reach London that some major new act of German aggression was in preparation. Especially alarming were reports that Germany was about to launch sudden air attacks on London, or alternatively to invade the Netherlands. Although now known to be false, these reports were taken very seriously at the time, especially by those in the British government who took the most pessimistic view of German intentions, and who were anxious to step up British preparations for war. A point was being reached where it could be argued that Britain would suffer more by not fighting than by going to war. The Chiefs of Staff highlighted the British dilemma at the time of the Dutch invasion scare when they agreed that it was vital to fight for the Low Countries although Britain's state of preparedness meant that she might lose a war.[45] There were other causes, too, for the greater sense of urgency that was beginning to develop in London. Halifax was among those who, as early as November 1938, began to fear that the French might be losing heart and might refuse to fight for the Low Countries. The French were also becoming too obsessed with their quarrels with Italy for British comfort. Such fears encouraged a reappraisal of British defence policy. To boost French resolve against Germany the French had to be assured of a significant British military contribution at the start of any war. 'Limited liability' had to go. The British began to think in terms of a sizeable contribution to the land war on the Continent. Overtures for closer military co-operation were made in Paris on 4 February 1939, and on the 6th Chamberlain publicly underlined Britain's determination to stand by France. In the same month the Treasury conceded that defence must now have priority even at the expense of the nation's balance of payments. This was accepted despite the realization that if the strain were prolonged American loans would be the only solution – and these for the moment were ruled out by Congress. Halifax perhaps offered some comfort with his belief that the matter must soon be settled one way or the other – the strain on the German economy must soon force Hitler to fight or compromise.[46]

American diplomats noted the growing pessimism in London and the determination of many to make a stand.[47] Chamberlain was an exception, and the end of February found him clinging to the hope that a prosperous Germany might yet develop a vested interest in peace. But on 14 March Hitler ordered his forces into Prague, and two days later a German protectorate was proclaimed over Bohemia and Moravia. Slovakia was encouraged to break away, and signed a treaty of protection with Berlin on 23 March. Chamberlain at first seemed uncertain how to respond. His first public comments were too cautious for the taste of many in Parliament and elsewhere. Harold Nicolson commented on the 17th: 'The feeling in the lobbies is that Chamberlain will either have to go or completely reverse his policy.' There was talk of a coalition headed by Halifax. Chamberlain later confessed: 'As soon as I had time to think I saw that it was impossible to deal with Hitler after he had thrown all his assurances to the wind.'[48] Some historians have been tempted to attribute the change in British policy following the German occupation of Prague to this outcry in Parliament and among the public. Undoubtedly Chamberlain and Halifax were impressed by the strength of feeling generated by this latest crisis, but it is also clear that government thinking and planning had begun to change before the break-up of Czechoslovakia. Chamberlain's reluctance to abandon the policy of appeasement must be emphasized, but so too must the fact that the events of mid-March confirmed and accelerated (they alone were not responsible) new trends in British foreign and defence policies.

The pace quickened still more in the second half of March in response to further rumours and developments. Given the state of mind in London credence was readily given to reports that first Rumania and later Poland as well stood in grave danger from Germany. The reliability of much of this information is even now a matter for debate. In particular there was the mysterious warning of 17 March from the Rumanian ambassador that his country was facing a virtual ultimatum from Germany. Rumania had for some months been seeking British political and military aid. It was certainly under pressure of some kind from Germany, and was forced to make concessions. But Bucharest denied the existence of anything resembling an ultimatum.[49] Nevertheless rumours continued to circulate concerning German ambitions in south-eastern Europe, and there were now those in the Foreign Office who were anxious to exploit any opportunity to prove to Germany that Britain intended to stand firm. The Chiefs of Staff were more cautious, warning of the threat from Italy and Japan, and of the need for Russian and Polish assistance in the event of war with Germany. Nevertheless as early as 18 March the Cabinet agreed that if sufficient allies could be found Germany should be warned that the next act of aggression would mean war.[50] A reluctant Chamberlain was even persuaded to address an appeal on the 20th to Russia as well as France and Poland to join a consultative pact in anticipation of future threats to the security and independence of European states. The Poles, however, refused to co-operate with Russia: they wanted a bilateral agreement with Britain. The Cabinet was easily persuaded that efforts to include Russia in any anti-German front were premature, but action of some kind seemed imperative. Halifax argued on the 25th that a line must be drawn. It must include Poland, Rumania and Yugoslavia – otherwise Germany would become too strong. At least the British received a hint of American co-operation at this time, with Washington agreeing to further naval talks and to the concentration of the American fleet in the Pacific to free the Royal Navy for possible operations in European waters. The Foreign Office argued that Britain must continue to take a strong line against Germany if she was to retain American support and confidence.

In the last days of March the Cabinet received still more confusing information from eastern Europe. On the one hand some 'mad-dog' act of aggression seemed possible: on the other there were fears that Hitler and Poland might reach an agreement which would rob Britain of an important ally in the east in the event of war. Either way Britain seemed to be confronted with the danger that Germany was about to become the dominant power in eastern Europe, and once Germany controlled eastern Europe she would feel free to turn west. Britain and France would then be unable to wage a two-front war against Germany, or maximize the effects of economic warfare – except perhaps in conjunction with Russia. Quick action seemed imperative, and the Cabinet therefore overrode the doubts of the Chiefs of Staff who were reluctant to countenance British commitments in eastern Europe unless Russia was included in some way in the arrangements. The haste with which the Cabinet decided to give a guarantee to Poland suggests that international factors weighed more heavily with the policy-makers than the parliamentary discontent which is stressed by some historians.[51] The Cabinet was desperately trying to recapture the initiative in Europe, though with still some hope even at this late stage that Hitler might be persuaded to see reason, or could at least be deterred from war.[52]

The Polish Guarantee, however, had no such effect. Hitler abandoned his efforts to conciliate the Poles (on his terms, of course): instead their country was scheduled for destruction as soon as possible. He ordered his forces to prepare for war by September 1939, and seven weeks later, on 23 May, he added that if the western powers intervened, 'then it will be better to attack in the west and incidentally to settle Poland at the same time'.[53] As we shall see, Hitler's final course of action in the summer of 1939 owed much to the actions of other states (including Russia and Japan), just as it was the Guarantee which produced his first major decision of 1939 as opposed to general preparations for and speculation about the future. Not surprisingly, in view of the subsequent Nazi–Soviet Pact and the failure of the western powers to aid Poland in September 1939 (in any meaningful way), the Guarantee has been widely criticized by historians. Certainly in their anxiety to assure themselves of Polish support the British threw away what might have proved a valuable bargaining counter in talks with both Warsaw and Moscow to establish a more comprehensive alignment against Germany in eastern Europe. The Guarantee enabled the Poles to obstruct talks with Russia: it also removed a major incentive for the Russians to come to terms with the western powers. Militarily the Guarantee lacked substance since Britain and France, in the immediate future, lacked the means and the will to give Poland significant aid in the event of war. But one must again stress that the two western governments still had hopes that the Guarantee would serve as a warning to Germany – that it might contribute to the ultimate stabilization of Europe and would not necessarily lead to war.

The Polish Guarantee was announced on 31 March. Joseph Kennedy, the American ambassador, noted soon afterwards how seriously the events of March had damaged Chamberlain's self-confidence and physical fitness. 'He walks like an old man and yesterday he talked like one.'[54] A British army of no less than thirty-two divisions was being contemplated, and the decision to introduce conscription was made public on 26 April. The creation of such an army would occupy several years, but it was hoped that this declaration of intent might impress opinion abroad. In general, however, the short-term military prospects were bleak. Germany was credited with a significant superiority in the air. In the event of war a German conquest of Poland seemed almost inevitable. Optimists thought Poland might resist for six months, but the country seemed doomed to conquest by Germany. Its role in war would be to buy time for the western powers. Poland would re-emerge as an independent state only after an allied victory which, given current plans, was unlikely to occur until the third or fourth year of a war.

Consequently there were still some even in the Foreign Office, as well as others more prominently in the Cabinet, who were reluctant to believe that an accommodation with Hitler was impossible. Cadogan and Kirkpatrick seemed prepared to negotiate so long as only Danzig and related issues of minor importance were at stake between Germany and Poland. Others thought this a futile course. Again there were hints from some German quarters that only a tough British policy would deter Hitler from war.[55] Indeed, some historians suggest that Chamberlain's continuing search for an accommodation with Hitler contributed to the Kremlin's suspicion of the western powers and its own decision to negotiate with Germany. Evidence certainly exists of American concern in the face of continuing Anglo-German contacts.[56]

THE RUSSIAN ENIGMA

A logical consequence of the Polish Guarantee was a new approach by Britain and France to the Soviet Union, if only to try to secure Russian supplies for the Poles in the event of war. The British Chiefs of Staff saw this clearly. The French government, which had been largely a bystander in the making of the Guarantee, viewed new talks with Moscow as distasteful but necessary. Feelings were still more mixed in the British Cabinet. It was tempting to hide behind the evident determination of the Poles to have nothing to do with the Russians; to argue that the Russian armed forces were of limited value, especially as a result of the Purges; and to deplore the basic untrustworthiness of the Russian government. Cadogan commented on 19 April that only a paper commitment was to be expected from Moscow, and this seemed poor compensation for all the drawbacks that Britain would experience as a result of association with communism.[57] Yet something had to be done. The British embassy in Moscow warned on 13 April that Russia and Germany might yet make a deal. Others were troubled by the advantages Russia would enjoy if she were able to stand aside in the event of war in western Europe. The Cabinet was also under parliamentary pressure to turn to Russia.

As critics have never been slow to point out, British approaches to Russia from March 1939 were confused and hesitant. The reasons for this were both good and bad – as we have seen and shall see again. But one cannot assume that a more determined and generous approach would have succeeded (perhaps even with access to the Russian archives one could not give an answer). It is possible that Stalin himself did not know whether to choose Germany, the western powers, or isolation until August 1939. Such evidence as there is suggests that the Russians were anxious to explore all available options, and gain room for manœuvre. Thus they disengaged from Spain late in 1938: they made soundings in Warsaw following Munich. A trade agreement was concluded with Germany on 19 December 1938. The American embassy on 22 February 1939 speculated on a possible improvement in Russo-German relations.[58] Stalin's report to the Eighteenth Party Congress on 10 March 1939 provoked much discussion. It was a skilful, equivocal speech. It spoke of 'strengthening business relations with all countries', of co-operation with lovers of peace and of support for victims of aggression. It also recommended caution: Russia must not pull 'the chestnuts out of the fire' for others. Many diplomats were struck by the emphasis upon the need for Russian self-help.

Published Russian evidence is highly selective. But there are authentic touches in the correspondence between Litvinov, the Foreign Minister, and Maisky in London, amid the many expressions of distrust of Britain, and of Chamberlain in particular. Litvinov claimed that Russia had been striving in vain for collective security for five years. It was now up to others to give a genuine lead. Even the Polish Guarantee failed to impress Litvinov. Maisky, though struck by the new mood in Britain, feared a change, especially in Conservative quarters, if the Ukraine should re-emerge as Hitler's basic objective. Litvinov complained that the Guarantee had strengthened Poland's position against Russia and was therefore 'an inimical act' on the part of Britain.[59] Russian suspicions are also highlighted by Maisky's rigorous interrogation of Halifax on 6 April as to the real meaning of the Guarantee.[60] The published Russian documents do not indicate if and when Moscow began to perceive the value of the Polish Guarantee to Russia, yet it meant that there was now a distinct possibility that Britain and France would fight to prevent German hegemony in eastern Europe. The Guarantee placed Britain and France in the position of the supplicants, rather than the Russians, in their relations with each other. The Guarantee might even serve as a lightning conductor from the Russian point of view – that is, a war over Poland might be fought mainly in the west, not the east. Indeed, the western powers soon went further, for Italy's occupation of Albania on 7 April was speedily followed by guarantees to Rumania and Greece, and Anglo-French talks opened with the Turks.

On 14 April the British asked Moscow for a public promise of support for a European neighbour against aggression if requested. The Russians on the 18th proposed nothing less than a three-power pact of mutual assistance supported by immediate staff talks. But on the previous day they had also made a delicate overture in Berlin. One of the most momentous games of diplomatic cat and mouse was beginning with all the players, including the Poles, until the middle of August, believing that they were cats. The Polish 'cat', indeed, pretended there was no game so far as Russia was concerned. It would have no dealings with Russia. The British were not quite so obdurate. Halifax summarized British desires on 24 April. Britain might want Russian aid in certain circumstances. She also needed a common front with Poland, and did not want to frighten the east European states with her dealings with Russia. Nor did she want to jeopardize the last hopes of peace with Germany. And Chamberlain's antipathy to Russia was as deep as ever. On 20 May Cadogan thought the Prime Minister preferred resignation to an alliance with Russia.

Nevertheless, until the end of May, the initiative perhaps lay with the British and French. Berlin was still looking for an alliance with Japan. Had this materialized, Russia might have been driven to accept a limited understanding with the British. On the other hand a German–Japanese agreement might have increased British interest in appeasement. Certainly so long as Germany had hopes of the Japanese alliance Russia's cautious signalling to Berlin failed to excite much attention, though Göring believed that Russo-German talks might persuade the British and Poles to give way. The concern felt in Moscow about the overall international situation is reflected in the replacement of Litvinov by Molotov (described by the British ambassador as Stalin's 'right-hand-man') early in May 1939. This did not mean that the Russians had decided on a line of action, but it was a sign of the importance now attached to foreign affairs. As it was they had to wait until the end of May when Hitler began to lose patience with the Japanese before they received the first slight hint of encouragement from Berlin. The possibility of Russo-German talks had not been forgotten by the British Foreign Office. It produced an impressive analysis on 22 May which reviewed the pros and cons of an Anglo-Russian pact.[61] It concluded that Germany must somehow be presented with the threat of a two-front war, and for this to be plausible there had, if necessary, to be some Russian backing for the Poles. This had to be achieved without alienating the existing friends of Britain and France in eastern Europe. The Foreign Office was also anxious to prevent a situation in which, in the event of a European war, the Russians could stand aside and maximize their opportunities for mischief. The British Cabinet was also under pressure from the Chiefs of Staff, France, Parliament and the press to make a positive overture to Moscow.

It was in these circumstances that Chamberlain was at last persuaded on 24 May to seek Russian support against German aggression. For him the bitter pill was slightly sweetened by reference to the virtually moribund League of Nations. The agreement also laid down that the act of aggression must be clear-cut, and that the victims must be willing to accept Russian help. Such proposals were thoroughly unsatisfactory from the Russian point of view. Understandably the Soviet Union wished to be free to decide when its interests were menaced in eastern Europe. Its interests might be menaced by something short of overt aggression by Germany – even by a neighbouring state entering into an agreement with Berlin. It also wished to be free to aid neighbouring states against their will. Moscow pointedly asked what the British would do if Belgium became pro-German. Not surprisingly Molotov subjected the British ambassador to a punishing interrogation concerning his government's proposals.[62]

The gap between the two powers was plain. The British wished to impress the Germans, and, if the worst came to the worst, exercise as much control as possible over Russian involvement. The Russians may or may not have been seeking an agreement, but in so far as they were, they were seeking as much freedom of action for themselves in eastern Europe as possible. Early in June some diplomats even thought the Russians, covered by the Polish Guarantee, were moving towards isolation.[63] The British embassy, despite rough handling from Molotov, advised against British concessions in the belief that a Russo-German deal was improbable.

Talks between the western powers and the Russians made little progress over the next two months. At one point an exasperated Halifax declared that the Russians could go and jump in the Baltic. Yet, as he informed Henderson in Berlin[64]:

> It would be folly for us not to conclude an agreement with Russia at the present time in view of our commitments in eastern Europe, and the Nazis themselves would be the first to despise us for omitting so obvious a precaution.

Towards the end of July the British resigned themselves to further concessions, including military talks, when the Cabinet was finally persuaded that Poland was too weak to form the core of an eastern front, and when there were rumours of new Russo-German contacts. Berlin and Moscow had in fact been using trade talks to test each other's seriousness, while Hitler, in default of progress with Japan, was becoming persuaded that a pact with Russia was necessary before he could bring the Polish question to a head. Time was pressing. He wanted to settle Poland before the autumn when military operations would be hampered by worsening weather.

A great flurry of German diplomatic activity from 2 August produced the Nazi–Soviet Pact of the 23rd. Any Russian effort to play for time was steamrollered aside by the Germans. Why did Germany succeed and the western powers fail? Obviously London and Paris could not compete with the single-mindedness of the Germans. Germany, by the secret provisions of the Pact of the 23rd, was prepared to give Russia an extensive sphere of influence in eastern Europe, including eastern Poland – Russia was being allowed to return to something akin to her pre-1914 position in Europe. The western powers, on the other hand, were hoping to deter or contain Germany, and yet at the same time prevent any significant advance of Russian or communist influence westward. But if Germany could always outbid Britain and France for Russian favour, why were the Russians not put off by the degree to which the Pact seemed likely to strengthen Germany, and cause her territory and influence to flow eastward so that the two powers would in future be in direct contact? Were the Russians misled by short-sighted greed? Did they think that they could coexist with Hitler's Germany? Or were they influenced, chiefly or in part, by strategic calculations? Given the lack of evidence, guesswork alone is possible.

For some writers the failure of the western powers, especially Britain, to extend the hand of friendship is explanation enough. Such conduct in all its failings from Munich to August 1939 is easily documented, but more positive approaches from London and Paris would not necessarily have succeeded. The tedious discussion of 'indirect aggression' and even the military talks bypassed crucial considerations. One can reasonably assume that the Russians knew of the intention of the western powers to stand on the defensive in the event of war and try to win a long conflict. In other words, the fundamental strategic calculations were totally different from 1914 when Russia and France each believed its security rested on the execution of the earliest possible offensive against Germany. In 1939 the Russians had reason to fear that if they became involved in a war in eastern Europe with Germany, they would be left to carry the main burden – perhaps, even the whole burden – for some unspecified time. But if Russia were neutral in a war affecting even eastern Europe, Anglo-French involvement should then mean that the main war would be fought initially at least in western Europe. Nor, unlike 1914, did the Russians have reason to fear that their neutrality would guarantee a French defeat and German hegemony in Europe. According to the conventional military wisdom of 1939 no quick German victory over France was likely. No policy is without its risks, and doubtless the Russians considered several scenarios in 1939. But given Russia's internal weaknesses and unpreparedness for war, given her fear of Japan in the east, given her distrust of France and Britain as well as Germany in the west, the Nazi–Soviet Pact was arguably the least risky of the available options – without the power to foresee the future, and especially the dramatic collapse of France in 1940. Such was (or should have been) the negative appeal of the Pact, even if less calculating minds in the Kremlin might also have been attracted by the gains in territory and influence for their own sake. In fact, such evidence as we have suggests that the Russians lived in fear of the possible consequences of their decision until the end of September 1939 when the Germans not only confirmed the partition of eastern Europe but made further concessions.[65]

THE OUTBREAK OF WAR AND THE FALL OF FRANCE

The announcement of the Nazi–Soviet Pact caused consternation in the west. But contrary to Hitler's hopes, Britain and France did not abandon the Poles, although they now seemed powerless to give them any meaningful help. He decided to delay his attack on the Poles for a few days to see if the British could be talked out of war. On the 25th he offered to guarantee the British Empire, talked of a reasonable limitation of armaments, and described Germany's western frontiers as final. Hitler was also disturbed to learn that Mussolini was not prepared to fight on his side unless Germany immediately delivered vast supplies of arms and raw materials. 'At our meetings the war was envisaged for after 1942', protested a rather pathetic *Duce*. Some of Hitler's advisers, perhaps Goring himself, were genuinely interested to see what could be obtained by diplomacy. Hitler may also have felt he needed 'an alibi' with the German people to prove to them he had done everything he could to preserve peace with the western powers. But he was determined that, come what may, Poland was to be eliminated as a force in European politics. He argued that Germany's economic situation meant that action in the near future was imperative. He talked of disposing of Poland to free his hands for action in the west. Fears of his own early mental and physical decline continued to plague him; while for many of his party war was seen as 'its true element', the indispensable means of winning the 'living space' which alone could satisfy the aspirations of the race. Important as Hitler was, his decisions were also 'the reflection and expression of the internal constitutional order and the external position of the regime'.[66]

No second Munich was possible. Hitler and his most ardent supporters were not interested in Danzig and the Corridor – they were merely excuses. The Poles themselves were determined to resist. In Britain Chamberlain and some of the Cabinet still wished to satisfy themselves that the future of Poland as a whole, and not simply Danzig and related issues, was at stake. But any efforts to negotiate or to buy time were viewed with growing concern and suspicion by important sections of opinion in Britain. Doubts in Paris were gradually being removed by the conviction that militarily it was better to fight now than later.[67] The German invasion began on 1 September: two days later the war became general.

Germany crushed Poland in two weeks. There followed six months of virtual inactivity – the so-called 'phoney war', a period when Russia's 'winter war' against Finland stole much of the limelight. This intensified fears in the west of Russia and communism as the ultimate and main beneficiaries from the conflict with Germany. The French government tried to exploit the Russo-Finnish War to embarrass the French Communist Party and to win support from the French Right. Indeed, the French were more eager to send help to the Finns than were the British, the latter seeing the war mainly as an opportunity to intervene in Scandinavia to interrupt the important Swedish iron-ore exports to Germany. Confusion and delay marked allied conduct at every turn, so that the Finns were forced to make peace on 13 March 1940 before any serious action was undertaken. Halifax gloomily concluded that the British could do no more than resume diplomatic contacts with Russia, and wait and hope for a Russo-German split, but he expected the Russians to try to sit out a long war and intervene at the most opportune moment. The Russian position was well expressed by Maisky when he remarked in 1940 that he added the German and allied casualties in the same column.[68] Not surprisingly there was continuing discussion in the west as to how a full-scale war with Germany might yet be avoided. An Australian politician, Robert Menzies, in February 1940 described the First Lord of the Admiralty, Churchill, as 'a menace', who threatened to perpetuate European instability with another Carthaginian peace. Menzies supported those who favoured a moderate peace and gave priority to the containment of communism. Chamberlain himself insisted that peace was possible only with a German government one could trust. He pinned his hopes on economic pressure on Germany. Perhaps its people could be persuaded by such means that Germany could not win, and this would lead to a change of government.[69] It was an extraordinary hope early in 1940 when Germany could draw resources from Russia, Scandinavia and other parts of Europe.

Meanwhile Hitler was determined to attack Britain and France 'at the most favourable and quickest moment'. He argued that Germany might not be able to rely on Russian neutrality for more than a few months. He rejected Mussolini's suggestions in January 1940 that he try to make peace. Mussolini doubted the possibility of victory in the west: he feared American intervention if the British and French appeared near to defeat. He argued that Russia and communism were the real danger. Hitler was unmoved, and in an astounding ten-week campaign – between 9 April and 22 June 1940 – his forces overran Denmark, Norway, Holland, Belgium and France, and placed the future of Britain herself in doubt. It was an extraordinary achievement, based not on superior forces, save to some extent in the air, but on superior strategy and tactics, the fragility of French morale and a great deal of luck. As in the First World War, in France and Belgium, initial allied strategy conformed closely to German needs – and this time with decisive results. The Anglo-French drive into Belgium in May 1940 facilitated their own encirclement and retreat to Dunkirk. Hitler was also able, thanks to his pact with Russia, to withdraw all but seven divisions from eastern Europe. With victory assured over France, Mussolini joined the war on the side of Hitler on 10 June.

Axis control of western Europe did not, however, guarantee the early defeat or surrender of Britain. Although an invasion force of sorts was improvised, its only chance of success rested on German mastery of the skies above southern England. On the whole in the close-run Battle of Britain in the summer of 1940 the advantages in leadership and luck lay with the British. Hitler himself did not show the same commitment to the campaign against Britain as in the struggle against France, or in the forthcoming war with the Soviet Union. As early as July 1940 his thoughts were already turning to the possibility of an invasion of Russia. Had some quick solution to the British problem presented itself, whether by war or diplomacy, Hitler would doubtless have seized it. As it was, Britain in the summer of 1940 seemed an annoyance and a distraction rather than a major problem. Hitler understood that even if Britain were defeated the main beneficiaries, especially with respect to the future of the empire, were likely to be Japan and the United States. The British navy in particular was likely to fall under American influence or control. True, the importance of the British Isles would become crucial if and when the United States entered the war, but Hitler did not regard this as imminent. In the summer of 1940 Hitler was not prepared to give absolute priority to the defeat of Britain. Already he was tempted to believe that the defeat of Russia would make Germany invincible, with the British being forced to make terms as one of its many by-products.

On the British side knowledge of the final outcome should not blind us to the desperate nature of the gamble on which the nation was embarking with the decision to fight on. Those who gave some thought to the question of peace should not be condemned out of hand.[70] Hopes of outright victory were based on the assumption of some form of American assistance, on the enforcement of a long-term blockade against Germany, on the aerial bombardment of Germany and on the efficacy of Resistance forces in occupied Europe. Strangely, in the light of what happened, little faith was placed in Russian resistance to Germany. Victory, it was normally assumed, would arise out of the combined effect of the above-mentioned strategies, which would ultimately make possible a British or Anglo-American landing on the Continent when Germany's forces were sufficiently dispersed by the Resistance movements, and her economic capacity to wage war was seriously impaired. In practice, of course, it was primarily the Russian front which facilitated the Normandy landings of 1944 – an invasion force far larger than anything contemplated in 1940. Indeed, had it not been for Hitler's decision to attack Russia in 1941, and the successful Russian opposition thereafter, one wonders how long Britain could have survived – even with American aid – against a concentrated German assault merely at sea and in the air. The British decision to fight on in the summer of 1940 was thus bold almost to the point of rashness. Churchill (and Ernest Bevin) personified the nation in that moment. Fortunately they could draw upon huge reserves of national confidence – built up over centuries of muddling through to victory, often with insufficient recognition of Britain's debts to her allies. The British faced the summer of 1940 not only in the spirit of John Bull but also of Mr Micawber. Churchill himself gambled on ultimate American involvement: he did not foresee the extent to which the war would be decided by Uncle Joe as well as Uncle Sam.

Meanwhile, in the summer of 1940, Germany's victories had world-wide consequences. They influenced policy-making in Tokyo, Washington and Moscow. The Russians hastily occupied the Baltic states and, before the end of June, took territory from Rumania. The militant expansionists in Japan became much more influential, while almost overnight Americans sensed a narrowing of both the Atlantic and Pacific oceans.

Although Roosevelt, with the outbreak of war in September 1939, was able at last to revise the Neutrality Legislation to the advantage of the western powers, Americans on the whole remained fairly confident that at worst Britain and France would survive to preserve some sort of balance of power in Europe. Roosevelt did not rule out the possibility of a German victory, and he lost no opportunities to try to persuade Americans that their nation should be as strong as possible at sea and in the air, and that aid short of war should be sent to Britain and France. Already his administration was preparing contingency plans for war, with much attention being given to the defence of the Philippines and the Caribbean. There were also indications that in the event of war with both Germany and Japan, priority would be given to the defeat of Germany, the stronger and more dangerous power. But it was the fall of France which created a real sense of urgency. At the end of May 1940 Cordell Hull warned that German hegemony in Europe could alter the whole character of the world economy, with Germany having at its disposal the forced labour of millions of conquered peoples and perhaps too the colonies of the defeated powers. The Nazis would be able to flood the world markets with cheap goods.

Roosevelt in a melodramatic speech of 10 June declared that the United States could become a 'lone island', threatened by the 'nightmare of a people lodged in prison, hungry and fed through the bars from day to day by the contemptuous, unpitying masters of the other continents'. Ex-President Hoover, who had declared not long before that 'America cannot correct the world every time it goes wrong' and who had recommended only *postwar* economic aid to Europe, began to favour cautious aid to the defenders of 'freedom' in the hope that the aggressors would finally overreach themselves. The Republican candidate for the 1940 presidential election was as much an internationalist as Roosevelt himself. Increasingly the talk was of American aid to Britain, short of war.

Even so, the service chiefs and, for a time, Roosevelt himself, hesitated in the summer of 1940 before they sent arms to Britain, a country that might soon fall to Germany and at a time when the United States had precious few arms to spare. Only six months might separate a British defeat from war between Germany and the United States. It was feared that the Germans might use French West Africa as a jumping-off point against the New World. The United States feared for the security of the Caribbean and Brazil in particular, but found it difficult to flesh out contingency plans with actual forces. Nevertheless British resistance in August 1940 increased American confidence, and finally made possible the famous destroyers for bases 'deal'. The United States introduced selective service in September, and Roosevelt reluctantly agreed that a large army was now a necessity as well as a two-ocean navy and the world's largest air force. But all this lay in the future. Marshall, the army Chief of Staff, calculated that the country would not be ready for war until March 1941: ideally war should be avoided until 1942. The navy chiefs, on the other hand, thought it vital to prevent a British defeat. Without Britain and her world-wide network of bases they feared even a fully mobilized America might be unable to defeat Germany and Japan. As Admiral Stark commented in November 1940: 'while we might not lose *everywhere*, we might, possibly, not win *anywhere*'. Roosevelt, however, was determined to keep in step as far as possible with American public opinion. He was also temperamentally averse to detailed blueprints. He preferred to improvise, and complemented his determination to retain for the United States a favourable position within the global balance of power with his characteristic optimism that his country would receive its fair share of lucky breaks. In the autumn of 1940 as he battled for re-election American policy remained all aid to Britain short of war.[71]

NOTES AND REFERENCES

1. Feiling, pp. 347–8
2. Telford Taylor, pp. 626, and see 621 ff.
3. Gibbs, pp. 642–7
4. Middlemas, p. 200; Dilks [1] I, 145–6
5. FRUS, USSR 1933–39, pp. 285–6, 398 ff., 447, 504–5, 514–18, 542–51, 588–9
6. DGFP, D, II, 426, 473–7, 629–31, 948–9. See also FRUS, 1938, I, 557–8, 737
7. Haslam, pp. 441–57; Weinberg [2] pp. 415–16; Telford Taylor, p. 447; Tolstoy, pp. 70, 76–7, 386 n. 17
8. Bullock, p. 450
9. Weinberg [2] pp. 313–19, 366–70, 431–56

10. Harvey, p. 128; see also p. 115, and Foster, pp. 441–65
11. See e.g. Dilks [1] ɪ, 149–50
12. Middlemas, pp. 331–2. See also R. J. Young, pp. 58–63, and for exaggerated fears of bombing, Bialer, *passim*
13. DGFP, D, ɪɪ, 238–9; Deist, pp. 87–8, 98–9
14. FRUS, 1938, ɪ, 549–51
15. FRUS, 1938, ɪ, 632; Telford Taylor, p. 750
16. FRUS, 1938, ɪ, 687. For Dominion fears, see Massey, pp. 259–61, and AD, ɪ, 459, 461, 473–5
17. FRUS, 1938, ɪ, 719; see also pp. 86–92
18. Telford Taylor, pp. 683, 705–13, 836–7
19. Adamthwaite [1] pp. 211, 219, 232; Bond [2] pp. 380–3; Telford Taylor, pp. 834–5. Note also Deist, pp. 68–9, 77–85, for German plans and state of preparations
20. Nicolson, p. 329
21. Gladwyn, p. 83; Harvey, pp. 202, 208; Weinberg [2] p. 439n
22. Middlemas, p. 456; Medlicott [2] p. 194
23. T. C. Kennedy, pp. 85–6
24. Schewe, ɪ, 61
25. Schewe, ɪ, 23
26. Schewe, ɪɪ, 355; see also ɪɪ, 239, 275a and b
27. Reynolds, pp. 16–19, 48–53
28. Gilbert [3] pp. 156–8. See also MacDonald, pp. 5–30, 79–81, 109–11, 165–7, and Reynolds above
29. Compare the interpretations of Roosevelt's foreign policy offered by J. MacGregor Burns, Melvin Small and Robert Dallek
30. Roskill [2] ɪɪ, 365, 367
31. Schewe, ɪɪɪ, 526, 530, 535
32. Schewe, v, 904. See also ɪv, 728, 825 and v, 1018
33. Schewe, vɪɪ, 1277. See also MacDonald, pp. 88–105. The German embassy in Washington was issuing warnings from May 1938 that Germany could not count on permanent American neutrality (DGFP, D, ɪɪ, 369–72, 981–2)
34. Schewe, vɪɪɪ, 1481
35. MacDonald, pp. 110–11. See also Reynolds, pp. 16–18, 22–3, 48–9
36. MacDonald, pp. 83–4, 126–7
37. Schewe, ɪx, 1616
38. Berle and Jacobs, pp. 183–4, 200–1, 206–10, 223–4, 230. See also MacDonald, pp. 107–39.
39. S. Newman, p. 6, and see Ch. 3
40. FRUS, 1938, ɪ, 85–6; Dilks [2] pp. 117–18. See also M. Newman, pp. 371 ff., and AD, ɪ, 128
41. S. Newman, pp. 45–9, etc.
42. Weinberg [2] pp. 503–14, 533–4, 551–2, 575–7, 580–1
43. DGFP, D. v, 152–8
44. Bullock, p. 497
45. Gibbs, pp. 499–500
46. Peden, pp. 103–4. See also Bond [1] pp. 292–301; Gibbs, pp. 495–6, etc.
47. FRUS, 1939, ɪ, 14–22, 32–3, 71

48. Feiling, p. 401; Nicolson, p. 393
49. Weinberg [2] pp. 536–7, 540–1
50. Aster, pp. 76–9
51. S. Newman, pp. 169–204
52. Hitler himself would probably have preferred a political settlement with the Poles at this stage (Fest, pp. 575–6)
53. Bullock, pp. 499, 509–10. For an interesting discussion of the influence of economic pressures on Hitler's policy, see Deist, pp. 111–12. It is true that by 1939 economic problems could have begun to threaten the regime's popularity, but Hitler had been deliberately running risks with the economy since 1936 to prepare for war, and he had repeatedly argued that predatory wars were the only permanent answers to Germany's problems.
54. FRUS, 1939, I, 16–17, 139–40
55. BD, 3rd series, V, 684–5; VI, 43, 295–8
56. Aster, pp. 259, 288; MacDonald, pp. 158, 165–7
57. S. Newman, pp. 215–16
58. FRUS, USSR 1933–39, p. 737; see also pp. 591–4, and FRUS, 1939, I, 318 ff.
59. *Soviet Peace Efforts*, pp. 159–61, 180–1, 206–7, 212–13, 221–3, 243–4, 253 ff., 282–3
60. BD, 3rd series, V, 53, 104
61. BD, 3rd series, V, 639–47
62. BD, 3rd series, V, 701–2, 722; Aster, pp. 186–7
63. BD, 3rd series, V, 736
64. BD, 3rd series, VI, 220. See also FRUS, 1939, I, 276–7, 282–8. On the Anglo-Soviet negotiations in general, see Manne [2] pp. 83–102. Note also Duroselle, pp. 416, 427.
65. See A. Seaton in Preston, p. 72; McSherry, I, 247–50. On Russo-German relations in the summer of 1939, see Sontag and Beddie, pp. 17 ff. Tolstoy (pp. 115–25) argues that Stalin opted for the Pact not out of stern necessity but out of greed, and for further hints of Russian interest in changes in the European equilibrium in 1939 see Weinberg [3] p. 7 and note. Roy Medvedev (pp. 440–3) agrees that Soviet historiography has yet to clarify the origins of the Pact, but sees it as a measure of self-defence, and is highly critical of Britain and France. For the story in detail, see McSherry, I, 156 ff. especially. For French policy, see Duroselle, pp. 416 ff.
66. Broszat, pp. XIII, 307, 359. See also Fest, pp. 607–13; Weinberg [2] pp. 618–22; Bullock, pp. 532–44
67. Adamthwaite [1] p. 328; R. J. Young, pp. 232–41
68. Woodward, I, p. xliv
69. AD, III, 20–34, 100–2; Bethell, pp. 357–401; Douglas [1] p. 147; Dilks [2] pp. 221, 228
70. For a convenient discussion of some Cabinet deliberations, see Grenville [2] pp. 473–9. See also Reynolds, pp. 103–4
71. Lowenthal, pp. 413 ff. See also Leutze, pp. 190–5; Pogue, pp. 76–9, 159–60; Dallek, Ch. 10

Chapter 9

GLOBAL WAR

THE FAR EASTERN BACKGROUND, 1938–40

Crises in the Far East and Europe in the early 1930s initially produced little interaction, and in so far as they affected the United States they encouraged a strengthening of isolationism. But by 1939–40 the world was rapidly becoming one. Never had the chancelleries in London, Berlin, Moscow, Tokyo and Washington been so conscious of the effect of a decision taken by any one of their number upon the remainder. There had been interplay before, often with major consequences, but never on the present scale. The stage was being set for a world war that was unequivocally deserving of the name, a world war whose origins in 1941 are incomprehensible unless one appreciates the interplay between the four capitals. Because of these complex ripple effects, much of what happened was not intended. Hitler, for instance, hoped to postpone any war with the United States until after the defeat of Russia. Roosevelt was not anxious to go to war – at least in 1941 – and if he fought anyone he wished to fight Germany, not Japan. Nor did the Japanese desire war with the United States until they found or felt themselves driven to it by circumstances beyond their control. As for the British, before the fall of France, most hoped that Germany could be tamed without the help of Russia and without the growth of undue British dependence upon the United States. They also wished to avoid war with Japan. Meanwhile the Russians in 1940 were probably viewing the world with a mixture of hope and fear.

As we have seen, the Japanese in the Far East in 1938 launched what they hoped would be a brief, decisive campaign against the Kuomintang. Their aim was not the conquest of China, but the creation of a political order in China which they could control. In their New Order for East Asia, proclaimed in November 1938, the Japanese invited the Chinese to become their partners – admittedly very junior partners – in a struggle against communism and western imperialism. This and other Japanese efforts to secure Chinese puppet allies largely failed, so that Tokyo found itself trapped in a costly and seemingly endless and unwinnable war, though with much of eastern China under its control. At times in 1940 the General Staff seemed tempted by the idea of an enclave strategy in south China – this would be less costly, and might persuade enough Chinese to return to the negotiating table. But as in the 1930s the Japanese leadership continued to be racked with divisions of all kinds as major interest groups and factions struggled for power. Those who favoured a more authoritarian and centralized regime, for instance, continued to be opposed by many business interests and the party politicians. Meanwhile the question of an alliance with Germany had produced a major battle within the elite in 1939.

The most enthusiastic support for the German alliance was centred in the army. The navy was divided, some fearing that it would lead to war with Britain and the United States. Many politicians also took this line. The value of such an alliance against Russia had more appeal, but even this aroused some opposition. In the summer of 1939 the anger of the pro-Germans was so extreme that the Navy Ministry was temporarily placed under special guard for its own safety.[1] On 8 August the navy warned that an alliance with Germany and Italy would have no chance against Britain, France, Russia and the United States. Japan's dependence on trade with the Anglo-American peoples was emphasized – about two-thirds of that conducted outside the yen bloc. But it was the Nazi–Soviet Pact of 23 August 1939 which finally brought negotiations with Germany to an end. Serious border fighting was in progress between Japanese and Russian forces at the time. On 28 August a new government took office and began a reappraisal of Japanese policy.[2]

For as long as there was a chance that Britain and France would frustrate German ambitions in Europe some western diplomats believed that moderate counsels would continue to prevail in Japan. Unfortunately British and Australian interest in a policy of economic appeasement encountered a hostile reception in Washington. Cordell Hull in December 1939 argued that such actions as the current moral embargo on certain American exports to Japan must continue to discredit the militants. If necessary the United States would continue with its present policy of disapproving Japanese actions in China for twenty-five years to compel compliance with the principles of the 'Open Door'.[3] Roosevelt feared that any relaxation of the American stance would work to the advantage of the isolationists. But not surprisingly, some groups in Japan, notably the navy, even before the dramatic German victories in Europe from April 1940, began to insist that Japan must secure more influence in the south seas and the East Indies. Japan needed more markets and raw materials. German victories prompted fears of the establishment of an American protectorate over the Dutch East Indies, and the Japanese navy for the first time began to develop an interest in Germany as an ally.[4] The advocates of a national defence state and a self-sufficient trading bloc gained more support. Japan, it was agreed, must put herself in the same league (in terms of resources) as Russia and the United States. But the intention was to deter, not to fight the United States. The fall of France, however, greatly strengthened the expansionists.

In July 1940 a new government under Konoye was much more representative of the pro-German factions, though Konoye himself was no mere tool of the extremists. He tried to establish a strong, centralized regime, but one which owed more to Japanese tradition than to European totalitarianism. In practice his government was a fairly broad-based coalition of interests which was subject to much criticism from the extreme factions, but which, unlike its predecessors, was now prepared to take bigger risks in foreign policy and was much more united on the question of an alliance with Germany. To the sceptics Matsuoka, the new Foreign Minister, insisted that the time had come to choose between Germany and the Anglo-Americans. To choose the latter would necessitate the forfeiture of Japan's great hopes in China. A new world order, he believed, was in process of formation, made up of four great regional blocks, each led by a major power, Germany, Russia, the United States and Japan. The Japanese were not alone in this view. Even Italy hoped to be the centre of a great area of autonomous 'living space' at the end of the war, while Sir Stafford Cripps as British ambassador in Moscow speculated in June 1940 on the emergence of four great regional blocs – an Asiatic one under Japan (or Japan and China), a Russian-dominated Euro-Asian region, a European grouping, and an American bloc, perhaps including Britain.[5]

On 26 July 1940 the Konoye government agreed that Japan must be prepared to use force in pursuit of her southern objectives (these included Burma, Malaya and the East Indies, as well as Indo-China): these objectives were given equal priority with the war with China. The same day saw the start of significant American economic pressure on Japan. This did not, as intended, deter the Japanese. Indeed they moved into northern Indo-China in the autumn. There was even some readiness in Tokyo to contemplate war with the United States to fulfil the southern ambitions. The navy, with a better appreciation of American strength and potential, had mixed feelings on the subject. It recognized, however, that time was on the side of the Americans – the latter could build a vastly superior navy; Japan's regional superiority was a wasting asset. The navy hoped that Japan's Greater Asia Co-Prosperity Sphere could be created without a major war, and to this end it began to sympathize with the pro-German factions in the hope that an alliance or agreement with Germany might deter the United States from war.

The Japanese conducted the negotiations with Germany in the autumn of 1940 with varying degrees of enthusiasm. The most ardent were the middle-ranking officers and officials of the General Staff and Army Ministry. The admirals were still hesitant, as were others in the government. The German ambassador, Ott, apparently without the knowledge of his own Foreign Ministry, signed a secret letter to the effect that Japanese involvement in a war with the United States would not be automatic.[6] Nominally mutual assistance was promised if one of the signatories were attacked by a power not at present involved in the war in Europe or China. But Konoye insisted that the 'basic aim of this pact is to avoid war with the United States'.He added: 'However, I think it is necessary for us to display firmness, because if we act humbly, it will only make the United States presumptuous.'[7] The Tripartite Pact of 27 September 1940 (the third member was Italy) was also intended by Japan to restrict Germany's expectations as a legatee of the European empires in Asia: both Hitler and Mussolini acknowledged Japan's leadership of a new order in 'Greater East Asia'. The pact did not impress the Americans, or even the British and Dutch, in the way that the Japanese had hoped. The Dutch refused to increase their oil exports to Japan. The British, though fully aware that they could send reinforcements to the Far East only at the expense of the war in the Mediterranean, reopened the Burma Road to supplies to China (this had been closed for three months in the summer of 1940 as a result of Japanese pressure). Churchill continued to bank on American involvement in the war sooner or later. The British service chiefs comforted themselves with false hopes about the state of Japan's armed forces. The latter had, after all, failed to achieve victory in China.[8] So one miscalculation followed another.

GRAND STRATEGY AND EUROPE, 1940–41

Hitler repeatedly affirmed that he would not repeat the German error of the First World War and fight on two fronts simultaneously. Anglo-French inertia in September 1939 obscured his departure from this assurance at that time. From the defeat of France until almost the end of the year there was a continuing debate as to Germany's next move, though how far Hitler himself was undecided is not clear. He later gave three different dates – spanning the period July–December 1940 – as the moment of his decision to attack Russia.

Preparations for a Russian war in 1941 began in the summer of 1940, but Hitler did not ignore proposals for the prior defeat of Britain. An early end to the war in the west would obviously be advantageous in itself, and would meet the criticism of service chiefs who strongly opposed any possibility of a war on two fronts.

Germany's failure in the Battle of Britain and her weakness at sea led Admiral Raeder in particular to advocate a Mediterranean strategy. With the help of Vichy France, Spain and Italy he hoped to clear the British from that region, and to reach eastward from there perhaps as far as the oil of the Middle East and even the Caucasus, and westward to secure Gibraltar and the Atlantic islands to weaken the position of Britain and the United States at sea. With Ribbentrop, Göring and General Keitel he opposed war with Russia at that time. Raeder himself later concluded that Hitler was already committed to war with Russia, and that he wanted no more than limited operations in the south to deny Britain and America the use of North Africa against his European empire. Nevertheless there were times when Hitler seemed ready to explore seriously the alternatives to an early war with Russia, though preparations for the latter continued. If he were indeed obsessed with Russia, he did enough to demonstrate to his colleagues that the Mediterranean strategy was not an easy option.

The Mediterranean strategy required the co-operation of Spain to take Gibraltar and the Atlantic islands, of Vichy France to hold north-west Africa and of Italy to secure Egypt and territory further east. Unfortunately the three prospective allies were territorial rivals in North Africa. Any threat to the colonial territory of France would alienate the Vichy regime, or perhaps even deliver North Africa into the hands of the Free French and de Gaulle. Spain, meanwhile, was too weak after the Civil War to back any but a certain winner, and her interests were protected with some skill by Franco in a meeting with Hitler on 23 October at Hendaye. Finally Mussolini's attack on Greece at the end of October misfired. These problems finally persuaded Hitler, if he needed persuading, that he should do no more than secure his southern flank while he dealt with Russia. Only a different outcome to his negotiations with the Russians in November 1940 could have saved the Mediterranean strategy. Nevertheless some historians have seen this decision as a great error on Hitler's part. Had he merely concentrated on the eastern Mediterranean the British would have been in grave danger. Germany had many potential allies in the Middle East, notably in Iraq.[9] She might even have reached the oil of the Caucasus by this southern route, with devastating consequences for Russia's military strength. This, of course, leaves out of account Russian reactions to a threat from this quarter, or Germany's immense logistic problems. All these might-have-beens are perhaps best left to war-games enthusiasts. Historians are well advised to concentrate on more tangible matters such as the deterioration in Russo-German relations in eastern Europe from the summer of 1940.

It is true that the many points of friction did not prevent negotiations in the autumn of 1940 on the possible inclusion of Russia in the Tripartite Pact. Professor McSherry argues that had the Russians been more conciliatory at this point in time they might have delayed the German attack on Russia for at least a year.[10] It is impossible, in fact, to decide how seriously Hitler took these talks. On 1 and 4 November 1940, for instance, he gave totally different impressions to General Halder of his intentions towards Russia. Perhaps he was genuinely puzzled. Of his determination to act against Russia sooner or later there can be no doubt. The appeal of the Mediterranean option was fading by this time, yet Hitler must surely have been tempted had the Russians accepted his terms concerning eastern Europe, and agreed to co-operate in the destruction of British power and influence from Egypt to India. The crucial talks began in Berlin on 12 November with Molotov representing the Soviet Union. Significantly, on the day of his arrival Hitler ordered the continuation of 'all preparations for the east already verbally ordered'.[11]

Hitler tried to tempt Molotov with what he described as 40 million square kilometres of 'bankrupt estate', the British Empire. Russia was invited to join the Tripartite Pact, and to centre her territorial aspirations 'south of the national territory of the USSR in the direction of the Indian Ocean'. Diplomatic assistance with Russia's border problems with Japan was promised. But the Russians would not abandon their interest in Europe – in Finland, Rumania, Bulgaria and Turkey. With hindsight this line of argument might seem unwise, but the Russians on the one hand were disturbed by the renewal of German activity in eastern Europe following the defeat of France, and on the other were apparently hopeful that Germany would not turn on them so long as the war with Britain lasted. Thus Molotov adopted a firm tone in Berlin, and even when the Russians offered on 25 November to join the Tripartite Pact they refused to disinterest themselves in eastern Europe. By then Hitler was talking of an attack on Russia in the spring of 1941, and rejecting Göring's advocacy of a Mediterranean strategy. The formal directive was signed on 18 December, with 15 May 1941 as the date for the completion of preparations. The ultimate aim was the creation of 'a defence line against Asiatic Russia from a line running approximately from the Volga River to Archangel'. Air power could be used to nullify any threat from beyond the Urals as necessary.

Hitler used different justifications at different times for the war with Russia. His repeated references to *Lebensraum* cannot be dismissed as mere day-dreaming, but the actual timing of the invasion of Russia was obviously determined by Hitler's assessment of the situation in the autumn of 1940. Whatever his own desires, he had to provide realistic political and strategic arguments to carry the German military leadership with him. Against their fears of a two-front war he claimed that the early defeat of Russia was the quickest route to victory over Britain – by depriving her of her one remaining potential European ally. With the resources of European Russia and the Caucasus Germany would be economically invulnerable. There are also indications that Hitler was anxious to defeat Russia before the United States became a real military threat in the west. Finally Hitler sometimes interspersed his remarks on the ease with which Russia could be defeated with warnings about the long-term Russian threat to Germany. He could exploit deep-rooted fears of the Slavs as well as the appeal of *Lebensraum* and economic self-sufficiency. Hitler was certainly correct to argue that time was not on Germany's side. Both Russia and the United States were preparing for war. Hitler of his own free will had placed himself in a position where he had no option but to go forward. It is true he might have chosen the Mediterranean strategy (with what results who can tell?), but in the autumn of 1940 his long-term aspirations and his assessment of the global balance appeared at last to coincide.[12]

Hitler's decision to attack Russia meant that the main German air offensive against Britain ended in May 1941 – apart from the later rocket bombardment – and insufficient German forces were sent to the Mediterranean to secure a decisive victory. The main military threat in Britain now came from the sea. The Battle of the Atlantic was fully as important as the Battle of Britain, and it was not until May 1943 that the struggle began to turn against the U-boats. On 8 December 1940 Churchill delivered a double warning to the United States. He wrote first of Britain's heavy shipping losses in the Atlantic and her consequent need for all possible American aid at sea. It was 'in shipping and in the power to transport across the oceans, particularly the Atlantic Ocean, that in 1941 the crunch of the whole war will be found'.[13] Secondly Churchill warned that Britain had almost exhausted the financial resources she needed to purchase American goods. Lord Lothian, the British ambassador to the United States, argued that Britain do her utmost in the next six months to rouse Americans to action. One had to take full account of the slow-moving character of the American political system.[14]

Roosevelt and others had already toyed with ideas of lending or leasing equipment to Britain, but the seriousness of Britain's problems with respect to dollar purchases had not been fully appreciated. Roosevelt now set out to convert ideas into reality. He used the homely illustration of lending one's fire-hose to a neighbour whose house was on fire – repayment could wait until the fire was out. Such was the origin of the Lend–Lease Agreement of 1941. The debate in Congress was not complete until March 1941, and much use was made of the argument that American economic interests would suffer if the world's trade fell under the domination of totalitarian powers. German influence in Spain, for instance, could have profound repercussions in South America. The Lend–Lease negotiations with Britain were also intended to protect American economic interests in the postwar world after the defeat of Germany. America did not give Britain something for nothing. Nor, in 1941, did Lend–Lease provide Britain with many additional arms (American food supplies were more important). It was not, as David Reynolds points out, particularly novel: it was 'a logical extension of F.D.R's defence and foreign policy since Munich'.[15] It was, nevertheless, a valuable boost to the morale of the beleaguered islanders, and more was to follow.

Thus Anglo-American staff talks were proceeding and becoming more elaborate. Information was being exchanged in many fields. The Americans were making no commitments, but it was agreed that in the event of war the United States would give priority to the defeat of Germany. American policy towards Japan, as we shall see, was not always carefully calculated, but the intention was to deter rather than to provoke. In the Atlantic the American naval chiefs were pressing for positive action given their fear that the German U-boat campaign might succeed before American power was brought to bear. From April 1941, therefore, American naval activity in the Atlantic was progressively stepped up. Greenland was proclaimed a temporary American protectorate. In June American troops replaced the British forces in Iceland, and American convoys began to run to that island. Even so some were of the opinion that Roosevelt was too cautious, and that the public was prepared to stomach even more vigorous action. Morgenthau, the Secretary of the Treasury, insisted that 'if we are going to save England we would have to get into this war . . . we needed England, if for no other reasons as a stepping stone to bomb Germany'. Roosevelt, however, was determined that Americans, if they went to war, should do so as a united people. If opinion sometimes seemed to creep ahead of him, this was often at his prompting. He encouraged the press and others to give a lead, even welcoming criticism of his own 'pusillanimous' policy, a word he himself once offered to a reporter.[16] In fact, Roosevelt had gone so far in support of Britain by 1941 that the German admirals were beginning to press for war with the United States. It was Hitler, for once, who showed restraint, though not for any benevolent reason – he wished to end the war with Russia first.[17]

Hilter also looked for assistance in the Far East to deter and distract the United States. In conversations with the Japanese in March–April 1941 he promised support if they became involved in war with the United States. He argued that this was a unique moment in history for the Axis: it was unlikely that so favourable an opportunity would recur for Germany, Japan and Italy. The defeat of Britain, he claimed, was only a matter of time: a Japanese attack on Singapore would be decisive. The United States was not yet ready for war, and an aggressive Japanese policy was more likely to encourage non-interventionism. Hitler at this time had no interest in Japanese help in his projected war with Russia. He was confident of victory, and had no wish to share the prize. Indeed, a Russian-controlled Siberia probably suited his geo-political ideas better than one that was under part Japanese control. He wanted Japan to weaken the British, and preoccupy the Americans while he struck at Russia. Only occasionally in the summer of 1941 did he seem receptive to the advice of some of his colleagues to seek Japanese help against Russia. The Japanese in any case were increasingly inclined to strike southwards, and in April 1941 they concluded a neutrality agreement with Moscow. This did not prevent discussion in Tokyo in June–July (after the German attack) of the possibility of war with Russia, and it was of the utmost importance to the Russians that Japan finally decided to give priority to her southern ambitions.

Russia was singularly unprepared for the German attack on 22 June. This was not for want of warning. The Russians were sufficiently alarmed from January 1941 for them to make repeated efforts to conciliate Germany. So rewarding for Germany was the new trade treaty of January 1941 that State Secretary Weizsäcker expected Germany to be a net loser 'in an economic sense' from a war with Russia.[18] When Germany struck in the Balkans in the spring of 1941, Russia briefly offered encouragement to Yugoslavia until the extent of German success was appreciated and the policy of appeasement was hastily reactivated. Meanwhile warnings continued to reach Stalin from many quarters of a probable German invasion. But Stalin was determined to buy time until at least 1942. Even Russian preparations for the defence of their western territories were carefully regulated so that the Germans were given no excuse to act. Stalin was determined to prevent an accidental war. Even when German aircraft infringed Russian air space Stalin chose to interpret this as all part of a war of nerves by Hitler – this was a prelude to a diplomatic offensive. Perhaps Stalin banked on German fears of a two-front war. He seems to have regarded British warnings of an imminent German attack as mischief-making – an attempt to provoke a Russo-German war to relieve Britain's problems. Stalin was reluctant even to order resistance in the first hours of the German attack on 22 June until he was convinced that Hitler had launched an all-out attack. Clearly he feared that war would prove a disaster for Russia, his regime and himself.

Stalin was perhaps pleasantly surprised by Britain's immediate offer of assistance. But further light is thrown on the relationship by

Churchill's private aside that he would have made a favourable comment on the Devil himself had Hitler invaded Hell. The response from the United States was even more equivocal. Anti-communist feeling was running much more strongly there. The State Department even touched on the probable extent of Russia's postwar territorial claims in eastern Europe should Germany be defeated. But in the summer of 1941 an early Russian defeat seemed much more likely. There was little America could do to help. American arms production was well below the nation's needs. Even if production were doubled, the current targets would not be met before September 1943. Nevertheless Roosevelt soon decided that it was in America's interest to contribute to Russia's survival in so far as she could. In November 1941 Russia joined Britain and China as recipients of Lend–Lease.

Even so, a Russian defeat in the winter of 1941–42 was still widely expected. The British, already badly mauled in the Middle East, feared a German thrust into the Caucasus. The Japanese threat to Malaya and Singapore was continually growing. Churchill could only look to the United States for more assistance, but his meeting with Roosevelt off Newfoundland in August 1941 was far less productive than he had hoped. With respect to Germany and the Atlantic the President ambiguously promised that he 'would wage war, but not declare it, and . . . become more and more provocative'.[19] Roosevelt's interpretation of his words was probably less generous than Churchill's. But at least from September 1941 allied ships were allowed to join American convoys sailing to Iceland, a concession which released about fifty British warships for other duties. American warships were also ordered to 'shoot on sight' at Axis submarines. On the other hand Roosevelt was still worried by the state of American public opinion. Its response to the Atlantic Charter, which he had negotiated off Newfoundland with Churchill, was tepid. The Charter proclaimed the general principles which should guide the postwar world: principles relating to democracy, self-determination and the development of a liberalized world economy. The British, fearing for their empire and Imperial Preference, signed with some reluctance, but accepted it as an exercise in public relations. They were disappointed to find no significant movement in the American opinion polls, although a majority now acknowledged that the defeat of Hitler was more important than the avoidance of war in all circumstances. The Senate, however, renewed Selective Service by only one vote: the House of Representatives relaxed the Neutrality Legislation by only ten in November. While the American naval chiefs tended to favour entry into the war to combat the German U-boat threat, the army wanted more time to prepare – especially against Japan in the Pacific.

AMERICA'S ENTRY INTO THE WAR

Developments in the Far East determined the date of American entry into the Second World War although, in general, neither Washington nor Tokyo wanted war. Nor were the hotheads among the Japanese military mainly responsible for what happened. Above all it was the politicians and the navy who directed Japan's drive to obtain increased control over the resources of south-east Asia, men who were usually well aware of the dangers they were running, given America's military potential and the acceleration in American preparations for war. Some lapsed into an uneasy fatalism, consoled by their concern for the nation's honour. The admirals saw that America was remorselessly eroding Japan's naval advantages: increasingly an early war seemed the only solution.

Japanese intellectuals, meanwhile, were doing their best to explain the current trends in world politics, and to justify Japan's own line of action. Once again one finds frequent use of the assumption that the world was being divided into four or five largely self-sufficient blocs. Where some writers remained obsessed with international rivalry and total war, others saw this as the necessary prelude to a new balance of power which might guarantee world peace. Similarly there were differences of opinion over the nature of Japan's relations with other peoples which would form part of her bloc. Japan would be the leader, but varying levels of partnership were envisaged – sometimes no more than limited local autonomy. In practice, as the first Burmese Prime Minister, Dr Ma Baw, later explained, although the Japanese by their invasion of south-east Asia did most to liberate the region from the western imperialists, the Japanese military proved 'so race-bound, so one-dimensional in their thinking', that they ruined most opportunities for partnership with the peoples of south-east Asia, just as they had failed in China. As early as 20 November 1941 the ministerial liaison conference decided that for the immediate future military needs must have clear priority in the newly acquired regions.[20] Asia for the Asiatics would have to wait.

Japan had occupied part of Indo-China in 1940. But Roosevelt recoiled from an oil embargo in case Japan struck at the Dutch East Indies. There was some American economic pressure, but in the first half of 1941 both Washington and Tokyo seemed anxious to negotiate. Some historians suggest that more American flexibility at this point might have averted war, but Washington refused to abandon China to the Japanese.[21] Given the virtual stalemate in China, given America's need to purchase time and to concentrate on the greater threat posed by Nazi Germany, one is bound to ask why Washington chose to make so dogmatic a stand on behalf of the 'Open Door'. In part the administration's obstinacy arose from its fear of giving hostages to its critics and the isolationists at home. Roosevelt was patiently creating a coalition for his policy of aid short of war to America's friends, and he feared that to yield on China might well weaken support for Britain. In addition there existed the fear that an appearance of American weakness might simply encourage Japanese aggression and demoralize the Chinese. In the case of Cordell Hull, questions of principle were also of real importance. Roosevelt gave the impression of wishing as usual to broaden his options, but was unable to translate his preference for flexibility into a practical policy. Nor must one forget that for ten years American and Japanese perceptions of each other's policies had been rapidly deteriorating; so much so that by 1941 it is difficult to see how this trend could have been reversed without the help of some dramatic change in the international scene – such as a major German setback in Russia, or a long period of relative quiescence in the Far East. Neither state, as it happened, found sufficient cause to change its policy, much though it regretted the worsening relations. It was easier to hope that the other would make the first conciliatory move. American attitudes, in any case, were being hardened by information derived from intercepted and decoded Japanese communications which fortified American distrust. Firmness continued to be seen as the only answer, encouraged by the widespread belief until the end of November 1941 that Japan would not dare to fight the United States.

Decisions of prime importance were taken in July 1941. Encouraged by German success against Russia, the Japanese occupied the rest of Indo-China. The United States replied with an embargo on trade with Japan on the 26th. The British and Dutch followed suit. About three-quarters of Japan's trade was affected. In particular she was denied crucial imports of oil and raw materials. Despite stockpiling it was soon evident that within two or three years Japan's economy, and therefore her ability to wage war, would begin to run down. Japan had little choice. If she was to fight, she could not delay beyond November or December 1941. The selection of this date was also influenced by the need to complete a wide range of amphibious operations against American, British and Dutch possessions before the onset of the 1942 monsoon. Finally with the passage of every month the Americans were becoming better prepared for war. Japan might perhaps have gambled on the inevitability of a war between Germany and the United States. As it was, she was encouraged by Germany's successes in Russia (Russian resilience became clear only after the Japanese attack on Pearl Harbor), and by Hitler's promises of support in a war with the United States. The Japanese were in no mood in 1941 to trust to luck that something would turn up to save them from decline or capitulation in 1942.

Nevertheless most of the Japanese leadership were still anxious to negotiate with Washington until the last possible moment. The deadline for war was pushed as close to the end of the year as was militarily feasible. Nor was Washington indisposed to talk. Some Americans saw that it made good military sense to try to buy time. The military chiefs were not averse to actual concessions to Japan to postpone war until 1942 – indeed, by 1942 they hoped to be able to deter Japan from conflict. Roosevelt and his advisers still saw Germany as the main threat. The embargo, however, was proving too effective a tool – it was forcing on the war Washington wished to avoid or at least postpone. In the closing months of 1941 diplomatic attention was centred on the possibility of a *modus vivendi*, however temporary, between the two powers in the Far East. Even the replacement of Konoye as Prime Minister by the hardline General Tojo Hideki in October 1941 did not put an end to the exchanges. Basically the search for a *modus vivendi* turned on the following points. Japan had to find a temporary solution to her declining reserves of strategic raw materials. There had to be some relaxation of the embargo. She had to find some relief in China, and at the very least the Japanese army was determined to force the Americans to abandon their support of Chiang Kai-shek. Once convinced of their isolation, Chinese resistance, it was hoped, would crumble. Japan also wished to check the American military build-up in the western Pacific. In return Japan offered on 20 November to pull out of southern Indo-China, and to confine its armed advances in the south to action against China. The Americans, for their part, were prepared to tolerate Japanese military action only in China and wished to impose a freeze on Japanese military preparations elsewhere, plus a Japanese withdrawal from southern Indo-China. The United States refused to abandon China totally, though it offered to help initiate Sino-Japanese talks, and given the assurance of peace in the Far East outside China it was prepared to allow some exports to Japan. Three and six months were mentioned as possible periods over which the *modus vivendi* might run.

Roosevelt was undoubtedly much influenced by the concern of his service chiefs to gain time. Real hopes existed that an effective American deterrent, with some British help, could be created in a few months. But his freedom of diplomatic manoeuvre was limited by American public opinion, by British and Chinese opposition to significant concessions to Japan, and by growing doubts in November as to the sincerity of the Japanese. The 'Magic' intercepts and other information concerning Japanese intentions and activities contributed to the abandonment of the American search for a truce on 26 November. Success in the talks was always improbable. China was the biggest single stumbling block. A settlement here required either that the Americans wash their hands of China, or that the Japanese tolerate the continuance of American aid. In isolation a compromise on Indo-China and trade might have been possible, but these could not be separated from other questions. Washington feared that Japan might honour the Tripartite Pact if the United States became involved in a war with Germany. The Japanese feared that with the passage of time America's growing military strength would rob them of the military option. One should also remember that just as Roosevelt felt his freedom of manœuvre to be limited by public opinion, so Konoye, before his resignation in October 1941, feared a military coup if he made significant concessions to the Americans. The mood in Japan late in 1941 is reflected in the comment of the President of the Council: 'The United States is being utterly conceited, obstinate and disrespectful.' America was denying Japan her right to live and grow as a great power. Admiral Nagano remarked: 'Nevertheless a nation which does not fight in this plight has lost its spirit and it is already a doomed nation.' Not surprisingly many Japanese historians have tended to interpret this period fatalistically, as did Admiral Yamamoto, the originator of the plan to strike at Pearl Harbor, at the time.[22]

War broke out in the Pacific on 7 December 1941. The attack on Pearl Harbor united Americans, but only against Japan. Roosevelt on the 9th pronounced Germany as guilty as the Japanese, and was clearly anxious to continue to give priority to the defeat of Germany. Hitler, who might have embarrassed Roosevelt by not declaring war, did so on 11 December, now being only too eager to back Japan once that country was committed to war. He underestimated American potential, but he also argued that this was the decisive moment of the war. The United States was only half-prepared: she was reeling under the Japanese assault. No better chance of victory on a global scale was likely to present itself.[23]

THE GRAND ALLIANCE AGAINST THE AXIS

Neither Germany nor Japan had kept the other informed concerning its main moves in 1941. Nor was strategy co-ordinated thereafter. Berlin and Tokyo did agree on 18 January 1942 that longitude 70° east should form the dividing line between their respective spheres of interest – broadly this placed Afghanistan and what is now Pakistan inside the German sphere. An invasion of India by way of Afghanistan had crossed Hitler's mind, but in 1942 his forces were still struggling to reach Moscow and the oil of the Caucasus. He ignored Japanese suggestions that an early Axis junction in the Indian Ocean gave the best prospect of victory and that he should make peace with Russia. By May 1942 Japan had no forces to spare for a major operation against India, and in June the navy suffered a disastrous defeat at the hands of the Americans off Midway in the Pacific. In the autumn of 1942, too, the Germans were checked, and lost their chance to take the Caucasus, a more valuable objective than Moscow according to General Timoshenko. Up until the battle of Kursk in July 1943 Hitler still perhaps had a faint chance of concluding a compromise peace with Russia, as Goebbels and Ribbentrop now advocated. But Hitler was not interested. Stalin's intentions remain obscure, though his fear of a long war and his suspicion of the Anglo-Americans (Russia might be left to bear the main brunt of the war while the United States became ever stronger) might have tempted him to weigh the pros and cons of a compromise peace with Germany very carefully. Be that as it may, in 1941–43 Germany and Japan lost whatever chance they had of winning the war.[24] Their greatest achievement was the formation of the improbable Grand Alliance of Britain, Russia and the United States.

No alliance is without internal tensions. Historians study, with ever increasing detail, the strains within the most successful in modern times – that between Britain and the United States. Given the history of Russia's relations with the western powers since 1917, it is remarkable that the wartime partnership was not riven with more difficulties. Nor is it surprising that Stalin and his western allies sometimes feared that the other might attempt to make a separate peace with Germany. Few have viewed their fellow men with such suspicion as Stalin, but in the early stages of the Russian war one must recognize how few means of leverage he possessed over the western powers other than their need that Russia should continue her desperate struggle. Understandably every effort was made to secure a Second Front from the western powers to divert German forces away from Russia. The issue was then and has been since something of a political football. The Russian pleas and complaints were both sincere and a political gambit. The western powers went back on promises made in 1942 and 1943, but usually for good military reasons, and while they were not engaging in massive land battles with the Germans, they were exerting no small pressure on German resources. The Anglo-American bombing of Germany had only a limited effect on German industrial production down to 1944, but it was a drain on German air defences and all the supporting services.

Any misapplication of resources on the part of the western powers arose not out of any hostility to the Soviet Union but from their own strategic preferences and prejudices. Heavy bombing was acquiring an obsessive quality and momentum all its own. The British did not wish to attempt a landing in northern France until they were sure of success, and had become heavily committed materially and emotionally to the Mediterranean. It was asserted that southern Europe represented 'the soft under-belly of the Axis',but at least north of Rome it was neither so soft nor so strategically rewarding as Churchillian rhetoric suggested. At the same time, given the state of British and American forces and their deployment by the summer of 1942 or the spring and early summer of 1943, it would have been a difficult, hazardous and possibly disastrous business to have attempted an earlier landing in Normandy. Ironically, had a successful Anglo-American landing taken place in northern France in 1943, this might well have worked to the long-term disadvantage of the Soviet Union. More of Germany and central Europe might have fallen to the western powers. Some Americans saw this as a reason to act in 1942–43.[25] On the other hand western leaders sometimes seemed genuinely embarrassed by their failure to do more to assist the Russians, and may at times have felt handicapped in their negotiations with Stalin.

One need not follow here all the shifts in Anglo-American feeling concerning relations with the Russians. There were few consistent patterns, save among the most adamant of anti-communists (even they could sometimes mellow, infected by the spirit of the times or fear of the Axis). If there were fears of the extent of postwar Russian influence in Europe, there were also occasions when it was feared that the Russians might be content to drive the Germans back to the frontiers of 1941 and no further. Yet the great wartime allied meetings tended to break up on fairly amicable and optimistic notes, notably at the Tehran Conference of November–December 1943, and to some extent at Yalta in February 1945. In any case, postwar Russian conduct did not yet preoccupy London and Washington to the exclusion of all else. There was no guarantee that Germany and Japan would not revive as aggressor states. Many expected serious Anglo-American dissension after the war over the future of the British Empire, Imperial Preference and trade policies in general.[26] During the war itself Americans were often distrustful of British interest in the Balkans. Militarily they saw this as a diversion from what they regarded as the decisive theatre – namely northern France. It also smacked of British imperialism – the defence of the route to India. When the anti-Russian American diplomat, William Bullitt, argued in 1943 for Anglo-American action in eastern Europe to exclude Russia, this was greeted by sections of the War and State Departments as 'sheer military fantasy'.[27] To be feasible, an alliance with Germany would be necessary. Well into 1945 the State Department often expected America's postwar role in Europe to be that of mediator between the British and Russians. Furthermore, it was only in 1944 that the British began to follow anything in the nature of a consistent anti-Russian policy in the Balkans. By then some American diplomats were beginning to share the alarm at the way in which.

as Russian forces advanced beyond their 1941 frontiers, so Moscow contrived to build up its influence in the liberated states. Conditions often seemed ripe for revolution. Marxists were usually the best organized of the groups battling for power, though the Russians also made astute use of some other parties. Indeed, in the winter of 1944–45, when British forces clashed in Greece with Communists and their Left-wing allies, there were some in Washington who were not sorry to see the British acting decisively.[28]

The alarm in the British Cabinet was shared by some of its Labour members. Ernest Bevin stressed the need to protect British interests in Austria, the Adriatic, Greece and the Straits. Nevertheless, so far as Greece was concerned, Stalin honoured his Moscow agreement of October 1944 with Churchill, although in Yugoslavia the fifty-fifty division of influence was nullified by the success of the local Communists under Tito. Stalin was embarrassed by Tito's independence, and by his clash with the British (and Americans) over Trieste in the early summer of 1945. Stalin preferred communist gains in eastern Europe to be made under his direction, and just as few could equal his ruthlessness when the occasion presented itself, so also he could proceed cautiously, pragmatically and patiently. His policy varied from country to country according to local circumstances and Russian needs. Thus the Finns, despite the Winter War of 1939–40, and their entry into the Russian campaign on the side of Germany, were granted an armistice on fairly lenient terms in September 1944. Doubtless Stalin anticipated difficulties if he tried to make Finland communist and recalled American sympathy for the Finns in 1939–40. Any material gains from a communist Finland might also have been outweighed by the effect on Sweden: Stalin could have had no wish to see Sweden abandon its neutrality. With the Czechs, too, Stalin was reasonably lenient, but elsewhere in eastern Europe Russian interests were pursued with varying degrees of vigour. Above all there was the question of the future of Poland.

From the start of Russian involvement in the Second World War they made clear their determination to recover the frontiers of 1941. Such a claim naturally aroused fierce opposition from the Polish government-in-exile in London. The British stalled at first, but on 7 March 1942 Churchill suggested to Roosevelt that the Russian demand be met. Roosevelt, however, feared the strength of the Polish vote at home, and wished in any case to avoid territorial commitments during the war. Hole-in-corner deals brought back unfortunate memories of the First World War. They ran counter to American aspirations concerning the postwar world, while many in the State Department were not anxious to make concessions to communism. Nevertheless at the Tehran Conference in November 1943 Roosevelt as well as Churchill basically met Stalin's demands on Poland's frontiers. The country was to be transposed westward at the expense of Germany. True, from the New Year, both the western leaders tried to secure for the Poles the right to settle their own affairs, given respect for Russia's security needs. But the Polish leaders in the west were uncompromising. They were proud and ambitious, but also persuaded that a policy of concessions would profit them little in their relations with Russia. This view had been reinforced by the discovery in 1943 of the mass graves of murdered Polish officers at Katyn. The claim that this must have been the work of Russians before the German attack of 1941 has never been disproved.

Churchill's efforts to produce a compromise between the London Poles and Stalin were thus unavailing. Roosevelt, with his domestic political worries, gave him little help. As usual one cannot read Stalin's mind with confidence. At times he seemed reluctant to offend the western powers, though he might also have calculated that time was on his side. He had few allies among the Polish people. The Polish Communist Party was extremely weak, as was the Polish Left in general. Stalin's first efforts to organize an alternative body to the London Poles were tentative and perhaps left the door open to other developments. The Union of Polish Patriots set up in March 1943 evolved into the Lublin Committee, but this did not proclaim itself a provisional government until the end of 1944.[29] Stalin was consistent in his demand for a friendly Poland. It was Poland's misfortune that she was the high road between Germany and Russia. With the best will in the world she could not become another Finland – or even a Czechoslovakia (1945–47 style). Postwar Russian influence in Germany was dependent on Russian influence in Poland. Stalin did not have to be Stalin to take a tough line on Poland.

The breach between Moscow and the London Poles widened in the summer of 1944. Russian forces were rapidly approaching Warsaw. Polish Resistance forces rose in the capital on 1 August, intent on the capture of the city themselves to strengthen their bargaining position with their Russian 'liberators'. The Russian armies stopped on the Vistula while the battle raged in Warsaw between the Poles and German forces. There were probably adequate military reasons for the Russian pause, but Russian conduct during the German defeat of the Warsaw rising suggests that Stalin was not sorry to see the non-communist Polish Resistance crippled. For Churchill this was a great blow to his hopes of narrowing the differences between Russia and the London Poles. But for others it was a moment of even greater disillusionment. George Kennan later insisted this was the moment when the western powers should have staged a showdown with the Russians.[30] This was hardly realistic. Germany – not to mention Japan – had still to be defeated. This was not a limited war of the kind waged by autocratic regimes in the eighteenth or nineteenth century.

Thus the Grand Alliance held together, with each of the 'Big Three' snatching such advantages as seemed safe and appropriate. Indeed, some western writers now argue that Stalin, well into 1945, might have preferred the continuance of the 'Big Three' partnership into the postwar era as the easiest way to promote Russian security and recovery after so devastating a war. Roosevelt and Churchill were partly reassured by his attitude during the meeting at Yalta in February 1945, and as late as the Potsdam Conference in July 1945 Churchill could say of Stalin, 'I like that man.'

EAST–WEST RELATIONS AND THE END OF THE SECOND WORLD WAR

Since 1945 there has been an on-going debate as to whether the United States towards the end of the war was too generous and too trusting towards the Soviet Union, or not generous and trusting enough – that the administration was too intent on making the world safe for American capitalism to make continuing co-operation with the Soviet Union possible. In these various analyses Roosevelt has appeared as both hero and villain, and his successor, Truman, either as too lacking in sophistication and subtlety to continue Roosevelt's policies successfully, or as embarking rather clumsily on a tougher line of his own. It can also be argued that the potential East–West divisions were so deep that no diplomacy, however skilful or imaginative, could have done much to lessen them. The defeat of Germany and Japan was creating a power vacuum in much of Europe and the Far East, and this was bound to cause a struggle for influence among the victors. Their needs and ambitions were bound to differ, and the clash of interest between communism and capitalism simply added one more component to an inevitable and complex rivalry. On this basis one might contend that the Cold War could at best have been moderated, not averted.

The abundance of American sources for the study of this period has not lessened the controversy over American policy, though part of this problem of evaluation arises from lack of knowledge of actual Russian perceptions of American strength and intentions. It has been suggested, for instance, that Roosevelt's efforts to conciliate and gain Stalin's confidence from Tehran to Yalta had the unfortunate effect of making the Russian leader over-confident, and causing him to seek more advantages than he might otherwise have done, the net effect of his more ambitious policy being to worsen East–West relations and therefore the Cold War in the longer term.[31] The Russians, it is argued, understood hard bargaining and were best handled by such methods. On the other hand it is said that Roosevelt gave up little that it was within his power to deny the Russians; that in his dealings with Stalin he was less innocent and optimistic than he appeared; and that, as in his approach to most problems, his policy is comprehensible only if the tactics are separated from the long-term strategy and full weight is given to their experimental character. Roosevelt, as usual, explained himself differently to different people. It is possible that he may at times have been carried away by vanity, optimism and enthusiasm (one must also take account of the serious deterioration in his health by 1944–45), and Stalin, like Churchill, could have had difficulty at times in comprehending his intentions. But for Roosevelt ambiguity and vague generalizations were often inescapable. He wished to keep in step both with the Russians and his own people – normally an impossible task. Often he was simply playing for time in the hope that something would turn up and work to his advantage, as he had done in 1937–39. Meanwhile he was doing his best to nudge people in the direction he wished them to go, though often in the knowledge that he might fail. Roosevelt was an idealist in the sense that he believed one should work for a better world in the knowledge that one might fail: he was a realist in the sense that he took due account of immediate needs and pressures but refused to be enslaved by them. Given time both the Russians and his own people might change: given encouragement both might move closer to acceptance of the sort of international order he desired. He preferred to clutch at straws rather than despair.

Roosevelt wished to lower the barriers between nations. He spoke of free ports of information as well as free ports for trade. He believed that world prosperity and peace were interdependent, and without being as dogmatic as Woodrow Wilson, he thought in much the same terms of a liberal capitalist world as his predecessor. But his world order was flexible enough to incorporate a co-operative Russia, despite its communist regime, so long as it was willing to become part of the 'civilized world community'. To the same end he wished to hasten decolonization and speed the development of backward areas of the world – if necessary through international trusteeships. In all this there was much exhortation and very little detail, and it was still a very American vision of the future. But Roosevelt believed in it for its own sake, in the conviction that one could not fight a world war without attempting to build barriers against another, and in the fear that without some unifying vision of a better world the American people might relapse into isolationism if faced with a repeat of the aftermath of the First World War.

These and similar ideas were widespread in his adminstration and in the diplomatic corps. For many the strongest attraction was the belief that such a world order would boost American trade and prosperity, and thereby stabilize the American way of life. Others thought in terms of rather stronger pressure on the Soviet Union than did Roosevelt himself. The American ambassador in Moscow, Averell Harriman, was especially interested in applying leverage to win Russia to 'our standards'. From within the State Department there emerged the following interesting comment on 3 February 1944:[32]

> . . . if by firmness, friendliness and positive action we can convince them that it is not only in our interest but theirs as well to join the family of nations as a fully fledged member, we may be able to cause them to drop at least the most odious aspects of their 'backdoor' methods of interference in the internal affairs of other countries.

Not surprisingly de Gaulle and Halifax were among the foreign observers to comment upon the dynamic crusading spirit exuded by the Americans. Soviet leaders must have reacted with a mixture of bewilderment, cynicism and amusement to American pleas for the extension of religious freedom, free speech and free institutions to the Soviet Union. George Kennan, from his long experience in the Moscow embassy, shrewdly concluded that Americans would have to learn to tolerate what could not be altered. He believed Russian and western conceptions of right and wrong were so far apart that few of his countrymen were likely to accomplish the 'philosophical evolution' necessary for 'any general understanding of Russia'. The American obstacles to such understanding were indeed formidable for, as Professor Michael Howard has commented, the United States bore more resemblance to a secular church than to a European nation-state. It found 'its identity not so much in ethnic community or shared historical experience as in dedication to a value system'.The result was an 'inward-looking community whose members could practise and bear witness to their faith' – from 1941 in the world as a whole as well as at home.[33] Roosevelt was well aware of the need to satisfy his people with generous helpings of idealistic rhetoric.

Roosevelt was much influenced by public opinion when considering the question of a successor to the League of Nations. His own initial preference was for a system which would be very much under the direction of the leading powers – with the United States, Russia, Britain and China as 'Four Policemen'. He argued, for instance, that large French and Polish armed forces would be unnecessary once Germany had been defeated. It was the State Department which showed more interest in the United Nations as a whole, while Roosevelt put his faith in the Security Council (essentially a great-power club) to which France was only belatedly admitted in 1945. Roosevelt had no great faith in the United Nations *per se*, but opted for the format that seemed most likely to appeal to the American people. As it was there was much embarrassing Republican criticism. The influential Senator Vandenberg wanted a satisfactory peace settlement to precede American participation, otherwise the country would be signing the 'most colossal "blank cheque" in history'. The President played down the difficulties, especially differences with Russia, fearful that Americans were about to be panicked into another bout of isolationism. People had also to be persuaded of the material benefits of international co-operation: it was not something that would require larger American hand-outs. Roosevelt thought it unlikely that Americans would permit the stationing of American troops overseas – except perhaps in another war. Influence could be exerted through American air and sea power, but in general he expected European affairs to be dominated by Britain and still more by Russia.[34]

This estimate of postwar Russian influence is important. Roosevelt's efforts to conciliate the Russians can be seen in a more realistic light if they sprang from the conviction that the United States, given its likely postwar interests and outlook, had no option but to try to work with the Soviet Union. In 1943 and 1944 the American military in Washington clearly anticipated that after the war Russia would dominate Europe perhaps as far west as the Rhine. Russia and the United States were each expected to be invulnerable in its own sphere, a situation which not even an Anglo-American alliance could alter. Even in so traditional a preserve as the Mediterranean the British might be too weak to resist the Russians. Roosevelt often acted as if he agreed with this reasoning. On the other hand some in his administration feared that British rivalry with Russia might be the cause of the next war, and that therefore America's main postwar diplomatic role might be that of mediator between the competing British and Russian empires. It was a theme in American policy-making which persisted well into 1945.[35] It is also interesting to note that until the end of the war the American service chiefs and planners seemed little concerned with the possibility of postwar rivalry with the Soviet Union. Yet future wars with totalitarian and militaristic enemies were expected, and it was argued that with the continual improvements in weaponry the United States could no longer rely on space and time as in the past in which to prepare its armoury. Forces in being, especially a powerful air force, were deemed essential to act as a deterrent, and to strike with devastating weight against an aggressor. Some thought was even being given to preventive war. As Professor Sherry argues, the strategy of preparedness and the Cold War mentality preceded the Cold War with Russia.[36]

But there was also a tougher side to American policy towards Russia even under Roosevelt. With British co-operation, Russia was denied an effective say in the running of Italy from 1943. Before the Yalta Conference Roosevelt had decided not to share Anglo-American nuclear secrets with Russia, at least for the time being. He had also apparently decided that there could be no postwar American loan to Russia without concessions in return. There were times, too, when Roosevelt seemed especially intent on building up British strength after the war. Those close to him were very conscious of his hopes and fears. They noted doubts concerning Russia and some feeling that he was gambling with none too favourable odds. On 11 January 1945 he left the Senate Foreign Relations Committee fully apprised of his awareness of Russian advantages in eastern Europe.[37] There was his weary acknowledgement to his Chief of Staff, Admiral Leahy, after Yalta of his dependence on Russian good faith. At Yalta, too, his efforts to woo Stalin were much influenced by his desire for Russian aid in the war against Japan once Germany had been defeated.

No tidy picture therefore emerges of Roosevelt and American policy. The Utopian and the pragmatist, the man with a long-term vision and the opportunist living from hand to mouth – these coexisted inside the same body. Confronted by an obstacle he almost seemed to relish the task of finding a way round, however great the diversion, provided there was no complete loss of direction. At the same time one cannot escape the feeling that with the approaching end to the war Roosevelt, the magician with his marvellous sleights of hand, was about to be exposed to his various audiences. He could not indefinitely speak one language to Stalin in private and another in public to the American people. Above all he was pinning his hopes on the possiblity that he could win sufficient Russian confidence for their fear of aggression to be diminished, and cultivate a degree of moderation in their conduct and demands that would reassure the American public. The Declaration on Liberated Europe, drawn up at Yalta to guarantee free elections, symbolized much of his work. There was too much reliance on clauses which could be interpreted in different ways, on postponements in the hope that something would make for a solution later, and on promises of good intent. It was a fragile edifice, but it would be wrong to assume that the President was wholly deceived. He was too good a politician for that. What he did was to refuse to despair of postwar co-operation until he was convinced there was no alternative. His fears of Russia were clearly growing shortly before his death in April 1945, but he still seemed determined not to rush into a confrontation. Had he lived his tactics might well have been more subtle and patient than those of his successor, although his interpretation of American interests and his determination to defend them would have been much the same.

Truman's introduction to world politics is thought of too much in terms of his famous verbal onslaught against Russian policy delivered to Molotov on the eve of the San Francisco Conference. His own advisers still ranged from hawks to doves on relations with Russia. Harriman, the American ambassador in Moscow, at first feared that

Truman might prove too conciliatory. At the end of April he thought him too strident. It seemed to Harriman that the Russian leadership itself was uncertain, even divided, on the question of future East–West relations, and he believed that it was up to America to find the right balance between the carrot and stick to encourage the trend towards co-operation.[38] Truman himself thought it necessary to get 'Churchill in a frame of mind to forget the old power politics'. In practice from April to the Potsdam Conference in the summer of 1945 the British and Americans were often out of step on East–West relations. The American fear that Britain's traditional and imperialistic approach to power politics might lead to unnecessary quarrels with Russia has already been noted. The British for their part wanted the Americans to take a more consistently tough stand against Russian policy in Europe. Thus the British repeatedly showed more concern than the Americans over Russian conduct in Poland. The Russians, despite certain assurances at Yalta, were determined to maintain a friendly and subservient government in Warsaw even at the cost of conflict with Polish parties which had formidable support in the country. The battle for power within Poland continued until January 1947, and extended far beyond the ballot box. But on 5 July 1945 the British had acquiesced in the American determination to recognize the Polish government although little had been done to revise its composition (Communists and their allies were still dominant) in accordance with Russian promises made at Yalta. Similarly in Germany the Americans overrode Churchill's desire to exploit as a bargaining counter the advance of Anglo-American forces into the intended Russian occupation zone. The Americans early in July insisted on withdrawal in the hope that this would provide a better basis for allied co-operation in the running of postwar Germany. They also wished to do nothing that would increase the tendency for Europe to be divided into eastern and western spheres of influence. As we shall see, an undivided Europe was expected to accord more satisfactorily with postwar American interests.[39]

Germany's surrender in May 1945 meant that the defeat of Japan was only a matter of time. But in the early summer of 1945 it was not clear how long Japan would continue to resist. The allies had a stranglehold on sea-borne supplies so that Japan's industry was faltering. Tremendous havoc was also being wrought from the air. Russian intervention in the war was only a matter of time. And from the spring of 1945 the Truman administration knew that it would soon have atomic weapons at its disposal. Nevertheless many still expected an allied invasion of Japan to encounter determined and desperate resistance by the Japanese army. Evidence that influential groups in Japan were seeking peace was not examined with the sensitivity it deserved – or so hindsight would suggest. Allowance must be made for the enormous momentum which the American war machine had acquired. A new President and an equally raw Secretary of State, Jimmy Byrnes, clung to firmly established lines of policy as the easiest way forward. It must also be recognized that the balance between the 'peace' and 'war' parties in Tokyo was so even that there remains ample scope for controversy as to the likely effect of a more imaginative American approach to the question of peace. There was hesitation in Tokyo even after the dropping of the first atomic bomb and Russia's entry into the war. But this combination enabled the 'war' party to accept defeat without loss of face. It was at this stage too that the Americans slightly qualified the demand for unconditional surrender; it was agreed that the imperial authority should be preserved, subject to the will of the Supreme Allied Commander.

Nevertheless the horrific nature of nuclear warfare, the continuing shadow of nuclear war to our own time and the onset of the Cold War soon after the defeat of Japan inevitably generated controversy as to the reasoning behind the dropping of the two atomic bombs over Japan early in August 1945 – how far they were necessary to hasten the end to the war, and how far they were dropped to provide the United States with diplomatic leverage over the Soviet Union? Historians can provide tentative answers, but they do not satisfy contemporary controversialists. What is clear is that by the early summer of 1945 there were some within the American administration who were beginning to regret the earlier eagerness to bring Russia into the war with Japan. Russia was expected to make considerable gains in the Far East, probably in excess of those conceded by Roosevelt at Yalta. While it had to be accepted in July 1945 that Russia would act as she thought fit, it was possible that a speedy end to the war might diminish her opportunities for advancement. Here atomic diplomacy had some practical appeal. In addition Churchill shared the hopes of those Americans who believed that in the world as a whole a demonstration of the new weapons would enhance the power of the West against the Soviet Union. But as good, if not a better case can be made out for the use of the atomic bombs against Japan because they had been devised at great cost and because Washington was determined to end the war as soon as possible. Given the American mood after three and a half years of war, Pearl Harbor, Bataan and Iwo Jima, one suspects that the bombs would have been dropped irrespective of the state of Russo-American relations.

Expectations that America's nuclear monopoly might somehow overawe the Russians and provide the West with more leverage were soon disappointed. The Russians in public refused to be impressed by the new weapons, though they were pushing ahead with a programme as rapidly as their own knowledge and resources permitted. The Americans, in contrast, tended to be complacent and confused: complacent because they expected a long monopoly with this weapon, and confused because foreign policy-making in Washington lacked clarity and leadership. Byrnes did not work well with his own department: he speedily fell foul of Republican critics, and was at odds with the President himself by the end of the war. Byrnes did not work with the British at the London Conference of Foreign Ministers in September 1945, and there were divisions within the American delegation. The Secretary of State was too intent on quick solutions, too easily persuaded that international politics were little different from domestic politics in the United States, and that he possessed a number of advantages (including the atomic bomb) which would persuade the Russians to make some concessions in their management of the affairs of eastern Europe. Molotov, however, stonewalled to excellent effect, showing both a superior tactical and strategic sense, and winning the admiration of John Foster Dulles, a future American Secretary of State, who attended the conference. Later in the year, at the Moscow Conference, Byrnes attempted a more conciliatory line with no real success, earning for himself in the process a good deal of criticism at home. An American Secretary of State had to be singularly adept at handling both the Russians and his own people simultaneously. Thus the year 1945 ended with a growing feeling in the United States that the government had somehow to devise a more effective policy in dealings with the Russians. As for the Kremlin's view of the United States, perhaps the veil is lifted a little if we can rely on an American intercepted and decoded message from Moscow to Bulgarian Communists late in 1945. This was a reply to Bulgarian alarm over western efforts to introduce non-communist elements into the government in Sofia as had been done earlier in Warsaw. Moscow bluntly commented: 'What if they do? It did not do them much good in Poland, did it?'[40]

A wide gulf thus often separated American aims and achievements. Naturally the pursuit of such aims, however half-heartedly, had some effect on the course of events and the perceptions of the two sides, but it is absurd to suggest – as have some writers – that American policy was the *main* as opposed to *a* cause of the Cold War, especially in 1945. Nor can American objectives be boiled down to the assertion that essentially the American postwar aim was to 'restructure the world so that American business could trade, operate, and profit without restriction everywhere'.[41] Bruce Kuklick has more shrewdly defined American policy as a quest for multilateralism in which ethical and political aims were inseparable from the economic. The State Department, for instance, stressed the need for equal economic opportunity in Poland and the Balkans if the United States were to have any hope of political influence in that region.[42] Political considerations were also causing the State Department in 1945 to question Roosevelt's desire to prevent a return of French rule to Indo-China. Roosevelt had been critical of the failure of the

French to realize the economic potential of the region – he was dismayed by its general backwardness – but American diplomats were beginning to stress the value of France as a 'world power' now that allies might soon be needed against Russia and communism.[43] Thus the 'Open Door' and Cold War were beginning to impose conflicting claims on American policy-making, and American economic interests were being weighed against concern for the world balance of power and American security.

NOTES AND REFERENCES

1.   Morley, pp. 92–107
2.   Morley, pp. 109–11, 175–6
3.   AD, ii, 466; iii, 101–2
4.   Silberman, pp. 284–5
5.   Mack Smith [1] pp. 239–40; Thorne [2] p. 104
6.   Morley, pp. 187, 245–55
7.   Morley, p. 256
8.   P. Lowe, pp. 182–4
9.   W. Carr [2] pp. 91–2. See also Leach, pp. 71, 73, 75n, 148
10. McSherry, ii, 248, etc.
11. Fest, pp. 641–2
12. Fest, pp. 645–7. See also W. Carr [2] pp. 93–4
13. Reynolds, p. 151
14. Reynolds, pp. 150–3
15. Reynolds, p. 166; see pp. 162–67 *passim*
16. Barron, p. 100; Blum, ii, 253
17. Herwig, pp. 221–34. For critiques of American policy, see Russett, *passim*, and Small, Ch. 5
18. Bullock, p. 647. See also Medvedev, pp. 447–54, on Stalin's reactions
19. Barker, p. 147
20. Lebra, pp. 114–16; see also p. 57
21. A good critique of American policy in 1941 is provided by Schroeder: compare with Dallek, Ch. 11. Note also Small, pp. 243 ff.
22. Silberman, p. 293; Borg and Okamoto, pp. 20–2. On American policy, see especially Dallek, pp. 299–311
23. Weinberg [3] pp. 85–95
24. Mastny [1] pp. 1365–88; Hildebrand, pp. 125–7; Warner [2] pp. 282–92
25. Stoler, pp. 37–9
26. See Louis [2] *passim*
27. Davis, pp. 79–80
28. Dallek, p. 469. Note also FRUS, 1944, iii, 1112 ff.; iv, 813 ff.
29. Dziewanowski, pp. 151 ff.
30. Kovrig, p. 18

31. Mastny [2] pp. 252–3, 309–11. See also Douglas [2] and Kettenacker, pp. 435 ff., for the view that the western powers failed to understand Russian policy and to exploit their own power. Appeasement was again being practised. On Stalin's foreign policy, note Taubman, Chs. 3–6
32. FRUS, 1944, iv, 813–19
33. Howard [3] p. 116. For Kennan's views, see FRUS, 1944, iv, 902–14
34. Campbell, pp. 5–21; Dallek, pp. 443, 507–8, 536, etc.
35. Kuniholm, pp. 96–100; FRUS, 1944, i, 700–2; FRUS, Malta – Yalta, pp. 107–8; FRUS, Potsdam, pp. 264–6
36. Sherry, p. 235
37. Campbell, pp. 85–6; Daniels, pp. 218–20; Yergin, p. 40
38. Kuklick, pp. 103–13; see also pp. 67–8
39. Nelson, pp. 93–8
40. Kovrig, p. 56
41. J. and G. Kolko, p. 2
42. Kuklick, pp. 3–17, 229–30; Nagai and Iriye, p. 48
43. G. Porter, i, 23–7

Chapter 10

THE COLD WAR IN EUROPE, 1946–1950

THE GERMAN QUESTION AND THE START OF THE COLD WAR

Many explanations of the origins of the Cold War have been offered by western scholars since 1945. Even when the Cold War was at its peak there were still a few who dissented from the orthodox view that Russia and revolutionary communist ambitions were the main, if not the only causes. The Vietnam War released a flood of revisionist writing, especially in the United States, and the needs of a capitalist American society were widely popularized as the prime cause of the Cold War. This in turn gave way to a more pragmatic school of thought which, while it might stress errors in American policy or examples of the ambition of American policy-makers, was unable to discover any grand design for the defeat of communism or the advance of capitalism. Writers of this school were more impressed by the difficulties and uncertainties which confronted the policy-makers. Like John H. Backer, in his critical study of American policy in Germany, they often concluded that policy was made through a series of 'small, or incremental, moves on particular problems rather than through a comprehensive long-range program'.[1] Some former protagonists of the orthodox and revisionist schools began to shift their ground and move to the 'incrementalist' centre. T. G. Paterson, for instance, once a severe critic of American policy, declared in 1979 that efforts to rank factors according to their importance in the origins of the Cold War had become 'a futile intellectual exercise', the causes being too interdependent and interrelated.[2] Arthur M. Schlesinger retreated from his earlier insistence on the inescapable importance of the revolutionary drive of Russian communism, with its sense of 'messianic mission', to an acceptance that Stalin's policy between 1945 and 1953 was primarily defensive.[3] Indeed, a Marxist writer, Fernando Claudin (*The Communist Move-*

ment from Comintern to Cominform) goes so far as to argue that Stalin was moved as much by *raison d'état* as the western powers, and that there was in effect a virtual East–West conspiracy to prevent genuine Left-wing revolutions in Europe at the end of the war.[4] He sees Stalin as the leader of a new ruling class in Russia, a bureaucratic oligarchy, which feared the destabilizing effects of revolutionary movements in Europe outside its own sphere of influence in eastern Europe. The Cold War arose by accident out of the confusion that prevailed in so much of Europe at the end of the war. In time the eastern and western blocs began to discover the limits of their power, and, once assured of their respective spheres of influence, found that coexistence was not impossible. If one discounts Claudin's romantic faith in the potential of the truly revolutionary Left and gives rather less weight to East–West connivance (while not forgetting such episodes as the Churchill–Stalin Balkan deal in 1944), one cannot but be struck by the amount of common ground which exists between the three above-mentioned writers.

Certainly historians can broadly agree that Stalin did little to assist the Chinese Communists in their drive for power in 1946–49, and that he encouraged communist disruption in western Europe only in the context of a general intensification of the Cold War from 1947. It was in Poland that Stalin made his most determined effort to secure a government to his liking. In eastern Germany he enjoyed a recognized base with his zone of occupation, and in 1945–46 he opportunistically sought what influence he could in the western zones. There is sketchy evidence that he may have hoped to create a united Germany under Russia's shadow, but in practice he concentrated upon the extraction of reparations from western Germany, and later upon trying to limit its usefulness to the western powers. Elsewhere in the creation of satellite states in eastern Europe one finds a mixture of careful probing for weaknesses and opportunities, or improvisation, and of decisive action only when the demoralization of the opponents of communism was far advanced – in Hungary, for instance, and still more so in Czechoslovakia.

To the western powers at the time Russian conduct appeared much more self-confident, aggressive, even revolutionary than it really was. Russian rhetoric and propaganda, notably as expressed in Stalin's speech of 9 February 1946 with its pessimistic assessment of East–West relations and the stress laid on the need to prepare Soviet strength against any eventuality, were easily misinterpreted. Stalin, it would seem, was anxious to portray the West as a threat to steel the Russian people for new sacrifices as they set about the reconstruction of their shattered country. Stalin had also to keep the West at arm's length for fear of its corrosive influence: it might inspire dangerously subversive ideas among the Russian people. There is no need to expand here on the extraordinary lengths to which Stalin went from the 1930s to the end of his life to root out any threat (real or imagined) to his authority.[5] Churchill was not far off the mark when he later commented that the Russians 'fear our friendship more than our enmity'. Yet, interestingly, Stalin might have hoped for a time at the end of the war that he could both insulate Russia and eastern Europe from western influence and yet secure help (perhaps a loan) from the United States in the reconstruction of the Russian economy. This has prompted some western historians to ask if the United States missed an opportunity here to check the postwar deterioration in East–West relations. One has, however, only to consider the difficulties experienced by the American administration when it tried to secure Congressional assent to a loan (on moderately onerous terms in the circumstances) to Britain in 1946. Congress would not have approved a loan to Russia after the war without a set of conditions which the Kremlin could not conceivably have accepted. In the end the passage of the British loan in 1946 was helped by growing Congressional fears of Russia and communism.

Given the emergence of the divide between East and West so soon after the war it is perhaps more tempting to take up the contemporary suggestion of the distinguished American columnist, Walter Lippmann, who recommended a blunt acceptance of eastern and western spheres in Europe as the best way to reduce fear and competition. The British were sometimes tempted by this solution, especially so long as they doubted the adequacy of American support. But they were also daunted by the prospect of trying to restore the economies of western Europe without access to the traditional markets and sources of supply in the east. Nor did they readily relinquish the hope of driving Russian influence as far to the east as possible. It is clear, too, that a division of Europe would have been politically unacceptable to all but a handful of Americans who were interested in the matter. So early a division of Europe would also have displeased the Russians, in that it would presumably have meant the loss of any say in the future of western Germany. In short, the powers had to learn from bitter experience that there was no alternative to the creation of a divided Europe, and that once divided there would in time be more scope for interchange between the two halves.

The occupation zones in Germany were intended to be temporary expedients – to endure only until the powers could agree on the future of the defeated enemy. But how could so potentially formidable or valuable a country be settled to the satisfaction of all? As Germany's defeat became imminent, so inter-allied rivalries and suspicions increased. At Yalta the 'Big Three' could only agree to 'study the question of partition but not prepare plans'. Germany, it was noted, should be required to submit to dismemberment if the victors so decided. Churchill was soon commenting, 'I hardly like to consider dismemberment until my doubts about Russia's intentions have been cleared away.' Already in July 1944 a State Department paper had warned that the creation of occupation zones would lead to a *de facto* division of Germany, with the former allies 'bidding for German support by promising to work for the reunification of Germany'.[6] The British Chiefs of Staff soon went further, arguing in the autumn of 1944 for the dismemberment of Germany both as a security against a revival of German militarism and to assure the West of the resources of western Germany in the event of future strife with Russia. The Foreign Office thought the consideration of such ideas premature, and had clearly not given up all hopes of postwar co-operation with Russia. This may explain its part in the forced repatriation of Russian citizens released from German control at the end of the war. At that time it expected the Russians to be assertive and difficult, but it did not take the revolutionary threat very seriously.[7] Churchill was usually more pessimistic, while the British Labour Party leader, Attlee, complained in May 1945 that the Russians were 'behaving in a perfectly bloody way, telling us nothing, but setting up Puppet Governments all over Europe as far west as they could'.[8] Stalin himself remarked, 'This war is not as in the past; whoever occupies a territory imposes on it his own social system. Everyone imposes his own system as far as his army can reach. It cannot be otherwise.'According to Marshal Zhukov, Stalin expected the western powers to try to create an 'obedient government' in Germany.

In practice economic considerations had most influence on the policies of the former allies immediately after the war. For Russia it was a question of drawing what she could – by some means or other – from the German economy to speed her own recovery. For Britain and the United States it was soon a matter of ensuring that their occupation zones represented as small a drain on their economies as possible. Later they became more interested in the potential contribution of Germany to the economic recovery and strength of western Europe. Even in 1945 the British Treasury was warning that the current Russian demands for reparations would slow the economic recovery of Europe, although its more immediate worry was with the provision of food for the British occupation zone – food which formerly had been supplied from eastern Germany.[9] The incompatibility of allied economic interests is evident, and the competition could only worsen once attention turned to the long-term future of a people who could not be trusted to determine their own destiny, but whose exclusive control by Russia or the western powers would have the most serious impact upon the balance of power in Europe.

Some American historians, in their anxiety to demonstrate the uniqueness of their country – for good or ill – have failed to note that a British Labour Foreign Secretary, Ernest Bevin, could take as serious a view of Russia and communism as the State Department. Indeed, in the summer of 1945, it was sometimes American diplomats who waited with apprehension when it was the turn of the stocky, pugnacious former trade union leader to speak at international conferences. On 23 September 1945, for instance, he complained to Molotov that 'it seemed to him that our relationship with the Russians about the whole European problem was drifting into the same condition as that which we had found ourselves in with Hitler'. He later diluted this to a warning that a lack of 'frankness' in East – West relations might lead to an irretrievable situation.[10] Bevin was also doing his best to alert more sceptical Cabinet colleagues to the dangers as he saw them, and if he sometimes seemed uncertain whether to put the German or Russian threat first the problem of Germany was discussed increasingly from 1946 in the context of a revived Germany as a partner of the Soviet Union.

Bevin complained that Russia was refusing to treat Germany as an economic unit (thus forcing Britain to supply her zone with food and raw materials). On 11 March 1946 he declared that Russia's ultimate aim was the control of all of Germany, while the following months found the Foreign Office and the Chiefs of Staff in agreement that Russia already seemed a more dangerous enemy than any Germany phoenix. The Chiefs of Staff again looked forward to the time when they would be assured of the resources of western Germany in any competition with Russia, and the Foreign Office now agreed that as much of Germany as possible must not be allowed to fall under direct Russian control. It was not yet clear how this was to be done, in that partition would mean a final breach with Russia, and no agreement was in prospect with France or the United States on the treatment of Germany. The French were preoccupied with their own recovery and with keeping Germany weak. The Americans still seemed intent on the restoration of Germany as an economic unit. Bevin himself did not rule out some Russian say in the management of the Ruhr if they provided adequate quid pro quos and behaved reasonably. But for the time being they were to be kept out, while in general he wanted to push Britain's strategic 'frontier' in Europe as far east as possible. Such was the state of opinion in Whitehall by May 1946.[11]

Given our knowledge of British and American priorities it is not unreasonable to assume that Russian thinking was much the same. The Russians were in even more desperate need of German resources to help in domestic reconstruction. They had as much, if not more incentive, to try to advance their strategic frontier. But increasingly the West saw Russian policy as one of pillage in eastern Germany supplemented by peremptory demands for a share of the milk produced by the western German cow which was being fed at no small expense by the British and the Americans. East and West could not co-operate in Germany since each wished to use her differently, and because each feared the other's influence on its own side of the divide. Such co-operation as did occur between the occupation forces (the Americans tended at first to complain more of their problems with the French than with the Russians) could not withstand these broader pressures. Thus the State Department argued on 9 May 1946 that, given Russia's current policies, Germany might, within two years, be seriously weakened by removals of capital equipment and be no nearer treatment as an economic unity. Russia, it was said, was trying to consolidate the division of Europe and to draw Germany under her exclusive influence, or at the very least was intent upon a free hand in her own zone.[12] The Americans therefore suspended interzonal deliveries in the hope that this would force the French and Russians to accept a common economic policy for Germany before the occupation zones hardened into a *de facto* division of Germany.[13]

Suspension, however, merely heightened the obstacles to co-operation, and in recognition of the impasse the British and Americans in the autumn of 1946 began to move towards bizonal co-operation as the first step in search of relief from the burdensome costs of occupation. Although the French did not follow the Anglo-American lead at first, by 1948 the stage was already set for the creation of a West German state. It was very much a product of the necessities of the moment. Kennan, in 1948, feared that a partition of Germany might alienate patriotic German feeling to the advantage of the Russians. The Joint Strategic Plans Committee of the Joint Chiefs of Staff were hardly more optimistic with their comment at the end of 1947 that events would 'force reluctant German acceptance of an unsatisfactory solution'.

TO THE TRUMAN DOCTRINE

The hardening of East–West relations in Germany from 1946 was accompanied by growing tension in other parts of Europe and in the Near and Middle East. Peace treaties, it is true, were painfully hammered out over Italy and the Balkan states. American party in-fighting late in 1945 and in the first half of 1946 sometimes suggested that the fear of Russia was more acute than it actually was – the Republicans were looking for opportunities to criticize the Democrats; the administration could not begin to develop a more positive foreign policy so long as the American public was obsessed with de-mobilization and lower taxes; consequently both parties were tempted to play up the 'Red Menace'. This must be remembered in connection with Republican assaults on Secretary of State Byrnes – one humorist asked how many destroyers the British wanted as extra payment if Byrnes were traded in for Bevin as Foreign Minister – and efforts by the administration to secure passage of the British loan. But at the same time there was an underlying growth of uneasiness about Russian intentions and a determination to assert American influence. There was, for instance, a rapid retreat from the view (approved by Truman as late as November 1945) that no quarrel existed between Russia and the United States in the Middle East.[14] The President, proud of his historical knowledge, began to talk in Palmerstonian terms. Russian interest in Turkey and Iran (Persia) caused concern. George Kennan's much quoted telegram from Moscow in February 1946 did not so much transform thinking in Washington about the danger from Russia as articulate what many already thought. The first months of 1946 brought elaborate warnings from the Joint Chiefs of Staff concerning various Soviet threats to American interests, especially in Iran and in the eastern Mediterranean. The implications were serious, for with Soviet control of Turkey and the Aegean the British would be under great pressure from Suez to Iraq. They might be forced to fight or face the eventual disintegration of their empire. The Joint Chiefs now wished to support the British Empire against the Soviet Union, arguing that without such an ally the United States and its remaining friends might lack the military potential to match that of an expanded Russia.[15] Anglophobia and dislike of the British Empire were rapidly becoming luxuries the Americans could no longer afford.

It is true that Churchill's Fulton speech in March 1946 has been credited by posterity with a positive impact on Anglo-American relations which it did not achieve at the time. Talk of a new Anglo-American partnership (in public) was premature. Bevin won more approval from public opinion in America by discussing the Russian 'threat' within the context of the United Nations. But Truman undoubtedly used Churchill's speech to test the water. The State Department put the case for close co-operation with Britain (with a few reservations) on 1 April 1946:[16]

> If the Soviet Union is to be denied hegemony in Europe, the United Kingdom must continue in existence as the principal power in Western Europe economically and militarily. The US should, therefore, explore its relationship with Great Britain and give all feasible political, economic, and if necessary military support within the framework of the United Nations, to the United Kingdom and the communications of the British Commonwealth. This does not imply a blank check to American support throughout the world for every interest of the British Empire, but only in respect of areas and interests which are in the opinion of the U.S. vital to the maintenance of the United Kingdom and the British Commonwealth of nations as a great power.

The Americans and British had already begun to co-operate in the defence of their interests in Iran when rumours of Russian activities, and troop movements to the north, caused some alarm. Communist control of the province of Azerbaijan was feared. This Iranian crisis from March 1946 enabled the American government to alert opinion at home, to impress the Russians with its vigilance and determination, and to gain a cheap victory. The government in Tehran was encouraged to act with more firmness, and by the end of the year Azerbaijan was firmly under its control.[17]

Meanwhile the Russians were also pressing the Turks for concessions at the Straits and in the Kars–Ardahan region. In August Turkey was promised American and British support in the face of unreasonable Russian demands. Civil war in Greece was also causing concern, and Washington was soon aware that the British could not afford to subsidize the Greek government indefinitely in this costly struggle against Left-wing forces. As early as 18 October 1946 Athens received an encouraging note from Washington, though not yet a promise of material aid. By this time, too, serious Anglo-American military talks had been resumed with respect to both Europe and the Near East. The British had hoped to continue the Combined Chiefs of Staff relationship beyond the war, but for much of 1946 contacts had become highly tenuous and largely unofficial. The State Department and President had been clearly fearful of domestic political repercussions if anything were formalised on a permanent basis. By the autumn of 1946 this clandestine approach to co-operation was no longer necessary.[18]

Some impression of thinking in Washington at this time can be gained from a report drawn up by Clark Clifford, Special Counsel to the President, and submitted to Truman on 24 September. This was based on wide-ranging consultations within the administration. The United States had to prepare for total war, one that would include the use of nuclear and biological weapons. The first American step, however, according to the Clifford Report, must be the provision of economic aid for friendly states, with military measures only as a last resort. There was some recognition of the scale of the obstacles which were impeding the economic recovery of the western world, and there was the usual interest in the removal of barriers to trade, plus an end to the division of states between occupying armies. A comprehensive strategy was needed to persuade the Russians of the disadvantages of being exposed to the enmity of the West. Economic aid to communist states and scientific exchanges were not ruled out in the appropriate circumstances.[19] But in practice, of course, any tentative hopes of *détente* were quickly overtaken by events. One need not, for instance, take very seriously the efforts of either the Americans or the Russians to place nuclear development under international control. It is true that there was as yet no acceleration in the American nuclear programme, the armed forces were not expanded, while the nettle of massive economic aid was not grasped until 1947. Nevertheless the Truman Doctrine was already foreshadowed, together with new thinking on the future of the British Commonwealth, the Middle East and even Germany.

On 21 February 1947 Washington received the famous British warning that they would be unable to continue to give aid to Greece and Turkey beyond 31 March. The State Department already thought an early Greek government collapse possible, and was arguing that a communist victory in Greece might be followed by the loss of all of the Near and Middle East.[20] The British appeal therefore arrived most opportunely to generate a real sense of urgency within the administration as a whole and more particularly in Congress. As it was, it was speedily assumed that a certain amount of alarmism would be necessary to stir Congress to prompt and effective action. Clark Clifford later admitted that the crisis was overstated to achieve the desired political results. Acheson similarly agreed that he had made more use of the communist bogy after 1945 than he would have liked in order to make people face realities as he saw them.[21] The deliberations of the Senate Foreign Relations Committee indicate how seriously its members took the problems of selling aid to their electors, while those who wished to take action through the United Nations seemed to do so not out of any faith in the institution but to reassure voters and to demonstrate in the longer term the limitations of that institution. Some Senators disliked the nature of the regime in Athens they were called upon to support, but accepted the reasoning of the influential Senator Vandenberg that an anti-communist line had to be drawn somewhere.[22] Here, and in later debates on Marshall Aid, one is also impressed by the anxiety to get value for money, to limit the inflationary effects on the United States and to promote the sale of American goods, especially those in surplus. The Senators were continually looking for satisfactory answers to the awkward questions they expected from voters, with the Republicans hoping to maintain their current momentum of electoral success, and with the Democrats conscious that they were on the defensive.[23] A cool, calculated government statement of policy was hardly to be expected in these circumstances.

The resultant Truman Doctrine of 12 March 1947 offered sweeping promises of aid for 'free peoples who are resisting attempted subjugation'. It was criticised by some Americans at the time as unnecessarily provocative, and it has attracted unfavourable comment from a number of historians since. Thus it has been described as 'a misleadingly simplistic view and model of the world', and one that was to prove remarkably difficult to change in the future, so adding to the rigidity in American foreign policy and in the popular perception of world affairs.[24] It also failed to evoke much popular enthusiasm for aid for Greece and Turkey at the time. Certainly it remains a classic example of the difficulty of creating a national consensus in favour of a new departure in American foreign policy when there exists no specific and widespread sense of imminent danger or of a challenge to the nation's dignity. One should also recognize that in practical terms the Truman Doctrine led only to American aid to Greece and Turkey, countries which the Russians were already largely disposed to accept as lying within the western world – unless the West showed no real determination to defend and assist them. In the longer term the Truman Doctrine was only one among many factors shaping the Cold War.

MARSHALL AID

When the Truman Doctrine was formulated, the American administration believed that prompt action was vital. The State Department, for instance, argued that if Britain was left unsupported for too long she might in desperation try to appease the Soviets. An Anglo-Russian compromise might not only injure American interests, but it might encourage a resurgence of American isolationism – a product of popular despair in the face of an unfriendly and unresponsive world. Alternatively, if Britain stood firm, the State Department hoped this would encourage internationalist sentiment in the United States. Unfortunately from this point of view the Truman Doctrine had no answer to Britain's worsening finances – save as a statement of principle. The American loan of 1946 was being expended more rapidly than anyone had anticipated, especially because of the unexpected surge in American inflation. But it was the American loan which was helping Britain to sustain so many overseas commitments. There were tentative warnings from the British in the spring of 1947 of the difficulties they expected to encounter if they attempted to fulfil their promise to make sterling convertible in the summer of 1947. The State Department, however, feared that any retreat from that liability under the terms of the 1946 loan would provoke an outcry in Congress, and wreck its own incipient hopes that some more comprehensive aid programme might soon be launched to give substance to the Truman Doctrine.

Pressures for a revolutionary change in American policy were coming from several quarters. There were disturbing reports of growing economic difficulties in much of western Europe. At first in 1946, apart from Germany, industrial production had begun to make an impressive recovery. But this was now threatened by growing food shortages (rations were lower in some places than during the war), by the inability of the French to obtain as much coal as they required from Germany, and by the evident inability of western Europe over the next few years to pay for the unusually large amounts of imports of all kinds which were required from dollar areas, especially the United States. Food, goods and materials normally supplied from within Europe, or from Europe's colonies were not available in the customary quantities, partly through the damage caused by the war, partly because of the division of Europe and partly from the constraints on German production. The situation was made worse by the harsh winter of 1946–47. A co-ordinating committee of the American armed forces and State Department concluded on 21 April 1947:[25]

> In 1947 the U.S. will probably export to the rest of the world $7.5 billion more goods and services than it imports. The outflow of dollars to finance this deficit will probably include $4.8 billion financed by the U.S. Government in loans, grants and expenditures in the occupied areas. The current volume of U.S. financing, . . . is not adequate to the full accomplishment of world economic stability, the type of world trading system the U.S. seeks, or U.S. political objectives in several countries.

The economic implications for the United States were serious. If America exported only 7 per cent of its gross national product at this time, no less than 13 per cent of American farm income came from abroad. Certain other sectors of the economy were heavily dependent upon exports. But there were political implications too. In an economic crisis Europe might move towards neutrality or, worse, towards the Soviet Union, unless substantial help were forthcoming from the United States.[26] Supporters of parliamentary democracy in western Europe similarly feared that a failure to maintain full employment, to improve rations and even to provide the hope of some warmth through the next winter, might produce a massive swing in electoral support to the communists, especially in France and Italy. There might be the makings of a revolutionary situation, leading to totalitarian rule by the Left or, perhaps in France, by the Right. American diplomats followed de Gaulle's fortunes in 1947 with no little concern. If he was preferable to the Communists, his advent as an all-powerful ruler of France was still expected to cause the United States a great deal of embarrassment. Finally the American service chiefs spoke out on the military importance of Britain and France as allies:

> No one can show . . . how the United States could live safely if France and/or Great Britain were under Soviet domination either by reason of military conquest or for the reason that communists had taken over control of their governments.

The Joint Chiefs also insisted that a western victory in Europe was dependent on the restoration of the German economy.[27]

There were thus several interlocking problems. Increased coal and industrial production in western Germany would relieve the economic situation in Europe as a whole, but any German economic revival was bound to excite the gravest concern among their neighbours, especially the French. France wanted German coal, but opposed American efforts to preserve the economic unity of Germany. The State Department, anxious to build up France as America's main friend on the Continent, had already made many concessions on the treatment of Germany in 1946. By 1947, however, the current policies seemed no more than palliatives. Reports of low morale in Europe abounded. This, and the threat of economic collapse, not direct action by Russia, represented the main threat to American interests in Europe. Russia and communism would benefit from the confusion, not create it, save in so far as Russian diplomacy was obstructing solutions to the problems of western Europe. Marshall had important yet unproductive talks with Stalin in Moscow on 15 April 1947. He did not find the Russian leader hostile, but Stalin's pleas for patience (given time he thought many East–West differences could be overcome) accorded ill with the American belief that time was now of the essence.[28]

Doubtless there was an element of exaggeration on Marshall's return from the Moscow Conference when he publicly asserted that the patient (that is, western Europe) was sinking while the doctors deliberated. But whatever Stalin's intentions, decisive action by the United States seemed essential if it was to stop the rot in Europe. At this point in time the United States was even assisted by the economic problems of France – the Americans enjoyed some leverage in Paris for the implementation of new policies in Germany. But it was a slow business for all that, with the French retreating only from necessity, and in their turn exploiting American anxieties concerning the situation as a whole in Europe. So brittle seemed the economic and political position in France, Italy and western Germany, so close to a revolutionary situation seemed much of western Europe that the United States felt it needed allies wherever they could be found if it was to make substantial progress. As for Russia and the European communist parties, even if these early in 1947 seemed to be thinking in terms of cautious, evolutionary policies, yet action of a very different kind might have been forced upon them had an economic and political collapse occurred in parts of Europe. It was the United States, however, which gradually seized the initiative.

Washington proceeded carefully. It had more time at its disposal than in the preparation of the Truman Doctrine. It appreciated the need to win western European support, both for its own sake, and to impress opinion in the United States that the Europeans were worth supporting – that a coherent and creative programme was in the making and that American money would be well spent. Above all the Europeans had to demonstrate their ability to work together. The subject was tentatively raised in the United States in low-key speeches by Acheson and Marshall in May and June respectively. But it was left to the British and French initially to set the pace with ideas on co-operation within Europe and across the Atlantic, a task which was admirably fulfilled by the British and French Foreign Ministers in June and July. Russia was not excluded from the talks, but both Bevin and Bidault were not sorry to see Molotov make his abrupt departure on 3 July. This was seen as a Russian tactical mistake. Bevin had feared that the Russians would act as a 'Trojan horse' in any European recovery programme, obstructing progress, and threatening one of America's basic objectives – the readiness of states to allow some of their key economic decisions to be guided by the needs of the programme. Indeed, so long as the Russians participated, it seemed unlikely that Congress would vote the necessary funds, whatever the hopes of the American administration. The Russian withdrawal thus seems surprising, unless it arose out of a sense of weakness. The recovery programme was attracting interest in eastern Europe, and the western leaders certainly hoped that its implementation throughout Europe might have the effect of weakening the Russian hold in the east.[29] Instead the Russians tightened their hold in the second half of 1947, notably with 'rigged elections' in Hungary, and with the establishment of the Cominform.

The Kremlin also tried to disrupt the movement towards greater co-operation between the main western European states and between western Europe and the United States. The permanent exclusion of western European communist parties from office was clearly becoming part of the price demanded for American aid, and one which a growing number of European politicians were equally happy to pay. Bevin, for instance, was increasingly impressed and relieved by the growing firmness of the French government in its handling of the French Communist Party.[30] The Russians in reply began to denounce French and Italian Communists for their 'passive' conduct, conduct which had in fact been determined by express orders to that effect since the war from Moscow. Thus in the middle of 1946 it had been Italian militants who had reacted unhappily to Stalin's insistence that there could be several roads to socialism, including the parliamentary one.[31] Even in the more aggressive phase from the autumn of 1947 the Russian concern appeared to be the discouragement of western unity under American leadership rather than an early overthrow of the existing order. Strikes, riots and demonstrations were used to probe the strength of those in power and to win the support of the discontented. The Russians were not prepared to run great risks, and showed caution even in Finland where a strong and popular government proved more than a match for the local Communist Party. Moscow seemed reasonably content so long as the Finns followed a foreign policy which did not conflict with Russian interests.[32]

Marshall Aid did not begin to flow from the United States until March 1948, but merely the promise of its coming did much to encourage western resistance to communism. The French government took a strong stand against strikes in the autumn of 1947, and so impressed the British that the latter dropped their objections to military talks (despite the Anglo-French Treaty of Dunkirk of March 1947) in the belief that there was now no longer a danger of a return of Communists to the French government. But for some months the situation in Italy looked much less promising. Elections were scheduled for the spring of 1948, and Washington warned that Italy could not expect Marshall Aid if communist influence continued to grow. Civil war seemed a possibility, resulting perhaps in the division of Italy with communist control in the north. American contingency plans provided for aid to the anti-communist forces and the seizure if necessary of the islands of Sicily and Sardinia. The British rather hesitantly took some part in these preparations.[33] On 13 September 1948 a Foreign Office assessment of communist strength outside the Soviet bloc was circulated to the British Cabinet. The armed strength of the Italian Communists was put at about 40,000 in the spring of 1948 – that is, those who could be mobilised at short notice. There was a much greater fear of strikes. The French 'fifth column' was put at between 100,000 and 150,000, but its activities were not expected to run much beyond industrial unrest and sabotage. This was only a tiny fraction of communist voting strength in France, but British Intelligence was convinced that the loyalty of most French workers was not in doubt – they voted Communist where their British counterparts voted Labour. An assessment made early 1949 was still more reassuring. The Italian militants, however, remained a threat. Their potential was described as 'serious' in March 1949.[34]

But it was a more aggressive image of communism which was swaying opinion in America, especially after the take-over in Czechoslovakia. An opinion poll of March 1948 found 73 per cent thought a third world war inevitable. In this atmosphere Congress moved swiftly early in 1948 to implement Marshall Aid. But for the American administration Marshall Aid served as more than a weapon in the Cold War. The American economy demanded a prosperous Europe. To strengthen western Europe for both politico-strategic and economic reasons the economy of western Germany had to be revived. To overcome French opposition (the French were appalled by the prospect of a strong west German economy) Marshall Aid was a useful lever and carrot. In short, Marshall Aid proved a singularly versatile and successful act of policy, even if in the longer term it helped to foster illusions concerning America's ability to influence developments in other parts of the world. Europe possessed unique skills, resources and potential: in 1948 it needed dollars and confidence, and these the European Recovery Programme provided.

ANGLO-AMERICAN STRATEGIC RELATIONS

Economic aid was the main strand in American policy towards western Europe down to 1948. Yet, as we saw earlier, there had been some convergence in Anglo-American military thinking, a partial revival of the wartime relationship, as early as 1946. This did not extend to nuclear weapons, and the British felt obliged to embark upon their own independent programme in 1947. An inner group of the Cabinet was convinced that Britain could not remain a great power without nuclear arms. Progress was slow at first, and it was the late 1950s before Britain possessed a significant nuclear capability, and it was then that Anglo-American nuclear co-operation was resumed in earnest. Meanwhile in 1946 the British were anxious to exploit any opportunity to relieve their overstretched armed forces and the strain which these imposed on their economy. Large British forces were deployed in Europe, the Mediterranean, the Middle and Far East despite repeated Treasury demands for cuts where practicable. For the Chancellor of the Exchequer and many Labour backbenchers the Middle East was a favourite target. The Prime Minister, Clement Attlee, seemed to sympathize with this suggestion early in 1946, but he added the important qualification that things might look very different if the Americans began to show more interest in this region. The Foreign Office and Chiefs of Staff were eager to secure American military assistance where possible, and the 1946 defence estimates were in fact prepared on the assumption that American aid would be forthcoming in a number of eventualities.[35]

Meanwhile American strategists, though not expecting an early war with Russia, were arguing that western Europe was likely to prove indefensible in the early stages of a hypothetical conflict without German assistance.[36] German support, however, was a political non-starter for the foreseeable future, and since military planners are expected to find answers to any problem they readily took up a peripheral strategy as the best substitute for a continental defence. This led naturally to a consideration of the strategic potential of the Middle East and North Africa – Britain being the already long-accepted linchpin in the north. The Americans began to forget their wartime criticisms of British preoccupations with the southern flank of Europe once they themselves had possible need of bases, and especially air bases, against an occupied Europe and a hostile Russia. North-west Africa was needed to help protect allied sea lanes across the Atlantic. American interest in Anglo-French handling of their relations with the peoples of North Africa now embraced the determination that nothing should be done to open that area to Russian influence. British and French imperialism was not necessarily a bad thing.[37] Major Anglo-American differences by 1947 over the future of Palestine and the treatment of Jews should not be allowed to obscure the strategic convergence that was taking place at the same time. The State Department and Joint Chiefs were often embarrassed by the strength of the Jewish lobby in the United States and its influence with the politicians, and worked to some effect with their British counterparts to mend fences broken by rampaging politicians and pressmen. Progress was also made in the resolution of Anglo-American oil rivalries in the Middle East.

In 1947 the American services and the State Department began to rank the Middle East immediately after Europe in their strategic priorities.[38] From bases in Britain, the Middle East and the eastern Mediterranean (notably Turkey and Egypt), about 80 per cent of Russian industry lay within reach of American B-29 bombers. The Russian oil industry in the Caucasus was especially vulnerable to attack from the Middle East. But no consensus existed as to the efficacy of such air attacks, with or without nuclear weapons. Some twenty Russian cities were selected as targets for atomic bombs late in 1945, but in the spring of 1947 the United States may have had no more than twelve bombs. Nor was there any great sense of urgency given the estimate that 1953 was the earliest date the Russians might be in a position to launch a nuclear attack on the United States. Few planners expected a short war – one that would be decided primarily with nuclear weapons, and most advocated the acquisition of strategic stockpiles for a five-year struggle. Middle Eastern oil, for instance, might be required to supplement American oil production which had been sorely strained during the Second World War. When this is taken in conjunction with the fear that much of the continent of Europe would be overrun at the start of a war with Russia, it is not surprising that the Joint Chiefs, while stressing the need for flexibility in planning, suggested on 1 May 1947 that 'it appears at the present time that initial establishment of Allied forces in the Middle East is the most promising course of action'.[39]

It must be reiterated that neither the American nor British governments thought war probable with Russia in the foreseeable future in 1947. But they did anticipate a keen struggle for influence in many parts of the world 'by other means'. The European colonies in much of Africa did not seem at risk, but the West could look forward to serious competition in the Middle East. This was a major reason why Britain was reemerging as America's main ally. Thus the America ambassador in London was asked on 17 May 1947 to explain how far he thought the United States could rely on Britain as an ally in the global struggle against communism. He was also asked if Britain would pursue a more liberal trading policy in return for more American aid.[40] The ambassador replied that Britain's current economic problems meant that she must cut some commitments or receive more support from the United States or Commonwealth countries. But he was able to reassure Washington that the British were determined to try to hold certain key points. Thus Indian independence was not diminishing the importance of the Middle East and the Mediterranean, although under pressure the British might be able to hold only Gibraltar, Malta and Cyprus. In the Middle East itself the best defence against communism was the improved welfare of the local peoples, and here American economic help was much needed. In the long term Kenya might become Britain's largest base east of Gibraltar, a new 'British "heartland"' where strategic industries could be dispersed and soldiers trained. Nor did the British forget to project themselves as a liberal imperial power, promising concessions to their colonial peoples, and encouraging the French and Dutch in the Far East to do likewise.[41]

An economic crisis in the summer of 1947 led to renewed discussion by the British Cabinet of the wisdom of trying to preserve a strategic presence in the Middle East. But the Prime Minister and Foreign Secretary were now fully at one with the Chiefs of Staff, while the possibility of American support in this region, as well as hope of Marshall Aid, made the decision to remain an easier one. This was important, as in other respects the outlook was discouraging. Palestine had attracted some service interest as an alternative base to Suez where the British were under notice to quit by the Egyptians. But the British were losing control of Palestine as the Zionists intensified their efforts to create a homeland for themselves. The British finally opted for a policy of evacuation by May 1948. Their efforts to negotiate new defence treaties with Egypt and Iraq were also failing, but for the time being they hoped to retain their bases in those countries. If deprived of Suez it seemed possible that the British might use their position in the Sudan and Cyrenaica as alternatives. Nevertheless, any study of British strategy in the Middle East had to be profusely punctuated with question marks. The Treasury was also pressing for economies in the services with some success late in 1947, and the Chiefs of Staff were directed to concentrate only on those forces which would 'give us the best chance of survival' in the event of war. They were told to plan on the assumption that there was little risk of a major war for ten years – despite all the unfortunate experience with the inter-war Ten-Year Rule.[42] The British therefore needed to know as much as possible about

American policy towards the Middle East. It was noted in the State Department on 5 November 1947:[43]

> ... Although the British Government has decided that the maintenance of the security of the Mediterranean and the Middle East is vital to British security, they have not made plans to implement that policy and one of the most important reasons for their indecision has been lack of knowledge of United States policy in respect of that area.

The British pursued this matter in the Pentagon talks with the Americans late in 1947. Finally on 4 December 1947 Secretary of State Marshall, while declining to make any positive commitments, agreed that the two powers should pursue 'parallel policies'. Britain must not offend Middle Eastern nationalist sentiment, nor pursue exclusive economic policies. But the United States encouraged British efforts to preserve their base at Suez, and agreed that bases were also desirable in Cyrenaica, the Sudan, Iraq and Kuwait.

For a time from the winter of 1947–48 the American services began to share something of the enthusiasm of the British Chiefs of Staff for the offensive and defensive potential of the Middle East. Emergency plans were drawn up in Washington to hold at least Cairo, Suez and Khartoum as a strategic triangle from which bombers could operate against targets in Russia.[44] Indeed, American interest ranged from French North Africa to Iran, though with the proviso that it would be 'unrealistic' for the United States to proceed without an assurance that 'the British maintain their strong strategic, political and economic position in the Middle East and Eastern Mediterranean, and unless they and ourselves follow parallel policies in that area'.[45] A study approved by the Joint Chiefs of Staff and passed to the National Security Council on 16 May 1949 described British and American strategic interests as 'practically the same', and added that, 'In the event of global war, the United States would probably wish to use facilities in the Cairo–Suez areas in conjunction with the British' – that is, for long-range air attacks on Russia.[46] Although, as we shall see, by 1950 circumstances were once again causing the American services to concentrate their attention on Europe, there had been a significant, if temporary, Anglo-American convergence in the Middle East which had contributed to the British decision (and ability) to remain in the Middle East with important consequences in the future.

Not all was smooth in the Anglo-American relationship even at this time. The American ambassador noted on 11 August 1948 that the British, including the government, could become almost 'pathological' on the subject of the United States. Britain and her Commonwealth, it was argued, deserved special support from the United States given their importance to the western cause. At the same time the British looked forward to a future when their own restored strength would entitle them to a more equal place in the western alliance. American leadership was accepted for the moment, but it was a 'bitter pill' to swallow.[47] But despite British complaints and behaviour which in American eyes could resemble that of a frustrated, and faded prima donna, Britain and her Dominions and colonies stood high in the estimation of Washington at this time. She had no rival as yet among America's other friends and allies. The British were described as the 'outstanding example' of a 'like-minded' people, and even a Labour government had its uses as a demonstration that a leftish government need not be anti-American. Britain and her Commonwealth constituted a 'world-wide network of strategically located territories of great military value' whose integrity the Americans wished to maintain.[48]

THE FORMATION OF NATO

Many British politicians had become convinced during the war that there could be no stability in Europe without some degree of American involvement on a long-term basis. The measure of American commitment would largely determine that of the British. True there were some who advocated the formation of an Anglo-European Third Force to offer an alternative to Russian or American domination in world politics. Many western Europeans certainly looked to Britain for a lead. But the resources and will were lacking, and talk of an Anglo-French customs union led nowhere. British insular and imperial preferences were very evident, and in 1947–48 when the European Recovery Programme was being negotiated the British did their best – though unsuccessfully – to secure special concessions from the United States. Nevertheless the British did play a vital part in the complicated train of events which led to the North Atlantic Alliance of 1949. Indeed, Bevin and the Foreign Office perhaps did more than anyone to set things in motion in the winter of 1947–48. They were influenced not so much by fear of any early Russian assault as by the feeling that western European morale was so low, despite the promise of Marshall Aid, that an economic recovery programme would succeed only if it were accompanied by the promise of military security and political stability in the future.

As the Foreign Office anticipated, no progress was made in negotiations with the Russians at the London Council of Foreign Ministers late in 1947, notably on the question of Germany. Bevin consequently informed Marshall on 17 December that there ought to be 'some western democratic system, comprising the Americans, ourselves, France, Italy, etc., and of course the Dominions'. This would not be a formal alliance, but it must have the power and resolve to show Russia that she 'could not advance further'. Western confidence must be built up. Similarly it was necessary to ensure western control of any future German revival or irredentist bid for unity.[49] There was cautious encouragement from Washington during the winter, perhaps best expressed in the comment: 'You are in effect asking us to pour concrete before we see the blueprints.'[50] Meanwhile Bevin was bombarding the Cabinet with suggestions for action. Early in January 1948 he circulated three important memoranda to his colleagues. He noted the probable division of Germany, but feared that German nationalism would prove too strong for this to be a permanent state of affairs. Germans must be attracted to the West and away from Russia. But as concessions were made to the Germans, so one had to reassure the French as to their future. In a paper of 4 January 1948 entitled 'The first aim of British foreign policy', Bevin argued that the West faced a desperate struggle with the Soviet Union. The Kremlin hoped that the West would fail to solve its economic problems. While the European Recovery Programme provided one answer to this, the West would need all its political and spiritual strength to create a position of all-round security. Hence the need for some kind of Western Union, a union which should ultimately embrace even Germany and Spain. Bevin did not rule out the possibility of a communist *putsch* in Italy. Indeed, Russian influence might spread throughout Europe, the Middle East and, if China succumbed to communism, much of south-east Asia. Bevin doubted the readiness of the Russians to risk open war: the threat lay in the use of Cold War methods, and these might suffice unless there was a decisive western response.[51] Like Clark Clifford and Dean Acheson in the United States, Bevin was probably exaggerating his fears for political effect – the Cabinet was not easily diverted to a consideration of foreign affairs, except in the hope of saving money. But it is interesting that Bevin should have chosen to take so vigorous a line even before the communist take-over in Czechoslovakia. He sensed both dangers and opportunities in this global struggle.

Britain, France and the Benelux states were soon making good progress towards the conclusion of the Brussels defence treaty (this was signed on 17 March 1948), but the communist coup in Czechoslovakia of 22 February suggested that something much more substantial was required. Bevin began to talk of the creation of an Atlantic security system that would stretch from Greenland and Newfoundland to the Azores and Casablanca. He warned on 3 March that 'the cardinal error is ever to let them (the Communists) into a Government in the vain hope that they will play the game according to Westminster rules'. He also feared that inadequate defence spending would dishearten friends and lead them to make 'the best terms they can with our enemies'. In another memorandum of 3 March dramatically entitled 'The threat to world civilisation' he painted a dark picture of how the Russians were aiming to secure 'physical control . . . of the whole World Island'. One could not tell when or where the next crisis might occur. But Bevin was still interested in European co-operation to provide some sort of counterweight to the dominance of the United States in the western world, and he also warned that whatever strength Britain drew from the Commonwealth was no compensation for the continuance of instability in Europe.[52] Although in practice Europe remained the least important of the 'three circles' within which Britain moved, Bevin's tentative exploration of the potential of the European option is worthy of note. While one sought security against communism, it was also thought wise to try to find leverage against the United States and to work in the long run for other than a bipolar world.

Meanwhile, as over Marshall Aid, it suited Washington that Europe should make much of the running in the creation of some sort of defence community. Marshall was anxious to restore the balance of power in Europe and Asia, but even after the Czech coup the Truman administration was not sure how far it could carry Congress and the American public in any policy of underwriting the security of western Europe. Yet action seemed vital, especially as for a time the fear existed that communist success in Czechoslovakia might be repeated in Italy and Norway. Even Kennan, who stressed that American policy must be selective (above all he wished to restore Europe to economic and political health), accepted that the time had come for covert CIA countermeasures.[53] On 12 March 1948 the administration agreed to discuss the establishment of an Atlantic security system, the main object being to improve European morale and combat communist subversion. The Brussels Pact showed that the Europeans were prepared to make a start by themselves, while Bevin's activities and flood of suggestions offered further encouragement. Intricate political maneouvres at home finally produced the Vandenberg Resolution of 11 June 1948, which was carried in the Senate by sixty-four votes to four – there was a significant number of abstentions. This cumbrously permitted American association with the collective security arrangements of peace-loving nations. Americans were still far from agreed among themselves as to how deeply they wished to commit themselves in Europe. But at least specific talks for the formation of NATO could now proceed, encouraged by a further deterioration in East–West relations from the middle of 1948.

Negotiations over the future of Germany had already reached an impasse by the end of 1947. Both sides were determined to hold what they already controlled. The European Recovery Programme demanded a revival of the German economy, and it was soon evident that it would only be a matter of time before the western powers proceeded to the creation of a separate West German state, firmly aligned with themselves. The Russians could not fail to be alarmed by such a prospect. Such a state would menace Russian influence in eastern Germany and perhaps elsewhere in eastern Europe. There must have been similar fears in Moscow to those in the West of an irredentist Germany aligned with the East. Thus, whatever Russia's long-term hopes in Europe in 1948, the immediate need was to frustrate the efforts of the United States in particular to revitalise western Germany. As it happened, the steps which were leading to the formation of a separate West German state were also dismaying many Germans, who foresaw permanent partition. There was much uneasiness in France, but any chance the Russians might have had to exploit these western divisions was thrown away by their decision to concentrate in 1948 on the interruption of the vulnerable western communications with West Berlin.

Restrictions were imposed intermittently from January 1948 on western traffic to Berlin, and the dispute over the currencies to be used in the city precipitated a full-scale 'blockade' in the summer of 1948. There was much anxious speculation in the West as to the extent of Russian aims. Bevin at times feared the situation might escalate out of control (he admitted to some sympathy with Chamberlain in 1938), and watched the conduct of Washington with some apprehension. But advocates of an armed convoy to test the Russian resolve (they included the leading representative of the Left-wing of the Labour Party in the British Cabinet, Aneurin Bevan) were defeated by those who believed in the feasibility of supplying West Berlin from the air. Western unity and confidence grew with the success of the airlift: it was sustained, too, by the conviction that this was a battle for the hearts, minds and stomachs of the Germans. The British Cabinet agreed that 'we are now faced by the menace of Germany allied to or occupied by the Soviet Union'. The abandonment of Berlin, it was said, would mean the loss of western Europe.[54] The western airlift was supplemented by a counter-blockade of the Russian zone by the West. The stalemate was finally broken by a hint from Stalin on 27 January 1949 that he was willing to lift the blockade if the West would do the same, and if the establishment of a West German government were postponed until there had been a further meeting of the Council of Foreign Ministers. The blockades ended on 12 May, and the Council met on the 23rd. Ultimately the foreign ministers could only agree to differ, so that the Federal and German Democratic Republics came formally into being in September and October 1949 respectively.

The Berlin crisis was a great stimulant to the formation of NATO. Even so the Americans proceeded hesitantly. They were warned by the British in the autumn of 1948 that with modern weapons, and given the vulnerability of Britain to air attack, the United States must be involved in a war from the outset. The British were doing their best to encourage the view that their island provided the Americans with an unsinkable aircraft carrier off the coast of Europe. The Americans had few forces they could send to Europe at short notice, and American planners by September 1948 were putting increasing emphasis on nuclear weapons, both in war and as a deterrent to war – either way they needed British bases. But the debate on American strategy was far from complete, and extended to a consideration of the possibility of holding the Russians on the Rhine, or at least delaying their further advance.[55] It was necessary for a variety of reasons to offer some comfort and hope to the French. The heterogeneous Centre parties continued to be harried by Communists and Gaullists, and the country's morale remained low. The Brussels treaty had given the French only limited reassurance, and Paris argued that only the Americans could provide 'real strength' in Europe. The French had no wish to be liberated a second time by the Anglo-Saxons: they wished the Rhine to be held, whatever British and American strategists might say (given the forces at their disposal). The French also saw an Atlantic alliance as an instrument through which to control and contain Germany, a point appreciated by the new American Secretary of State, Dean Acheson. Even so, NATO, as instituted in the spring of 1949, contained no automatic American guarantee: indeed, each member was free, according to its own constitutional processes, to decide how to respond to an attack. Of the five NATO planning groups which were set up, the Americans were full members of only two – those relating to North America and the Atlantic.[56]

Nor was the institution of NATO followed by any significant gains in western military strength. The debate continued in the United States between the military and economic advisers of the President as to what defence forces the nation needed and what it could afford.[57] The services continued to argue that they were overstretched, and that the overall military balance was moving in favour of the Russians. War might come by accident, or through a Soviet calculation that their military advantages would soon be at their peak. So constricted was the current American mobilisation base that a year might elapse before major reinforcements were sent to Europe. In the second half of 1948 the State Department and the newly formed National Security Council largely supported the military. The Policy Planning Staff of the State Department accepted that the Kremlin preferred 'concealed domination' to other methods, but thought the Russians always likely to be tempted by military weakness. In any case, the European peoples who lay between the Soviet Union and the United States would always be influenced by the 'shadows' cast by the armed strength of each. The National Security

Council claimed that the Russians could overrun all continental Europe and the Near East as far as Cairo in six months, not to mention gains in the Far East. By the mid-1950s the Russians were expected to be able to mount a sizeable air threat to the United States itself. The whole global balance was menaced by Russia: it might secure control of Eurasia – the world island. This could only be countered by greater American military preparedness, by Europe's economic recovery, by safeguards against internal subversion (precautions were necessary in the United States as well as in Europe) and by a counter-offensive against the Soviet bloc so that the initiative did not always lie with the Kremlin. Ideas here were vague, but they included propaganda and subversion against communist regimes (there was an ill-fated Anglo-American venture in Albania in 1949), and the stirring up of dissension between Russia and her satellites.[58]

Others in Washington had different worries. Truman himself wrote to the National Security Council on 1 July 1949 concerning the various threats to 'a sound fiscal and economic program'. The extent of the probable budget deficit in the early 1950s was worrying. The economic effects would be serious, and there could be damaging political and social consequences. Even the National Security Council agreed at the end of August 1949 that defence spending might safely be cut to $13 billion in 1951, though it wished to defend the Military Aid Programme to Europe. Short-term savings could mean larger costs in the long run. Early in September the Council approved the first-use of nuclear weapons in the event of war involving NATO (NSC 57), while Truman himself favoured the development of this arm, partly at least because of its apparent cost-effectiveness. It was only in the course of this month that a shocked administration learned of the first Soviet nuclear test. The Russian nuclear programme was progressing much more rapidly than had been anticipated.

WESTERN STRATEGIC PLANNING BEFORE THE KOREAN WAR

Estimates of Soviet armed power in 1949 still vary, though it might reasonably be assumed that some twenty-five or thirty Russian divisions were stationed in eastern Europe compared with only ten poorly organised ones in western Europe. The Russians could have reinforced their armies more easily and quickly – a much more important point of comparison with NATO. The cosmetic nature of NATO at its inception in April 1949 has already been stressed, and much reliance was placed on the deterrent power of the Strategic Air Command, and on the assumption that Russia neither wanted nor was ready for war. By the end of 1949, as a result of the Soviet test in August 1949, and the development by Russia of a long-range bomber, it was assumed that Russia might be ready for nuclear war as early as 1954. It was also expected that in a future conflict chemical and biological weapons would be used.[59] Western pessimism was further increased by the victory of the Communists in China. Communist-led revolutions or civil wars were in progress in Malaya and French Indo-China. Although Stalin and Tito had quarrelled, and the Russians had been unable to bring the dissident Yugoslavs to heel, elsewhere in eastern Europe they had consolidated their hold. It is true that, helped by the Russo-Yugoslav split, the Greek Communists had been defeated, and while Austria was still divided among the powers even in the Russian zone communism was not making real progress. Nevertheless the feeling that the West was under pressure was strengthening, and the planners began to cast around for ways to fortify the anti-communist world. The thinking, as we shall see, was not entirely defensive. Especially in Washington the desire to seize the initiative was strong.

The rift between Tito and Stalin, however, was approached with some caution. Tito was still a Communist: he was not 'our friend'. In September 1949 his conduct was likened to that of Franco in the Second World War. Heretical regimes were an improvement, although the Americans still hoped to end totalitarianism in eastern Europe. More subtly it was recognised that enthusiastic western support might even weaken Tito in Yugoslavia and the Balkans.[60] There was some division among the American policy-makers as to what pressure (in theory) should be exerted on communism in eastern Europe, and whether there was any danger of precipitating the very war the administration wished to avoid. If it came to a war, the difficulty of imposing America's will on so vast a territory as the Soviet Union was fully recognised. Hence the emphasis that was placed on the destruction of Russia's military potential. Control might be exercised through economic instruments – that is, if Russia could be made sufficiently dependent on the world economy. The National Security Council had little expectation of the emergence of a democratic Russia – the necessary political forces did not exist. The United States would be unwise to interfere in the 'strange and inscrutable' political processes of Russia. Obviously some Americans recalled their relations with the White Russians in 1919. Indeed the Russo-German Treaty of Brest-Litovsk of 1918 was cited as a possible model for a peace settlement with a defeated Russia, though with the reservation that only viable separatist movements should be encouraged.[61]

Speculation of this kind, however, did nothing to resolve the more immediate question concerning the security of Europe. George Kennan continued to argue that political and economic rather than military instruments would determine the fate of Europe. But the Soviet nuclear test in August 1949 strengthened those who believed that some increase in western armed strength was vital. Nuclear deterrence was not enough. At the very least NATO required more conventional forces to slow a Russian advance beyond the Rhine. Such a capability in itself might act as a deterrent, and would help to improve French morale. Nevertheless France and her continental neighbours were still expected to provide the bulk of the land forces – the British and Americans would make major contributions only in the later stages of a war. Indeed, at the start of a conflict, America's limited conventional forces (governed by a $14 billion peacetime defence budget) would have to give priority to the protection of lines of communication with Britain, Gibraltar, central Africa, Japan and Okinawa. Despite earlier American interest in the Middle East, this region was now to be left to the British (initially), although bases within 2,500 miles of key targets in Russia were still essential for the envisaged bombing offensive. Nuclear attacks were planned against seventy key areas. These, it was hoped, would cripple about 30 per cent of Russian industry (casualty estimates ranged from 2 to 7 million), but even devastation on this scale was expected to have little effect on the offensive capabilities of Russian armies in Europe.[62] Indeed, doubts concerning the ability of NATO to defend France led the Joint Chiefs of Staff in the spring of 1950 to laud the merits of Spain as an ally, and to touch on the question of making more use of West German resources. The State Department condemned such suggestions as divisive and premature, and argued that war was unlikely before 1954, though some planners thought the period of maximum danger was only two or three years distant.[63]

At the beginning of 1950 Truman authorised the start of the thermonuclear programme. There were some critics both on grounds of morality and usefulness, though General Bradley thought the first power to acquire the H-bomb would gain an important psychological advantage.[64] Pressure also continued to build up within the administration in favour of a general increase in armaments, and this gave rise to the famous National Security Council report of 7 April 1950 (NSC 68). Acheson, for instance, argued that American foreign policy needed more muscle if it was to be effective, while early in 1950 the American embassy in Moscow was reporting growing Soviet self-confidence. Russian policy seemed to be moving into a more active phase in which accidental war (unless there were a strong western response) would be more likely.[65] Doubtless there was an element of exaggeration in many of the papers circulated at this time, but the advocates of change feared the inertia of other government departments and of Congress. The Treasury remained a major obstacle, and some defence experts argued that current western defence programmes gave no promise of security even by 1960.

NSC 68 was an ambitious document. It argued that the American economy could easily bear a large increase in defence spending. It also did more than ask for additional resources with which to defend the status quo. Russian conduct, it claimed, could not be moderated by negative policies. 'Containment' must be interpreted to include the rolling back of communism as well as the prevention of further Russian aggression. The power and influence of Russia must be reduced to limits that would no longer threaten the peace of the world.[66] Free institutions must spread to eastern Europe. George Kennan at the time criticised NSC 68 for its 'zero-sum' interpretation of East–West relations. He thought it exaggerated Russia's aggressive potential and intentions, and gave undue weight to military solutions. Over time he expected the Russians to encounter more and more regional resistance, even within their own current spheres of influence. Resistance also came from fiscal conservatives who did not agree with the optimistic economic forecasts for the American economy provided by the main authors of NSC 68.[67] One cannot attempt to guess how much of NSC 68 would have been implemented had it not been for the outbreak of the Korean War in June 1950 and the acute intensification of the Cold War later in the year. Certainly NSC 68 must be read as a political document, and not literally. Its authors did not expect total success. It must be seen in the context of American politics. Genuine fears underlay it, both foreign and domestic. Thus Assistant Secretary of State Edward Bennett commented that even a psychological 'scare campaign' might not have a sufficiently lasting effect on the public to enable a democracy to 'outlast' a dictatorship in a long-haul struggle.[68]

The State Department in the first half of 1950 was also trying to persuade the Europeans to increase their contributions to NATO. It feared a loss of momentum in the build-up of western strength, military and economic. Bevin and the British Chiefs of Staff shared some of these fears. Strong pressures for further cuts in British defence spending were fought off at the end of 1949. Even then the projected strength was only sufficient provided there was no increase in the tempo of the Cold War.[69] Bevin, on 2 May 1950, argued that the West could not negotiate satisfactorily with the Russians until it could do so from real positions of strength – Acheson has been criticised by a number of American historians for taking this view.[70] Nevertheless all European governments were understandably reluctant to sacrifice economic and social development for armaments. Nor did Washington relish the thought of any check to European recovery because of the arms race, as this would prolong European dependence on American aid – a sore point with the American electorate! Difficulties were also anticipated if the European (and Japanese) economic recovery began to outstrip the available markets and to offer uncomfortable competition to American producers. But such problems seemed preferable to stagnation, and the indefinite continuation of Europe (and Japan) as American pensioners.

One problem as usual led to another. A healthy and viable European economy required the full assistance of West Germany. To reassure Germany's neighbours, and to strengthen Europe in general, the Americans favoured European integration – preferably including Britain. The end-product, in the eyes of the State Department, should mean a reduction in America's world-wide responsibilities and progress towards a 'world-wide multilateral convertible system' of trade.[71] Such a step might also help to combat the apathy which seemed so prevalent in West Germany – Washington feared the impact of Russian promises of reunification and economic gain (if Moscow recognised its opportunity).[72] The French, alive to the way the wind was blowing, and anxious to find some way to control the German economy, came up in the spring of 1950 with plans for a European Coal and Steel Community. This was a step in the right direction from the Americans' point of view, but they were disappointed by the British refusal to participate. Indeed in the first months of 1950 Europe was but one of several causes of a deterioration in Anglo-American relations. Just as a Canadian general had earlier suggested that the best guide to his country's defence spending was the lowest level that would satisfy the United States, so the British tended to do just enough in Europe to satisfy Washington – a policy of 'limited liability'.[73] Bevin preferred to talk in terms of Atlantic, not European co-operation, although as he said to the Cabinet on 25 May 1950, if Europe was 'the kernel' of American policy, 'it must also be ours'.[74]

There were other Anglo-American bones of contention. The Sterling Area continued to cause concern in the United States, yet the State Department was driven to admit that it was doubtful whether the United States was 'willing to face the consequences which would result from a widespread loss of confidence in the future of sterling'.[75] Britain and the United States were not always in step in the Middle and Far East. Certainly there was agreement in principle by May 1950 that Russia would be stronger and could therefore be expected to be more provocative from the mid-1950s. The Soviets might even try to stir up civil war in Germany, or more probably in parts of south-east Asia. A general war, however, still seemed improbable, and the British refused to increase their defence spending despite American requests to that effect. Bevin, on German rearmament, would only promise that it might be discussed in the future. Thus the NATO planners continued to press in vain for a fifty-division army at a cost of $30 billion in new equipment spread over the next five or six years. Nor could Acheson win Anglo-French assent even in principle to the adoption of the liberation of eastern Europe as a specific western objective.[76] Thus intensive NATO talks in April–May 1950 gave little comfort to the activists behind the recommendations of NSC 68.

Had it not been for the Korean War, Russian policy towards Europe might soon have fortified those who argued that a drastic strengthening of NATO was unnecessary. In 1949–50 the Kremlin certainly had cause to review its strategy. Recent efforts to consolidate Russian influence in eastern Europe and to shake western European ties with the United States had helped to worsen East–West relations and to confirm the division of Europe. In addition, Russia's gross national product had only just returned to the level of 1940, and an effective nuclear arm still lay some years in the future. The Kremlin, in short, was hardly in a position to embark on adventurous policies in western Europe, and this may explain its growing attention to propaganda and the encouragement of peace movements. Doubtless it hoped to divide and confuse western opinion, slow or reverse the integration of West Germany into the western bloc, and similarly reduce the military threat from NATO to a minimum. Doubtless, too, the Kremlin would have continued to probe for western weak points, just as some on the western side would have continued to try to build up positions of strength. But as it happened the future was determined less by developments in Europe than in the Far East. For an explanation of the dramatic increase in arms spending and the arrival of one of the darkest periods in the Cold War we must turn our attention to events at the other side of the Eurasian world island.

NOTES AND REFERENCES

1.   Backer, pp. 171 ff.
2.   Paterson (1) p. 173: compare with his (2) *Cold War Critics*
3.   *The London Review of Books*, 25 Oct. 1979
4.   For a dissenting view, see Medvedev, pp. 471–2
5.   See Medvedev in Tucker, pp. 220–9; for Stalin's suspicions concerning Mao Tse-tung, see pp. 229–30. On Stalin's foreign policy in the years 1943–53, compare Mastny (2), McCagg, and Taubman
6.   Backer, pp. 25–7
7.   Woodward, v 203–10; Ross, pp. 536–8
8.   Burridge, p. 161
9.   Woodward, v 226–7, 292–3, 325–42

10. CAB 129/3 CP(45) 218. For a full discussion of Bevin's attitudes towards Russia and Germany, see Rothwell, Chs 4–6. Bevin opposed the formation of an anti-Soviet western bloc until the end of 1947, and while always firm in the defence of western interests, did not despair of co-operation for some time after the war.
11. CAB 129/8 CP(46) 139, 186; 129/13 CP(46) 386; 129/20 CP(47) 209–10, 226
12. FRUS, 1946, v 505 ff., 528, 535; vi. 550
13. Clay, i. 202–17, 243–4, 281–97, 321–31; Backer, pp. 141 ff.
14. FRUS, 1945, viii, 14–16
15. Cohen, pp. 68–70
16. FRUS, 1946, i, 1170
17. Kuniholm, pp. 336–42, 384–95. See also Anderson, pp. 134–7
18. Hathaway, pp. 264–9
19. Etzold and Gaddis, pp. 64–70, 72
20. FRUS, 1947, v, 29–30
21. Kuniholm, p. 413; McLellan, pp. 50–1, 83, 92–5
22. SFRC, no.3, pp. vii–xii
23. SFRC, no.6, pp. 186–95, 209 ff.
24. Kuniholm, p.415
25. FRUS, 1947, iii, 207
26. Etzold and Gaddis, pp. 102–11; Theoharis, pp. 146–7
27, FRUS, 1947, i, 734–46
28. FRUS, 1947, ii, 337–44
29. FRUS, 1948, iii, 304
30. CAB 129/19 CP(47) 188, 197
31. McCauley, pp. 165–6, 180–1
32. McCauley, Ch. 8
33. FRUS, 1948, iii, 727–9, 765–71, 810, 844, 849–50
34. CAB 129/29 CP(48) 223; 129/34 CP(49) 72. For US assessments, see NSC 1/1, 15 October 1947, and revisions, 1/2, 1/3
35. CAB 129/7 CP(46) 65
36. FRUS, 1947, i, 738 ff.
37. Etzold and Gaddis, pp. 288, 310–11, 319–20
38. FRUS, 1947, i, 742
39. Etzold and Gaddis, p.310; see also pp. 302–11, and Herken, pp. 196–244
40. FRUS, 1947, i, 750–1
41. FRUS, 1947, i, 751–8
42. CAB 129/21 CP(47) 226, 272. See also 129/23 CP(48) 7; 129/29 CP(48) 206; FRUS, 1948, v, 1530–2
43. FRUS, 1947, v, 578
44. FRUS, 1948, v, Part 1, pp. 2–3
45. FRUS, 1948, iii, 766
46. NSC 47. See also NSC 45/1 (15 April 1949) on airfield construction
47. FRUS, 1948, iii, 1113 ff.
48. FRUS, 1948, iii, 1091–1108
49. FRUS, 1947, ii, 815–22; see also p. 687
50. FRUS, 1948, iii, 22
51. CAB 129/21 CP(47) 326; 129/23 CP(48) 5–8. See Rothwell, pp.433–56,

for the evolution of British policy leading up to the Brussels Pact and the first hints of NATO

52. CAB 129/25 CP(48) 71–2, 75
53. Donovan, pp. 341, 366
54. Medvedev (p. 479) describes the Berlin Blockade, like the later Korean War, as a 'reconnaissance in force'. On British policy, see CAB 129/27 CP(48) 134; 129/29 CP(48) 203; 129/31 CP(48) 306. See also FRUS, 1948, ii, 804 ff., 827 ff., 924–5, 1147–8
55. Herken, pp. 247–88
56. Ireland, Chs 3–4, and pp. 162–3. See also Gaddis (2) pp. 73–4
57. Note Etzold and Gaddis, pp. 173–209; Herken, pp. 298–303; Gaddis (2) pp. 27–88; Freedman, pp. 52–5
58. Gaddis, (2) pp. 27–88. For American interest in the geopolitical theories of Mackinder, see Parker, pp. 173 ff., 184 ff.
59. Etzold and Gaddis, pp. 315–67
60. NSC 18, 6 July 1948; see also NSC 58, 14 September 1949, when Tito's role was compared to that of Franco in the Second World War. The desirability of heretic regimes was stressed, though only non-totalitarian regimes would ultimately satisfy the United States
61. Etzold and Gaddis, pp. 153 ff.
62. Etzold and Gaddis, pp. 315–67; Ireland, p. 167; FRUS, 1949, iv, 355–6
63. NSC 72, 15 June 1950; FRUS, 1950, iv, 688–9, 1184
64. Herken, pp.306–17
65. FRUS, 1950, iv, 1083–4, 1099–1101, 1150 ff., 1164–84
66. Etzold and Gaddis, pp. 383 ff.
67. FRUS, 1950, i, 298 ff. See also Gaddis (2) pp. 89–106
68. Theoharis, pp. 180–1
69. CAB 129/37 CP(49) 245
70. CAB 129/39 CP(50) 115; McLellan, pp. 163–4, 173–4
71. FRUS, 1950, iii, 957; see also 833, 858–60
72. FRUS, 1950, iv, 597–602, 609–10
73. Clarke, pp. 208–10
74. CAB 129/40 CP(50) 118
75. FRUS, 1950, iii, 873
76. FRUS, 1950, iii, 21–64, 845 ff., 955 ff., 1101 ff., 1598 ff. For British defence policy, see CAB 129/38 CP(50) 19; 129/39 CP(50) 92

Chapter 11

NEW DIMENSIONS TO THE COLD WAR

THE UNITED STATES AND CHINA AT THE END OF THE SECOND WORLD WAR

The end of the war in the Far East found the main powers relatively well agreed as to their respective areas of influence. The United States was determined to settle the fate of Japan unilaterally, and despite Russian and British complaints it was admirably placed to do so. It was not long before the Americans decided that Japan, disarmed and liberalized, should play a significant part in the world economy. The Cold War only hastened the implementation of this policy. Meanwhile Russia's last-minute entry into the war against Japan had given her something approximating to the position enjoyed by the Tsars before the Russo-Japanese War. Thus Port Arthur once again became a leased naval base. The Russians secured special privileges in the two chief railways in Manchuria: these were to be jointly operated with the Chinese. Nevertheless the Kremlin also recognized Chiang Kai-shek as the leader of China, and its attitude towards the Chinese Communists was at times sufficiently ambiguous to suggest that it might not interfere very actively in China's internal affairs. In July 1945 the Americans suddenly awoke to the likelihood of Russian penetration into postwar Korea, and this led to an agreement between the two powers to divide the peninsula along the 38th parallel for occupation purposes. Differences soon developed as to the future governance of Korea, but neither superpower was willing to take risks on behalf of their respective Korean clients each of whom hoped to unite Korea under communist or non-communist rule. Neither superpower sought a confrontation in Korea.[1]

South-east Asia was at this time left largely to the European colonial states which had been evicted in 1941–42 by the Japanese. American dislike of colonialism was already being displaced by fear of chaos and communism, especially in Indo-China.[2] Nor did the

Americans wish to offend states whose friendship and stability were vital in Europe. Given this relative absence of great-power competition in the Far East, the main pressures for change came from the indigenous peoples – in China, south-east Asia and in Korea.

Any explanation of the 1945 balance of power in China between the Communists and Kuomintang under Chiang Kai-shek must take due account of the effects of the war with Japan since 1937 upon China. Stuart Schram, one of Mao Tse-tung's best biographers, concludes that in the long run this was 'perhaps the most important single factor in Mao's rise to power'. The Long March (1934–35) must not be allowed to conceal the fact that in 1936 the Chinese Communists controlled a population of perhaps no more than 1.5 million, with a party membership of some 40,000 and an army of less than 100,000. By 1945 the population had grown to some 90 million, party membership to over 1 million and the army to around 500,000. True, if Japan had done much to weaken the Kuomintang, the Communists had demonstrated a remarkable ability to take their chances as they came – in contrast to their rivals. American personnel of all kinds in China during the war remarked continually on the corruption and inefficiency of the Kuomintang, its apparent inability to protect the interests of other than its own leading members and the conservative landlord class, and the weakening of the support it had enjoyed in the 1930s among businessmen, professionals and intellectuals. Inflation was already serious, the price index rising from 100 to 10,000 between 1941 and 1945 despite American financial aid. In contrast, most Americans were impressed by the honesty and efficiency of the Communists, their skilful efforts to cultivate support among the middling classes as well as the peasants, and their successful blend of moderate reform policies with an appeal to Chinese nationalism. Some Americans, indeed, saw them as agrarian, nationalist reformers rather than as Communists. One American observer commented in November 1944:[3]

> The communist governments and armies are the first governments and armies in modern Chinese history to have positive and widespread popular support. They have this because the governments and armies are genuinely of the people.

As the war progressed, so Washington, including Roosevelt, learned more of the failings of the Kuomintang. The only alternatives to its rule, however, appeared to be chaos or communism. Meanwhile the United States wished to keep China in the field against Japan, though its strategic importance declined during the war as the Americans found that they could defeat Japan by a combination of island-hopping in the Pacific, naval pressure and air attack. Expectations also began to decline concerning China's postwar value as an ally and as one of Roosevelt's 'Four Policemen'. Increasingly the

Americans were content to keep China in the field to tie up large Japanese forces, though Roosevelt, with his eyes on the future, still argued that one must not forget the enormous potential of China, with the world's largest population and its unique history. He feared, with some British and American experts on foreign affairs, that other anti-White and anti-western forces might well develop in Asia in succession to the Japanese militarists.[4]

In 1945 it was still impossible to gauge the respective strengths and potential of the Kuomintang and the Chinese Communist party. The leadership of the latter was uncertain as to its prospects, the unknowns early in 1945 embracing not only the strength of the Kuomintang but the date of the ending of the war with Japan, and long-term relations with Russia and the United States. Not surprisingly some Chinese Communists were prepared to explore the possibility of closer relations with the United States, and found some American agents responsive. They were frustrated by the dogmatic American ambassador in China, Patrick Hurley, who believed that a settlement broadly favourable to the Kuomintang was feasible. He even entertained hopes of Russian assistance to this end. Some of his advisers however, saw that he was crudely exaggerating Kuomintang strength and underestimating that of the Communists. They believed that more concessions to the latter were needed to win their support and to draw them away from the Russians.

But Hurley would not listen to such advice. Furthermore his diagnosis and remedy were approved by Roosevelt himself. Though Hurley's critics, such as Service and Davies, had allies in the Office of Far Eastern Affairs in the State Department, they could not gain a hearing elsewhere in Washington.[5] Fears of communism were already increasing, and had some weight with Roosevelt. Already he was concerned over the long-term consequences of Russian involvement in the war against Japan. He asked Harriman on 10 November 1944, 'If the Russians go in [to China], will they ever go out?' What better, then, than to secure Chinese Communist subordination to Chiang, especially if as Hurley claimed it could be achieved with the blessing of the Kremlin? Roosevelt therefore cold-shouldered overtures by and on behalf of the Chinese Communists for American aid in the winter of 1944–45. He feared such aid would make them less amenable, would increase the risk of civil war and would excite political controversy in the United States where many continued to admire Chiang Kai-shek and to dream of a pro-American China.

But Roosevelt failed to anticipate the uncooperativeness of Chiang himself. The Chinese leader was confident that in the last resort he would always have American backing. Any compromise with the Chinese Communists seemed suicidal, and in 1945 he believed he could make an arrangement with the Russians which would give him a free hand against Mao.[6] Both Chiang and Hurley underestimated the independence and strength of the Communists. Whether a greater attempt at even-handedness by the Americans at this stage between the Kuomintang and Communists would have achieved worthwhile results must also be open to doubt, but would have been preferable by any diplomatic criteria. Certainly the thinking in Washington began to change a little in the course of 1945 as the defeat of Japan in August led to greater American involvement in China and familiarity with its problems. The Communists could not be ignored or easily crushed. Chiang now had to take a little more account of the wishes of his great benefactor – he required American assistance to occupy and control the vast areas which the Japanese still held in China at the end of the war. In the winter of 1945–46 Chiang agreed to negotiate with the Communists. A cease-fire was concluded between the warring Chinese parties in January 1946.

General Wedemeyer reported to Washington from China on 20 November 1945 that while the Kuomintang could hold southern China, the recovery of the north in the face of communist opposition would be a slow and costly business. The reoccupation of Manchuria would be still more difficult. For the Americans, whose main concern was to exclude Russian influence and to avoid expensive commitments, it made sense to press for a compromise between the Kuomintang and the Communists. At the end of 1945 General Marshall, the widely respected army Chief of Staff, was sent to mediate. Unfortunately his ability to exploit Chiang's dependence on American aid was limited. Washington, though now ready to make a few more concessions to the Communists, was not prepared to abandon Chiang to his fate if he proved unreasonable. Consequently Chiang could, and would, call any American bluff. Even the sceptics and pessimists in Washington agreed that it was too early or too late to cut Chiang adrift. On the other hand, early in 1946, Mao was probably sufficiently uncertain of his own strength, and of the aid to be expected from the equivocal Russians, for him to have been genuinely interested in a compromise. Recent research, for instance, suggests that the Kuomintang on its return to the coastal cities after the defeat of Japan was not seriously challenged by the Communists for popular favour until it alienated support by its own gross incompetence and misconduct. The Kuomintang created a vacuum which the Communists did not begin to fill until later.[7] Naturally in so far as the Communists were interested in the formation of a coalition government, with themselves as junior partners, they were not prepared to deliver themselves bound hand and foot to Chiang. Unfortunately this was all Chiang had in mind.[8] Despite Marshall's efforts, and some American attempts to restrain the Kuomintang by withholding supplies, the civil war was resumed in the second half of 1946.

The Russians would probably have welcomed a compromise in China. Their hands were full in Europe and with their own recovery. Mao's independence might even have persuaded Stalin that his interests in the Far East would best be served by a situation in China which compelled the Chinese Communists to look to Russia for some help. In contrast a civil war and too much communist success would propel Chiang into the arms of the United States and increase American influence in China. Thus a weakish Chinese Communist Party might have appeared the ideal solution, giving Russia influence over both Mao and Chiang, and reassuring and even neutralising the United States. Certainly Moscow seemed anxious to give Mao no more than the minimum of assistance to keep his party in being, while the Kuomintang was carefully cultivated until late in the civil war. It is worthy of note that the Americans themselves hoped that the Marshall mission, while it might produce a China that largely met American interests (which as we have seen were already becoming more modest), would also impress the Russians with its moderation. Washington had few expectations of China as a great market or ally in the foreseeable future: it wanted to minimise Russian and communist influence, and appreciated that a coalition government might be the cheapest solution. As for the Chinese Communists, even after the renewal of the civil war, they stressed the need for self-reliance. They intended to work out their own destiny. The American threat was played down in their press. Only towards the end of 1947 did the party move openly in favour of the Soviet Union and a two-camp world, and even then reservations continued to appear. Russian interest and support remained tepid.

THE 'LOSS OF CHINA'

American attempts at mediation persisted into 1947, but the Kuomintang, after being helped by the Americans to establish itself in northern China and Manchuria, was gaining in confidence. It was intent on victory. In fact it had fatally over-committed its forces. The control of major cities was offset by communist strength in the countryside. The Chinese Communists received some help from the Russians, but it was their own strength and the failings of the Kuomintang which were decisive. Non-communist China was suffering from galloping inflation, and its corrosive effects on society were increased by the inefficiency and dishonesty which permeated the Kuomintang regime. Militarily the Kuomintang also suffered a major setback in 1947 when it failed to establish a direct rail link between north China and Manchuria. Its strength was beginning to wither, and still more rapid was the disintegration of the morale of its huge forces.

George Marshall, now Secretary of State, became increasingly pessimistic. He complained of Chiang's misrule and of America's inability to secure reforms. Already the belief was growing in the State Department that China was a lost cause, although no one as yet foresaw the speed of the Kuomintang collapse. The administration was increasingly reluctant to pour resources into China to be wasted by Chiang and his crooked friends. It was counting the cost of its many commitments in the world, and was trying to establish a list of priorities. Indeed, in April 1947 the Joint Chiefs of Staff ranked the Far East last among American strategic interests. Of sixteen countries ranked in order of their military importance to the United States, China was placed fourteenth, well below western Europe and the Middle East. Even if China were lost to communism, the service chiefs hoped to isolate the infection with an 'economic quarantine' provided their policies were successful elsewhere. Japan was already rated as of more potential importance.[9] In August 1948 Marshall commented that the Chinese Communists could only be defeated if the United States virtually took over Chiang's government.[10] Comfort was sought in the belief that no regime in the foreseeable future would be able to turn China into a formidable power. Europe was regarded as the key theatre in the Cold War, followed by the Middle East. Japan was the front runner for American attention in the Far East.

Not all Americans took this view. There was a strong China lobby in Congress – abetted by some Republicans for partisan reasons – which continued to plead the case of the Kuomintang. Their influence was such that the administration, in its anxiety to rush aid to Europe, had to buy support in Congress by sending more aid to China than it wished. The importance of these Congressional pressures can easily be understood by reference to the deliberations of the Senate Foreign Relations Committee in 1948–50[11] Most of the senators had few illusions concerning the nature of Chiang's regime or the possibility of saving him, but none was anxious to shoulder the responsibility in the United States for his fall. Some freely complained that they were being blackmailed to give aid to Chiang to avoid delays in the Senate to the European Recovery Programme. The Committee's problem from 1948 was to decide how much to pay out to protect itself.

Both the State Department and the British Foreign Office tried to draw some comfort from their contemplation of the huge economic problems which would confront the Chinese Communists when they attained power. Both thought there was a possibility that even a Marxist regime might in time be driven to seek western aid. Both, partly for this reason, were anxious to prevent the extension of communist influence to south-east Asia. The loss of this 'rice-bowl' to China and communism would upset the economic balance in the Far East to the advantage of communism, and would greatly relieve the problems facing the rulers of an impoverished China. The Foreign Office at the end of 1948 also warned that the loss of this region would make it harder for the West to combat poverty in the Far East: the people of Asia in consequence would be more open to communist influence, and there could be repercussions as far afield as India and Pakistan. Nor did it appear that the United States was as yet prepared to make a contribution to the defence of this area. The State Department was looking for tenable positions of strength in the Far East from 1948, and its attention was directed to Japan, the islands of the western Pacific, and the Philippines, all of which could easily be defended provided they were internally secure. American forces were happily pulled out of Korea, six months after the Russians. Further American intervention was not ruled out, but the unstable if authoritarian regime in South Korea did not excite any enthusiasm. As for China, the National Security Council agreed on 13 October 1948 that the Kuomintang should be recognised until its overthrow, but already there were hints of open-mindedness concerning its successor – that is, if the Chinese Communists were prepared to behave as nationalists first and not as Russian satellites.[12]

American policy towards the Chinese Communists in 1949 was a mixture of public obduracy and earnest deliberation within government departments. The Communists themselves made a number of tentative and roundabout overtures in the course of the year, touching on American recognition in the middle of the year and later on the question of economic aid. There were hints of divisions within the leadership into liberals and radicals, or pragmatists and dogmatists. After the Communists proclaimed the Chinese People's Republic on 1 October 1949 American consuls in China were soon picking up rumours of Chinese disillusionment with and even hostility towards Russia. On the whole these overtures and rumours were treated with a great deal of suspicion by the American officials in question, especially as at best the Chinese seemed willing to offer nothing in return and at worst communist Chinese treatment of American subjects and interests in China, together with the public attitude adopted towards the United States, all worked against a better relationship.[13] The Communists received no overt American encouragement. Truman himself showed no interest in the possibility of recognition, perhaps because he feared a Republican outcry.[14] But within the State Department and the National Security Council the matter was given some consideration. The State Department, for instance, disliked the continuance of aid – even on a restricted basis – to the Kuomintang in 1949. The National Security Council opposed those like General MacArthur who still wished to continue the fight against communism in China. The Council insisted that Russia was the main enemy: the Chinese leadership might be divided on the question of the closeness of their relationship with Russia. Above all nothing should be done to unite Chinese nationalist feeling against the United States. In time the Chinese Communists might be forced by Chinese nationalist pressures to take a less friendly attitude towards the Soviet Union, or face the possibility of overthrow at the hands of a new nationalist movement. The example of Tito in Yugoslavia was not forgotten.[15] There was further discussion of the role of economic weapons – economic leverage might yet be used for political purposes. The United States itself had no significant trading hopes in China, but Washington could not ignore the probability that as the Japanese economy recovered so Sino-Japanese economic relations would once more become very important.[16]

Some thought was inevitably given to the question of recognition of communist China. The reaction of the American public was not encouraging. An opinion poll in July 1949 found only 19 per cent in favour, but among the press *The Wall Street Journal* expressed interest. In time even Republicans such as Vandenberg and Dulles hinted that their opposition might melt in the light of changing circumstances. Acheson and the State Department were in no hurry. At the very least they hoped to trade recognition and admission to the United Nations for general acceptance by the Chinese Communists of the norms of international conduct and relations as understood by the United States. It was important that the Communists should prove that they could govern China and that they were not threatened by any rivals. Time would also show whether they intended to follow an independent foreign policy. Late in 1949 the administration had no reason to suppose that it would lose by a policy of delay. Indeed, it could hope that if Chinese affairs began to evolve on something akin to the lines described above, recognition would no longer carry with it any penalties in American domestic politics.

This policy of delay, however, was also dependent upon the course of events elsewhere in Asia. Much of the region was in a state of turmoil. The Americans had given the Philippines independence in 1946, but the islands were plagued by the Hukbalahup insurrection until 1954. American pressure also hastened the Dutch grant of independence to their East Indian colonies in 1949, Washington believing that the Indonesian nationalists would prove more effective defenders of the islands against communism, and hopeful too that independence would open up and speed the development of the island economies. Nevertheless the political future of the Indonesian federation was still very uncertain at the end of 1949. Similarly, despite the current American control of Japan, Washington was by no means confident that Japan could be permanently tied to the West. The democratic experiment might fail, especially without rapid economic progress. It was possible that Japan might be directly subverted by communism, or drawn into the Russian orbit if communism came to dominate many of Japan's key markets and sources of supply in the Far East. Alternatively, economic problems might generate another authoritarian regime whose foreign policy would be unpredictable and unscrupulous. Indeed, the National Security Council commented in December 1949 that in the very long run China and India, as well as Japan, might all pose problems for the United States once they began to realize their potential. But for the foreseeable future it was stressed that Russia and Russian communism were the only serious threats, and although it was admitted that even if the Communists enjoyed general success in Asia, from Japan to India, it would be a long time before this region could be turned into a strategic force against the American homeland. Washington remained determined to deny Russian communism as many of the resources of the Far East as possible. Western Europe, too, would be weakened if it were denied access to the markets and raw materials of south-east Asia in particular, while the United States itself was dependent upon it for certain strategic raw materials such as rubber and tin.

The National Security Council's warning of 23 December 1949 that south-east Asia was now 'the target of a co-ordinated offensive directed by the Kremlin' was paralleled by many similar warnings in the British Cabinet papers.[17] Both London and Washington speculated apprehensively on the likelihood of Russian control of the Eurasian world island in phraseology that might have been used by Halford Mackinder, and by earlier prophets of the inevitability of a partition of the globe. The potential of Asian nationalism was not yet appreciated, despite the grants of independence to India, Burma and Indonesia. Given sufficient communist influence in Asia it was assumed that even Japan and India, though not necessarily communist themselves, would be vulnerable to economic leverage, and overawed by communist political influence and prestige. Titoism or nationalism in China was seen as a possible corrective, but given these perceptions of international rivalries, with expectations of the monolithic character of communism running so high and complemented by the assumption that the largest powers would continue to dominate the rest as easily as in the past, it is understandable that there should have been so much anxiety to prevent communist gains, especially in so important a region economically as south-east Asia. The Japanese had come close to creating their own self-sufficient empire earlier in the decade. It was still logical to assume that Communists directed from Moscow or Peking could do the same, especially when Peking could draw upon the services of Chinese expatriates in many parts of south-east Asia. The bulk of the communist insurgents in Malaya were Chinese. Furthermore, Washington was impressed by the fact that Asian nationalism was usually anti-western, and therefore seemed peculiarly vulnerable to communist influences. This was especially the case in French Indo-China. Americans noted indignantly that Russia, 'the most voracious and evil imperialist in history', was able to accuse the West of imperialism and draw great benefits from the charge.

There is now no reason to assume that communist insurgency in south-east Asia was master-minded by either Moscow or Peking: its origins were essentially local. If from the end of 1947 there had been signs of Russian interest in 'the sharpening crisis of the colonial system', Russia had been only a marginal influence at the Calcutta Conference of the World Federation of Democratic Youth in February 1948. Amid the vast unrest that permeated so much of Asia and the colonial world in the late 1940s Soviet strategy was ambiguous, sluggish and uninspired.[18] It is true that in January 1950 Moscow did express support for the Chinese revolutionary doctrine of armed struggle as the main form of struggle against imperialism, but if Stalin's tactics in Europe are taken as a guide there is still good reason to doubt his enthusiasm for any communist movement which lay outside his control. On the other hand he doubtless welcomed the damage such parties inflicted on the western powers at this time. Nevertheless it was the Chinese who first recognised theVietminh in their struggle against the French in Indo-China. The Russians followed suit a few days later. Recognition took place during Mao Tse-tung's visit to Moscow early in 1950, but such evidence as we have of the talks does not suggest an atmosphere of any great cordiality or co-operation. Mao later claimed that the treaty of alliance and friendship of February 1950 was signed by Stalin only with reluctance after much discussion, and that Stalin feared that Mao would become another Tito.[19] Interestingly some Chinese publications at this time hint at a debate among the Chinese leaders as to how far they should align themselves with Russia. Nevertheless it seems reasonable to conclude that Mao himself saw no prospect of aid in China's reconstruction from any other quarter save Russia, and China's internal problems were such that she could not afford to stand friendless in the world. Stalin and the Soviet Union in any case still enjoyed enormous prestige as the centre of the communist world, and at that time the Chinese and other Asian communist parties needed the legitimising stamp and approval of Moscow.

As we have seen, the State Department was not totally unaware of possible divisions in the communist bloc, or within individual parties. Some American agents reported from Indo-China that they could find no evidence that the Vietminh leader, Ho Chi Minh, was controlled by Moscow. A few in Washington were tempted by the argument that Ho might prove a nationalist rather than a Russian tool and were impressed by his popularity and influence. But

Acheson had replied that a red flag was still a red flag although it might be decorated with 'yellow stars'. Even if Ho proved another Tito, this was still the worst of the acceptable alternatives. As early as 18 July 1949 Acheson had insisted that 'the United States does not intend to permit further extension of communist domination on the continent of Asia or in the southeast Asia area'.[20] Although the domino theory was not given public and popular currency until 1954 by President Eisenhower, it was fully articulated within the government by 1949 if not before.

French setbacks in Indo-China brought increasing American criticism. Washington believed that the Vietminh could be effectively resisted only if the French succeeded in generating a pro-western nationalist movement, and to achieve this liberal reforms were necessary. Briefly they hoped that the Emperor Bao Dai, the Indo-Chinese leader under French control, would be accepted as a true nationalist by other Asian states as well as the Indo-Chinese themselves. But the Thais dismissed him as a French tool, and the Indians were still more critical. Washington continued to look for ways to strengthen the anti-communist forces in Indo-China despite repeated disappointments at the hands of the French who refused to relax their influence to any significant degree. All problems, however, tended to prompt the same response in most parts of the American administration – the long-term effects of communist advances in south-east Asia would outweigh the costs of resistance. Nevertheless American military intervention was not among the options being considered at this time. Strategically the Americans wished to minimise their commitments in the Far East – an offshore island defence perimeter had many attractions. What was agreed early in 1950 was that substantial economic and military aid should be given to the French in Indo-China in the hope that French and Indo-Chinese forces would be equal to the task in hand. This was the first fatal American step towards the Vietnam War. It is also important to note that the first aid agreement was reached with the French in May 1950 – that is, before the outbreak of the Korean War.

Meanwhile the American government was also deliberating over the future of Formosa (Taiwan). Chiang Kai-shek and the rump of the Kuomintang forces had retreated to this island in 1949. Communists and Kuomintang alike insisted that Formosa was part of China, and there could be no question but that the Communists would seize the first opportunity to invade the island. The United States wished to deny Formosa to communist China for strategic and political reasons, but the State Department also wished to do nothing to increase Chinese dependence upon the Soviet Union, or to outrage mainland Chinese nationalist opinion. For America to support the Kuomintang on Formosa would have just this effect. Many in Washington in any case were thoroughly disenchanted with the Kuomin-tang – its incompetence and corruption – and Acheson was scathingly critical when he appeared before the Senate Foreign Relations Committee as late as 29 March 1950.[21] The service chiefs reluctantly admitted in 1949 that they had no forces to spare for the island's defence – it ranked below Iceland in American strategic priorities. Chiang was not expected to hold out for long against an assault from the mainland.[22] Thus American policy on Formosa remained in an unhappy state of uncertainty. Limited aid to Chiang was continued for the time being – partly in deference to Congress – but in the longer run it seemed possible that the United States would stand aside if and when the Communists attempted to overrun the island. Priority was still given to the hope that the paths of Russia and China might ultimately diverge.

In the spring of 1950 the CIA forecast that a communist seizure of Formosa was probable before the end of the year.[23] Circum-stances, however, were now beginning to favour those Americans who had always been reluctant to give up the island to communism. The idea of some form of neutralization or a UN protectorate was again put forward.[24] MacArthur from Tokyo and Chiang's supporters in Congress urged resistance, and were encouraged by the latest intensification of anti-communist feeling in the United States as Senator McCarthy took his first steps towards public notoriety as the leading crusader against the 'Red menace'. The popularity of the Truman administration was at a low ebb, and within the adminis-tration pressures were building up in favour of tougher policies against communism in general. On Formosa, Dean Rusk, an Assistant Secretary of State, argued on 30 May 1950 that no more grey areas should be given up to the Communists – such surrenders merely encouraged communist advances elsewhere. Japan or the Middle East might be next.[25] Given such pressures and attitudes, it is not surprising that when the Korean War broke out at the end of June 1950 it brought an immediate toughening of American policy on Formosa (American warships were promptly deployed to 'neutralise' the Formosa Straits, the main effect of this action being to prevent a possible communist Chinese invasion of the island). Yet after the outbreak of the Korean War the State Department did not even then give up its hopes of a breakthrough to better relations with China.

THE KOREAN WAR

Speeches by Truman and Acheson in January 1950 had placed only

Japan, the Philippines and a number of islands in the western Pacific specifically within the American defence perimeter in the Far East. South Korea and Formosa were not included, though Acheson referred to the security of the latter in the context of the United Nations. Obviously this defence perimeter was only an agreed minimal American posture. American interests could and did stretch beyond it, but to what extent was a matter for continuing debate. Nevertheless it is possible that this perimeter speech, with such episodes as the temporary defeat in Congress of the administration's aid programme for South Korea, contributed to the belief of the North Koreans and the Russians that South Korea could be safely invaded later in the year.[26] Acheson's difficulty was that he was trying to satisfy several audiences simultaneously, and having to do so before the United States had developed an agreed policy on all areas in the Far East.

In South Korea, early in 1950, the main object of the Truman administration was to encourage reform policies to lessen internal discontents. Unrest would encourage communist subversion from the North. But the government under Syngman Rhee was oppressive, and far too interested in the acquisition of American arms with which to attack the North. Rhee, like Chiang before him, seemed to believe that the United States could not afford to abandon him, whatever his policies. Foster Dulles visited Seoul in the middle of June 1950 and tried to persuade Rhee that communist subversion was more to be feared than a 'shooting war'. Rhee should adjust his policies accordingly. It is true that the CIA at this time was aware of the North's advantage in tanks, guns and aircraft, but thought such forces equal only to limited operations, such as the capture of Seoul. A northern victory over the South by war or even by subversion seemed improbable.[27] The United States would certainly have welcomed a united, pro-western Korea, but in 1950 it lacked the means or the incentive to act. Attempts to implicate Washington in the origins of the war remain unconvincing, though some suspicion still attaches itself to Rhee and his supporters. Indeed, the competition between the two regimes in Korea was such that sooner or later one was likely to make a bid for overall control, unless both were held back by the superpowers.

Historians are no longer content with the original western interpretation of the origins of the Korean War – a simple case of communist aggression master-minded by Stalin. More weight is now given to local rivalries. The Russians appear hesitant and cautious – very much in line with their generally ambiguous conduct in the Far East from 1945. There are hints that the Russians might have been interested in a two-China solution as late as 1949. Mao's victories were given only sketchy publicity in the Soviet Union, and his reception in Moscow on 16 December 1949 was on a modest scale. According to Khrushchev it was the North Korean leader, Kim Il-sung, who first broached to Stalin the idea of an attack on South Korea, arguing that this would touch off a revolt against Rhee, and that his success would be complete before the Americans could intervene. There are other wisps of evidence to suggest that Stalin mulled the matter over carefully before he was persuaded it was safe to approve and support the operation. Only then were Russian aircraft, heavy guns and tanks supplied in the numbers necessary for the North Koreans to take the offensive.[28] The Kremlin might also have been prompted by fears of the consolidation of American influence in Japan through the negotiation of a generous peace treaty – a united communist Korea would be some compensation, and might even encourage neutralism in Japan. The place of Korea in Russo-Japanese relations before 1904–5 must not be forgotten. But the most likely leading determinant of Soviet policy must remain the expectation that a northern attack would result in no more than a short-lived 'civil war' since the Americans seemed neither predisposed nor able to intervene.

The Korean War began on 25 June 1950. Within a matter of hours northern forces were advancing rapidly and were able to sustain that advance without difficulty. Washington was taken by surprise, but promptly despatched air and naval support to aid the hard-pressed South Koreans. When these proved inadequate, land units were hurriedly scraped together and thrown into the battle. There existed a genuine and widespread belief in America that the mistakes of the 1930s must not be repeated. This was 'America's Rhineland'. Henry Wallace, who had been sacked by Truman in 1946 when he disagreed with the new 'get tough' with Russia policy, supported the Korean decision. For Truman and his advisers in June 1950 this war seemed a calculated test of American will-power by the Kremlin. Inaction would only encourage further communist moves elsewhere in Europe or Indo-China. Japanese opinion might begin to favour neutrality in the Cold War if the United States appeared weak.[29] Acheson commented: 'To back away from this challenge, in view of our capacity for meeting it, would be highly destructive to the power and prestige of the United States. By prestige I mean the shadow cast by power, which is of great deterrent importance.'[30] In the harsh world of power politics, and given the then state of East–West relations, the American reaction was not surprising. The execution of American policy over the next six months, however, was not always so wise.

Although the first stage of the Korean War soon found American and other forces desperately clinging to a foothold around Pusan in the southern extremity of the peninsula, as early as 1 July a State

Department official mooted the possibility of a crossing of the 38th parallel into North Korea once the tide began to turn. Interest in the elimination of the parallel soon spread, although Kennan, the Policy Planning Staff and the CIA were more sceptical, and stressed the dangers of an advance into North Korea. But there was more sympathy for the argument that restraint would simply encourage further aggression, that appeasement did not pay, that aggression must be punished if it was to be discouraged, and that a return to the status quo would leave South Korea open to further attack from the North. There was not a little moralising on the wickedness of the enemy. Chinese and Russian peace moves failed to meet the American requirement that aggression must be seen to fail. They were also seen, not unreasonably, as attempts to sow dissension between America and her European allies.[31] The North Koreans had to be thrown back before the West could negotiate from a position of equality. At this time, too, the United States was well placed in the United Nations where, apart from allies and dependants, so independently minded a state as India voted with fifty-two others (out of a total of fifty-nine) for a return of the northern forces to the original dividing line – the 38th parallel. The Yugoslavs, fearful of a sudden Russian move against them, discreetly indicated their sympathy with UN action.[32] The British spoke of naked communist aggression, and gave some military support in Korea. In so far as London had reservations they were that the Americans might overreact, or allow too many forces to be diverted to the Far East, so endangering Europe and the Middle East. In fact both Washington and London were anxiously scanning many potential trouble spots in the world to try to anticipate where the Communists might strike next.[33] A third world war began to seem a less distant possibility. A paper prepared by the British Joint Planning Staff in August 1950 bluntly stated: 'The Russian aim in cold and hot war is to establish a communist world dominated by Moscow.'[34]

By the end of August 1950 there was general agreement in Washington that the parallel should be crossed, if America's allies agreed, and so long as Russian or Chinese intervention seemed unlikely. Much wishful thinking was evident, with a blind eye being turned to Chinese troop movements and their explicit warnings through New Delhi. It was too readily assumed that America's 'limited' aims in Korea would be recognised as constituting no threat to others, and that China would be too much preoccupied with internal problems of reconstruction to intervene. The CIA as late as 12 October 1950 thought the Chinese unlikely to move unless Russia was ready for global war, and according to CIA estimates it was not until 1952 that the military balance would most favour the Russians – this would be the year of greatest military danger for the West.[35] Over and above such calculations there was an evident desire on the part of many in Washington to win a real victory over communism, and there was a growing temptation to interpret the sequence of events in Korea in the autumn of 1950 as providing such an opportunity.

Indeed western spirits as a whole rose when MacArthur took his opponents in Korea by surprise with an amphibious landing at Inchon on 15 September. Inchon, located on the Korean west coast just below the 38th parallel, provided MacArthur's forces with a base from which they could drive across the peninsula and cut the North Korean supply lines. The northern armies disintegrated, and at the beginning of October the crossing of the parallel became the question of the hour. A vague UN resolution on 7 October loosely permitted both political and military action to effect the unification of Korea. There were 47 votes in favour, 7 against, and 5 (including India) abstentions. This opened the door to an invasion of the North, which the Americans (and still more MacArthur) seized with both hands. The British Foreign Secretary, too, was increasingly optimistic and ambitious at this stage. He believed that the United Nations could seize the diplomatic initiative in Korea to bring about reunification, discreetly using just enough military force to make this possible. He feared Russia politically rather than militarily, and was ambitiously trying to keep in step with both the United States and India. He acted in this manner despite warnings from the Foreign Office of probable Chinese military movements in Manchuria and into Korea, and from Chou En-lai by way of the Indian ambassador in Peking on 3 October that China would intervene if the parallel were crossed. The British Chiefs of Staff were also uneasy, and opposed any UN advance beyond the readily defensible 'waistline' in North Korea, well short of the Manchurian border.[36]

But discreet or cautious military action was the last thing which the allied commander, MacArthur, had in mind. He advanced his forces towards the North Korean borders with China and Russia without regard for the political implications – or indeed the military ones should the Chinese, for instance, launch a counter-stroke. His widely deployed troops were in no condition to engage a determined enemy. Even so it is possible that the Chinese intervened only after much debate. Mao, it has been suggested, had to dispel fears of America's nuclear power. The Chinese might have received encouragement and reassurance from the Russians. Once at war the Chinese received Russian arms – but later complained concerning the price they were required to pay for them. Nevertheless their intervention was so effective from the end of November that they not only recovered North Korea but in the winter of 1950–51 seemed likely to occupy the whole peninsula. It took time for American fire-power to stabilise the battle-line roughly along the 38th parallel. In the first months of 1951 the Truman administration began to think in terms of a draw – a return to the status quo in Korea. MacArthur was dismayed: he insisted there was no substitute for victory. He was finally sacked by Truman for insubordination in April. In June the long search for a cease-fire began.

At home the Truman administration was sorely embarrassed by public sympathy for MacArthur, and by the witch-hunts inspired by Senator McCarthy. Nevertheless its case was effectively defended by the army Chief of Staff, General Bradley, when he described the Korean War as the 'wrong war, at the wrong place, at the wrong time, and with the wrong enemy'. The administration was anxious not to expend too much strength against the lesser enemy, China. It argued that to use the Strategic Air Command in this theatre, for instance, might entail losses which it would take two years to replace, with a consequent weakening of the the the allied nuclear deterrent against Russia. In the first half of 1951 the administration finally managed to secure acceptance by Congress of its selective strategy in the Far East, and of the priority it wished to give to the defence of Europe. But events since October 1950 had destroyed whatever hopes the State Department still had of driving an early wedge between Russia and China. America drew closer to Japan and Chiang Kai-shek, and early in 1951 the condemnation of communist China as an aggressor was pushed through the UN.

The Korean War dragged on for another two years, militarily a stalemate, but with each side trying to wring advantages from the cease-fire talks. The Americans, as we shall see, also feared that an early end to the war might release Chinese forces for 'aggression' elsewhere, notably in south-east Asia. But all were tiring of the war. Eisenhower's presidential victory in 1952 owed much to the popular hope that he would find an early solution to the war. The Chinese faced an enormous task of domestic reconstruction, and were perhaps interested in a cease-fire by the end of 1952.[37] Stalin died early in 1953, and his successors had good reason to work for a period of calm in international affairs as they battled for power in Russia. The new Eisenhower administration adopted a tough pose, and issued vague threats of a readiness to escalate the war – even to the nuclear level.[38] What effect such threats had upon the thinking in Moscow and Peking, if any, cannot be established, but an armistice was finally signed at Panmunjom on 27 July 1953. Korea remained divided much as it had been in 1950, but with much of its terrain devastated. The casualty estimates have run as high as 4 millions, including civilians as well as all belligerents. Easily described as an 'unnecessary' war, especially in the light of the outcome in the Far East, it nevertheless affected the international scene far beyond its own locale. In particular it intensified the Cold War in Europe, and transformed paper plans for arms increases into realities.

THE WAR SCARE OF 1950–51

Fear and opportunism guided American policy from June 1950 until the late summer of 1951. At first the alarm centred on the possibility that the Korean War might prove merely the first of several aggressive communist moves in various parts of the world. Later more emphasis was placed on the expected worsening of the East–West military imbalance in the early 1950s: this temporary advantage might tempt the Russians to push more vigorously for openings than usual, and even general war could not be ruled out.[39] But alarmist speculation of this kind was also prompted by the determination of the State Department and the American services to exploit the current crisis to secure the implementation of as much as possible of the proposed defence programme, NSC 68. The crisis was similarly played up to drive America's European allies along a rearmament path they were reluctant to follow, and to make possible the rearmament of West Germany. Some Americans have since written of these manoeuvres in highly critical terms. Yet allowance must be made for the political environment in which American policy-makers concerned with foreign and strategic affairs were called upon to act. They had difficulty in mobilising support from within certain sections of the administration, notably the Treasury, not to mention problems with Congress, the American public, and allies overseas.

Undoubtedly hopes existed that the United States might, given the resources of the western powers as well as its own, be able to seize the initiative in some aspects of the Cold War – that positions of strength, even of superior strength, might be created. At the same time there existed genuine fears of what the Soviet Union might do, unless constrained, and there was a deep appreciation of the difficulty of persuading democracies to sustain an expensive defence programme over a long period of time. The administration had also to balance between those in America who were mainly interested in the war in the east and European allies who feared an excessive diversion of American strength away from their continent. Yet if it was with some reluctance that the British agreed to brand the Chinese as aggressors early in 1951, such a move helped Truman to win support in Congress for a considerable increase to the American commitment in Europe.[40] British assessments of the Russian threat varied, and there was a singularly pessimistic report from the War Office in February 1951 which thought war 'possible' in 1951, and 'probable' in 1952.[41] Even Aneurin Bevan, who took a sceptical view of such warnings, favoured a western guarantee to Yugoslavia to deter a possible Russian attack.[42] A brief examination of the negotiations which brought about a significant strengthening of NATO in the early 1950s will help to highlight the extent and character of western fears at this time.

At first, on 12 July 1950, the American ambassador in London reported that the western European reaction to the Korean crisis had been excellent. Earlier in the year Washington had been fearful of a revival of the 'neutrality complex' in some European circles.[43] Now there were hopes that communist aggression and the American response to it would encourage the Europeans to rearm. Furthermore Europe seemed highly vulnerable. General Montgomery thought the two American divisions in West Germany the only truly effective land units in Europe. Other assessments by western military experts were equally bleak. There was renewed talk of some form of German rearmament, if only the development of paramilitary police units to counter those being formed in East Germany. Even the French now seemed willing to consider the question!

But no consensus could easily be created. The Germans themselves feared that rearmament would make reunification impossible. Nor were they yet assured of the protection of NATO in the event of war.[44] Bevin asked on 7 August 1950 if German rearmament would not precipitate the very Russian attack it was designed to discourage. When, a month later, he feared that a Korean-type situation might develop in Germany, he still favoured a strengthened West German police force. The British Chiefs of Staff, however, recommended a twenty-division army, with ten more in reserve, and a tactical air force of 1,100 planes.[45] The State Department, aware of the explosive nature of the German question, trod warily. On the one hand in August 1950 it feared the development of a 'fear and resignation psychosis' in Europe, but on the other it believed that this was perhaps the right psychological moment to seize the initiative.[46] With eighteen divisions in Europe one could begin to think of defending Germany on the Elbe. If German units were merged in a European army, France might be reassured and persuaded to accept German rearmament. The State Department therefore attempted to bargain with the Europeans. In return for European and German rearmament the United States would send extra troops to Europe, and agree to the appointment of an American as the Supreme Allied Commander in Europe (SACEUR).

The allied negotiations from September 1950 were by no means amicable. The British were hesitant. French fears of Germany threatened to prevail over their desire for American support. Step by step the Americans were forced to offer their contributions to the proposed package (including the integration of American troops in NATO to give the French more security against Germany) before the French were even prepared to concede the principle of German rearmament, let alone agree on how it should be implemented. This French obstructionism complicated the task of the American administration at home as it battled for Congressional support. There were many objections to the extent and permanence of the American military involvement in Europe. But the administration finally prevailed in the spring of 1951, and it was only then that NATO became for the Americans a truly entangling alliance. The Europeans, and especially the French, had had their way to a remarkable degree, and it is important to note that European policies were shaped by fears of Germany as well as of Russia.[47] Thus in 1951 the Americans found themselves contributing the lion's share of the additions to the strength of NATO, and although their European allies began to step up their military preparations, the question of German rearmament continued to hang fire. There is no need to discuss here the ill-fated attempt to establish the European Defence Community, the hope being that the merging of German forces within such an organization would remove objections to German rearmament. But this project was finally vetoed by the French in 1954. It was only in 1954–55 that agreement was reached on West German rearmament, and there was a further lapse of time before German forces made a major contribution to western defence. Fortunately for NATO, West Germany's policies were under the firm direction of Chancellor Konrad Adenauer. He was convinced that integration with the West was preferable to German reunification on terms which might increase Russian influence in the heart of Europe.[48]

The German problem, however, must not be allowed to obscure the very real fears of Russia which existed in the West, and which intensified as the Korean War took a turn for the worse at the end of 1950. Speculation as to Russian intentions was rife throughout 1950.[49] High-level inter-departmental deliberations in Washington produced the National Intelligence Estimate of 11 December 1950. This declared: 'the over-all situation is such that the possibility cannot be disregarded that the USSR has already made a decision for general war and is in process of taking steps preliminary to its inception'. At the very least the Russians were expected to use war scares to try to decrease the western will to resist. Russian confidence in their current military–political position was said to be high, and the Kremlin was bent on advancing communist influence at the expense of the West in Japan, south-east Asia and West Germany.[50] The Policy Planning Staff agreed early in 1951 that there was a real danger of major Russian moves in the next year. The western powers needed time to gather their strength, and the Russians might be tempted to strike before they could accomplish this. Alternatively conflicts in the Far East might be escalated to divert the United States and to demoralise western Europe.[51] A Czech defector, Karel Kaplan, claimed in 1977 that he had seen evidence in the Czech archives of a secret meeting of Stalin with the east European leaders in January 1951 at which he argued that by 1955 the Americans would be too strongly entrenched in Europe for Russia and her friends to win a pre-emptive war. Stalin revealed plans to overrun western Europe before that consolidation could take place, and the east European leaders agreed in writing to place their forces under Soviet command.[52] If true, this might have been no more than a contingency plan. It seems out of character with Stalin's postwar foreign policy as a whole, though some historians are convinced that Stalin was becoming more unpredictable and irrational in his later years – even in his handling of foreign affairs.[53] His daughter, Svetlana, records his embittered feelings against the whole world. Nevertheless the attack was not made, and certainly in 1952 Stalin was putting some faith in a diplomatic initiative to try to counter the threat of West German rearmament and the strengthening of NATO.

Even in 1951 not all Americans took a thoroughly pessimistic view of Soviet intentions. Admiral L. C. Stevens, who had served as naval attaché in Russia in 1947–50, returned convinced that the West was exaggerating Russian power and intentions. The Kremlin's first concern was the security of the USSR itself. He did not believe any specific expansionist plan existed. The Russians were taking a long view in their foreign policy. They preferred other means than war to attain their ends unless they were sure of instant victory.[54] Charles Bohlen, a diplomat, took the same line later in the year, even suggesting that the Korean War might have arisen from a miscalculation on the part of Moscow. He thought the war demonstrated 'the extraordinarily pragmatic and opportunistic nature of Soviet policy and the absence of any fidelity to a blueprint, or even a design'. He agreed that it might be necessary to arouse the American public to support rearmament by exciting fears of a Russian bid for world domination, but the government should not become a victim of its own rhetoric – indeed he thought parts of NSC 68 might have been more cautiously drafted. Bohlen agreed that the situation was dangerous, and would certainly continue to be so for a very long time. Consequently he was very critical of the argument that the maximum period of danger might pass in two or three years. He thought the best guide to western arms preparation was that level of defence spending which the western economies could reasonably be expected to sustain in the long term. As for Russia, 'the internal situation', he concluded, 'is the single greatest controlling force in its foreign policy'.[55]

General Eisenhower had returned from his tour of Europe in January 1951 with very similar views. He thought the Russians were averse to war at the moment, and that what was most needed was a force of ten or twelve American divisions stationed in Europe until western morale and economic strength had been built up and the Europeans were able to defend themselves. In the event of war he, as SACEUR, intended to rely very much on the strength of his forces on the Russian flanks – in the North Sea and Mediterranean.[56]

American intelligence estimates continued to differ in 1951 as to the nature and immediacy of the Russian threat. The supposed military imbalance over the next two or three years (which might tempt the Russians to engage in a pre-emptive war) continued to be stressed, but as the year wore on there was more agreement on the opportunistic character of Russian policy. In contrast to the pessimism of Churchill, Montgomery and the CIA earlier in 1951, Eisenhower insisted in December that Russia would ultimately lose a war, and therefore would not take the risk. His successor as SACEUR, General Gruenther, later spoke of the reluctance of the Russians to gamble, and did not think they could even begin to think in terms of a wager on war before 1960.[57] The situation outside Europe, however, remained less hopeful, with the CIA fearing that Chinese forces, once released from the war in Korea, might be used in southeast Asia. The Joint Chiefs of Staff took much the same view in October 1951. They also expressed concern at the weakening cohesion, power and influence of the British Commonwealth. They wanted to see Britain's disputes with Egypt and Iran resolved in favour of the West, and the emergence of a Middle Eastern defence organization based on Turkey, Egypt and Iran. This would still require Commonwealth reinforcements, forces which did not as yet exist. In consequence it was not clear what line might prove defensible in the Middle East.[58]

Attention was also given to the feasibility of a surprise Russian attack on the United States, using TU-4s on one-way missions and carrying nuclear bombs. A surprise attack might 'blast the heart out of United States industry' and kill up to 4 million people.[59] The Russians, however, showed few signs in the early 1950s of developing such a capability, and one breathing space followed another. Similarly, although figures were produced at the end of 1951 to suggest that NATO had only half the conventional forces which were needed to defeat a Russian conventional attack, most NATO representatives at a meeting in London on 13 November expected Russia to rely on Cold War and localised activities in the foreseeable future. A general war appeared so much less likely that at a NATO Council meeting in Rome at the end of November it was agreed that a gradual build-up over a period of years (rather than with the year 1954 as the target) in accordance with political and economic possibilities would now suffice.[60] Instead of a frantic two- or three-year spurt in defence preparations, the planners now thought in terms of limited mobilisation, and a long period of competition with the Soviet Union. Accordingly there was growing concern as to how to sustain public support and morale in such circumstances.[61] The search for defence economies began before the much heralded cost-cutting under the Eisenhower administration (from 1953). Already tactical nuclear weapons were being developed in the hope that these would make possible the defence of western Europe against superior Soviet forces, while dismay over the consequences of general war encouraged interest in deterrent strategies and tactics designed to localise any conflict which did break out. Constructive talks with the Kremlin still seemed improbable until the West had acquired a much stronger military position, and there were abiding fears that any Russian moves in favour of *détente* would be designed to tempt the West to lower its guard, to encourage divisions within the alliance and to excite popular criticism of western governments and their policies.

THE FIRST HINTS OF A 'THAW' AND A NEW INTERNATIONAL ORDER

The Cold War reached one climax in 1950–51, and though further crises lay ahead (notably over Cuba in 1962) there was soon some evidence to suggest that the world was not doomed to partition into two impermeable, unchangeable, ideological blocs. Separate national identities became more important within each alliance, while the growing forces of nationalism in what was to become known as the Third World increasingly demonstrated their reluctance to conform to the prescriptions of East and West. It took time for this developing state of affairs to be widely recognised – full acceptance did not materialize until the 1970s – but there were hints of realization once the fears of 1950–51 that a third world war was neither inconceivable nor perhaps all that far off began to lessen, and no longer dominated the thinking of the policy-makers.

One of the most dramatic examples of the more relaxed and flexible approach to politics was the Russian proposal of 10 March 1952 that Germany should be neutralized and reunited. An intercepted message from Moscow to the East German government in 1952 even suggested that the Kremlin was considering the possible sacrifice of a communist East Germany for a united Germany that would not present a military threat to the Soviet Union and its interests in eastern Europe.[62] Scholars have naturally been intrigued by this overture and the failure of the western governments to make a positive response. Was this perhaps the one moment in the postwar era when German history might have taken, or been pushed into a different channel? Were the western states unnecessarily suspicious and intransigent? It is easier to speculate than to provide answers, especially in the absence of useful information on the thinking behind the Soviet move. An American study, NSC 114/2, in the late summer of 1951 had indeed suggested that a time might come when German unification might seem preferable to the Russians to German rearmament.[63] In the spring of 1952 Stalin spoke of four-power control of Germany as one prerequisite for East–West peaceful coexistence, though in general it was not made clear how a united Germany would be governed and what limits would be placed on its independence. Nevertheless it seems reasonable to assume that the Russians might have been well satisfied with a Germany which was subdued and denied the means to become in the foreseeable future a powerful force in the heart of Europe. East Germany under Russian control was a less attractive solution in the light of the advantages the western alliance might expect to derive from a strong, rearmed West Germany. The Russians had good reason to test the water at this stage, if only in the hope of encouraging divisions in the West, and in West Germany itself.[64] Each side in fact followed the obvious policy in the light of its perceived needs.[65] The West preferred a rearmed West Germany to one that was united but neutralised.

Even before Stalin's death in March 1953 the caution in Russia's foreign policy outside its own spheres of influence was becoming evident. Peaceful coexistence, or East–West competition by all means short of major war, was not entirely the invention of Stalin's successors, though it was elaborated and emphasized by them in the special circumstances of the middle 1950s. The struggle for power in Russia after Stalin's death was not finally resolved until October 1957, and even then Khrushchev never attained a position that could be compared with that of Stalin. From 1953 Russia continued to face massive economic problems, especially in agriculture, and no rational government would have chosen to embark upon a perilous policy abroad when there were so many other calls upon the nation's resources. The years 1953–54 also witnessed the start of the H-bomb era, and the Russian leaders were soon stressing in public the revolutionary importance of thermonuclear weapons. At the Twentieth Party Congress early in 1956, Khrushchev insisted 'there is no fatal inevitability of war'. From 1954 the Russians regularly produced extensive proposals for disarmament (conventional and nuclear) or arms control, reaching a climax with Khrushchev's proposal to the General Assembly of the UN in 1959 that there should be general and complete disarmament. The propagandist intention behind most of these suggestions is evident, but there were also occasions when some western experts thought they detected a desire to escape from some of the burdens of the arms race and an anxiety to prevent an accidental nuclear war. For a time in 1955 East–West relations improved sufficiently for journalists to write of a 'thaw' in the Cold War. This measure of optimism did not last for long, but there was no immediate return to the winterish temperature of 1950–51.

From 1953–54 all the leading capitals of the world had to take account of the development of weapons with an explosive strength which had to be measured in millions of tonnes compared with the ten or twenty thousands of their predecessors of the atomic age. The inter-continental bomber was operational, and the inter-continental rocket was only a few years away. Together these represented a much greater change in the character of total war than that envisaged by most strategists when thinking of the atomic bomb and its B-29 carrier. As we have seen, in the years immediately before and after 1950–51, western planners assumed that, important as atomic weapons were, vast numbers of conventional arms would be required to fight a third world war of several years' duration. In stark contrast, by the mid-1950s it seemed likely that a total war would be over in a matter of days, leaving vast areas devastated, even greater areas menaced by radiation, and with casualties which would run into tens of millions and more. Not only had the powers to prepare for a very different sort of war, but total war was ceasing to be a usable instrument of policy. Many argued that only deterrent strategies made sense for the future.

At first the public pronouncements of the new Republican administration under Eisenhower suggested that it was reluctant to come to terms with the new technology. Secretary of State Foster Dulles spoke of 'massive retaliation' and 'brinkmanship', and at times frightened his western allies if not his eastern opponents. Some consideration was certainly given to the use of atomic weapons in the closing stages of the Korean War, during the Indo-Chinese crisis of 1954, and the offshore island crisis with China in 1954–55. Preventive war was not ruled out in 1953, but the idea was dropped a year later.[66] In fact the 'New Look' strategy of the Republicans was never quite so simple as it seemed. Basically the aim was to reply to communist advances in places and ways best suited to the United States. Nuclear weapons were only part of the answer sought to the question how the United States could pursue a global policy at something considerably less than the heavy defence costs envisaged by the Truman administration in its final strategic study, NSC 141.[67] When Eisenhower entered office his country still appeared to possess some usable nuclear advantages, and Dulles was anxious to seize the initiative from the Communists, or at least to throw them off balance with a display of American resolve. But however attractive such ideas seemed in theory, they were very difficult to put into practice in a way that was both controlled and convincing. Nor was Dulles at his best on the public platform. He was often dogmatic and unbending at the conference table, prompting Eden, who often worked with Dulles, to describe him as 'a preacher in world politics'. Even Eisenhower was sometimes troubled by Dulles's adversarial approach, and once remarked that Foster was too anxious not to suffer the fate of his predecessor, Acheson, at the hands of diehard Right-wing politicians. Dulles was certainly determined to retain the support of the Right, and he also played up the communist threat in the belief that otherwise Congress, American public opinion and the Europeans might favour a less determined stand in the Cold War. But if Eisenhower left the detail and presentation of American foreign policy to Dulles, he was in overall charge. He was most content when in pursuit of some happy medium between militancy and conciliation. Eisenhower was inaccurately caricatured by contemporary critics as naive and indolent. Crises usually found him at his best, notably during the Suez crisis of 1956. Also he showed a commendable interest in the restraint of American defence spending.

Initially the Eisenhower administration, unlike its predecessor, had an abundance of nuclear weapons (and theoretically at least could contemplate their use in a variety of situations). For a year or two, also, the American nuclear lead over the Soviet Union was large enough to persuade the administration that nuclear weapons were usable and would not provoke general war with the Soviet Union. It was asserted early in 1955:[68]

> So long as the Soviets are uncertain of their ability to neutralize the
> U.S. nuclear-air retaliatory power, there is little reason to expect them
> to initiate general war or actions which they believe would . . .
> endanger the regime and the security of the USSR.

This expectation led the administration to cut conventional forces, and to agree to reductions in the build-up of NATO. Tactical nuclear weapons were deployed in Europe from 1953, it being noted in NSC 162/2 in October 1953 that the main deterrent against aggression in western Europe was 'the manifest determination of the United States to use its atomic capability and massive retaliatory striking power if the area is attacked'. Eisenhower as late as 1956 confidently declared that the tactical use of atomic weapons against military targets 'would be no more likely to trigger off a big war than the use of twenty-ton "block busters"'.[69]

The same policy was adopted outside Europe. The National Security Council's Planning Board concluded on 1 June 1953 that while there was still a serious risk of a general war, western strength was much more likely to be eroded by local aggression, covert operations or economic assistance to developing nations. Russia's tone might be more conciliatory, but its basic aims were unchanged. Nuclear weapons were therefore included in America's diverse armoury to meet such challenges, and this policy was formally restated by the National Security Council on 7 January 1955 (NSC 5501). Eisenhower remarked:[70]

> . . . the United States cannot afford to preclude itself from using
> nuclear weapons even in a local situation, if such use will bring the
> aggression to a swift and positive cessation, and if, on a balance of
> political and military consideration, such use will best advance U.S.
> security interests.

The presidential reservations, however, should not be forgotten, while the growth of the Soviet nuclear armoury was carefully analysed year by year in the expectation that Russia would soon have sufficient weapons to decrease the value of the American nuclear deterrent against local aggression. Warnings to this effect appeared as early as 1953.[71] By 1956 it was estimated that the Russians were making significant progress. The United States could reduce life in Russia to 'chaos' in a few hours, but the Russians could now deliver a 'crippling' (though not a decisive) blow in return. America's period of recovery to the level of a great industrial nation would be prolonged.[72] As the decade advanced so it seemed increasingly probable that neither side would be able to achieve a meaningful victory in a general war. No defence was conceivable against intercontinental ballistic rockets with their megaton payloads. Priority had now to be given to the creation of indestructible deterrent forces to ride out any surprise attack. In this new stage of the arms race America's technological lead over Russia began to seem more important than its industrial superiority; such a lead was vital to prevent a surprise Russian breakthrough which might threaten the state of mutual deterrence. By the late 1950s a growing number of question marks were being placed beside the administration's strategy, with its heavy reliance on nuclear arms. Private doubts were multiplying behind public expressions of confidence that limited nuclear wars could be kept limited. But there could be no overt change in strategic thinking so long as Eisenhower clung to his resolve to limit defence spending and yet uphold so many foreign commitments.[73]

Nevertheless appreciation of the intractability and variety of the real world grew during the decade. There had always been a propagandist element in Republican talk in the early 1950s of rolling back communism in eastern Europe, and it was in fact accepted by the National Security Council as early as October 1953 that the satellite states could be freed only by general war or by the Russians themselves. Neither seemed plausible. No other short cuts to the resolution of the Cold War in favour of the West presented themselves. Instead there was anxious study of projections of the long-term economic potential of the eastern and western blocs to try to establish which was the better equipped to withstand a struggle of attrition. Strains within the western alliance were closely examined. Every European state was subject to its own peculiar internal and external problems and pressures: each was naturally tempted by any easing of East–West tension to give more energy to such matters and less to the needs of the western alliance against 'the communist threat'.Similarly the non-communist world outside Europe was full of divisions and weaknesses. In September 1953, for instance, American hopes were already beginning to fade that Egypt might act as the pacemaker in the creation of a Middle Eastern Defence Organisation against communism. In the course of the decade the administration became ever more conscious of the difficulty of moulding allies and the non-aligned to serve its purposes.

The global conflict took on new dimensions. America's nuclear arms were of no use against the Soviet political and economic offensive from the autumn of 1953 to try to gain influence among peoples who were escaping from the old European empires and spheres of influence. Hitherto Lenin's theories that the downfall of capitalism could be hastened by the encouragement of colonial revolts against their imperial overlords had enjoyed little success in practice. Indeed, colonial and semi-colonial areas had been largely neglected by Stalin after the 1920s, while in the early years of the Cold War the bourgeois nationalist leaders of most independence movements had been written off as imperialist lackeys. Opportunities for influence in India and many parts of the Arab world had been neglected. Quarrels with Turkey and Iran, and initial support for Israel, had worsened Russia's prospects. A new strategy was possibly in formation before Stalin's death, but it was his successors who began to cultivate India, Egypt and Afghanistan in particular from 1953 to 1955, and to seek influence through arms sales and help in the development of the national economies. Early in 1956 Khrushchev proclaimed the existence of a 'zone of peace', and acknowledged the independent role in world affairs of former African and Asian colonies. He spoke of the new threat to these countries posed by multinational western corporations and other instruments through which the West strove to maintain its influence and profits. Russia was joining battle with this neo-colonialism, and at the same time was trying to reduce the number of Third World countries which might otherwise provide the West with valuable bases for use against the Russian homeland and for the general conduct of the Cold War. A new global struggle for influence was in progress in which the Russians strove to leapfrog any lines of containment erected by their opponents, or to find means to neutralise western positions of strength. For Afro-Asian states in search of economic aid and for opportunities to diminish their dependence on the West, these Russian offerings were very welcome. For some, in addition, there were important military and political advantages as well.

Eisenhower and Dulles, before they took office in 1953, were fearful of the appeal of communism to colonial and ex-colonial but impoverished peoples. In reply they concentrated on the discovery and encouragement of allies among such peoples. Dulles in particular disliked neutrals and the non-aligned. The administration, as in its defence policy, was wary of indiscriminate foreign aid expenditure, and like its predecessor often hoped that aid to build up a friend would produce savings in American expenditure in the long run. Nevertheless the growing importance of political and economic weapons in the Cold War was stressed in a NSC document of 15 March 1956. Third World countries might come to doubt the relevance of western models and institutions to their own problems if Russia and China began to enjoy marked economic progress at home. A NSC paper of 3 June 1957 argued that more flexibility and imagination was essential as the global conflict took new turns.[74] The Middle East in particular prompted some new thinking. The Eisenhower Doctrine of 1957 and the intervention in the Lebanon in the summer of 1958 had been clumsy moves, although the latter had done something to advance the uneasy peace which was beginning to develop (temporarily) in that region. On 13 August 1958 Eisenhower promised economic aid to states which devised viable development plans and which were at peace with themselves and with their neighbours. A NSC paper of 4 November 1958 argued that if the United States was to increase its influence it had to show more respect for Arab feelings and aspirations. It was necessary to consider how best to compete with Russia for Pan-Arab sympathy. It might be necessary, for instance, to confine the military dimension to co-operation with the British in the Persian Gulf.[75]Many interesting ideas, of course, did not get beyond the paper on which they were written, while Senator Fulbright, for instance, complained in 1958 that the United States tended to deal with almost everyone in the newly emergent states except 'the common man'. A Senate-sponsored study in 1958 concluded that American foreign policy to date had relied overmuch on military alliances with conservative regimes. It stressed the need to find more ways whereby the United States could align itself with the forces of change, while seeking always to create a more 'rational world order'.[76] Those actually engaged in the running of American policy might have raised a weary eyebrow or two in response to some of these suggestions, but the next President, John F. Kennedy, surely had reason to complain when he found that the State Department wished to continue the American ban on the formation of Centre–Left governments in Italy.[77]

Yet the deliberations within the Eisenhower administration were not totally without effect. If the 1955 hopes of an East–West 'thaw' proved short-lived, the possibility of coexistence in some shape or form was beginning to attract attention. As early as September 1953 the NSC's Planning Board had suggested that, given time, Russia's revolutionary zeal might begin to flag. The popular demand for consumer goods, the rise of bureaucratic and other vested interests might force a reallocation of Russian resources.[78] By 1955 it seemed safe to play down the risk of general war for at least the rest of the decade.[79] In an age of nuclear stalemate, subversion seemed the more likely threat. While even small communist gains might be politically damaging, these were balanced by hopes that the Russians and Chinese might come to agree that coexistence was the only rational choice in a nuclear world. Communists might even be persuaded to follow policies which, while they were not out of step with their own national interests, would not threaten American security. There had, of course, to be strict reciprocity and no premature concessions by the West, but it was thought conceivable that once Soviet policy began to move along such lines, consumer and other interests in Russia might prevent a reversal.[80] In so far as the West could hope for positive gains in the future, these seemed most likely to result from the exploitation of potential internal differences within the communist bloc. Admittedly such suggestions failed to move the administration towards a more flexible policy on China, for instance, and the public image of Dulles in particular remained one of almost complete rigidity. Nevertheless some historians have subsequently become persuaded that Republican diplomacy in the 1950s was not entirely unconstructive. There were limits to what could be achieved while each side was consolidating its position, especially in Europe. But even there the period was not totally barren. Interestingly Professor Gaddis commends the handling of the Berlin crisis in 1959 by Dulles and Eisenhower, describing it as an effective blend of menace and reassurance towards the Russians which, although it appeared to end in disaster in the abortive Paris Summit in 1960, nevertheless legitimised the practice of talks with the Russians without causing unacceptable splits in western opinion.[81]

Naturally no comparable portrait of thinking in Russia is possible. But the Yugoslav ambassador to Moscow (1956–58), Veljko Mićunović, who saw much of the Russian leadership, kept a detailed diary of his impressions. He witnessed the last two years of Khrushchev's struggle to become the most powerful figure in Russia. Mićunović doubted if Marxist–Leninist theoretical disputes, or the labelling of persons as Stalinists or anti-Stalinists, provided much guidance concerning the nature of the struggle. Khrushchev himself was above all an opportunist, happier explaining his policies with stories and jokes than by invocations of theory. In foreign policy Mićunović was repeatedly struck by Russian fears lest they should appear weak in the eyes of the West, while over Hungary in 1956 Khrushchev claimed that he would be in danger from critics at home unless he took a firm line. In Europe the stress appeared to be on winning western acceptance of the status quo: outside Europe there were, however, hopes of socialist gains as colonialism crumbled. Throughout Khrushchev showed himself as erratic and volatile, blowing hot and cold as he tried a variety of tactics to get his way. But in all the changes of mood and tactics, the normal underlying assumption appeared to be one of continuing competition with the West short of all-out war, with East–West relations themselves assuming a variety of forms as each side manoeuvred for advantage.

Nuclear tests, strong words, economic aid and conventional diplomacy were all part of the armoury. But whatever the weapons, the emphasis was on long-term, controlled and calculated rivalry.[82] In particular, efforts continued to devise a situation in Germany – and central Europe as a whole – that was favourable to the Soviet Union.

NOTES AND REFERENCES

1. Nagai and Iriye, pp. 126–7
2. G. Porter, I, 128, 139–40
3. Ch'en, p. 254
4. Thorne (2) pp. 539 ff.
5. FRUS, 1945, VII, 349
6. Schaller, pp. 177–216
7. Pepper, *passim*. For the debate inside the Chinese Communist Party, see Reardon-Anderson, *passim*
8. Schaller, pp. 288–300
9. FRUS, 1947, I, 737–8, 745–6, 749
10. Tsou, pp. 476, 488
11. SFRC, no. 5, pp. 343, 441–59; no. 8, pp. 97–9, 134–6
12. CAB 129/31 CP(48) 299; Etzold and Gaddis, pp. 240–7; Ovendale, pp. 447 ff.
13. Segal, p. 1; FRUS, 1949, VIII, 357–9, 363–4, 537–42, 586–93, 632–6, 643–5, etc.
14. Borg and Heinrichs, pp. 206–9, 232, 235 ff., 275
15. FRUS, 1949, IX, 494, 545
16. NSC 41, 12 February 1949
17. Compare NSC 48/1 (23 December 1949); NSC 51 (1 July 1949); NSC 64 (27 February 1950) with CAB 129/32 CP(49) 39, 67; 129/33 CP(49) 52; 129/36 CP(49) 180. Note Ovendale's (pp. 447–64) argument that Britain was more interested in the security of this region at this time than was the United States
18. Nagai and Iriye, pp. 334–5, 363 ff.
19. Nagai and Iriye, pp. 243–4
20. Jessup, p. 29
21. Borg and Heinrichs, p. 73; McLellan, pp. 188–216; Etzold and Gaddis, pp. 269–76; FRUS, 1949, IX, 261 ff., 376 ff., 463 ff.; FRUS, 1950, VI, 302 ff., 348 ff.
22. FRUS, 1949, IX, 261–96, 356, 376 ff.
23. FRUS, 1950, VI, 330
24. FRUS, 1950, VI, 348–51
25. FRUS, 1950, VI, 349–51
26. Nagai and Iriye, pp. 285–6
27. FRUS, 1950, VII, 32–3, 107 ff; Nagai and Iriye, pp. 287–8
28. Nagai and Iriye, pp. 315–17, 320; Stueck (1) pp. 622 ff.
29. FRUS, 1950, VII, 149 ff.
30. FRUS, 1950, VII, 405

31. FRUS, 1950, vii, 272, 312–39, 386–7, 393 ff.
32. FRUS, 1950, vii, 215–16, 322; see also pp. 1419–20
33. FRUS, 1950, vii, 215–16, 232, 280, 319, 419–20
34. *The Times* 14 April 1981
35. FRUS, 1950, vii, 667–721, 760–800, 933 ff., 980 ff.
36. CAB 129/41 CP(50) 193, 200, 215; 129/42 CP(50) 215–16, 220–1. See also *The Times* 3 January 1981
37. Shulman, p. 189
38. NSC 147, April 1953, discusses the pros and cons of the use of nuclear weapons in Korea
39. NSC 73, 1 July 1950; NSC 73/7, 29 July 1950
40. Williams, pp. 243–5
41. Williams, p. 245
42. For other evidence of British concern over Yugoslavia, see CAB 129/42 CP(50) 234
43. FRUS, 1950, iii, 21–64
44. FRUS, 1950, iii, 1278–9
45. FRUS, 1950, iii, 265–6; iv, 718–21. For earlier pleas from British and American soldiers, see Ireland, pp. 169, 176–86. See also FRUS, 1950, iv, 687, 691–5, 702 ff.; NSC 71, 8 June 1950
46. FRUS, 1950, iii, 200, 211–19
47. Ireland, pp. 183 ff.
48. FRUS, 1950, iv, 674–5
49. FRUS, 1950, iv, 1220–1, 1224–9, 1230–2
50. FRUS, 1951, i, 4–7
51. FRUS, 1951, i, 19–20, 37–40
52. *The Times* 6 May 1977; Williams, p. 245n
53. See e.g. Tolstoy, p. 359; Deutscher, pp. 621–4
54. FRUS, 1951, i, 42–4
55. FRUS, 1951, i, 107–8, 166–72, 180–1
56. FRUS, 1951, iii, Part 1, pp. 451–6
57. Sulzberger, pp. 523–4, 553–4, 577–8, 614, 726; FRUS, 1951, i, 124–7, 182–206
58. FRUS, 1951, i, 193–206, 240–4
59. NSC 100, Chairman of the National Security Resources Board to NSC, 11 January 1951
60. FRUS, 1951, iii, Part 1, pp. 708–9, 731, 748, 754
61. FRUS, 1951, i, 230–1; NSC 114/3, 18 October 1951
62. Kovrig, pp. 83–6
63. FRUS, 1951, i, 190–1
64. For an example of the debate in the West, see Kennan, ii, 253
65. Shulman, pp. 240–54; Wolfe, pp. 28–32
66. Gaddis (2) pp. 149–50
67. Gaddis (2) pp. 121–5, 147–63. See also Freedman, pp. 76–90
68. Gaddis (2) p. 151
69. Gaddis (2) p. 167
70. Gaddis (2) pp. 149–50. See also NSC 5501, 7 January 1955
71. NSC 162, 30 September 1953; see also NSC 141
72. NSC 5602/1, 15 March 1956
73. Gaddis (2) pp. 165–75, etc. See also NSC 153, 1 June 1953
74. NSC 5602/1, 15 March 1956; 5707/8, 3 June 1957

75. NSC 5820/1, 4 November 1958
76. US Senate, Cong. 86, sess. I, Committee on Foreign Relations, *United States Foreign Policy, the operational aspects* (Study no. 6, Washington DC 1959), *passim*
77. Schlesinger, pp. 433–42
78. NSC 162, 30 September 1953
79. NSC 5501, 7 January 1955
80. NSC 5602/1, 15 March 1956; 5707/8, 3 June 1957. In practice in 1958–60 the US turned down several opportunities to increase trade with Russia
81. Gaddis (2) p. 196
82. Mićunović, especially pp. 133, 153–7, 215, 338, 341–3, 431–2

Chapter 12

WORLD RIVALRIES, 1954–1968

THE UNITED STATES AND THE FAR EAST IN THE 1950s

Among the many developments which were necessary before people could begin to speak hopefully (some would now say prematurely) of an ending or at least a genuine lessening of the Cold War, four stood out. These were the relative (if temporary) stabilization of the nuclear arms race in the early 1970s, the general acceptance of the implications of a divided Europe, the rift between Russia and China, and the American search for an 'honourable' way out of the Vietnam War from 1968. It was not until the late 1960s and early 1970s that these began to interact in such a way as to encourage talk of East–West *détente*, and an end to the postwar era. Together they also encouraged a greater appreciation of the limits to the powers of even the greatest and richest of states. Ideology might still matter, but it was also essential to recognize the diversity of the communist and capitalist worlds. Intervention, direct or indirect, by the superpowers might still be successful, in Santo Domingo, Czechoslovakia and Chile, but Cuba and Yugoslavia as well as China were equally significant pointers to the future. If well into the 1950s it did not seem unreasonable to write of a Soviet threat from the 'heartland' to the Eurasian 'world island',such language seemed increasingly out of place by the end of the next decade. Revolutions by the Left were not master-minded by the Kremlin, and neither did the writ of Washington, Wall Street or multinational corporations run unchecked through the western world and its spheres of influence. Indeed, images of power politics which had broadly served since the 1890s (that is of a global game played by fewer and fewer participants) now needed qualification or replacement. To understand this new world one must understand the evolution of the four great issues mentioned above. One can conveniently start with American policy in the 1950s towards south-east Asia and towards China.

The first great test of the diplomatic skills of the major powers, once a peace of resignation and exhaustion had descended upon Korea, was the future of Indo-China, where the French resolve to continue the struggle against the Vietminh was clearly crumbling by the beginning of 1954 despite massive American aid. The thing which Washington had feared for some years – that the whole western position in south-east Asia might be about to crumble – seemed close to realization. Since at least 1949 the Americans had been in search of a policy for Indo-China. Reports from the region were often discouraging, and as early as 20 November 1950 the Deputy Director of the Mutual Defence Assistance Programme had suggested to Acheson that America might weaken itself elsewhere in the world if it backed a lost cause in Indo-China.[1] The Joint Chiefs of Staff at first opposed direct American military involvement, while the National Security Council on 17 May 1951 concluded that American intervention might do no more than buy time 'to build up the defense of the off-shore chain', and increase the price the Communists would have to pay for success in Indo-China. Many put their faith in American air and sea power, based on the offshore islands, notably Japan.[2] At the same time the Joint Chiefs and the President did not want to appear too defensively minded in the Far East. The services wanted to prevent, 'by all appropriate means, the further spread by force of Communism on the mainland of Asia . . . ' especially in Indo-China.[3] Truman approved a tough National Security Council (NSC 48/4) statement of 17 May 1951 which stressed the need to 'deflate Communist Chinese political and military prestige by inflicting heavy losses on Chinese forces in Korea', and which looked for ways to embarrass the Chinese leadership at home.

The economic importance or potential of south-east Asia continued to attract attention. It provided 90 per cent of the world's rubber and 60 per cent of its tin.[4] America's existing stockpiles were inadequate. The CIA argued that with control of south-east Asia the Communists would be self-sufficient in the Far East, with great bargaining power over Japan, and ultimately the West. Admittedly if Japan became Communist it seemed improbable that three such powerful (or potentially powerful) states as Japan, China and Russia could coexist indefinitely – a triangular rivalry of some sort was likely to develop.[5] There were hopes, too, that Malaya might remain part of the British Commonwealth. But a battle for opinion as well as territory was being waged: it was vital to show that communism could be resisted – even pushed back. It must not be seen as the tide of the future, especially in India and Japan. But against such calculations had to be set the unpleasant fact as stated by the American minister in Saigon on 24 February 1951 – Ho Chi Minh was the only Vietnamese who enjoyed 'any measure of national prestige'.[6] The weaknesses of the anti-communist forces throughout Indo-China were all too evident.

Nevertheless Washington was increasingly determined to believe that Americans might succeed where the French were failing. The latter, indeed, were looking hopefully for signs that the Vietminh (or Moscow, fearful of Chinese influence in south-east Asia) might be interested in a compromise peace.[7] In contrast an American inter-departmental committee claimed on 17 March 1954 that there was no substitute for victory. There was a growing consensus in Washington that at the very least America should make a show of its strength and resolve. Dulles was exploring a number of possibilities: the Joint Chiefs insisted on 12 March 1954 that the United States must on no account be associated with a compromise peace. They stressed the 'domino' danger: this might even extend to Japan, 'the keystone of US policy in the Far East'. China, with the resources of south-east Asia and Japan, would be more formidable than the Japanese Empire at its height. China would, it was claimed, ultimately control 'the entire Western and Southwestern Pacific region and would threaten South Asia and the Middle East'. It would be cheaper to fight in Indo-China than to quit.[8] But it was easier to say this than agree how it was to be done.

Admiral Radford's proposals for air strikes (and the possible use of nuclear weapons) to rescue the beleaguered French garrison at Dien Bien Phu were not supported by the other Chiefs of Staff or by the President. Dulles hoped to discourage the Communists by the creation of a position of overwhelming strength – a united stand by much of the free world in support of the French and the anti-communist indigenous forces in Indo-China. But for the French their impending defeat at Dien Bien Phu seemed the last straw. They were interested in American support, not to continue the war in Indo-China, but to strengthen their hand in cease-fire talks with the Vietminh. The British were dismayed by the thought of any involvement in Indo-China, and at times were sorely troubled by the apparent belligerence of the Americans. They were prepared to study only the defence of Thailand and perhaps other parts of south-east Asia (but excluding Indo-China), and above all they were anxious to explore the possibility of peace at the impending Geneva Conference. American uncertainties were also increasing as they took more account of the weakness of the indigenous anti-communist forces in Indo-China. Dulles reported from Europe on 29 April 1954 that the Russian and Chinese attitudes suggested that American intervention would be followed by that of China 'with [the] consequence of general war in Asia'. He concluded that a strong American lead was still essential, though not necessarily a military one.[9] Meanwhile in Washington Eisenhower opposed Radford's proposals for unilateral American action, and fully agreed with Congressional leaders that America must act only with allies.[10]

Dien Bien Phu fell on 8 May. Washington vainly sought concerted action with the French, Australians and the New Zealanders – leaving the British aside for the moment. The Joint Chiefs now favoured only air and naval intervention, arguing that the 'allocation of more than token U.S. armed forces in Indochina would be a serious diversion of limited U.S. capabilities'. At this time the strategic reserve consisted of only six divisions. Possibly twice as many would be needed if the United States became seriously involved in Indo-China.[11] Dulles therefore had no option but to work in the longer run for the formation of some sort of south-east Asian defence grouping (the British seemed inclined to co-operate here once the situation in Indo-China had been clarified). In the meantime he struck as tough a posture as he dared, surrounding American policy with an air of menace and uncertainty in the hope that this might impress the communist negotiators at Geneva. Eden, though often troubled by American policy, also appreciated that its nuclear power and its policy in general probably improved the bargaining position of the West, while Molotov certainly seemed to be keeping a somewhat apprehensive eye directed towards Washington.[12] Dulles indeed warned the Chinese in June that their involvement in Indo-China 'would be a deliberate threat to the United States itself' and that 'we could not escape ultimate responsibility for decisions closely touching our own security and self-defense'. Washington was in fact prepared to use nuclear weapons against Chinese military targets, though again only with Congressional approval and allied support.[13] There was much agonizing among the American leaders. Eisenhower wondered if any opportunity to internationalize the struggle against communism had been missed since 1950. The mood in Washington was a mixture of pessimism and frustrated militancy. Some acknowledged the danger of precipitating another war with China, which might produce a second Korean situation or initiate a slide towards a third world war. Some wished to maximize Asian support for American policies, and saw the need for restraint and caution in that context.[14]

Meanwhile at Geneva negotiations edged with painful slowness towards the cease-fire and other arrangements of 20–21 July 1954. These include a *de facto* partition of Vietnam along the 17th parallel, with provision for elections for a single government in 1956. Neither the interim regime in the South nor the United States was a signatory. Washington merely agreed not to use military force to upset the agreements but stated that it would view any violation with grave concern. Both the Russians and the Chinese seemed satisfied with the outcome – at least for the time being.The Chinese feared that a continuing war might result in the establishment of American bases in Laos. Both Moscow and Peking seemed troubled at times by the menacing attitude of the United States, and both in any case had plenty to preoccupy them at home. The Russians, too, may have feared that too hard a line would drive France into the arms of the Americans both in Asia and Europe (in the latter case this could tip the balance in France in favour of the European Defence Community).

As a temporary and uneasy peace descended on Indo-China from the end of July 1954, the western powers began to co-operate in the formation of the rather loose South East Asian Treaty Organization (SEATO). This came into being in September, and included the United States, Britain, France, Australia, New Zealand, Thailand and the Philippines. But Washington was also unilaterally pushing its interests in South Vietnam, displacing French influence, and – not without controversy in its own ranks – seeking to construct a solidly pro-American regime led by Ngo Dinh Diem. When General Lawton Collins reported sceptically on 7 April 1955 from Saigon concerning the prospects of the new government, Dulles angrily retorted that Diem was the best man available – an alternative leader might lean on the French rather than the United States.[15] Meanwhile American contingency plans continued to refer to the need to weaken China and to achieve the withdrawal of North Vietnam from the communist bloc. Mention was again made of the use of nuclear weapons in certain circumstances – such as against military targets within 'aggressor' states.[16] There was still more emphasis on the injury that American interests would suffer unless the trend in favour of communism in south-east Asia was reversed. Yet oddly enough some Americans also drew encouragement at this time from Russia's relative lack of interest in the region.

In their determination to find allies against communism, the Americans often found themselves in strange company. In the heat of the Korean War former criticisms of the Kuomintang were rapidly forgotten. Taiwan was now seen as an undisputed military asset, not least because it tied down Chinese troops which Peking might have liked to deploy elsewhere. The loss of the island, it was said, would encourage further Chinese aggression; it would injure western standing in Japan, the Philippines and Indonesia; communism would appear to be the wave of the future. This was not mere anti-communist emotionalism. No one in the mid-1950s could have foreseen the political geography of east Asia in the 1960s. Meanwhile the possibility of a Sino-Soviet rift was not forgotten, but little or nothing was done to encourage its development. Indeed, perhaps the most that can be said for Sino-American relations after 1953 is the degree to which the two powers learned a little of the arts of crisis management. Thus the two crises over the offshore islands held by the Kuomintang, though they had their dangerous moments, were handled with rather more skill and restraint than the public rhetoric of the two sides suggested. In the 1954–55 incident, one group of islands, the Tachens, was abandoned to the Communists as indefensible, but Quemoy and Matsu were retained by the Kuomintang as defensive outposts. Kuomintang efforts to use them offensively were discouraged by the Americans. The Chinese in 1954–55 stepped up the pressure on the two islands, but although there was some reference in Washington to tactical nuclear weapons, Eisenhower and his army Chief of Staff opposed even conventional bombing of the mainland, save *in extremis*. Both powers were able to pull back from the brink. The Chinese were doubtless disappointed by the lack of Soviet support (American pressure here was a way of underlining Sino-Soviet differences of interest), but they could still hope to find a more opportune time for action in the future.[17]

Unfortunately before 1958 Washington did not explore with any seriousness Chinese signals to the effect that they wished to enter into some sort of dialogue. The British picked up hints from the Russians as early as 1955 that they were not entirely satisfied with their relationship with the Chinese. The latter, meanwhile, were assiduously courting Asian neutralists with promises of peaceful coexistence. American diplomacy appeared heavy-footed in comparison. Jan Kalicki suggests that the strength of anti-communist feeling in the United States, and the influence of those in Congress who were particularly anxious to make an anti-communist stand in Asia, need not have inhibited the administration. There were plenty of Democrat votes to be picked up in Congress. Eisenhower did refuse to bind himself to the non-recognition of communist China in all circumstances, and by 1958 even Dulles seemed responsive to Peking's overtures. But by then it was too late as a new radical mood began to grip China. Indeed the Chinese were soon testing Russian and American feeling with new bombardments of Quemoy and Matsu. They were also provoked by the growing strength of the Kuomintang on the islands. Chiang Kai-shek was again able to hold the Americans captive since, although Washington was embarrassed by his actions, the American government had no wish to see Chiang suffer a major defeat. Thus there followed a second round of (fortunately 'controlled') 'brinkmanship'. Both the Chinese and Americans exercised restraint under cover of a great deal of sound and fury. There was no direct Chinese assault on the islands. The Americans devised means to keep the islands resupplied under fire, and sent in 8-inch howitzers as a pointer that tactical nuclear weapons could be used if necessary. The Russians gave the Chinese no significant support and the crisis gradually faded away. The Kuomintang presence on the islands, under American pressure, slowly became less provocative.[18]

THE SINO-SOVIET DISPUTE

Despite some western speculation concerning the durability of the Sino-Soviet alliance, and despite some hints that all might not be well between the two communist powers, western policy was not as yet influenced by the possibility of a rift between Moscow and Peking. Nevertheless this profoundly important development in the communist bloc was well under way by the late 1950s. It is not easy to separate reality from rhetoric, material causes from ideological rivalries, in any attempt to explain the origins of this dispute. With hindsight it is tempting to stress the apparent inevitability of the rift and the importance of underlying trends and basic differences, yet the fortuitous, circumstantial and immediate causes must not be forgotten.

Given China's size, vast population and proud history, together with the fact that Mao Tse-tung and his party had won their way to power largely by their own efforts, Russia could not expect Peking to accept for long a truly subordinate position in the communist bloc. Tito's Yugoslavia had pointed the way. But in the early 1950s Russia and China were being pushed together for a variety of reasons. The Cold War was at its height. China needed Russian arms when it became involved in the Korean War. In addition the Chinese Communists had inherited a massive task of economic reconstruction and development at home, and in the 1950s could expect to obtain foreign aid only from the Russians. The latter's share of Chinese trade rose from under one-quarter in 1950 to nearly 60 per cent in 1956 – its highest point. Russia provided short-term credits for about one-quarter of the goods supplied, and China continued to import more from Russia than she could export in return until 1956. She could obtain advanced equipment from almost no other source, and about half the machinery needed for the first Five Year Plan had to be imported. Russia was giving loans to no other country at this time. The machinery exported to China represented 2 per cent of her total production: exports to China represented nearly 1 per cent of her gross national product – not insignificant figures given Russia's own needs.[19] For a while after 1953 the Chinese were assisted by the death of Stalin and the uncertainties surrounding the future leadership of Russia. Khrushchev was welcomed by the Chinese as a hardliner compared with his rival, Malenkov, and Khrushchev in return made considerable concessions to the Chinese in October 1954.

Nevertheless the ending of the Korean War removed a vital common interest. As early as March 1954 the French thought the Russians were fearful of Chinese adventurism.[20] Later in the year the Chinese had cause to feel let down by Moscow over the question of the offshore islands. By this time both capitals were trying to broaden their options by the cultivation of Third World opinion, and a competitive element was soon to creep into these policies. Furthermore, in so far as the Chinese welcomed the rise of Khrushchev, they also sympathized to some extent with the desire of eastern European states to see some reduction in Russian influence over their affairs. A delicate balance had to be struck between the freedom of action of each individual state in the management of its affairs and the unity of the communist bloc as a whole. Thus, in Chinese eyes, the Yugoslavs were outlaws, whereas the Poles in 1956 received some support from Peking against Moscow. The Chinese, however, agreed with the Russian intervention against Hungary in 1956 – Hungarian actions were threatening the unity of the communist bloc. Khrushchev welcomed Chinese sympathy in that crisis, and was careful to woo Peking so long as his own position in Russia was in doubt – at least until October 1957. At the same time he was also giving aid to the Chinese in the hope that this would provide Russia with more influence over Chinese policy. In 1955, for instance, the Russians began to assist in the construction of a Chinese atomic reactor and cyclotron. Chinese nuclear physicists were admitted to a Russian nuclear research centre near Moscow. There were other examples of aid being given or withheld between 1957 and 1960 in an attempt to sway Chinese policy, and to influence the interplay of factions within the Chinese leadership.

The immediate origins of the Sino-Soviet dispute are to be found to a great extent in the bargaining processes whereby each sought to influence or gain advantages over the other. A bargaining relationship exists in any alliance, but in this case, for various reasons, it began to run out of control, almost certainly against the original intentions of the policy-makers. The Chinese themselves in 1963 attributed the start of the rift to Khruschchev's famous speech at the Twentieth Party Congress in February 1956 when he denounced Stalin and emphasized the 'peaceful transition' to socialism. Their claim should not be taken literally: they wished to present their case in terms which would appeal to Marxists. But at the same time the Chinese were probably troubled by Khrushchev's sudden, unilateral move. It was a blow to Chinese dignity. Had they to fall immediately into line behind every tactical shift by the Kremlin? They had no great reason to defend Stalin themselves, but they perhaps feared that Khrushchev's assault on the 'cult of personality' might damage Mao's standing.

In 1956–57 Sino-Soviet relations continued to turn on the question of reconciling the interests of individual communist states within the communist bloc under the leadership (but not the dictatorial leadership)of Russia. An agreed statement on these questions emerged from the Moscow Conference in November 1957, though probably only after difficult negotiations, and with the two countries tending to put their own gloss on the agreement, the Russians emphasizing their authority as the centre of the alliance, and the Chinese cherishing their autonomy. Certainly the Yugoslav ambassador in Moscow, Mićunović, was convinced that Sino-Soviet relations were not as they were said to be. He noted the first serious Chinese complaints against the Russians in his diary on 14 April 1957, and was struck by Sino-Soviet rivalry in Mongolia during his visit of June 1957.[21] In the autumn the Chinese leader was insisting that the East wind was prevailing over the West, and he gave more prominence to the Russian space success with the Sputnik, together with its military and political importance, than the Russians themselves desired. Mao argued that the time was ripe to step up the world revolutionary process. If the worst came to the worst in a general war, communism would still survive and triumph: mankind would not be annihilated by nuclear war. Mao's outspoken claims seemed designed to embarrass the Russians who, as a nuclear power (and one that knew its limitations compared with the Americans), appreciated that militant rhetoric must not be carried too far.

Mao, for his part, had gone to Moscow in November 1957 in the hope of extra support for both his domestic and foreign policies. China was suffering from many internal problems. An effort to accelerate economic growth had encountered many obstacles, including a poor harvest, heavy debt repayments to Russia and the strength of discontent revealed in the brief period of Chinese liberalization – the period of 'a hundred flowers'. For China this was a critical period, and the way forward was unclear. The Chinese delegation to Moscow in November 1957 included personnel who were interested in the acquisition of advanced Soviet equipment of all kinds. But there were signs too of a reluctance to become too dependent on Russia aid.[22] To modernize after the Russian model would require massive Russian help, but at what price to Chinese independence? The repression which followed the 'hundred flowers' also meant that China was even shorter of the professionals and experts of all kinds needed to implement a Russian-style modernization programme. On the Russian side, an agreement in October 1957 to supply nuclear arms to China must have included the intention to exert considerable control over Chinese foreign policy and strategy, and to prevent the emergence of China as an independent nuclear power. Thus by the end of 1957 the Russian and Chinese leaderships were often pulling in different directions, yet both sides still hoped to benefit from continued co-operation. Unity was needed in face of the West. Russia might expect to exert more influence over China through aid and co-operation. A breach with China would encourage centrifugal tendencies in the communist alliance as a whole. As for the Chinese, their foreign and domestic policies required more Russian support, but only on their terms.

From the spring of 1958 it seemed for a time as if the Chinese were opting for a radical and independent solution to their problems. The 'Great Leap Forward' campaign, with its mass mobilization and backyard industrialization, was publicized as a direct move towards communism; the socialist stage would be bypassed. To the Russians it had all the marks of a direct challenge to their authority and policies, and was criticized accordingly. Differences over foreign affairs also became more apparent in the summer of 1958. Internal unrest in the Lebanon and Jordan finally resulted in American and British intervention, encouraged by a successful revolution in Iraq. Washington and London believed that a show of western power and resolve was necessary to check the progress of radical Arab movements in the Middle East. But Khrushchev feared western intervention in Iraq as well. The new regime in Iraq was not communist, but Khrushchev feared for Russian prestige in the Middle East if the radicals suffered a major defeat. At the same time he clearly wished to avoid a major crisis with the United States. He therefore appealed to Eisenhower on 18 July 1958:

> We address you not from a position of intimidation but from a position of reason. We believe at this momentous hour that it would be more reasonable not to bring the heated atmosphere to boiling point; it is sufficiently inflammable as it is.

In contrast, the Chinese *People's Daily* on the following day was much more militant:[23]

> ... if the United States–British aggressors refuse to withdraw from Lebanon and Jordan, and insist on expanding their aggression, then the only course left to the people of the world is to hit the aggressors on the head!

This is a good example of the efforts of the Chinese to court radical and revolutionary opinion in the world – in competition with the Russians. In August and September 1958 they renewed their bombardment of the offshore islands held by the Kuomintang, and doubtless included in their calculations were hopes that the Russians would either be shamed into support of some kind or would be humiliated if they failed to act. In contrast, the Russians were interested in the possibility of a new defence relationship with the Chinese in the Far East, with themselves as the senior partner. Chinese conduct of this kind was not at all to their taste, and they were content to save face as best they could over Quemoy and Matsu when they felt it was safe to do so.

The collapse of the 'Great Leap Forward' and the temporary eclipse of Mao himself in the first half of 1959 brought a temporary improvement in relations. Khrushchev offered more aid, evidently in the hope that this might strengthen the 'pragmatists' among the Chinese leaders. P'eng Te-huai, the Minister of Defence, was pro-Russian and was anxious to secure Russian equipment to modernize the Chinese armed forces. But in June 1959 the Russians withdrew whatever offer they had made to the Chinese concerning nuclear weapons, while in a renewed battle within China P'eng fell from power and was disgraced soon after he had made his bitter attack on the radical policies of the recent past at the Lu Shan plenum in August 1959. At the Bucharest Conference in 1960 Khrushchev was reported as speaking up for P'eng, claiming that his only offence had been to oppose Mao's incorrect policies towards the Soviet Union. In September 1959 Sino-Soviet relations worsened when the Russians adopted a neutral stance over a border conflict between the Chinese and Indians, and when Khrushchev not only visited the United States (and appeared to make some progress towards a better relationship) but compounded his crime, when in Peking at the end of the month, by making thinly disguised complaints against Chinese militancy in foreign affairs. He attacked those who wished to 'test by force the stability of the capitalist system', and implied that the Chinese should temporarily accept the separation of Taiwan from the mainland. Nor can the Chinese have been ignorant of rumours that Khrushchev was hoping for an agreement with the West which would include the denial of nuclear weapons to the Chinese. Peking apprehensively watched the preparations for the Summit Conference in Paris between Russia and the western powers. Indirect and implicit criticism of Khrushchev's hopes of an agreement with the United States increased. The ninetieth anniversary of Lenin's birth in April 1960 was used by the Chinese to publicize their faith in uninterrupted revolution at home and in enthusiastic support for revolution abroad.

From 1957 Russia and China had been clearly exerting mounting pressure on each other in the hope that each would follow policies more in accord with the wishes of the other. But no compromise was possible when the Russians wanted essentially an obedient and dependent China, whereas Mao wished to be a revisionist in foreign affairs (and indulge in at least revolutionary rhetoric), a major force within the communist bloc, and a radical with distinctive policies at home. It is true that China's stance on nuclear weapons and revolution was less militant than it appeared, but its encouragement of revolutionaries, even if it stressed that they must be self-reliant, was injuring its relations with some Third World states which it had carefully cultivated in the mid-1950s. The question of Tibet and border disputes produced tension with India in particular.

From 1960 Khrushchev was branding Mao as another Stalin, an ultra-Leftist, an ultra-dogmatist and a Left revisionist. He added for good measure that China's dispute with India was purely a national quarrel which injured the cause of world communism. The Chinese retorted that Khrushchev was the revisionist and that it was his foreign policy which threatened the cause of communism. Although only the Albanians openly supported the Chinese, some other communist parties were troubled by Khrushchev's vehemence. Even the Russians and Chinese were reluctant to publicize their differences to the rest of the world, but the furious debate at the Third Congress of the Communist Party of Rumania in June 1960 was followed by the withdrawal of Russian experts and advisers from China. They took with them even their blueprints, causing considerable economic disruption in the process.

A veiled press war began to develop between Russia and China. Yugoslavia and Albania served as surrogates for Russia and China as the verbal conflict was intensified. Differences burst fully into the open at the next meeting, the Twenty-Second Party Congress in Moscow in October 1961, when the Chinese melodramatically laid a wreath on Stalin's tomb to demonstrate their defiance of the Russians. The latter replied by removing Stalin's body from its place of honour. Soon after this some western communist parties began to publish accounts of the split, and by 1963 even the pseudonyms of Yugoslavia and Albania for Russia and China were dropped as Peking and Moscow intensified their exchange of polemical broadsides.

The extent of Sino-Soviet differences was also highlighted by the 1962 Cuban missile crisis and the brief war between India and China. In March 1963 the Chinese claimed that they, and not the Russians, were the true heirs of Marx and Lenin. In a paraphrase of the *Communist Manifesto* of 1848 the Chinese asserted: 'A spectre is haunting the world – the spectre of genuine Marxist–Leninism, and it threatens you [Khrushchev]. You have no faith in the people, and the people have no faith in you. You are divorced from the masses. That is why you fear the truth.' Another bitter attack followed on 31 July 1963. The Chinese were dismayed by Russia's role in the nuclear test-ban talks which finally resulted in a limited agreement with the West. China, however, was able to carry out its own nuclear test in October 1964. The fall of Khrushchev in the same month triggered off only the briefest speculation that a new start might be possible in Sino-Soviet relations with the disappearance of so controversial and provocative a figure. The breach was complete, with the Chinese now looking for support in particular among the less developed peoples of the world.

Though the dispute was waged with much reference to Marxist ideology, national interest was clearly the main determinant. Doubtless the perceptions of the leaders were coloured to some extent by ideology, yet even this may be questioned in the case of Khrushchev. In Mao one senses a continuing struggle between the romantic and practical revolutionary, the Sino-Marxist theoretician and the day-to-day leader. In the earlier rift between Russia and Yugoslavia, Dedijer thought that it began as a power struggle, but that it was subsequently fought out 'with a strange kind of fire, like the disputes between medieval Christian sects'.[24] But ideology was used above all to legitimize the positions of the two governments, and to try to win friends and influence people. Nor did the collision arise primarily because the two countries were at different stages of economic development. This mattered mainly in the sense that it was a cause of the original dependence of China on Russia, so that Russia was encouraged to try to make use of this dependence to influence Chinese conduct. It is more revealing to ask what drove the two governments into the close working relationship of the earlier 1950s. At that stage common interests were clearly in the ascendant with the Cold War at its worst, with China's dependence on outside assistance being at its peak for both internal and external reasons, with Russia being clearly inferior to the United States in nuclear weapons, and with the Russian leadership in some disarray following the death of Stalin. For various reasons in the mid-1950s the two countries could hope that partnership might still be useful, though even then the elements of rivalry were rapidly resurfacing. Soon each was demanding too much of the other, and thereafter the divisive trends became dominant. The differing priorities and interests of Russia and China finally drove them apart.[25]

THE VIETNAM WAR

Given the palpable existence of the Sino-Soviet split by the early 1960s, and the appearance of other, lesser divisions in the communist monolith of the previous decade, it may seem surprising to posterity that the United States should still have embarked upon the tragic and horrific struggle in Indo-China to try to stem the further advance of communism in south-east Asia. True, American policy was not formulated at this time without a measure of debate and soul-searching. Doubts and reservations were expressed: alternative strategies were mentioned. But the United States had already become so committed to the containment of communism in this region that a change of policy was not easily contemplated in the absence of some compelling new development which would have forced a reappraisal of American priorities. The Sino-Soviet rift failed to arrest the momentum of existing policy: indeed, at times it may have increased American hopes of success.

Nevertheless, as we have seen, American involvement in southeast Asia had developed in piecemeal fashion from the late 1940s, and always under the influence of American global perceptions of the Cold War and the threat of communism. The American commitment to the Diem regime in South Vietnam from the mid-1950s had a touch of desperation about it. Dulles argued in 1955 that Diem should be supported, if only to buy time. The Joint Chiefs were often critical of the Diem regime, arguing that the United States needed as friends governments which were capable of promoting peaceful change in Asia.[26] How such governments were to be found or created was another matter. Washington, though often disappointed by India's anti-American attitudes, became increasingly interested in its success as a non-communist country. Economic aid was granted to India in the hope that it would prove an attractive Asian alternative to communist China – that is, as a model of economic and political progress.[27] Meanwhile in Vietnam the Americans were encouraged when the year 1956 passed without any serious communist efforts to insist on the elections promised by the 1954 Geneva agreements to determine the future of the whole of Vietnam. There were rumours in 1957 that the Russians might be willing to recognize South Vietnam. But major disappointments soon followed. The North Vietnamese Communists were steadily overcoming their internal problems, whereas no comparable consolidation was taking place in the South. By 1959 Communist and other forms of opposition to Diem were gaining ground. Aid from the North was not significant at this stage, though in the long run it was to be of prime importance that South Vietnam, unlike South Korea, because of its long borders, was so vulnerable to infiltration from Laos and Cambodia as well as from North Vietnam.

In so far as the Americans recognized the nature of the gamble upon which they had embarked in Vietnam, they justified it with the argument that the loss of the South would be far more serious than the loss of, say, South Korea.[28] By the early 1960s there was a new consideration. The fear was growing in Washington that the main threat to the West might now come from 'wars of national liberation' which even Khrushchev professed to support. It was argued in the National Security Council on 25 July 1960 that the will of south-east Asians to resist communism was dependent on their confidence in American military backing.[29] But in the Eisenhower era the funds were not available to encourage the armed forces to think in terms of serious military involvement in such areas, and many of the military themselves were not anxious to repeat the

Korean experience. This began to change as the situation continued to deteriorate in South Vietnam. So divided were the anti-communist forces that the North Vietnamese government described the political struggle as the primary one and, given time, it expected the Diem regime to collapse in the face of a general popular uprising.[30] The new Kennedy administration which took office in January 1961, however, was much more willing than its predecessor to spend money on military aid and on America's own defence forces. It argued that the American ability to resist communism was restricted when undue reliance was placed on nuclear weapons. The United States needed larger and more versatile conventional forces to give its diplomacy credibility in lesser as well as the most serious emergencies. The strategy of 'flexible response' (that is, the substitution of conventional weapons as far as possible for nuclear weapons) was to be applied globally, and Kennedy himself took a personal interest in the literature on guerrilla warfare and its possible antidotes. One of his most influential military advisers, General Maxwell Taylor, was a well-known advocate of large conventional forces, including those suited to 'brushfire' operations to prove that the West could defeat 'wars of national liberation'. Another influential figure, Professor Walt Rostow, who – at least in print – had taken a dangerously simplistic view of American 'appeasement' of Stalin in eastern Europe at the end of the war, was anxious to 'face down' communism wherever it was to be found, especially in the Third World.[31] It is important to remember that, despite the tension in Europe – notably over Berlin in 1961 – the administration was reasonably confident that its lead in nuclear weapons, with small increases to NATO's conventional strength, would enable it to meet any Russian challenge. The Kremlin under Khrushchev was not seen as fanatically or fatally aggressive, but as engaged in a desperate search for remedies to the many weaknesses in the Russian position. America had resources to spare for the struggle in south-east Asia.

Communist influence in Laos appeared to confirm the truth of the 'domino' theory, while at an inter-departmental meeting on 29 April 1961, Chester Bowles spoke of the probability of war with China within ten years. Curtis Le May for the air force commented that if that were the case it would be wiser to fight before China acquired nuclear weapons.[32] Here was language reminiscent of Germany in 1912–14. But this meeting, like the German 'War Council' of December 1912, was inconclusive. On Laos at least Kennedy was ready to work for a compromise with the Russians, but more than a year was to elapse before a settlement of sorts was achieved. Indeed, in the autumn of 1961 the Chiefs of Staff advocated military intervention, despite the current crisis over Berlin, on the grounds that American forces in Laos would check infiltration from North Vietnam into the South, and would also help to protect the Thai border. Kennedy, however, preferred to protect South Vietnam through a policy of military aid to Diem. The need for political and other reforms was stressed by some of his advisers – military solutions were not enough. Even a hardliner such as Secretary of State Dean Rusk could ask whether Diem would take advantage of American assistance by introducing reforms, and commented that the United States might find itself backing the wrong horse. Maxwell Taylor agreed that American intervention could become open-ended, but was already inclined to seek an answer in direct pressure on North Vietnam, Robert McNamara, the Secretary of Defence, accepted that it might be possible to prevent northern involvement in the South only with the threat of American retaliation. He also antici-pated that the South might require the support of up to 200,000 American troops. The President agreed, however, to no more than new contingency plans.[33] American efforts to coax reforms from Diem in the winter of 1961–62 were unsuccessful, and an intelligence estimate of 21 February 1962 gloomily concluded that the Commu-nists could hope to win by primarily political methods, so ineffectual was the opposition.

By this time, too, the United States was displaying increasing awareness of Russian caution and even lack of interest in south-east Asia. But this did not reduce American concern. Rather, this was followed by the argument that any separation of Russia from North Vietnam and China would enable the last two to pursue even more militant policies.[34] Even if the Chinese showed restraint (and this was thought likely), a communist advance achieved by North Vietnam alone would still impress neighbouring states and enhance the pres-tige and influence of communism. Thus the debate, however struc-tured, tended to circle back to the same conclusion. This occurred although the new administration in Washington was perhaps even more conscious of the strength of nationalism than its predecessor, and despite its awareness of the growing pressures and diversity within the communist world. It had more sympathy for the non-aligned, and was a little troubled by the character of the Right-wing extremist regimes with which the United States was associated. Yet it could not bring itself to run the risk of unopposed communist gains. Kennedy to the end argued so long as neither Russia nor China controlled Europe and Asia, 'then our security was assured'. The fear that one power or alliance could master the 'World Island' was still present.[35]

Yet there are occasional hints that Kennedy wished to explore alternative possibilities, and that he was trying to keep an open mind. Thus Senator Mike Mansfield visited south-east Asia at his request, and reported at the end of 1962. Mansfield, a former admirer of Diem, feared that America was about to be drawn into a disastrous and unwinnable war. He conceded that if south-east Asia were deemed an 'essential' American interest the country must act accordingly (but as time passed he was to press with growing conviction for a political solution).[36] Kennedy sometimes talked of American disengagement, and always insisted that it was South Vietnam's war. But he was anxious to give the South every chance to win, and the aid programmes were thus stepped up. He also claimed that he dared not show himself as 'soft' on communism – or certainly not until he had been re-elected in 1964. Kennedy, however, was assassinated on 22 November 1963, and it is idle to speculate on his policy had he lived. Certainly he possessed some advisers who were looking for alternatives to the policy that was being pursued. In addition ideas for the neutralization of the South were circulating in Paris, Hanoi and even Saigon. Some form of coalition government was mooted.[37] But the hardliners in Washington questioned the durability of such a solution, and under a new President, Lyndon B. Johnson, they set out to prove that communism could not win. In the light of what followed the United States would have been wiser had it explored the political possibilities in 1963–64.

As it happened, Kennedy's assassination took place soon after the overthrow of Diem by dissident Vietnamese generals, a step favoured by many Americans in the hope that a stronger government would emerge in Saigon. In practice the political condition of the South rapidly deteriorated. The American Joint Chiefs recognized the scale of the political and economic as well as the military problems, but drew some comfort from the current agricultural crisis in China and from the Sino-Soviet rift. These, they hoped, would discourage serious Chinese intervention. They continued to insist that communist faith in 'wars of national liberation' had to be destroyed otherwise outbreaks in Africa and Latin America would follow. The new President agreed to the preparation of plans for the exertion of 'graduated pressure' on North Vietnam, and strongly opposed all 'neutralist' talk. Instead he hoped that a Russo-Chinese 'showdown'would soon occur as this might make action against the North 'more practicable'.[38]

De Gaulle's suggestions for a great international conference to tackle the Vietnamese question therefore came to nothing. He correctly doubted if the Chinese were as expansionist as the Americans claimed, but he could not circumvent the American fear that talks *of any kind* might wreck such resolve and strength as remained in South Vietnam, and deliver the country to communism.[39] Already in June 1964 the Johnson administration was talking of the desirability of a Congressional Resolution to give the President special powers to take action in south-east Asia. A naval 'incident'in the Gulf of Tonkin provided the opportunity in August 1964 and the Resolution was duly secured. Nevertheless some critical voices were still to be heard inside the administration. A CIA report of June 1964 even questioned the 'domino' theory: it thought it possible to confine communism to Indo-China, given the power that the United States would still be able to wield with its air and sea forces – a return, in other words, to the peripheral strategy. In November a National Security Council working group concluded that if the general management was centred in Hanoi, the 'primary sources of Communist strength in South Vietnam . . . [remained] indigenous'. It also stressed the difficulty of trying to reverse the situation in south-east Asia.[40] But to arguments of this kind William Bundy, for instance, replied early in 1965 that while the proposed strategy of 'graduated response' was not assured of success, it was better to try and fail than to do nothing. It was vital to demonstrate to other friends of America to what lengths Washington was prepared to go on their behalf. Bundy finally argued that even if a communist Vietnam were to prove independent of Russia and China, a communist victory of any kind would still be a grave blow to American standing and influence.[41] In so far as the American leadership ever produced a justification for its policy in Vietnam which made sense in an imperfect world, especially a world of *realpolitik*, this was it. The Communists had to be taught that even if they were to win, it could only be at enormous cost. Divisions in the communist world, it was argued, made no difference, since any form of communist success encouraged others, and threatened the strength and morale of their opponents. Yet this was a form of *realpolitik* which a Bismarck would have dismissed as simplistic, just as he had opposed demands for preventive war in 1887.

McNamara commented in July 1965 that the United States had three options: to withdraw, to fight on broadly as at present, or to try to prove to the Communists that they could not win. He thought the last the best policy, especially as there seemed to be little risk of war with Russia or China – given restraint in American bombing of the North. Care was also needed here so as not to alarm America's main allies. McNamara was not always so decided, and was to conclude in 1966 that the 'reasons why we went into Vietnam . . . are now largely academic'.[42] Expectations of success certainly varied in the administration, but the year 1965 saw the start of a massive deployment of American military strength in South Vietnam, and the beginning of the bombing of the North. The plan was to intensify this step by step until the North was driven to negotiate, though many feared that even in those circumstances the United States would be able to do no more than prevent a complete communist victory in the South. Not surprisingly many historians have asked why the American government, especially given the deplorable political condition of South Vietnam from the end of 1963, did not opt for a policy of gradual disengagement. Apart from the reasoning touched on above, it is clear that President Johnson was haunted by the political furore which had accompanied the 'loss of China' in the late 1940s. He was determined not to be the first American President to lose a war. The easier political choice in the mid-1960s was to fight on, especially when it seemed that such a decision would have no serious budgetary or military consequences for the United States. The economic cost of the war was grossly underestimated, and there were no emergencies elsewhere in the world to make a significant call on American military strength to encourage a reappraisal of American strategic priorities. Thus in June 1967 the Chiefs of Staff were still opposing any 'major realignment of US objectives' in southeast Asia, or any lessening of the American military pressure on North Vietnam.[43]

On the other hand criticism of the war within the United States was increasing rapidly. The country was also torn by recurrent violence over civil rights from the summer of 1965. By 1967–68 opinion in America was more divided than at any time since the Civil War. A growing number of American intellectuals insisted there must be an end to international crusades. Senator Fulbright was an early leader in this field with his aptly named book, *The Arrogance of Power* (1967). McNamara joined those who favoured withdrawal – with honour. Johnson, however, continued to hope that real military progress would be achieved before the 1968 presidential election. Thus the turning-point did not come until the beginning of that year when the Vietcong launched a spectacular, if militarily unsuccessful offensive. But it was the moral effect of the Tet offensive which mattered. The American commander in Vietnam began to talk in terms of half a million American troops to achieve a victory of sorts. To acquire such numbers Johnson realized that he would have to appeal to Congress. It would be necessary to call up reserve units. Nor was it possible any longer to ignore the economic cost of the war. Other government policies, at home and abroad, were in danger as Vietnam devoured more and more resources. At last the 'hawks' in Washington began to take heed of warnings from various sources that America's bombing of the North and South, and its extravagant ground offensives against the Vietcong were inflicting much less damage on the enemy than was commonly believed. It was the United States which was finding the costs of the war unacceptable.

On 31 March 1968 Johnson announced that he would not run again for the presidency, suspended the bombing north of the 20th parallel and reiterated his interest in peace. Although the war, for America, continued until January 1973, this was the essential confession of failure – the acceptance of defeat by the world's strongest power at the hands of a small Asiatic people. It is true that North Vietnam was dependent upon Russian and Chinese aid. The United States was never free to throw its full weight against North Vietnam in case the communist giants to the north felt obliged to step in to ensure its survival. But with these reservations this was still a remarkable triumph for North Vietnam and its allies in the South – one quite without parallel in modern times. It was the outstanding, though not the only demonstration of the enhanced capabilities of disciplined, strongly motivated nationalist forces in the face of a superstate. The contrast with the fate of lesser peoples under serious military pressure from a major power before 1945 was complete.

BERLIN, CUBA AND THE TEST-BAN TREATY

To the peoples of south-east Asia, ravaged by American fire-power, a description of the Vietnam War as a limited conflict must seem a classic example of imperialist hypocrisy. Nevertheless this war fits into the largely unwritten rules, conventions and understandings which had grown up between the superpowers from 1945, and which together imposed some restrictions on their rivalries. Thus the war in Korea had been geographically localized, the communist forces being allowed a sanctuary in Manchuria, while the West was not harassed by submarines at sea. Gradually from 1945 much was accepted, mostly informally, concerning the rights and privileges of each superpower within its own clearly delimited sphere of influence. Although fear of general war, and increasingly of nuclear war – especially from the 1950s – encouraged caution and restraint behind the rhetoric and displays of power, one must not discount the contribution of other stabilizing forces.

Historians cannot hope as yet to assess the significance of the reiterated expressions of Marxist–Leninist confidence that history was on their side (whether the imperialists resorted to war or not), or the restraining influence of liberal, humanitarian opinion on policy-makers in the West. In practice it can only be noted that neither western nor eastern leaders were inhibited in the use of force when interest demanded and circumstances permitted, as in Vietnam, Korea, Hungary, Czechoslovakia, Egypt (Suez) or, more recently, in Afghanistan, to mention but the most obvious examples. Force, however, was used primarily within spheres of influence, or – usually with a wary eye on major rivals – in the grey areas of the world. Furthermore, although reciprocal nuclear deterrence began to operate effectively and comprehensively only from the mid-1950s, in the preceding decade war-weariness and the enormous task of postwar reconstruction had done much to discourage adventurous foreign policies. It is true that neither the Russians nor the Americans were well satisfied with the postwar world, yet neither was sufficiently dissatisfied (or hopeful of relatively easy success) for a general war to seem a plausible line of policy to any but the most fanatical and ignorant. There were indeed some western advocates of a preventive war against communism (for a time Bertrand Russell exemplified the limitations of logic as a guide to political action), particularly as long as the United States held a monopoly in nuclear weapons. This, as we have seen, was not viewed as a realistic military or political option by American policy-makers. The power equation between East and West at that time was extraordinarily complex, especially if one includes political and economic as well as military factors. It meant little to add up numbers of atomic bombs, army divisions, steel production figures and many other statistics in isolation from each other. What is plain to the historian is that each side was more intent on consolidation than expansion beyond the lines broadly established at the time of the defeat of Germany and Japan in 1945. Limited adventures alone seemed permissible.

But what might appear self-evident to the historian did not necessarily appear so to contemporaries on either side of the Iron Curtain. Each was more aware of its weaknesses than were its opponents: each had difficulty in evaluating the capabilities and still more the intentions of the other. As we have already seen, intentions and capabilities may combine in very different ways to produce a decision for war. Thus no power in the twentieth century tried so ruthlessly to match intentions and capabilities, or to maximize its opportunities as Nazi Germany. In contrast, Japan in 1904, and to a lesser extent Germany in 1914, went to war rather than see a temporary military advantage eroded. It is interesting that in the early 1950s some western planners feared that Russia might think herself in a similar position. Unfortunately one cannot tell how Soviet planners viewed the United States during its years of atomic monopoly. Nevertheless, if there were some resemblances between the calculations of the British government at the time of Suez in 1956 and those of Austria-Hungary in 1914, the United States in 1956 did not share the feelings of Wilhelmine Germany nor the Soviet Union those of Tsarist Russia. Indeed, neither superpower from 1945 had cause to see its problems or future in quite such stark life-and-death terms as Germany and Japan in the first half of the twentieth century. Neither had cause to see its place in the world in the form of a briefly opened window of opportunity, an opportunity to be snatched or lost forever. Each had more, if not total reason to feel that time was on its side – if not necessarily to achieve exclusive supremacy, then at least to secure a shared if uneasy and highly competitive position at the top.

Not surprisingly the achievement of even a small measure of confidence and stability in the relationship of the superpowers took time. Each viewed the other's advances within its own sphere – and still more in the grey areas of the world – with the utmost jealousy and concern. But in Europe, in the 1950s, the Russians could not prevent the gradual integration of West Germany within the western alliance. Russia chose not to risk a general war to prevent this happening. Equally unrest in eastern Europe in 1953, and Russia's intervention in Hungary in 1956, demonstrated – if any demonstration were necessary – that the United States possessed no effective means of challenging Russia's influence in the east other than through general war. Nevertheless no solid progress in East–West relations was possible until both sides were not only reconciled to the division of Germany, but also were reasonably satisfied that their respective shares of Germany were securely attached to one or the other alliance. By the later 1950s the West was making more rapid progress towards this object than the Russians. Whatever the delays over rearmament, the economic recovery of West Germany was remarkable, and its attachment to the western alliance provided much hope for the future. Very different was the situation in East Germany where large numbers of the population, especially among the professional and skilled groups, were voting with their feet in an exodus to the West. The injury to the economy of East Germany was serious, and politicial confidence was shaken. For the Russians this was a highly disturbing state of affairs, and by 1961 a solution had become imperative.

Khrushchev provoked the first mini-crisis over Berlin in November 1958 when he demanded the transformation of West Berlin into a 'free city' and its evacuation by western occupation forces. But Khrushchev's efforts to impose a time-limit on the negotiations, and his threats of a separate agreement between Russia and East Germany, though creating periods of tension, all ran into the sand as the western powers, not without some discord and uncertainty, managed to stand firm. Khrushchev's volatile personality and his abrupt tactical shifts from conciliation to belligerence made it difficult for the West to assess his real intentions. Thus Macmillan, the British Prime Minister, was to be found anxiously speculating at times whether Khrushchev was really a megalomaniac – another Hitler – or someone with whom one could do business. But at other times it was the seeming underlying subtlety of the Russian diplomatic strategy which was most worrying. If the West adopted an entirely negative attitude over West Berlin, the continuing tension seemed likely to excite divisions among opinion in the West – to lead to complaints that the game was not worth the candle, to agitation in favour of a compromise and to renewed suggestions for a fresh approach to the whole German question. Alternatively, if the West made concessions over West Berlin, this might well be interpreted as a sacrifice of West German aspirations, thus causing injury to the western alliance. In western eyes, therefore, far more was at stake than the recognition and consolidation of the new status quo in

Germany – the problem was affecting the unity and strength of the western alliance. Thus, whether the prime Russian aim was the relief of the problems of East Germany or the weakening of the overall western position in Germany, the effect was much the same. The western leaders groped for policies which would retain the confidence of West Germans, yet sought to present them in such a way as to minimize unease elsewhere among western opinion.

In fact as the year 1959 wore on neither the Russians nor the Americans seemed anxious to box themselves into a corner. Khrushchev's Camp David talks with Eisenhower in September 1959 were inconclusive, but agreement to hold a Summit Conference in Paris in the spring of 1960 generated some optimism. This conference, however, collapsed before it had formally begun, ostensibly because of Khrushchev's demands for an American apology following the shooting down of an American spy plane over Russia – the U-2 incident. But it is possible that Khrushchev used the episode to wreck the conference because he foresaw that no worthwhile western concessions would be forthcoming on Berlin or Germany. The war of nerves continued, though in November 1960 both the American State and Defence Departments were reasonably confident that Russian pressure over Berlin would stop short of war.[44] Small cuts to American forces in Europe, and relatively modest increases in American defence spending overall reflected this assurance. The new Kennedy administration took a more expansionist approach in 1961, but it did so in the belief that Russia's conventional strength had been exaggerated, and that with some additions NATO would be able to move over to a strategy of 'flexible responses' and thereby become much less dependent on nuclear weapons in the face of a Russian attack.[45] The building of the Berlin Wall in August 1961 by the Russians and East Germans, though it produced a temporary crisis, was basically an acknowledgement of defeat by Khrushchev. The accelerating flight of East Germans to the West demanded instant action if there was to be any hope of stability in East Germany. Khrushchev no longer had the time to hope and work for western concessions or western dissension. But however ruthless the 'Wall' as a solution to East Germany's loss of people, it was one which worked. The problems of East Germany were gradually brought under control in the 1960s, and as the confidence of its government grew, so the West Germans were driven to accept the fact of a divided Germany, and the possibility of a more constructive East – West dialogue in Germany and Europe as a whole began to emerge. But it must be reiterated that constructive negotiations were possible only when both sides broadly accepted the status quo which had been emerging since 1945, and when both sides believed they had nothing vital to lose by entering into such talks.

Tension over Berlin and Germany between 1958 and 1962 was

complemented by the fears aroused by the arms race. There had, it is true, been a variety of negotiations on disarmament throughout the 1950s, and from 1958 special attention was devoted to the question of banning nuclear tests, partly in response to public concern over the radioactive contamination of the atmosphere. Indeed, an informal moratorium on nuclear testing was in existence for almost three years from October 1958. It was broken by the Soviet Union at the end of August 1961 as the Russians tried to lessen the American nuclear lead. At this time it was becoming increasingly apparent that, far from there being a 'missile gap' which placed the West at a disadvantage, the United States was once more pulling rapidly ahead of the nuclear armoury of the Soviet Union. As Kennedy's Secretary of Defence, Robert McNamara later conceded, the Russians might have feared that the United States was trying to secure a first-strike capability – that is, the ability to knock out the bulk of the Soviet nuclear force before it could be used against the United States – and thereby attain a position to win a nuclear war.[46] Indeed, of the current scenarios for the outbreak of nuclear war, perhaps the most plausible was that of one side letting loose its arsenal in the mistaken belief that it was about to fall victim to a preemptive strike by the other superpower. Bombers, it was true, could be launched and then recalled. But not missiles! Thus the peace of the world – and its whole future – could hang on the correct interpretation of radar signals, on the perfect control of all nuclear delivery systems and on safeguards against the most improbable accidents and mistakes. The possibilities of human error, mechanical malfunction, atmospheric oddities (wild geese over the North Pole were once taken for a rocket salvo on a radar screen), let alone the intervention of a deranged personality or a group of fanatics, generated understandable alarm. Nor could sufficient assurance be found in the argument that Moscow and Washington were equally alive to these problems, and that sufficient understanding would exist in each of these capitals for both to pause even in a moment of acute crisis. Indeed, everything that related to pre-emptive or first-strike warfare was highly damaging to international confidence, from fears of war by accident to the desperate remedial actions of any power which feared it was being thrust towards a position of palpable inferiority to its rival without the assurance of being able to strike back with devastating, and therefore deterring, effect.

As early as 1946 Bernard Brodie in contributions to *The Absolute Weapon: Atomic Power and World Order* had argued that a state could guard itself against nuclear attack provided it could always retaliate in kind. An attacker had to be sure that it would not suffer on the same scale as its victim. The 'survivability' of the American nuclear arsenal had not been overlooked in the Eisenhower era once the Russians began to pose a significant threat to the homeland, but it was Churchill who gave the notion its most colourful expression at this time. He spoke on 1 March 1955 of 'the value of deterrents, immune against surprise and well understood by all persons on both sides . . . who have the power to control events'. Given the fulfilment of these conditions he believed that safety might prove 'the sturdy child of terror, and survival the twin brother of annihilation'. He concluded hopefully that after a certain point had been reached in the arms race, 'The worse things get, the better.' It was not to be as simple as that, with certain ideas requiring elaboration and certain weapon technologies requiring development before a mutual state of deterrence was created. In the late 1950s, for instance, 'survivability' in the Strategic Air Command took the crude form of maintaining a number of heavy bombers in the air at all times, with a number at short stand-by notice on the ground. This was expensive, but it was also effective and made full use of the flexibility provided by the manned aircraft. The Russians, with great difficulty, were acquiring a long-range bomber force by the mid-1950s, but they recoiled from the cost of acquiring anything comparable with the Strategic Air Command, and chose instead to put their faith in long-range rockets. Their initial success, however, merely encouraged the Americans to accelerate their own programmes, and by 1961 it was evident that in this field, too, the Americans were well ahead.

Although the American missile programmes of the 1950s were much influenced by inter-service rivalry, out of this struggle emerged revolutionary weapon systems which promised to reduce the risk of accidental nuclear war. Three developments were of crucial importance. The first generation of missiles were liquid fuelled. They were unreliable, and could not be maintained in a state of high alert. This made them vulnerable to a pre-emptive first strike. The next generation had solid fuel and could be maintained in a high state of readiness. The provision of silos for land-based missiles, and nuclear submarines (which could launch missiles from the ocean depths) meant that an almost indestructible nuclear deterrent was at the disposal of the United States in the early 1960s. Certainly it was safe from a Russian first strike in the foreseeable future. Unfortunately the Americans were making such rapid progress in the early 1960s that the Russians began to feel dangerously exposed. They were well behind the Americans in the acquisition of comparable weapons, and understandably began to look for ways in which to redress the balance as quickly as possible. It was this consideration above all which led to the most dramatic East–West confrontation of the whole Cold War – the Cuban missile crisis of 1962.

Soviet conduct in Cuba in 1962 was out of character – even of Khrushchev at his pyrotechnic worst. The decision to place missiles in Cuba was extraordinarily reckless – which strengthens the argument that it was prompted by feelings of desperation. It is of course impossible to know what allowances Russian contingency planning made for miscalculation – the possibility of an extreme American response, and the need for a Russian bolt-hole. Although the Russians achieved partial success in their attempt to introduce the missiles secretly into Cuba, the operation as a whole at times suggested poor co-ordination between the various units involved, not least in the efforts at camouflage. The thoroughness of some of the planning must be questioned, but in particular the Soviets seemed blind to the emotional importance of Cuba in American politics. Khrushchev must have hoped that the successful deployment of the missiles would improve his bargaining strength on a number of issues. Nevertheless the most plausible explanation for the Russian move must remain the Kremlin's desire to find a quick (and cheap) answer to the growing nuclear lead of the United States.[47]

In the course of 1961 the Kennedy administration learned beyond all doubt that the much discussed Soviet lead in rockets was a myth. But its own ambitious programme continued unchecked. In his presidential campaign Kennedy had promised bold action on a number of fronts to lift the United States out of what was described as the inertia of the Eisenhower years. The missile programme was one attractive and convenient way of doing this. McNamara was keen to impose more discipline on the American services in the procurement of new weaponry, and generous funding of certain programmes was one way of buying off opposition to the cancellation of others. The pressure from the services, and especially from the air force, for more nuclear arms was considerable. The administration itself was far from indifferent to the appeal of possessing a clear nuclear lead over the Russians, though McNamara later claimed that he dissented from the air force's desire to acquire a first-strike capability against the Soviet Union. At the same time he conceded that the Russians probably feared that this was the American aim. 'If I had been the Soviet secretary of defence, I'd have been worried as hell at the imbalance of forces.'[48] The Russians had no ready answer to the American threat with inter-continental forces of their own. They deployed few of their first generation of inter-continental missiles, and were well behind the Americans in the development of a second. Russia faced a long period of exposure if she tried to match like with like. Quite apart from first-strike fears, Khrushchev must have been troubled by the political and psychological advantages which the Americans might appear to hold as a result of their nuclear lead. He may not have been reassured by his own failures when he had tried to exploit the 'missile gap' a few years before. Furthermore, any growth in the vulnerability of his position abroad was likely to be repeated at home. In these circumstances Khrushchev's readiness to undertake the Cuban gamble becomes more comprehensible, for the deployment of shorter-range missiles (which were readily available) on the island promised to double Russia's first-strike capability against the United States. Indeed, it has been argued that these rockets would have secured for Russia in 1962 much the same strategic position as she secured only at the end of the decade and at much greater cost to herself with new inter-continental missiles. Even so it is possible that not all the Russian leadership were happy with this bold solution, but the sceptics were for the time being carried along by the exuberant Khrushchev.[49]

The Americans obtained hard evidence of the Russian rocket preparations in Cuba only in the middle of October 1962. There had been a flurry of concern at the end of August prompted by other evidence of Russia's increasing activities in Cuba. Contingency plans for 'pinpoint attack' or 'outright invasion' had then been ordered in case nuclear missiles were stationed on the island.[50] Nevertheless the surprise expressed by the administration early in October was genuine, and Russian preparations were so well advanced that speed was of the essence in Washington. Critics who argue that there should first have been secret negotiations with Moscow ignore the time factor and the problem of 'leaks'. Apart from the 'enemy' in the Kremlin, Kennedy was only too well aware that the Republicans would exploit any signs of weakness on his part to the full. He had publicly accepted Russian assurances that no offensive missiles would be installed in Cuba, so that his position at home was already vulnerable. Imminent elections made it all the more important to seize the initiative. McNamara queried the military importance of the Cuban missiles – the Russians, he argued, would catch up sooner or later in the nuclear arms race. But it was the political aspect which mattered. The administration feared for its credibility at home and abroad if it failed to face down this challenge. Relevant too was the fact that around Cuba the United States possessed an overwhelming advantage in conventional weapons. If it failed to act here, where would it act? Or so the argument ran in the world of *realpolitik*.

But if the administration was resolved to act, there was still the question of how. Graham Allison argues that it was fortunate that those who favoured an air strike against the missile sites wrongly believed that they could not guarantee complete success at this stage. An air strike would have caused casualties and inflamed the situation to a degree that was improbable with the initial line of action which was finally chosen – naval blockade, or naval 'quarantine' as it was delicately described. Kennedy announced the blockade and demanded the withdrawal of the missiles on 22 October. The United States was able to exercise complete command over the seas around Cuba. Vessels not carrying missiles were allowed to proceed. Fortunately none carrying rockets tried to run the blockade. But the deployment of missiles already on the island continued, and the Russians at first gave no sign of yielding. In the second stage of the crisis, therefore, Washington began to prepare air strikes and an invasion of Cuba. On the 27th an American U-2 reconnaissance plane was shot down by a newly installed Russian surface-to-air missile. But intense diplomatic activity was also taking place: furthermore, the United States could achieve its aims in Cuba with conventional weapons alone unless there was an escalation of the crisis to a general war. Of this no one could be sure. Mundane events began to acquire a special poignancy for people who felt themselves very near to a nuclear holocaust. McNamara and others remarked on the brilliance of the sunset and sunrise. of 27–28 October when the tension was at its height, and preparations for the American attacks were nearing completion.

Just how near the world was to disaster at the end of October 1962 cannot yet be established. Certainly there was no other moment of comparable tension in the history of the Cold War. And yet it is tempting to ask if the danger was as great as many imagined. The Russians could not hope to win a limited and localized war in the Caribbean. The missiles had been sent in a desperate attempt to offset America's nuclear advantage. It made no sense to fight a nuclear war to support a move which the Americans were now able to frustrate. Neither did it make sense for the Americans to escalate the war to areas outside Cuba and its waters. There remained, of course, always the danger of war by accident and miscalculation. The Russians might have been tempted to reply to an American move against Cuba with pressure, say, on Berlin. Bluff and counter-bluff might have interacted with disastrous consequences. Graham Allison also stresses the importance of the built-in rigidities, prejudices and special interests of the various organs in both governments, all of which limited the freedom of the policy-makers at the top. One could not rely on the automatic triumph of reason however rational Kennedy and Khrushchev and their closest advisers tried to be. Indeed some of Kennedy's advisers were disturbingly confident and bellicose, and it is likely that Khrushchev too had his 'hawks'. As it was, Moscow and Washington exchanged a 'myriad of "signals" – some compatible, and others contradictory' through a variety of channels. Informal contacts often played an important part. On the credit side the crisis seems to have developed a sense of fellow-feeling between Kennedy and Khrushchev – each knew that his error would destroy both. They began as rivals, and yet as the crisis unfolded so they became increasingly like climbers on a rockface – if one fell, the other fell too, so fragile were their holds and so insecure the lines by which they sought to save themselves. It was fortunate that earlier crises had not eradicated Kennedy's belief (as a result of other contacts with Khrushchev) that the latter was basically a rational person. But if Kennedy had faith in Khrushchev, he still feared that miscalculation or loss of control could lead to disaster.[51]

The crucial Soviet concessions were made on 28 October. The offensive and offending missiles were finally withdrawn in return for an American intimation that Cuba was not in danger of invasion. There were also informal assurances about the early removal of obsolete American missiles in Turkey. But equally important among the results of the Cuban crisis was the desire in both capitals to avoid a similar eyeball-to-eyeball confrontation in the future. As a twentieth-century Dr Johnson might have said, the missile crisis had concentrated the mind wonderfully. Both Kennedy and Khrushchev had been troubled by the difficulties of communication when time and mutual comprehension were at a premium. These fears encouraged the establishment of the so-called 'hot-line'between the two capitals to facilitate rapid and clear communication. There were other possible repercussions. No more was heard of Khrushchev's threats to conclude a separate peace with East Germany, and embarrass the West by placing control of western access routes to West Berlin unequivocally in the hands of the East Germans. Progress also began to take place – if accompanied by much hard bargaining – on the question of nuclear testing. Although the Russian acceptance of the principle of inspection did not lead to anything in practice, the superpowers and the British did reach agreement on a partial test-ban treaty on 5 August 1963. This put an end to nuclear testing by the three signatories in the atmosphere. Nuclear weaponry had in fact reached the point where the advanced nuclear powers (in comparison with the French and Chinese) could be content with underground testing. The year 1963 also witnessed extensive American wheat sales to Russia to ease the latter's food problems: both powers agreed to the demilitarization of outer space (a cosmetic gesture since neither wished to extend their competition to that region), and tacitly accepted the use of satellites for reconnaissance purposes over each other's territory (again they had no option). Such surveillance, however, was to make it possible for each power to follow the other's land-based missile deployment with considerable accuracy. The vexed question of inspection and fears of cheating were thus sufficiently circumvented for the later Strategic Arms Limitation Talks (SALT) to take place, and achieve some limited success in 1972.

Cuba was not, however, followed by any relaxation of the arms race. The Russians, denied a short cut from inferiority in 1962, were forced to build land and submarine-based inter-continental missile systems, and take a long, hard and expensive road to parity with the United States. The American missile programmes also continued, though the initial hopes of the administration that it would be able to achieve some sort of meaningful nuclear superiority over the Russians began to fade in the mid-1960s. McNamara in particular began to develop doubts, and later conceded that his programme might have triggered off a new stage in the arms race. Khrushchev had certainly been anxious to economize on defence spending in the early 1960s, given the many other calls upon his country's resources. Pressures for consumer goods, for instance, were mounting, and there was the continuing crisis in Russian agriculture. But even if the Democrat administrations from 1961 had been content with the missile build-up envisaged under Eisenhower (this programme was about half their own), the Russians would still have been anxious to acquire at least a comparable nuclear force, made up of almost invulnerable, solid-fuelled missiles, to provide Russia with an assured retaliatory force – one that could ride out any American first strike and still inflict an unacceptable level of damage in return. Nor were Russian conventional forces forgotten in this period. Thus Russian defence spending was rising sharply even before the fall of Khrushchev in October 1964. Between 1965 and 1970 it rose by 40 per cent at a time when more and more of the increases in American defence spending were being devoted to the war in Vietnam. Thus, although American defence spending doubled during the Democrat period (1961–69) in office, because of Vietnam and the Russian response the military balance between the two superpowers did not move in America's favour. Indeed the Russians made some significant gains at sea, and still more so in the creation of a nuclear deterrent which by the end of the decade enabled them to think in terms of approximate nuclear parity with the United States. The era of Mutual Assured Destruction (MAD) had arrived.[52]

NOTES AND REFERENCES

1. G. Porter, I, 299–303
2. G. Porter, I, 186, 204, 319–20, 349, 354–5
3. NSC 101, 5 January 1951
4. FRUS, 1951, VI, Part 1, pp. 1–31
5 FRUS, 1951, VI, Part 1, pp. 107–14
6. FRUS, 1951, VI, Part 1, p. 385
7. FRUS, 1952–54, XVI, 520
8. FRUS, 1952–54, XVI, 472 ff.; 1953, I, 431, 536–7; NSC 177, 30 December 1953. Note also Sulzberger, pp. 837–8
9. FRUS, 1952–54, XVI, 605–7
10. FRUS, 1952–54, XVI, 623, 628–9. An opinion poll of 19–22 May 1954 found only 21 per cent in favour of unilateral action; 69 per cent for action with allies; 46 per cent in favour of a truce; and 40 per cent insistent on a Communist defeat
11. G. Porter, I, 535–6; Divine, pp. 47–8
12. FRUS, XVI, 875

13. Divine, p 51. See also FRUS, 1952–54, xvi, 397 ff.; G. Porter, i, 504–49
14. FRUS, 1952–54, xvi, especially pp. 1021–3, 1047–9, 1189–93, 1281–2, 1374
15. G. Porter, i, 687, 694–7. See also FRUS, 1952–54, xvi, 1134–6. For US policy in South-east Asia, July–December 1954, see FRUS, 1952–54, xiii, Part 2, pp. 1867 ff.
16. G. Porter, i, 666–8, 690–2
17. Kalicki, pp. 135–55
18. Kalicki, pp. 170–209
19. Cowan, pp. 156–8, etc.
20. FRUS, 1952–54, xvi, 483–4
21. Mićunović, pp. 187–8, 197–8, 228, 243, 322–3, 354. See also Nogee and Donaldson, p. 107, and for the debate in China, MacFarquhar, i, *passim*
22. Adomeit and Boardman, p. 125
23. Crankshaw, p. 81
24. Dedijer, p. 36
25. On the border issue, see Ginsburgs and Pinkele, *passim*. A Soviet view of the Sino-Soviet dispute as a whole can be found in Borisov and Koloskov. A good up-to-date account is provided by Thornton, while for divisions in the communist world as a whole, see Bromke and Rakowska-Harmstone *passim* (eds)
26. Warner [3] pp. 614–15
27. NSC 5612/1, 5 September 1956; 5617, 7 December 1956; 5701, 10 January 1957
28. See above, notes 3–8
29. NSC 6012, 25 July 1960
30. G. Porter, ii, 52–82
31. Rostow, pp. 89–148. See also Gaddis [2] pp. 200, 211
32. It is reassuring to find that Kennedy thought Le May almost impossible (Schlesinger, pp. 449–50. See also pp. 451–2)
33. G. Porter, ii, 90–101, 124–45
34. G. Porter, ii, 148–55
35. Gaddis [2] pp. 198–211. Note Segal, especially Chs. 2 and 3, for the claim that the Kennedy administration showed little ability to recognize and exploit the emerging triangular relationship between the United States, Russia and China
36. G. Porter, ii, 174–6, 229–30, 237–9, 391–2
37. On the other hand Kennedy authorized a plan in August 1963 to overthrow Diem partly because of fears of a secret deal between Diem and Hanoi (Gaddis [2] p. 246). Kennedy's successor, L. B. Johnson, was even more fearful of being thought weak, especially by opponents at home, according to Kearns, pp. 252–9. For the situation at the end of 1963, see Schlesinger, Ch. 31
38. G. Porter, ii, 235–7, 258–9, 261
39. G. Porter, ii, 279–81
40. G. Porter, ii, 326–31
41. G. Porter, ii, 341–3, 349–57
42. G. Porter, ii. 385–91, 396; Gaddis [2] pp. 241, 258–9

43. Gaddis [2] pp. 242, 258–63; G. Porter, ii, 470–2
44. NSC 6017, 17 November 1960
45. Gaddis [2] pp. 207–8
46. *The Guardian* 9 August 1982
47. Allison, pp. 110–11. See R. N. Lebow, in O'Neill and Horner, pp. 227–8, for the suggestion that Khrushchev's policy was influenced more by the degree of support it received among influential groups in the Russian government than by its own intrinsic merits, and that subjective hopes and perceived needs were more important than attempts at objective assessments of the situation. See also Nogee and Donaldson. pp. 120–7
48. *The Guardian* 9 August 1982. Compare Schlesinger, pp. 420–32 with Ball, *passim*
49. Allison, pp. 40–56; Schlesinger, p. 504 and note
50. NSC Action Memo. no. 181, 23 August 1962. Mention of a blockade came early in September, Schlesinger, p. 471
51. Allison, pp. 210–15; Schlesinger, pp. 529–30
52. For the evolution of thinking on nuclear war and strategy, see especially Freedman, pp. 97–196, 228–56

Chapter 13

A NEW PATTERN OF RIVALRIES

A number of efforts had been made during the Cold War to turn East–West rivalries into less dangerous channels. Sometimes these had been primarily exercises in propaganda: in others the purposes of the powers had been too asymmetrical for real progress to be possible. But if the Geneva Conference of 1954 had bought only a few years of troubled peace in south-east Asia, the Korean cease-fire had held, as had the test-ban treaty as it affected the Soviet Union, the United States and Britain from 1963. Tentative exchanges began to take place between West Germany, Russia and some east European states in 1962, and rather more seriously from 1966. In the winter of 1966–67 the United States raised the question of strategic arms limitation talks (SALT), and a year later a NATO statement described military security and *détente* as two sides to the same coin. The Russians began to show interest in SALT in June 1968, and on 1 July the Treaty on Nuclear Non-Proliferation was signed. Progress was sharply, but only temporarily, interrupted by the Czech crisis in the summer of 1968 and the Russian intervention which began on the night of 20–21 August. There was no repetition of the bloody battles in Budapest in the autumn of 1956. In March 1969 the Soviet ambassador in Bonn referred meaningfully to Chinese 'aggression' on the Ussuri River, and a few days later at a meeting of the Warsaw Pact in Budapest there was a renewal of the Soviet proposal for a general European conference on questions of security and co-operation. There was increasing evidence of Russian interest in western equipment and expertise to help accelerate the modernization of crucial sections of Russian industry. In West Germany a new coalition led by the Social Democrats under Willy Brandt came to power in October 1969, and quickly demonstrated its determination to regularize relations with Russia and its eastern neighbours – in ways which were compatible with German pride, security and also hopes of trade – and formalize the central European status quo. Over the same period the United States, as already noted, had begun (from March

1968) to seek ways to disengage from an unwinnable war in south-east Asia, while in October 1968 there appeared the first Chinese hints for more than a decade of an interest in contacts with Washington. Thus at the very end of the 1960s a number of events, interests and processes began to interact in a highly creative manner to make possible a considerable change in the international environment, and for a time even its atmosphere, over the next few years.

Contemporary talk in the early 1970s of the dawning of an era of *détente* should not blind us to the hard-headed calculations of the policy-makers who carried through these interesting and important negotiations which temporarily lessened the fear of nuclear war, created feelings of greater confidence and stability in central Europe, encouraged East–West trade and which, in the Far East, finally ended the Vietnam War (early in 1973) and produced a diplomatic dialogue between the United States and China. Each contributor to these developments was working with maximalist and minimalist objectives in mind. The Americans, for instance, hoped to avoid so quick and total a collapse of anti-communist forces in south-east Asia as actually occurred. The Russians initially appeared to be hopeful of weakening the cohesion of NATO and especially of West Germany's relationship with that alliance, but in the end were content to settle for West German recognition of the existing frontiers in Europe, effective acceptance of the division of Germany and its renunciation of nuclear weapons, all sugared for Russia by access to western technology and credits. On the western side these new economic openings in the East were welcomed not merely for the extra trade which they provided, but hopefully as a way of enmeshing Russia to some extent with the western economies so that Moscow would develop an interest in peaceful coexistence which was more in accord with western needs.

Clausewitz had written of war as the continuation of politics by other means: similarly *détente*, arms limitation, peaceful coexistence and even trade agreements might all be employed in the continuation of rivalries by other methods. As history had not come to 'a full stop' when the United States became 'top nation' in the aftermath of the First World War, neither did the global struggle cease when Russian nuclear parity with the United States was recognized by the first SALT agreement of May 1972. Similarly one should not forget Russia's fear of China, and still more China's fear of Russia, as contributory factors to the changes which were taking place at this time, nor the popular and economic pressures which were persuading the Johnson and later the Nixon administrations in the United States to seek less expensive policies to contain communism throughout the world. Meanwhile *Pravda* acknowledged at the end of 1969 that Russian industry must be made more productive, and there was other evidence of dissatisfaction with managerial conservatism. The agricultural problems seemed as intractable as ever, while at the Twenty-Fourth Party Congress in 1971 it was deemed advisable to promise that more consumer goods would be made available in the future.

The negotiations which led to the Moscow accords of 26 May 1972 (SALT I) have been described as 'probably . . . one of the most intensive, complex, and crucial periods of diplomatic activity ever recorded'.[1] Yet they only restrained – temporarily – they did not end the nuclear arms race. As at Washington in 1921–22, the signatories agreed essentially not to do what they had no great wish to do. The costs of certain programmes – such as the anti-ballistic missile defence systems – outweighed their likely advantages. Both powers had good reason to concentrate on the completion of invulnerable second-strike inter-continental nuclear delivery systems – whether land or sea-based. The great aim was mutually assured deterrence and retaliation, though more ambitious strategies continued to attract attention, and were soon to attract more. Under SALT I the two superpowers simply expanded and refined their nuclear armouries more selectively than they might otherwise have done. The search for advantages over the other continued, though there was also some acceptance of the desirability of other accords to reduce the risks of misunderstanding and to close off undesirable areas of rivalry. Thus in October 1969 the two powers had agreed to ban the use of nuclear weapons on the sea bed. East and West edged towards conferences on security and co-operation in Europe and on mutual balanced force reductions, the Russians being encouraged to move in this direction by the need to station a larger proportion of their forces in the Far East. Unrest in Poland led to the downfall of the government in December 1970, and was a further incentive for the Russians to think in terms of consolidation, and also of economic development which would lead to a higher standard of living in the East, and so lessen popular discontent. Even in the Middle East, where the Arab –Israeli war of 1967 had triggered off new, and intensified existing, problems, and led to more direct Russian involvement in the region, both superpowers proceeded with no little caution, and clearly hoped to avoid a direct confrontation. In September 1971 agreement was reached to improve communications between the two governments in periods of crisis (an advance on the 'hot-line' arrangements of 1963). Agreements followed in May 1972 concerning co-operation in the exploration and use of outer space for peaceful purposes, on the prevention of incidents on or over the sea, as well as the SALT agreement itself. These understandings failed to prevent a brief but serious crisis between Russia and the United States at the height of the Middle Eastern War of October 1973 when for a time the Israelis were pressing for too complete a victory over Egypt. The crisis demonstrated the limitations and the usefulness of the work of the past few years, and it was a reassuring sign, if little resulted from

their labours, to see the Russians and Americans co-chairing negotiations between the Arabs and Israelis in Geneva at the end of 1973.
Meanwhile Russian and American diplomats continued to seek
further agreement on the prevention of war, control of nuclear
weapons, the peaceful use of atomic energy and the promotion of
trade.

Similarly in Europe the main obstacles to better relations between
West Germany, Russia and eastern Europe were being steadily overcome by the end of 1973. West Germany accepted the Polish frontier
in 1970; agreement was reached on the future of Berlin, and on the
relations between the two Germanies in 1971–72. At the end of 1973
West Germany established diplomatic relations with Bulgaria,
Hungary and Czechoslovakia. Rumanian and Yugoslav recognition
of West Germany had taken place in 1967. The Moscow treaty
between West Germany and Russia of 12 August 1970 was followed
by an agreement on 19 May 1972 on economic, industrial and technical co-operation. These agreements, especially on the future of
Berlin and the two Germanies, were not without their limitations and
ambiguities, but the contrast with the preceding decades was striking,
and it is not surprising that a genuine mood of optimism began to
develop. The Central Committee of the Communist Party of the
Soviet Union in April 1973 described peaceful coexistence as 'a
general rule'for inter-state relations despite the existence of different
social systems: it stressed the value of Summit Conferences and
international trade. It subsequently emphasized the links between
good foreign relations and Russian domestic prosperity. Alastair
Buchan entitled a book published in 1974, *The End of the Postwar
Era*, and referred to the feeling that 'a new and unfamiliar landscape'
was taking shape in international relations. For the first time since
1931 among the leading powers there was a sense of something akin
to peace.[2] Michael Howard, a year earlier, suggested that grand
strategy as practised by Napoleon and in the two world wars was
dead. Eighteenth-century models were becoming more relevant. At
that time policy had been in the hands of men 'who had much to lose
and little to gain from war, who fearfully committed their forces to
battle and manoeuvred them cautiously; men with limited resources
and often divided public opinion within their domains'.[3] Many
writers were struck by the emergence of a multipolar balance – even
if the superpowers remained in a different league from the rest. But
the economic strength of the European Economic Community and
of Japan was too great to ignore, especially given the current
economic difficulties of the United States, while China, though poor
and backward, and with only limited military strength (conventional
and nuclear), was nevertheless a force to be reckoned with. Marshal
Grechko, for instance, in May 1969 ranked China with West

Germany and the United States as a major threat to the Soviet Union.

As far back as January 1962 the American State Department had shown some interest in the possible implications of the Sino-Soviet rift. One member spoke of 'an intellectual thaw' as the ice of twelve years began to snap and crackle.[4] But in general China was still seen as dangerously militant and aggressive, a view that was strengthened by the Sino-Indian War of 1962. Although in practice the Chinese fought a model, limited war, Kennedy was more impressed by the growing strength of China and of what he described as Stalinist tendencies within it. He was disturbed by the ability of the Chinese leadership to start and stop a conflict without fear of any domestic repercussions – here was an authority that was answerable only to itself. At times he seemed to regard China as a greater threat to world peace than Russia. Thus, although under Kennedy and his successor there was occasional interest in the opening of a line to Peking, in general the administrations were intellectually and emotionally unprepared to exploit any openings that did occur. A number of historians are convinced that the Russo-Sino-American triangular relationship which began to develop from 1969 might have come into being much earlier had Washington been more open-minded and alert.[5] This may be so, but one should also note that from 1965 to 1968 China was preoccupied with the Cultural Revolution as Mao and others strove to rally the more radical forces in China in a great internal power struggle. This was not a situation in which much progress towards better relations with the United States was likely. The Vietnam War was also at its height.

So matters remained throughout the Johnson administration. It was not until 26 November 1968 that Peking indicated a readiness to resume talks in Warsaw, the last centre of contact between Chinese and American diplomats. Although the Cultural Revolution was not properly at an end until April 1969, China could hardly continue to treat the rest of the world as if it did not exist. The threat of a border confrontation – or perhaps something worse with Russia – was steadily growing. Some western observers suggested that 1969 was the last year the Russians would have an opportunity to cripple or destroy China's growing nuclear capabilities before the damage from retaliation became unacceptable. But even the conventional confrontation was assuming dangerous dimensions. Between 1966 and 1970 Russia's eastern border forces were increased from twelve under-strength divisions to forty modernized ones. Many border incidents preceded the important clash over Damanski Island on the Ussuri River in March 1969. The Chinese might also have been disturbed by the Russian intervention in Czechoslovakia. Nevertheless Peking took no hasty steps. The United States continued to wage war in south-east Asia with tremendous vigour, and the Chinese doubtless wished to take the measure of the new Republican administration headed by Richard Nixon – a famed hardliner against Communism – and to establish whether a genuine transformation of American policy with respect to the Far East was in progress. Discreet American signalling at first prompted no response, and Henry Kissinger, Nixon's special adviser on foreign affairs, later claimed that the administration was surprised when a deal suddenly began to seem possible. 'We were convinced that the Chinese were fanatic and hostile.' At the same time he felt that some American officials still exaggerated the importance of Chinese ideology and militancy. The Chinese, as a people of 800 million, would, insisted Kissinger and Nixon, be a 'geopolitical' problem whoever governed them.[6]

The tension between Russia and China in the summer of 1969 became so serious that Moscow itself seemed anxious for American understanding. Washington was sufficiently alarmed to prepare contingency plans for a Sino-Soviet war: the United States could not allow Russia to cripple China.[7] At the same time Washington could not but hope that the situation, short of the catastrophe of war, would work to its advantage. If both Moscow and Peking began to court the United States, one or the other (the Russians seemed the better bet) might try to restrain Hanoi and help the United States out of the morass in south-east Asia.[8] The Chinese, for their part, were not only under pressure from Russia, but must have feared that developments such as the Nuclear Non-Proliferation Treaty of July 1968 might encourage Russian and American interest in a global condominium. Although border tension with the Russians began to ease from October 1969, the Chinese, having opened the door slightly to American contacts, continued to explore the situation. Kissinger elegantly describes the secret diplomatic exchanges which followed as[9]

> . . . an intricate minuet . . . so delicately arranged that both sides could maintain that they were not in contact, so stylized that neither side needed to bear the onus of an initiative, so elliptical that existing relationships were not jeopardized.

The Pakistanis, for instance, proved a particularly useful avenue of communication. Serious talks were under way by the beginning of 1970, although support for *détente* was by no means general in Peking. It was one of the many issues in the 1971 power struggle which led to the mysterious death of Lin Piao in September 1971, the leader of the radicals. Vietnam remained something of an impediment, and it took time for the Americans to persuade the Chinese that they were sincerely bent on an honourable escape despite the continuing intensity of the war. Nevertheless, despite American invasions of Cambodia and Laos in 1970–71, Kissinger was able to visit China (in the utmost secrecy) in 1971, and the way was opened for President Nixon's epoch-making visit in February 1972.

Meanwhile Russo-American relations survived the shock of this new development in international relations without noticeable strain. Russia could not allow Peking to monopolize the attention of the United States, nor could it forget its needs in Europe, from consolidation of the status quo to access to western goods, credits and expertise. The Americans, similarly, were on the defensive, one of the main problems of the administration in the early 1970s being to sustain sufficient public support to enable it to carry through even its more selective defence of America's overseas interests. There was pressure, for instance, to cut American forces in Europe – Senator Mansfield from May 1971 was urging that they be cut by a half. The Russians, strangely, made no move to encourage such withdrawals. Nevertheless an upsurge of neo-isolationism seemed possible in America, with a Gallup poll in June 1973 recording that opinion was evenly divided on the question of fighting in defence of western Europe. American balance of payments problems strengthened criticism of expensive foreign commitments, while the Watergate crisis, which finally drove Nixon to resignation in August 1974, absorbed more and more attention from 1973.

The lessening of East–West tensions was accompanied, and even anticipated, by a notable de-emphasis of ideology. In 1969 William Zimmerman argued that a considerable convergence appeared to be taking place in the Soviet and American attitudes to international relations. He believed that ideology in Russia was increasingly performing a legitimizing function rather than serving as a guide to policy in a world where workers in the developed countries clearly had far more to lose than their chains, where nuclear weapons, Third World nationalism and the Sino-Soviet rift all demanded flexibility and pragmatic handling if Russia was to gain even small advantages in an intricately competitive, volatile and unpredictable world. In ideological terms the Soviets might perhaps find consolation in the fact that the replacement of feudalism by capitalism had taken several centuries: the replacement of capitalism was proceeding at 'a significantly more rapid tempo'.[10]

It was under Khrushchev that Soviet writing on international relations began to break free from the strait-jacket thrust over it by Stalin. As Khrushchev himself had said, 'the atomic bomb does not observe the class principle'. The rise of a more pragmatic approach was reflected in the work of some Soviet analysts who, in 1963–65, began to discuss the role of interest groups in the formation of policy in the United States, with the White House, the Pentagon and the intelligentsia all being seen as autonomous forces, distinct from Wall Street. Old theories concerning the role of class, and the inevitability of divisions within the capitalist world were no longer adequate. The diversity of the bourgeoisie received some attention, especially the so-called peace and war groups in the United States. The lobbying power of non-business elements was recognized. Meanwhile the Sino-Soviet split was also generating new ideas on the relations of socialist states. One contributor to the *World Marxist Review* (August 1964) feared that the abnormal relations created between states by capitalism would continue for some time beyond its decline. Indeed, he hinted that the 'oneness of will and action' created in socialist states could lead to an even more virulent form of nationalism: only under socialism could a nation feel itself truly 'a single whole', so that international rivalries might be even more extreme than in the capitalist era.[11] The Russians in their eagerness for allies among Third World people began to offer a very generous interpretation of the word 'socialist' so that it could be applied as frequently as possible to their new friends.[12] It could mean as little as anti-imperialist.

The 1960s and early 1970s also witnessed a temporary advance of the pragmatists at the expense of ideologues and Cold War warriors in the United States. Kennedy's American University speech of June 1963 was an early example.

> We must conduct our affairs in such a way that it becomes the
> Communists' interest to agree on a genuine peace . . . to . . . let each
> nation choose its own future, so long as that choice does not interfere
> with the choice of others . . . If we cannot now end our differences,
> at least we can help make the world safe for diversity.

The new departures in relations between Russia and China were helping here, but it was the great debate precipitated by the Vietnam War which did most damage to the post-1945 orthodoxy on the question of America's relations with communism, and created widespread doubts concerning America's chosen role as a world crusader and policeman. American motives, as well as its methods, became suspect. Senator Fulbright warned in 1966 that 'our puritan spirit has tended to break through, leading us to look at the world through the distorting prism of a harsh and angry moralism'. America, with the best intentions, could destroy the very societies it was professedly trying to defend. Communism was fanatical, not evil: in time the fanaticism might exhaust itself.[13] Thus by the late 1960s many Americans were mentally prepared for the Nixon–Kissinger approach to foreign affairs to a degree that would have been unthinkable a few years earlier. Thus Nixon in 1969 expressed the hope that the 'isms' would lose their vitality, while Kissinger spoke of the need 'to build a moral consensus which can make a pluralistic world creative rather than destructive'. The need as he saw it was to encourage as many people as possible, and especially the most powerful, to develop a vested interest in stability, in peaceful change and in a balanced world order. By such means the status quo would be legitimized. This is not the place to discuss how far he achieved his aims, or how intelligently he pursued them.[14] Suffice to say that to an unusual degree (and admittedly helped by many special circumstances),Americans, Russians, Chinese and Europeans were all willing to make a greater effort than usual to remove some major causes of international friction in the period 1969–75, or thereabouts. Kissinger aptly described Russo-American relations in October 1973: 'We are at one and the same time adversaries and partners in the preservation of peace.'

The feeling that caution and restraint were being forced on the leading powers was much in evidence at a meeting between President Nixon and the British Prime Minister, Edward Heath, in December 1971. Kissinger recorded a discussion of what was described as 'perhaps the most profound philosophical question' facing the West. Heath expressed it thus: 'We are moving more and more into a state of world affairs in which effective action is no longer possible.'[15] The West was inhibited by the fear of nuclear war and by the strength of Third World nationalism. Indeed, E. H. Carr suggests that 'the world revolution which will complete the downfall of capitalism, will prove to be the revolt of colonial peoples against capitalism in the guise of imperialism rather than a revolt of the proletariat in the advanced countries'.[16] This is prejudging the future with a deterministic and eschatological eye with a vengeance, but one can accept that by the early 1970s 'the revolt of the colonial peoples' was lessening in some degree that extreme imbalance in the world which had so accentuated the global struggle among the leading powers as virtually to eclipse local and regional rivalries.

The period from the late nineteenth century had been one of unparalleled imbalance, and had witnessed staggering economic, technological and political changes. The turbulence of these years is reflected in the many transformations which took place in the political geography of the world. In that time the maps of eastern Europe, the Middle East, southern Asia, and Africa were all drastically redrawn – in some cases more than once. Yet the long anticipated partition of the world had not occurred. George Orwell in his famous *Nineteen Eighty-Four*, published in 1949, had thought it not implausible to envisage a world dominated by three totalitarian superstates waging limited war among themselves from Africa to Indonesia. He included a hint or two of strategic calculation which would not have been out of place in a paper submitted to the National Security Council (or the Defence Committee responsible to the British Cabinet) in the late 1940s or early 1950s. On the other hand he expected nuclear weapons to deter the superpowers from direct assaults on each other's territory or spheres of influence. *Nineteen Eighty-Four*, of course, was written as a warning, not as an exercise in futurology, but his assumptions are interesting for all that. With the rise of Afro-Asian nationalism it seemed possible by the early 1970s that the superpowers might be inhibited almost as much by this new force as by their fear of nuclear war. Indeed, where Orwell had envisaged a demi-world of violence regulated by the superpowers, Hedley Bull, reflecting in 1981 on the emergence of a plural world, the strife in the Middle East, the turmoil in parts of south-east Asia since 1973, the conflicts in Africa and the waves of terrorist activity, suggested that the future might 'prove more Hobbesian, less moderated by the institutions of an international society' than it had been in the past.[17] As John Foster Dulles once remarked, one always knew when one was making progress because the problems changed.

It might be interesting, though it is idle in a work of this nature, to speculate further on the possibility that the combination of nuclear weapons with the new-found self-confidence and assertiveness of the former victims of the powerful has, for the foreseeable future, imposed some major restraints on the conduct of the great powers, and that the 1970s may prove something more than an interlude. As it is, historians can only guess at the extent to which nuclear weapons have contributed to the avoidance of war between the superpowers since 1945. Similarly they may note that the larger hopes of *détente* in the early 1970s have not been realized – though what this may augur for the future is beyond them. What historians can do is to stress that in the third quarter of the twentieth century it became increasingly evident that no state was in a position to attain an unchallengeable lead in the struggle for global power through territorial conquest, or even through the spawning of obedient satellites. The hierarchy of states still had meaning, and would continue to do so. Many levers of power were, and still are, open to the leading states. The rivalry of the superpowers must remain at the centre of any study of international affairs, and may take a catastrophic turn which will leave no part of the world unscathed. But local and regional affairs continue to demand more and more attention. The international history of the last decades of the twentieth century promises to be a more complicated and disjointed affair than that for the period when the global struggle between the leading powers so largely dominated the scene.

NOTES AND REFERENCES

1. Kahan, p. 186
2. Buchan, p. 3
3. Howard [5] p. 265
4. Hilsman, p. 344

5. Segal, pp. 27–34, 42, 65–72
6. Kissinger, pp. 163, 178
7. Kissinger, pp. 172–3, 179–83
8. Kissinger, pp. 163–4
9. Kissinger, p. 187
10. Hoffmann and Fleron, p. 27
11. Zimmerman, pp. 268–9
12. Zimmerman, pp. 273–4. See also Schwarz, *passim*
13. For an interesting analysis of the Vietnam debates in America, and their significance, see e.g. Garrett, pp. 478–508
14. See e.g. Gaddis [2] Chs. 9 and 10
15. Kissinger, p. 965
16. E. H. Carr [2] p. 275
17. O'Neill and Horner, p. 33

FURTHER READING
For full bibliographical details see pp. 366–81

An excellent introductory text is Grenville [2], *A World History of the Twentieth Century*, which deals with the great powers up to 1945 and includes a useful bibliography. A second volume on the postwar period is promised. Northedge and Grieve, *A Hundred Years of International Relations*, is uneven, but contains useful insights. Among many regional histories Joll, *Europe since 1870*, and Hughes, *Contemporary Europe*, complement each other admirably. For the Far East see Vinacke, *A History of the Far East in Modern Times*, and Fairbank et al., *East Asia: the modern transformation*, while the interaction of East and West is interestingly explored by Storry, *Japan and the Decline of the West in Asia, 1894–1943*. American foreign policy is studied in detail by Bemis, *A Diplomatic History of the United States*, and in a manageable and stimulating fashion for students by Cole, *An Interpretive History of American Foreign Relations*. The rise of the two superpowers can be followed in Ulam, *Expansion and Co-existence: Soviet foreign policy, 1917–73*, and Ambrose [2], *Rise to Globalism: American foreign policy since 1938*.

For the period of the 'new imperialism' one should compare the works of Robinson and Gallagher, *Africa and the Victorians*, H. M. Wright, *The 'New Imperialism'*, and Fieldhouse, *Economics and Empire*. The European diplomatic background is provided by Taylor [1], *The Struggle for Mastery in Europe*, while Gillard, *The Struggle for Asia*, provides an excellent corrective to the obsession with Africa in the late nineteenth century. For more detailed treatment of British policy see Grenville [1], *Lord Salisbury and Foreign Policy at the Close of the Nineteenth Century*, and Bourne, *The Foreign Policy of Victorian Britain*, with his valuable selection of documents. French policy is interestingly handled by Brunschwig, *French Colonialism*, and Cooke, *The New French Imperialism*, and that of Germany by Woodruff D. Smith, *The German Colonial Empire*. Russia must not be forgotten, and here one should consult Malozemoff, *Russian Far*

Eastern Policy, and Kazemzadeh, *Russia and Britain in Persia*. For the activities of the non-European powers see Storry, *Japan and the Decline of the West in Asia*, and on the United States, Iriye, *From Nationalism to Internationalism*.

The general background to the First World War can be studied in Taylor [1], *The Struggle for Mastery in Europe*, and in a stimulating recent work by Langhorne, *The Collapse of the Concert of Europe*. The problems of Austria-Hungary deserve special attention, and on these see Bridge [1], *From Sadowa to Sarajevo*. Fischer [2], *War of Illusions*, is a must on Germany: for some insights into the controversy excited by this work, see also Moses, *The Politics of Illusion*, and for a critical view of Russian policy see L. C. F. Turner, *Origins of the First World War*. On the war itself, note the provocative study by Ferro, *The Great War*, and Fischer's massive [1], *Germany's Aims in the First World War*. Barry Hunt and Adrian Preston, *War Aims and Strategic Policy in the Great War*, have put together much recent and important material, while American policy is conveniently explored in May, *The World War and American Isolation*. American entry into the war is handled controversially by Small, *Was War Necessary?* Other unusual angles on the war can be found in C. Jay Smith, *The Russian Struggle for Power*, and Busch, *Britain, India and the Arabs*.

S. Marks provides a good overview of the aftermath of the war in Europe in *The Illusion of Peace, 1918–33*. On the peacemaking, note Dockrill and Goold, *Peace without Promise: Britain and the Peace Conferences, 1919–23*, Stevenson, *French War Aims against Germany*, Levin, *Woodrow Wilson and World Politics*, J. M. Thompson, *Russia, Bolshevism and the Versailles Peace*, and Mayer, *The Politics and Diplomacy of Peacemaking*. The Russian question can be studied in great detail in Ullman, *Anglo-Soviet Relations, 1917–21*, and the Washington Conference in the relevant chapters of Nish [2], *Alliance in Decline*, and briefly in Storry, see above. For the international economy down to 1929, see Aldcroft, *From Versailles to Wall Street*. Note also Silverman, *Reconstructing Europe after the Great War*. The period of modest optimism is assessed by Jacobson, *Locarno Diplomacy, 1925–29*, while for the British role in its creation see Orde, *Great Britain and International Security*.

Useful introductions to the deteriorating situation in the Far East are provided by Storry, see above, and Louis [1], *British Strategy in the Far East*. The first crisis is admirably analysed by Ogata, *Defiance in Manchuria*, and thereafter one should use Crowley, *Japan's Quest for Autonomy* and Pelz, *Race to Pearl Harbor*. Note also Borg and Okamoto, *Pearl Harbor as History*. On Europe there is Adamthwaite [2], *The Making of the Second World War*, which includes a useful selection of documents, Hildebrand, *The Foreign Policy of the Third*

Reich, Baumont, *The Origins of the Second World War*, and
Robertson [3], *The Origins of the Second World War*. Dilks [1],
Retreat from Power, vol. i, contains several reassessments of British
policy, while the best detailed treatment of Germany's foreign policy
is to be found in Weinberg, *The Foreign Policy of Hitler's Germany*,
2 vols. Interactions between Europe and the Far East can be studied
in Morley, *Deterrent Diplomacy: Japan, Germany and the USSR*,
while the origins of the war between Germany and Russia are
comprehensively explored by McSherry, *Stalin, Hitler and Europe,
1933–41*, 2 vols. For the American entry into the war, see Drummond, *The Passing of American Neutrality*.

In the vast literature on the Second World War it is important to
note Dallek, *Franklin D. Roosevelt and American Foreign Policy*,
Gaddis [1], *The United States and the Origins of the Cold War*, and
Mastny [2], *Russia's Road to the Cold War*. G. Kolko's *The Politics
of War* is ambitious and thought-provoking, as is the sequel on the
postwar period, with J. Kolko, *The Limits of Power*. An interesting
introduction to the Cold War in general is provided by Paterson [1],
On Every Front, while for developments in eastern Europe see
McCauley, *Communist Power in Europe, 1944–49*. *The Origins of the
Cold War in Asia* (edited by Nagai and Iriye) is a very important and
wide-ranging work, while for the communist rise to power in China
one can consult Harrison, *The Long March to Power, 1921–72*. The
growing American involvement in the Far East is well explained by
Rose, *Roots of Tragedy: the United States and the struggle for Asia,
1945–53*.

For a general treatment of the whole postwar era, see Calvocoressi, *World Politics since 1945*, and for stimulating discussion of
major themes in this period see Brodie, *War and Politics*, Freedman,
The Evolution of Nuclear Strategy, and Spanier, *World Politics in an
Age of Revolution*. For an introductory account of American foreign
policy, see Ambrose [2], *Rise to Globalism*, while for a thoughtful
and comprehensive assessment of American policy-making in matters
of national security see Gaddis [2], *Strategies of Containment*. Amid
the vast literature on the Truman era, the documentary collection
edited by Etzold and Gaddis, *Containment*, and supplemented with
much informed comment, should not be overlooked. The Eisenhower era has been succinctly analysed by Divine, *Eisenhower and
the Cold War*, and for the period from 1961 Gaddis [2], see above,
is a good starting point. For Russia since 1945 there are complementary studies by Rubinstein, *Soviet Foreign Policy since
World War II*, and Nogee and Donaldson, *Soviet Foreign Policy
since World War II*. For more specific detail on Russia and Europe,
see Wolfe, *Soviet Power and Europe, 1945–70*, while Russo-
Chinese relations can be studied in general in Clubb, *China and*

Russia: the 'Great Game', and more specifically for the years since 1949 in Thornton, *The Bear and the Dragon*. The interrelations of Russia, China and the United States, especially in the 1960s, are interestingly discussed by Segal, *The Great Power Triangle*. A work which ranges more widely (and in an interesting style) than its title suggests is Taubman, *Stalin's American Policy*.

BIBLIOGRAPHY

Note: Place of publication is London unless otherwise stated

Abramsky, C. (ed.), *Essays in Honour of E. H. Carr*, Macmillan, 1974

AD: *Documents on Australian Foreign Policy, 1937–49*, Canberra: Australian Government Publishing Service, 1975 ff.

Adamthwaite, A. P. [1], *France and the Coming of the Second World War*, Frank Cass, 1977

Adamthwaite, A. P. [2], *The Making of the Second World War*, Allen and Unwin, 1977

Adler, S., *The Uncertain Giant, 1921–41*, Collier-Macmillan, 1969

Adomeit, H. and Boardman, R. (eds), *Foreign-Policy Making in Communist Countries*, Saxon House, 1979

Aldcroft, D. H., *From Versailles to Wall Street: the international economy, 1919–29*, Allen Lane, 1971

Allen, G. C., *A Short Economic History of Modern Japan*, Allen and Unwin, 1962

Allison, G. T., *Essence of Decision: explaining the Cuban Missile Crisis*, Boston: Little, Brown, 1971

Ambrose, S. E. [1], *The Supreme Commander: the war years of David D. Eisenhower*, Cassell, 1971

Ambrose, S. E. [2], *Rise to Globalism: American foreign policy since 1938*, Penguin, 1971

Anderson, Terry, *The United States, Britain and the Cold War, 1944–47*, University of Missouri Press, 1981

Andrew, C., *Théophile Delcassé and the Making of the Entente Cordiale*, Macmillan, 1968

Artaud, Denise, *La question des dettes interalliés et la reconstruction de l'Europe, 1917–29*, Lille, Paris: Université de Lille, 1978

Ash, B., *The Lost Dictator: a biography of Field-Marshal Sir Henry Wilson*, Cassell, 1968

Aster, S., *The Making of the Second World War*, Deutsch, 1973

Backer, J. H., *The Decision to divide Berlin*, Duke University Press, 1978

Ball, Desmond, *Politics and Force Levels: the strategic missile programme of the Kennedy administration*, University of California Press, 1981

Barker, Elisabeth, *Churchill and Eden at War*, Macmillan, 1978

Barron, Gloria J., *Leadership in Crisis*, New York: Kennikat Press, 1973

Bartlett, C. J., 'Great Britain and the Spanish change of policy towards Morocco in June 1878', *Bulletin of the Institute of Historical Research*, November 1958, pp. 168–85

Baumont, M., *The Origins of the Second World War*, Yale University Press, 1978

BD: *Documents on British Foreign Policy, 1919–39*, HMSO, 1946 ff.

Beale, H. K., *Theodore Roosevelt and the Rise of America to World Power*, New York: Collier Books, 1962

Bemis, S. F., *A Diplomatic History of the United States*, New York: Holt, Rinehart and Winston, 1965

Berger, G. M., *Parties out of Power in Japan, 1931–41*, Princeton University Press, 1977

Berghahn, V. R., *Germany and the Approach of War in 1914*, Macmillan, 1973

Berghahn, V. R. and Kitchen, M. (eds), *Germany in the Age of Total War*, Groom Helm, 1981

Berle, Beatrice B. and Jacobs, T. B., (eds), *Navigating the Rapids: from the papers of Adolf A. Berle*, New York: Harcourt Brace Jovanovich, 1973

Bethell, Nicholas, *The War Hitler Won: September 1939*, Allen Lane, 1972

Bialer, Uri, *The Shadow of the Bomber*, Royal Historical Society, 1980

Blum, J. M., *From the Morgenthau Diaries*, 3 vols, Boston: Houghton Mifflin, 1959–67

Bond, Brian [1], *British Military Policy between Two World Wars*, Oxford: Clarendon Press, 1980

Bond, Brian [2] (ed.), *Chief of Staff: the diaries of Lieutenant-General Sir Henry Pownall*, vol. I, *1933–40*, Leo Cooper, 1972

Borg, Dorothy and Heinrichs, W. (eds), *Uncertain Years: Chinese–American relations, 1947–50*, Columbia University Press, 1980

Borg, Dorothy and Okamoto, Shumpei (eds), *Pearl Harbor as History*, Columbia University Press, 1973

Borisov, O. B. and Koloskov B. T., *Soviet–Chinese Relations, 1945–70*, Indiana University Press, 1975

Bosworth, R. J. B., *Italy, the least of the Great Powers*, Cambridge University Press, 1979

Bourne, Kenneth, *The Foreign Policy of Victorian Britain, 1830–1902*, Oxford: Clarendon Press, 1970

Bourne, Kenneth and Watt, D. C. (eds.), *Studies in International History*, Longman, 1967

Bovykin, V. I., 'The Franco-Russian alliance', *History*, February 1979, pp. 20–35

Boyle, J. H., *China and Japan at War, 1937–45*, Stanford University Press, 1972

Bridge, F. R. [1] *From Sadowa to Sarajevo: the foreign policy of Austria–Hungary, 1866–1914*, Routledge and Kegan Paul, 1972

Bridge, F. R. [2] *Great Britain and Austria–Hungary, 1906–14*, Weidenfeld and Nicolson, 1972

Brodie, B., *War and Politics*, Cassell, 1973

Bromke, A. and Rakowska–Harmstone, Teresa (eds), *The Communist States in Disarray, 1965–71*, University of Minnesota Press, 1972

Broszat, Martin, *The Hitler State: the foundation and development of the internal structure of the Third Reich*, Longman, 1981

Brunschwig, Henri, *French Colonialism, 1871–1914*, Pall Mall Press, 1966

Buchan, Alastair, *The End of the Postwar Era*, Weidenfeld and Nicolson, 1974

Buckley, Thomas H., *The United States and the Washington Conference, 1920–1922*, University of Tennessee Press, 1970

Bullock, Alan, *Hitler: a study in tyranny*, Penguin, 1962

Burk, K. M., '*British War Missions to the United States, 1914–18*', unpublished D. Phil., Oxford, 1976

Burns, J. MacGregor, *Roosevelt: the lion and the fox*, New York: Harcourt, Brace and World, 1956

Burridge, T. D., *British Labour and Hitler's War*, Deutsch, 1976

Busch, B. C., *Britain, India and the Arabs, 1914–21*, University of California Press, 1971

Busch, B. C., *Mudros to Lausanne: Britain's frontier in west Asia, 1918–23*, State University of New York Press, 1976

Butler, J. R. M., *Lord Lothian*, Macmillan, 1960

Butterfield, H., *History and Human Relations*, Collins, 1951

CAB: British cabinet memoranda and papers, 1945–50, CAB 129/1–43, PRO, London

Calvocoressi, Peter, *World Politics since 1945*, Longman, 1971

Campbell, Thomas M., *Masquerade Peace: America's United Nations policy 1944–5*, Florida State University Press, 1973

Carlton, David, *Anthony Eden*, Allen Lane, 1981

Carr, E. H. [1], *The Twenty Years Crisis, 1919–39*, Macmillan, 1946

Carr, E. H. [2], *From Napoleon to Stalin and other Essays*, Macmillan, 1980

Carr, William [1], *A History of Germany, 1815–1945*, Edward Arnold, 1969

Carr, William [2], *Hitler, a study in personality and politics*, Edward Arnold, 1978

Ch'en, Jerome, *Mao and the Chinese Revolution*, Oxford University Press, 1965

Ciano's Diary, 1937–8, transl. by A. Mayor, Methuen, 1952

Ciano's Diary, 1939–43, M. Muggeridge (ed.), Heinemann, 1947

Ciano's Diplomatic Papers, M. Muggeridge (ed.), Odhams Press, 1948

Clarke, Sir Richard, *Anglo-American Economic Collaboration in War and Peace*, Oxford: Clarendon Press, 1982

Clay, Lucius, *The Papers of Lucius Clay (Germany, 1945–9)*, 2 vols. Indiana University Press, 1974

Clubb, O. E., *China and Russia: the 'Great Game'*, Columbia University Press, 1971

Cohen, Raymond, *Threat Perception in International Crisis*, University of Wisconsin Press, 1979

Cole, W. S., *An Interpretive History of American Foreign Relations*, Homewood, Illinois: the Dorsey Press, 1968

Collins, D. N., 'The Franco-Russian alliance and Russian railways, 1891–1914', *Historical Journal*, 1973, pp. 777–88

Cooke, J. J., *The New French Imperialism, 1880–1910*, Newton Abbot: David and Charles, 1973

Coox, A. D. and Conroy, H. (eds), *China and Japan: a search for balance since World War I*, Santa Barbara: Clio Books, 1978

Coverdale, J. F., *Italian Intervention in the Spanish Civil War*, Princeton University Press, 1975

Cowan, C. D. (ed.), *The Economic Development of China and Japan*, Allen and Unwin, 1964

Craig, Gordon A., *Germany, 1866–1945*, Oxford: Clarendon Press, 1978

Crankshaw, Edward, *The New Cold War: Moscow v Pekin*, Penguin, 1963

Cross, J. A., *Sir Samuel Hoare*, Jonathan Cape, 1977

Crowley, J. B., *Japan's Quest for Autonomy: national security and foreign policy, 1930–8*, Princeton University Press, 1969

Dallek, Robert, *Franklin D. Roosevelt and American Foreign Policy, 1932–45*, Oxford University Press, 1979

Daniels, Jonathan, *White House Witness, 1942–5*, New York: Doubleday, 1975

Darwin, John L. [1], 'Imperialism in decline? Tendencies in British imperial policy between the wars', *Historical Journal*, 1980, pp. 657–79

Darwin, John L. [2], *Britain, Egypt and the Middle East, 1918–22*, Macmillan, 1981

Davis, Lynn E., *The Cold War Begins*, Princeton University Press, 1974

Dayer, Roberta A., *Bankers and Diplomats in China, 1917–25*, Frank Cass, 1981

DDF: *Documents Diplomatiques Français, 1932–39*, Imprimerie Nationale, 1962 ff.

Dedijer, V., *The Battle Stalin Lost*, New York: Viking Press, 1970

Deist, Wilhelm, *The Wehrmacht and German Rearmament*, Macmillan, 1981

de Santis, Hugh, *The Diplomacy of Silence: the American foreign service, the Soviet Union, and the Cold War, 1933–47*, University of Chicago Press, 1980

Deutscher, I., *Stalin*, Oxford University Press, 1967

DGFP: *Documents on German Foreign Policy, 1918–45*, HMSO, 1948 ff.

Dilks, D. [1], *Retreat from Power: studies in Britain's foreign policy of the twentieth century*, 2 vols, Macmillan, 1981

Dilks, D. [2] (ed.), *The Diaries of Sir Alexander Cadogan, 1938–45*, Cassell, 1971

Divine, R. A., *Eisenhower and the Cold War*, Oxford University Press, 1981

Dockrill, M. L. and Goold, J. D., *Peace without Promise: Britain and the Peace Conferences, 1919–23*, Batsford, 1981

Donovan, Robert J., *Conflict and Crisis: the presidency of Harry S Truman, 1945–8*, New York: W. W. Norton, 1977

Douglas, Roy [1], *The Advent of War, 1939–40*, Macmillan, 1978

Douglas, Roy [2], *From War to Cold War, 1942–8*, Macmillan, 1981

Drummond, D. F., *The Passing of American Neutrality, 1937–41*, New York: Greenwood Press, 1968

Dugdale, E. T. S. (ed.), *German Diplomatic Documents, 1871–1914*, Methuen, 1929

Dunn, W. H., *J. A. Froude*, 2 vols, Oxford University Press, 1961–63

Dupuy, T., *A Genius for War: the German army and general staff, 1807–1945*, Macdonald and Jane's, 1977

Duroselle, Jean-Baptiste, *La Décadence, 1932–39*, Imprimerie Nationale, 1979

Dziewanowski, M. K., *Poland in the Twentieth Century*, Columbia University Press, 1977

Edwards, Jill, *The British Government and the Spanish Civil War*, Macmillan, 1979

Egerton, G. W., 'Britain and the "Great Betrayal"', *Historical Journal*, 1978, pp. 885–911

Egremont, Max, *Balfour*, Collins, 1980

Elcock, Howard, *Portrait of a Decision: the Council of Four and the Treaty of Versailles*, Eyre Methuen, 1972

Eldridge, C. C., *Victorian Imperialism*, Hodder and Stoughton, 1978

Eley, Geoff, *Reshaping the German Right: radical nationalism and political change after Bismarck*, Yale University Press, 1980

Emmerson, J. T., *The Rhineland Crisis*, Maurice Temple Smith, 1977

Etzold, T. H. and Gaddis, J. L. (eds), *Containment:documents on American policy and strategy, 1945–50*, Columbia University Press, 1978

Fairbank, J. K., Reischauer, E. O. and Craig, A. M., *East Asia: the modern transformation*, Allen and Unwin, 1965

Farago, L., *The Broken Seal: the story of 'operation magic' and the Pearl Harbor disaster*, Arthur Barker, 1967

Farrar, L. L. [1], *The Short War Illusion*, Santa Barbara: Clio Books, 1973

Farrar, L. L. [2], *Divide and Conquer: Germany's efforts to conclude a separate peace, 1914–18*, Columbia University Press, 1978

Feiling, Sir Keith, *The Life of Neville Chamberlain*, Macmillan, 1947

Ferro, M., *The Great War, 1914–18*, Routledge and Kegan Paul, 1973

Fest, Joachim C., *Hitler*, Weidenfeld and Nicolson, 1974

Feuchtwanger. E. J. (ed.), *Upheaval and Continuity: a century of German history*, Oswald Wolff, 1973

Fieldhouse, D. K., *Economics and Empire, 1830–1914*, Weidenfeld and Nicolson, 1973

Fischer, Fritz [1], *Germany's Aims in the First World War*, Chatto and Windus, 1967

Fischer, Fritz [2], *War of Illusions: German policies from 1911 to 1914*, Chatto and Windus, 1975

Foster, Alan, '*The Times* and Appeasement: the second phase', *Journal of Contemporary History*, 1981, pp. 441–65

Fowler, W. B., *British–American Relations, 1917–18: the role of Sir William Wiseman*, Princeton University Press, 1969

Fraser, Peter, *Lord Esher*, Hart-Davis MacGibbon, 1973

Freedman, L., *The Evolution of Nuclear Strategy*, Macmillan, 1981

Frodsham, J. D., *The First Chinese Embassy to the West*, Oxford: Clarendon Press, 1974

FRUS: *Foreign Relations of the United States*, Washington, DC: Government Printing Office

Fry, M. G., *Lloyd George and Foreign Policy, 1890–1916*, McGill – Queen's University Press, 1977

Fulbright, J. W., *The Arrogance of Power*, Jonathan Cape, 1967

Gaddis, J. L. [1], *The United States and the Origins of the Cold War, 1941–47*, Columbia University Press, 1972

Gaddis, J. L. [2], *Strategies of Containment: a critical appraisal of postwar American National Security Policy*, Oxford University Press, 1982

Garrett, S. A., 'The relevance of great debates: an analysis of the discussion over Vietnam', *Journal of Politics*, 1971, pp. 478–508

Gatzke, Hans W., *Germany's Drive to the East*, Baltimore: Johns Hopkins Press, 1950

Geiss, I. [1], *German Foreign Policy, 1871–1914*, Routledge and Kegan Paul, 1976

Geiss, I. [2], *July 1914: the outbreak of the First World War: selected documents*, Batsford, 1967

Gibbs, Norman, *Grand Strategy*, vol. I, HMSO, 1976

Gilbert, Martin [1], *Winston Churchill, 1916–22*, Heinemann, 1975

Gilbert, Martin [2], *Sir Horace Rumbold*, Heinemann, 1973

Gilbert, Martin [3], *The Roots of Appeasement*, Weidenfeld and Nicolson, 1966

Gilbert, Martin [4], *Plough My Own Furrow*, Longman, 1965

Gillard, David, *The Struggle for Asia, 1828–1914*, Methuen, 1977

Ginsburgs, G. and Pinkele, C. F., *The Sino-Soviet Territorial Dispute, 1949–64*, New York: Praeger, 1978

Gladwyn, Lord, *The Memoirs of Lord Gladwyn*, Weidenfeld and Nicolson, 1972

Gooch, G. P. and Temperley, H. W. V. (eds), *British Documents on the Origins of the War, 1898–1914*, HMSO, 1926–38

Gooch, John, *The Prospect of War*, Frank Cass, 1981

Goschen, *The Diary of Edward Goschen, 1900–14*, C. H. D. Howard (ed.), Camden 4th series, vol. xxv, Royal Historical Society, 1980

Grant, A. J. and Temperley, H. W. V., *Europe in the Nineteenth and Twentieth Centuries*, Longmans Green, 1947

Grathwohl, Robert P., *Stresemann and the DNVP: reconstruction or revenge in German foreign policy, 1924–28*, Regents Press of Kansas, 1980

Grenville, J. A. S. [1], *Lord Salisbury and Foreign Policy at the Close of the Nineteenth Century*, Athlone Press, 1970

Grenville, J. A. S. [2], *A World History of the Twentieth Century*, vol. I, Fontana, 1980

Griffiths, Richard, *Fellow Travellers of the Right: British enthusiasts for Nazi Germany, 1933–9*, Constable, 1980

Hagglof, Gunnar, *Diplomat*, Stockholm: Norstedt, 1971

Harbaugh, W. H., *The Life and Times of Theodore Roosevelt*, Oxford University Press, 1975

Hardach, Gerd, *The First World War*, Allen Lane, 1977

Hardach, Karl, *The Political Economy of Germany in the Twentieth Century*, University of California Press, 1981

Harriman, W. Averell, *Special Envoy to Churchill and Stalin, 1941–6*, Hutchinson, 1976

Harrison, J. P., *The Long March to Power, 1921–72*, Macmillan, 1973

Harvey, John (ed.), *The Diplomatic Diaries of Oliver Harvey, 1937–40*, Collins, 1970

Haslam, J., 'The Soviet Union and the Czech crisis of 1938',*Journal of Contemporary History*, 1979, pp. 441–57

Hathaway, Robert M., *Ambiguous Partnership: Britain and America, 1944–47*, Columbia University Press, 1981

Hauner, M., 'Did Hitler want a world dominion?', *Journal of Contemporary History*, 1978, pp. 15–32

Haupts, Leo, *Deutsche Friedenspolitik, 1918–19*, Düsseldorf: Droste Verlag, 1976

Heinemann, John L., *Hitler's First Foreign Minister: Constantin Freiherr von Neurath*, University of California Press, 1979

Herken, Gregg, *The Winning Weapon: the atomic bomb and the cold war, 1945–50*, New York: Knopf,1980

Herwig, Hodger H., *Politics of Frustration: the United States and German Naval Planning, 1889–1941*, Boston and Toronto: Little, Brown, 1976

Hiden, John, *Germany and Europe, 1919–39*, Longman, 1977

Hildebrand, Klaus, *The Foreign Policy of the Third Reich*, Batsford, 1973

Hilsman, Roger, To Move A Nation: the politics of foreign policy in the administration of John F. Kennedy, New York: Doubleday and Co., 1967

Hinsley, F. H. [1] (ed.), *British Foreign Policy under Sir Edward Grey*, Cambridge University Press, 1977

Hinsley, F. H. [2], *British Intelligence in the Second World War*, HMSO, 1979

Hoffmann, E. P. and Fleron, F. J. (eds.), *The Conduct of Soviet Foreign Policy*, Butterworths, 1971

Hogan, Michael J., *Informal Entente: the private structure of co-operation in Anglo-American economic diplomacy, 1918–28*, University of Missouri Press, 1977

Hohenlohe-Schillingsfurst, C. C. V. von, *Memoirs of Prince Hohenlohe*, 2 vols, Heinemann, 1906

Howard, Michael [1], *The Franco-Prussian War*, Rupert Hart-Davis, 1968

Howard, Michael [2], *The Mediterranean Strategy in the Second World War*, Weidenfeld and Nicolson, 1968

Howard, Michael [3], *War and the Liberal Conscience*, Temple Smith, 1978

Howard, Michael [4] (ed.), *Restraints on War*, Oxford University Press, 1979

Howard, Michael [5], 'The relevance of traditional strategy', *Foreign Affairs*, January 1973, pp. 253–66

Hughes, H. S., *Contemporary Europe: a history*, Prentice-Hall, 1976

Hunt, Barry and Preston, Adrian, (eds.), *War Aims and Strategic Policy in the Great War, 1914–18*, Croom Helm, 1977

Ienaga, Saburō, *The Pacific War*, New York: Pantheon Books, 1978

Ireland, Timothy P., *Creating the Entangling Alliance*, Aldwych Press, 1981

Iriye, Akira, *From Nationalism to Internationalism*, Routledge and Kegan Paul, 1977

Irving, David J. C., *Hitler's War*, Hodder and Stoughton, 1977

Jacobson, Jon, *Locarno Diplomacy: Germany and the West, 1925–29*, Princeton University Press, 1972

Jessup, Philip C., *The Birth of Nations*, Columbia University Press, 1974

Joll, J., *Europe since 1870*, Penguin, 1976

Jonas, Manfred, *Isolationism in America, 1935–41*, Cornell University Press, 1966

Jones, Thomas, *A Diary with Letters, 1931–50*, Oxford University Press, 1954

Kahan, Jerome H., *Security in the Nuclear Age*, Washington: Brookings Institution, 1975

Kaiser, David E., *Economic Diplomacy and the Origins of the Second World War*, Princeton University Press, 1981

Kajima, M., *The Emergence of Japan as a World Power, 1895–1925*, Rutland, Vermont: Tuttle, 1968

Kalicki, J. H., *The Pattern of Sino-American Crises: political and military interactions in the 1950s*, Cambridge University Press, 1975

Kaufman, Burton I., *Efficiency and Expansion: foreign trade expansion in the Wilson administration, 1913–21*, Connecticut: Greenwood Press, 1974

Kazemzadeh, Firuz, *Russia and Britain in Persia, 1864–1914*, Yale University Press, 1968

Kearns, Doris, *Lyndon Johnson and the American Dream*, Deutsch, 1976

Kedourie, Elie, *In the Anglo-Arab Labyrinth: 1914–39*, Cambridge University Press, 1976

Kehr, E. [1], *Battleship Building and Party Politics, 1894–1901*, University of Chicago Press, 1975

Kehr, E. [2], *Economic Interest, Militarism and Foreign Policy*, University of California Press, 1977

Kennan, George, *Memoirs, 1925–63*, 2 vols, Hutchinson, 1968–73

Kennedy, Paul [1], *The Rise of the Anglo-German Antagonism, 1860–1914*, Allen and Unwin, 1980

Kennedy, Paul [2] (ed.), *The War Plans of the Great Powers, 1880–1914*, Allen and Unwin, 1979

Kennedy, Thomas C., *Charles A. Beard and American Foreign Policy*, University Presses of Florida, 1975

Kettenacker, L., 'The Anglo-Soviet alliance and the problem of Germany, 1941–5', *Journal of Contemporary History*, 1982, pp. 435–57

Khrushchev, Nikita S., *Khrushchev Remembers*, Deutsch, 1971

Kissinger, Henry, *The White House Years*, Weidenfeld and Nicolson, 1979

Kitchen, Martin [1], *The German Officer Corps, 1890–1914*, Oxford: Clarendon Press, 1968

Kitchen, Martin [2], *A Military History of Germany from the Eighteenth Century to the Present Day*, Weidenfeld and Nicolson, 1975

Kitchen, Martin [3], *The Political Economy of Germany, 1815–1914*, Croom Helm, 1978

Knox, MacGregor, *Mussolini Unleashed, 1939–41*, Cambridge University Press, 1982

Koch, H. W. (ed.), *The Origins of the First World War*, Macmillan, 1972

Kochan, L., *Russia in Revolution, 1890–1918*, Weidenfeld and Nicolson, 1966

Kolko, G., *The Politics of War: the world and United States foreign policy, 1943–45*, New York: Harper and Row, 1972

Kolko, J. and G., *The Limits of Power: the world and United States foreign policy, 1945–54*, New York: Harper and Row, 1972

Kovrig, B., *The Myth of Liberation: east-central Europe in United States diplomacy and politics since 1941*, Johns Hopkins University Press, 1973

Kuklick, Bruce, *American Policy and the Division of Germany*, Cornell University Press, 1972

Kuniholm, B. R., *The Origins of the Cold War in the Near East*, Princeton University Press, 1980

Langhorne, Richard, *The Collapse of the Concert of Europe, 1890–1914*, Macmillan, 1981

Laves, W. H. C., *German Government Influence on Foreign Investments, 1871–1914*, New York: Arno Press, 1977

Leach, Barry A., *German Strategy against Russia, 1939–41*, Oxford: Clarendon Press, 1973

Lebra, Joyce C., *Japan's Greater East Asia Co-Prosperity Sphere in World War Two*, Oxford University Press, 1975

Lee, Dwight E. (ed.), *The Outbreak of the First World War*, Lexington: D. C. Heath, 1975

Leffler, Melvyn P., *The Elusive Quest: America's pursuit of European stability and French security, 1919–33*, University of North Carolina Press, 1979

Leigh, Michael, *Mobilizing Consent: public opinion and American foreign policy, 1937–47*, Connecticut: Greenwood Press, 1976

Leutze, James R., *Bargaining for Supremacy: Anglo-American naval collaboration, 1937–41*, University of North Carolina Press, 1977

Levin, N. G., *Woodrow Wilson and World Politics*, Oxford University Press, 1968

Link, A. S. [1], *The Papers of Woodrow Wilson*, vol. xxx ff., Princeton University Press, 1979 ff.

Link, A. S. [2], *The Higher Realism of Woodrow Wilson*, Vanderbilt University Press, 1971

Lockhart, J. G., *Cecil Rhodes*, Duckworth, 1933

Louis, W. R. [1], *British Strategy in the Far East, 1919–39*, Oxford, Clarendon Press, 1971

Louis, W. R. [2], *Imperialism at Bay: the United States and the decolonization of the British Empire*, Oxford, Clarendon Press, 1977

Lowe, C. J., *The Reluctant Imperialists: British foreign policy, 1878–1902*, 2 vols, Routledge and Kegan Paul, 1967

Lowe, C. J. and Dockrill, M. L., *The Mirage of Power: British foreign policy, 1902–22*, 2 vols, Routledge and Kegan Paul, 1972

Lowe, Peter, *Great Britain and the Origins of the Pacific War, 1937–41*, Oxford: Clarendon Press, 1977

Lowenthal, M. M., 'Roosevelt and the coming of the War, 1937–42', *Journal of Contemporary History*, 1981, pp. 413–40

McCagg, W. O., *Stalin Embattled, 1943–48*, Wayne State University Press, 1978

McCauley, Martin (ed.),*Communist Power in Europe, 1944–49*, Macmillan, 1977

MacDonald, C. A., *The United States, Britain and Appeasement, 1936–39*, Macmillan, 1981

McDougall, Walter A., *France's Rhineland Diplomacy, 1914–24*, Princeton University Press, 1978

MacFarquhar, R., *The Origins of the Cultural Revolution*, vol. I, *1956–57*, Oxford University Press, 1974

Mackay, R. F., *Fisher of Kilverstone*, Oxford: Clarendon Press, 1973

Mack Smith, D. [1], *Mussolini's Roman Empire*, Longman, 1976

Mack Smith, D. [2], *Mussolini*, Weidenfeld and Nicolson, 1981

McLean, David, *Britain and her Buffer State: the collapse of the Persian Empire, 1890–1914*, Royal Historical Society, 1979

McLellan, David S., *Dean Acheson: the State Department years*, New York: Dodd, Mead and Co., 1976

McSherry, J. E., *Stalin, Hitler and Europe, 1933–41*, 2 vols, New York: World Publishing Co., 1968–70

Malozemoff, A., *Russian Far Eastern Policy, 1881–1904*, University of California Press, 1958

Mann, Golo, *The History of Germany since 1789*, Chatto and Windus, 1968

Manne, R. [1], 'The Foreign Office and the failure of the Anglo-Soviet rapprochement', *Journal of Contemporary History*, 1981, pp. 725–56

Manne, R. [2], 'Some British light on the Nazi–Soviet Pact', *European Studies Review*, January 1981, pp. 83–102

Marder, A. J., *From the Dreadnought to Scapa Flow*, vol. i, Oxford University Press, 1961

Marks, S., *The Illusion of Peace: international relations in Europe 1918–33*, Macmillan, 1976

Marquand, David, *Ramsay MacDonald*, Jonathan Cape, 1977

Marsden, Arthur, *British Diplomacy and Tunis, 1875–1902*, Scottish Academic Press, 1971

Massey, V., *What's Past is Prologue: the memoirs of Viscount Massey*, Toronto: Macmillan, 1963

Mastny, V. [1], 'Stalin and the prospects of a separate peace in World War II', *American Historical Review*, December 1972, pp. 1365–88

Mastny, V. [2], *Russia's Road to the Cold War*, Columbia University Press, 1979

May, E. R., *The World War and American Isolation, 1914–17*, Harvard University Press, 1963

Mayer, A., *Politics and Diplomacy of Peacemaking, 1918–19*, Weidenfeld and Nicolson, 1968

Mayer-Oakes, T. F. (ed.), *Fragile Victory: the Saionji–Harada memoirs*, Wayne State University Press, 1968

Medlicott, W. N. [1], *Bismarck and Modern Germany*, English Universities Press, 1965

Medlicott, W. N. [2], *British Foreign Policy since Versailles, 1919–63*, Methuen, 1968

Medvedev, Roy, *Let History Judge: the origins and consequences of Stalinism*, Macmillan, 1972

Meskill, J. M., *The Hollow Alliance: Germany and Japan*, New York: Atherton, 1966

Micaud, C. A., *The French Right and Nazi Germany, 1933–39*, New York: Octagon, 1964

Michaelis, Meir, 'World status or world dominion', *Historical Journal*, 1972, pp. 331–60

Mićunović, Veljko, *Moscow Diary,* Chatto and Windus, 1980

Middlemas, Keith, *Diplomacy of Illusion: the British government and Germany, 1937–39,* Weidenfeld and Nicolson, 1972

Middlemas, Keith and Barnes, John, *Baldwin: a biography,* Weidenfeld and Nicolson, 1969

Minger, Ralph E., *William Howard Taft and United States foreign policy, 1900–8,* University of Illinois Press, 1975

Mitsubishi Economic Research Bureau, *Japanese Trade and Industry: present and future,* Macmillan, 1936

Monger, G. E., *The End of Isolation: British foreign policy, 1900–07,* Nelson, 1963

Moorman, Mary, *George Macaulay Trevelyan,* Hamish Hamilton, 1980

Morley, J. W. (ed.), *Deterrent Diplomacy: Japan, Germany and the USSR, 1935–40,* Columbia University Press, 1976

Morrison, G. E., *The Correspondence of G. E. Morrison,* Lo Hui-min (ed.), 2 vols, Cambridge University Press, 1976–78

Moses, John A. (ed.), *The Politics of Illusion: the Fischer controversy in German historiography,* George Prior, 1975

Moulder, Frances V., *Japan, China and the Modern World Economy,* Cambridge University Press, 1977

Müller, Klaus-Jürgen, *Armee, Politik und Gesellschaft in Deutschland, 1933–45,* Paderborn: Ferdinand Schöningh, 1979

Nagai, Yonosuke and Iriye, Akira (eds), *The Origins of the Cold War in Asia,* University of Tokyo Press, 1977

Nekludoff, A., *Diplomatic Reminiscences, 1911–17,* John Murray, 1920

Nelson, H. I., *Land and Power: British and allied policy on Germany's frontiers, 1916–19,* Routledge and Kegan Paul, 1963

Néré, J., *The Foreign Policy of France from 1914 to 1945,* Routledge and Kegan Paul, 1975

Newman, M., 'The Origins of Munich: British policy in Danubian Europe, 1933–37', *Historical Journal,* 1978, pp. 371–86

Newman, Simon, *March 1939: the British guarantee to Poland,* Oxford: Clarendon Press, 1976

Newton, Lord, *Lord Lansdowne,* Macmillan, 1929

Nicolson, Harold, *Diaries and Letters, 1930–39,* Collins, 1966

Nish, Ian H. [1], *The Anglo-Japanese Alliance, 1894–1907,* Athlone Press, 1966

Nish, Ian H. [2], *Alliance in Decline: a study in Anglo-Japanese relations, 1908–23,* Athlone Press, 1972

Nish, Ian H. [3], *Japanese Foreign Policy, 1869–1942,* Routledge and Kegan Paul, 1977

Nogee, J. L. and Donaldson, R. H., *Soviet Foreign Policy since World War II,* New York: Pergamon, 1981

Northedge, F. S. and Grieve, M. J., *A Hundred Years of International Relations,* Duckworth, 1971

NSC: *Documents of the National Security Council, 1947–77,* Paul Kesaris (ed.), a microfilm project of University Publications of America, Washington DC, 1980

Ogata, S. N., *Defiance in Manchuria, 1931–32*, University of California Press, 1964

Okamoto, Shumpei, *The Japanese Oligarchy and the Russo-Japanese War*, Columbia University Press, 1970

Oliver, Roland, *Sir Harry Johnston and the Scramble for Africa*, Chatto and Windus, 1957

O'Neill, R. and Horner, D. M. (eds.), *New Directions in Strategic Thinking*, Allen and Unwin, 1981

O'Neill, R. J., *The German Army and the Nazi Party, 1933–39*, Cassell, 1966

Orde, A., *Great Britain and International Security, 1920–26*, Royal Historical Society, 1978

Ovendale, Ritchie, 'Britain, the United States, and the Cold War in South-East Asia, 1949–50', *International Affairs*, 1982, pp. 447–64

Pachter, Henry M., *Modern Germany: a social, cultural and political history*, Colorado: Westview Press, 1978

Parker, W. R., *Mackinder: geography as an aid to statecraft*, Oxford: Clarendon Press, 1982

Parrini, C. P., *Heir to Empire: United States economic diplomacy, 1916–23*, University of Pittsburgh Press, 1969

Paterson, T. G. [1], *On Every Front: the making of the Cold War*, New York: W. W. Norton, 1979

Paterson, T. G. [2] (ed.), *Cold War Critics: alternatives to American foreign policy in the Truman years*, Chicago: Quadrangle Books, 1971

Peden, G. C., *British Rearmament and the Treasury, 1932–39*, Scottish Academic Press, 1979

Pelz, S. E., *Race to Pearl Harbor*, Harvard University Press, 1974

Pepper, Suzanne, *Civil War in China: the political struggle, 1945–49*, University of California Press, 1978

Pogue, F. C., *George C. Marshall: ordeal and hope, 1939–42*, MacGibbon and Kee, 1968

Porter, A. N., *The Origins of the South African War*, Manchester University Press, 1980

Porter, Gareth, (ed.), *Vietnam: the definitive documentation of human decisions*, 2 vols, Heyden, 1979

Preston, A. (ed.), *General Staffs and Diplomacy before the Second World War*, Croom Helm, 1978

Purifoy, L. M., *Harry Truman's China Policy*, New York: Franklin Watts, 1976

Rauschning, H., *Germany's Revolution of Destruction*, Heinemann, 1939

Reardon-Anderson, James, *Yenan and the Great Powers, 1944–46*, Columbia University Press, 1980

Reynolds, David, *The Creation of the Anglo-American Alliance, 1937–41*, Europa Publications, 1981

Rich, Norman, *Friedrich von Holstein*, 2 vols, Cambridge University Press, 1965

Rich, Norman, and Fisher, M. H. (eds.), *The Holstein Papers: 1837–1909*, 4 vols, Cambridge University Press, 1955–63

Ritter, Gerhard, *The Sword and the Sceptre: the problem of militarism in Germany*, 4 vols, Allen Lane, 1972

Roberts, John G., *Mitsui*, New York: Weatherhill, 1973

Robertson, E. M. [1], *Hitler's Pre-War Policy and Military Plans, 1933–39*, Longman, 1963

Robertson, E. M. [2], *Mussolini as Empire-Builder: Europe and Africa, 1932–36*, Macmillan, 1977

Robertson, E. M. [3] (ed.),*The Origins of the Second World War*, Macmillan, 1971

Robinson, R. E. and Gallagher, J.. *Africa and the Victorians*, Macmillan, 1961

Röhl, J. C. G., *Germany without Bismarck, 1890–1900*, Batsford, 1967

Rose, Lisle A., *Roots of Tragedy: the United States and the struggle for Asia, 1945–53*, Connecticut: Greenwood Press, 1976

Roskill, S. [1], *Hankey: man of secrets*, 3 vols, Collins, 1970–74

Roskill, S. [2], *Naval Policy between the Wars, 1919–39*, 2 vols, Collins, 1968–76

Ross, G., 'Foreign Office attitudes to the Soviet Union, 1941–45', *Journal of Contemporary History*, 1981, pp. 521–40

Rostow, W. W., *The United States in the World Arena*, New York: Harper and Row, 1960

Rothwell, Victor, *Britain in the Cold War, 1941–47*, Jonathan Cape, 1982

Rubinstein, A. Z., *Soviet Foreign Policy since World War II*, Cambridge, Mass.: Winthrop, 1981

Russett, B. M., *No Clear and Present Danger: a skeptical view of the United States entry into World War II*, New York: Harper and Row, 1972

Ryder, A. J., *Twentieth Century Germany from Bismarck to Brandt*, Macmillan, 1973

Sanderson, G. N., *England, Europe and the Upper Nile, 1882–99*, Edinburgh University Press, 1965

Schaller, Michael, *The United States Crusade in China, 1938–45*, Columbia University Press, 1979

Schewe, Donald B. (ed.), *Franklin D. Roosevelt and Foreign Affairs, 1937–39*, 10 vols, New York: Garland Publishing Inc., 1979

Schlesinger, A. M., *Robert Kennedy and his Times*, Deutsch, 1978

Schram, S., *Mao Tse-tung*, Penguin, 1966

Schroeder, Paul W., *The Axis Alliance and Japanese – American Relations 1941*, New York: Ithaca, 1958

Schwarz, M., *Soviet Perceptions of the United States*, University of California Press, 1978

Seabury, P., *The Wilhelmstrasse: a study of German diplomats under the Nazi regime*, Connecticut: Greenwood Press, 1976

Seeley, J. R., *The Expansion of England*, Macmillan, 1883

Segal, Gerald, *The Great Power Triangle*, Macmillan, 1982

SFRC: *Senate Foreign Relations Committee's Historical Series, 1947–50*, New York: Garland Publishing, 1979:
    No. 3, *The Legislative Origins of the Truman Doctrine;*
    No. 5, *The Foreign Relief Assistance Act, 1948*;
    No. 6, *The Vandenberg Resolution and the North Atlantic Treaty*;

No. 7, *Economic Assistance to China and Korea, 1949–50*;

No. 8, *Reviews of the World Situation, 1949–50*

Shai, A., *Origins of the War in the East: Britain, China and Japan, 1937–39*, Croom Helm, 1976

Sheehan, J. J. (ed.), *Imperial Germany*, Franklin Watts, 1976

Sherry, Michael S., *Preparing for the Next War: American plans for postwar defense, 1941–45*, Yale University Press, 1977

Shulman, M. D., *Stalin's Foreign Policy Reappraised*, Harvard University Press, 1963

Silberman, B. S. (ed.), *Japan in Crisis*, Princeton University Press, 1974

Silverman, D. P., *Reconstructing Europe after the Great War*, Harvard University Press, 1982

Small, Melvin, *Was War Necessary? National security and United States entry into war*, Sage Publications, 1980

Smith, C. Jay, *The Russian Struggle for Power, 1914–17*, New York: Greenwood Press, 1956

Smith, D. M., *The Great Departure: the United States and World War I, 1914–20*, New York: John Wiley, 1965

Smith, Woodruff D., *The German Colonial Empire*, University of North California Press, 1978

Sontag, R. J. and Beddie, J. S. (eds), *Nazi–Soviet Relations, 1939–41*, Connecticut: Greenwood Press, 1976

Soviet Peace Efforts on the Eve of World War II, USSR, Ministry for Foreign Affairs, Moscow: Progress Publication, 1973

Spanier, J. W., *World Politics in an Age of Revolution*, Pall Mall Press, 1967

Spinner, T. J., *George Joachim Goschen*, Cambridge University Press, 1973

Steinberg, Jonathan, *Yesterday's Deterrent: Tirpitz and the birth of the German Battle Fleet*, Macdonald, 1955

Steiner, Zara, *Britain and the Origins of the First World War*, Macmillan, 1977

Stern, Fritz, *The Failure of Illiberalism*, Allen and Unwin, 1972

Stevenson, D., *French War Aims against Germany, 1914–19*, Oxford University Press, 1982

Stoff, Michael B., *Oil, War, and American Security, 1941–47*, Yale University Press, 1980

Stoler, M. A., *The Politics of the Second Front, 1941–43*, Connecticut: Greenwood Press, 1977

Storry, R., *Japan and the Decline of the West in Asia, 1894–1943*, Macmillan, 1979

Stueck, W. W. [1], 'The Soviet Union and the origins of the Korean War', *World Politics*, July 1976, pp. 622–35

Stueck, W. W. [2], *The Road to Confrontation: American policy towards China and Korea, 1947–50*, University of North Carolina Press, 1981

Sulzberger, C. L., *A Long Row of Candles*, Macdonald, 1969

Taubman, W., *Stalin's American Policy*, New York: Norton, 1981

Taylor, A. J. P. [1], *The Struggle for Mastery in Europe, 1848–1918*, Oxford: Clarendon Press, 1954

Taylor, A. J. P. [2], *Politicians, Socialism and Historians*, Hamish Hamilton, 1980

Taylor, Telford, *Munich: the price of peace*, Hodder and Stoughton, 1979
Thaden, Edward C., *Russia and the Balkan Alliance of 1912*, Pennsylvania State University Press, 1965
Theoharis, A., *The Truman Presidency*, Heyden, 1979
Thompson, J. M., *Russia, Bolshevism and the Versailles Peace*, Princeton University Press, 1966
Thompson, Wayne C., *In the Eye of the Storm: Kurt Riezler and the crisis of modern Germany*, University of Iowa Press, 1980
Thorne, Christopher [1], *The Limits of Foreign Policy: the West, the League and the Far Eastern crisis of 1931–33*, Hamish Hamilton, 1972
Thorne, Christopher [2], *Allies of a Kind: the United States, Britain and the war against Japan, 1941–45*, Hamish Hamilton, 1978
Thornton, R. C., *The Bear and the Dragon, 1949–71*, New York: American – Asian Educational Exchange, 1972
Tolstoy, Nikolai, *Stalin's Secret War*, Jonathan Cape, 1981
Trachtenberg, M., *Reparation in World Politics: France and European economic diplomacy, 1916–23*, Columbia University Press, 1980
Trask, David P., *Captains and Cabinets: Anglo-American naval relations, 1917–18*, University of Missouri Press, 1972
Trotter, A., *Britain and East Asia, 1933–37*, Cambridge University Press, 1975
Tsou, Tang, *America's Failure in China, 1941–50*, University of Chicago Press, 1963
Tucker, Robert C. (ed.)*Stalinism: essays in historical interpretation*, New York: W. W. Norton, 1977
Turner, H. A., *Nazism and the Third Reich*, New York: Quadrangle, 1972
Turner, L. C. F., *Origins of the First World War*, Edward Arnold, 1970

Ulam, A. B., *Expansion and Co-existence: Soviet foreign policy, 1917–73*, New York: Praeger, 1974
Ullman, Richard H., *Anglo-Soviet Relations, 1917–21*, 3 vols, Princeton University Press, 1961–73
USMI: *United States Military Intelligence*, 30 vols, New York: Garland Publishing Inc., 1978
Uzoigwe, G. N., *Britain and the Conquest of Africa*, University of Michigan Press, 1974

van Creveld, M. L., *Hitler's Strategy, 1940–41: the Balkan clue*, Cambridge University Press, 1973
van der Poel, Jean (ed.), *Selections from the Smuts Papers*, vol. VI, Cambridge University Press, 1973
Vernadsky, G. (ed.), *A Source Book for Russian History*, vol. III, Yale University Press, 1972
Vinacke, H., *A History of the Far East in Modern Times*, Allen and Unwin, 1962
Vinson, J. C., *The Parchment Peace: the United States Senate and the Washington Conference, 1921–22*, University of Georgia Press, 1955
Vladimirov. P., *The Vladimirov Diaries, 1942–45*, Robert Hale, 1975

Waites, Neville (ed.), *Troubled Neighbours: Franco-British relations in the twentieth century*, Weidenfeld and Nicolson, 1971

Waley, Daniel, *British Public Opinion and the Abyssinian War, 1935–6*, Maurice Temple Smith, 1975

Warner, Geoffrey [1], *Pierre Laval and the Eclipse of France*, Eyre and Spottiswoode, 1968

Warner, Geoffrey [2], 'From Pearl Harbor to Stalingrad: Germany and its allies in 1942', *International Affairs*, April 1978, pp. 282–92

Warner, Geoffrey [3], 'The United States and Vietnam', *International Affairs*, July 1972, pp. 379–94; October 1972, pp. 593–615

Watson, David R., *Georges Clemenceau*, Eyre Methuen, 1974

Watt, D. C., *Too Serious a Business: European armed forces and the approach of the Second World War*, Temple Smith, 1975

Weinberg, G. L. [1], *The Foreign Policy of Hitler's Germany, 1933–36*, University of Chicago Press, 1970

Weinberg, G. L. [2], *The Foreign Policy of Hitler's Germany, 1937–39*, University of Chicago Press, 1980

Weinberg, G. L. [3], *World in the Balance: behind the scenes of World War II*, University Press of New England, 1981

Westlake, John, *Chapters on the Principles of International Law*, Cambridge University Press, 1894

White, S., *Britain and the Bolshevik Revolution, 1920–24*, Macmillan, 1979

Whitman, Sidney, *German Memories*, William Heinemann, 1912

Widenor, William C., *Henry Cabot Lodge and the Search for an American Foreign Policy*, University of California Press, 1980

Williams, Philip, *Hugh Gaitskell: a political biography*, Jonathan Cape, 1979

Wolfe, Thomas W., *Soviet Power and Europe, 1945–70*, Johns Hopkins Press, 1970

Woodward, E. L., *British Foreign Policy in the Second World War*, 5 vols, HMSO, 1970–76

Wright, Gordon, *Raymond Poincaré and the French Presidency*, New York: Octagon Books, 1967

Wright, Harrison M. (ed.), *The 'New Imperialism': an analysis of late-nineteenth century expansion*, Lexington: Heath, 1976

Yapp, M. E., *Strategies of British India: Britain, Iran and Afghanistan, 1798–1850*, Oxford University Press, 1980

Yergin, Daniel, *Shattered Peace: the origins of the Cold War and the National Security State*, Boston: Houghton Mifflin, 1977

Young, K. (ed.), *The Diaries of Sir Robert Lockhart*, vol. I, Macmillan, 1973

Young, M. B., *The Rhetoric of Empire: American China policy, 1895–1901*, Harvard University Press, 1968

Young, R. J., *In Command of France: French foreign policy and military planning, 1933–40*, Harvard University Press, 1978

Zedlitz-Trützschler, Count Robert, *Twelve Years at the Imperial German Court*, Nisbet, 1951

Zeman, Z. A. B., *A Diplomatic History of the First World War*, Weidenfeld and Nicolson, 1971

Zimmerman, W., *Soviet Perspectives on International Relations, 1956–67*, Princeton University Press, 1969

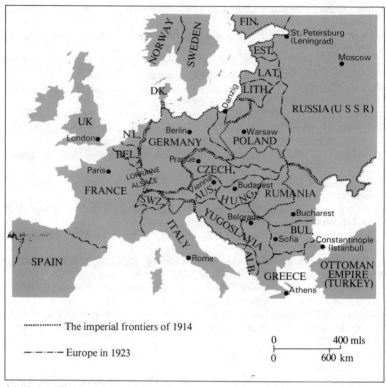

The imperial frontiers of 1914

Europe in 1923

0		400 mls
0		600 km

MAP 1. The break-up of the Russian, German and Austro-Hungarian empires, 1914–23

MAP 2. Europe from the beginning of 1938 to June 1940

The Rhineland (remilitarized March 1936)

Austria annexed by Germany, March 1938

German gains from Czechoslovakia, October 1938

Czech regions annexed by Germany, March 1939

Russian gains 1939-40

German conquests, September 1939

German conquests, April - June 1940

0   400 mls

0   600 km

The global conflict

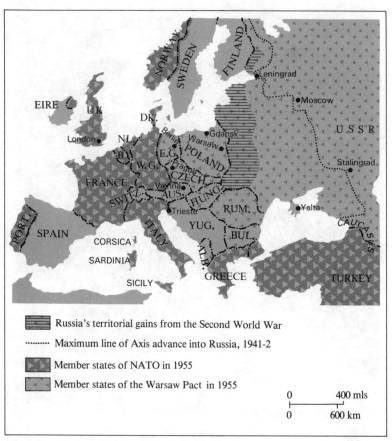

MAP 3. Europe showing post-1945 frontiers

MAP 4. The Far East

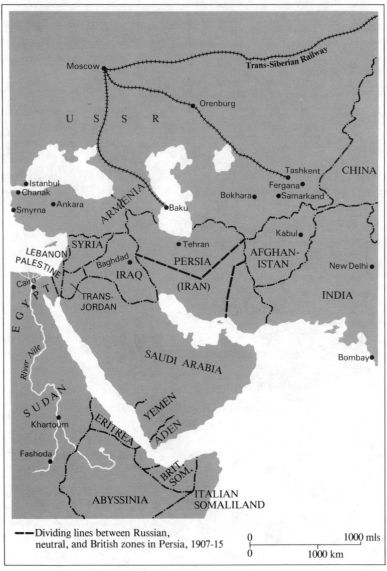

MAP 5. The Middle East showing inter-war boundaries

INDEX

Note: Most subentries are listed in chronological order